Asset-Backed Securities

Edited by

Anand K. Bhattacharya
Senior Vice President
Director of Fixed Income Research
Prudential Securities Inc.

and

Frank J. Fabozzi
Adjunct Professor of Finance
School of Management
Yale University

Published by Frank J. Fabozzi Associates

This publication is designed to provide accurate and authoritative information in regard to the subject matter covered. It is sold with the understanding that the publisher is not engaged in rendering legal, accounting, or other professional services.

ISBN: 1-883249-10-4

Printed in the United States of America
1 2 3 4 5 6 7 8 9 0

AKB

*To my wife Marcia
and
my children
Christina and Alexander*

FJF

*To my wife Donna
and
my son
Francesco Alfonso*

Contributing Authors

Jonathan Adams	Prudential Securities Inc.
Anand K. Bhattacharya	Prudential Securities Inc.
Len Blum	Prudential Securities Inc.
Leo Burrell	Prudential Securities Inc.
Morton Dear	The Money Store Inc.
Chris DiAngelo	Dewey Ballantine
John N. Dunlevy	Hyperion Capital Management, Inc.
Frank J. Fabozzi	Yale University
Donna Faulk	Prudential Securities Inc.
Lina Hsu	Prudential Securities Inc.
Robert Karr	Prudential Securities Inc.
Inna Koren	Prudential Securities Inc.
John Lucas	
Henry C. McCall III	United Companies Financial Corporation
Suzanne Michaud	Fitch Investors Service
Evan Mitnick	Prudential Securities Inc.
Cyrus Mohebbi	Prudential Securities Inc.
Vincent T. Pica	Prudential Securities Inc.
Greg Richter	Prudential Securities Inc.
Andrew Shook	Hyperion Capital Management, Inc.
R.J. Shook	Prudential Securities Inc.
Carol Sze	Prudential Securities Inc.
Paul Taylor	Duff & Phelps Credit Rating Co.
Lirenn Tsai	Prudential Securities Inc.
Thomas Zimmerman	Prudential Securities Inc.

Table of Contents

Acknowledgements

This book could not have been completed without the support of several individuals and organizations. First and foremost, we would like to thank the contributors to this book.

We thank Prudential Securities Inc. for its continued support in all phases of this project. On a more specific note, we thank Leland Paton, President, Capital Markets, and Howard Whitman, Executive Vice President, Taxable Fixed Income Division, for their sponsorship of this project. Robert Johnson, National Sales Manager, and Jeff Theodorou, Co-Head, Fixed Income Trading, provided continued encouragement — sometimes in unconventional form — and advice. We owe a debt of gratitude to the structuring, modelling, analytical development, and research professionals at Prudential Securities Inc. for their involvement in this project. The market insights of the ABS trading desk, headed by Greg Richter, and the efforts of the banking group, led by Len Blum, had a profound influence on this project.

A good number of the chapters in this book were authored or coauthored by professionals in the asset-backed securities research and structuring groups at Prudential Securities. Vincent Pica, President of Capital Finance at Prudential Securities, played a major role in establishing the infrastructure for these groups. We gratefully acknowledge these efforts.

We would like to specifically acknowledge the efforts of Lisa Pendergast, Miriam Cohen, Mike Valente, Emely Gallo, Dina Cotroneo, and Kyle Webb for their hard work in editing the chapters contributed by the authors employed by Prudential Securities Inc. Gladys Cardona is owed a special mention for her work on various tasks related to this book.

Finally, we acknowledge the feedback provided by several issuers and investors in the asset-backed securities market who shared their thoughts on various topics with us and the contributors.

Anand K. Bhattacharya
Frank J. Fabozzi

Index of Advertisers

Part I: General

Chapter 1

The Expanding Frontiers of Asset Securitization

Anand K. Bhattacharya
Senior Vice President
Director of Fixed Income Research
Prudential Securities Inc.

Frank J. Fabozzi
Adjunct Professor of Finance
School of Management
Yale University

The authors wish to thank Thomas Zimmerman for his significant contribution to this chapter.

INTRODUCTION

The securitization of assets is broadly defined as the process by which loans, consumer installment contracts, leases, receivables, and other relatively illiquid assets with common features are packaged into interest bearing securities with marketable investment characteristics. Using securitization, financial institutions can create assets suitable for resale from loans that might otherwise have been held to maturity. In this sense, asset securitization may be used strategically for a myriad of purposes, such as liquefying the balance sheet, improving leverage ratios, and creating alternative sources of capital, especially if the process leads to favorable gain on sale accounting treatment and lower costs of funding. Securitized assets have been created using a diversity of collateral, including home mortgages, commercial mortgages, manufactured housing loans, leases or installment contracts on personal property (such as computers, trucks, automobiles and credit card receivables, marine loans, recreational vehicles), small business administration loans, and health care receivables.

Investors are attracted to such engineered securities mainly because of their desirable investment and maturity characteristics. However, the higher yield is associated with investors bearing some degree of prepayment, early amortization, credit, and liquidity risk. From the point of view of the issuer, the securitization of assets permits institutions to reduce leverage, improve asset performance, enhance credit quality, and concentrate on asset and business creation rather than on asset management. Additionally, in the U.S. market, the types of assets converted to the securitization fold continue to expand with parallel developments geared toward increasing the investor base for such products. On the international front, securities are being structured that specifically appeal to the global community, such as yen and London interbank offered rate (LIBOR) indexed floating-rate bonds created out of U.S. dollar denominated assets, especially fixed-rate mortgages and credit cards. At the same time, competitive, regulatory and environmental changes occurring globally, especially in Europe and, to some extent, Japan, indicate that there is significant potential for using securitization technology, perhaps with a local flavor, to account for specific accounting, regulatory, and credit enhancement issues in other countries.

This chapter discusses the reasons for the growth of securitization, addresses the investment characteristics of asset-backed securities (ABS), explores the macro-economic benefits of securitization, and evaluates the issues raised by the growth of asset securitization.

DEVELOPMENT OF ASSET SECURITIZATION

While the securitization of consumer installment loans, receivables, leases, credit cards, automobile contracts, home equity loans, manufactured housing loans, and the like is a relatively recent phenomenon, the concept of securitizing mortgages in the U.S. has existed for decades. The growth of the mortgage-backed securities (MBS) market grew out of a public policy concern of channeling funds into the private sector to spur home owner-ship. Traditionally, the mortgage lending function was the sole domain of thrift institutions, which used deposits raised locally to extend mortgage credit. However, due to changing demographic and economic conditions, this localized form of providing mortgage funds was inadequate in address-ing regional and national imbalances in the supply of and demand for mort-gage funds. Also, cyclical credit crunches brought about in part by regulatory rate ceilings periodically devastated the housing market.

The national secondary mortgage market was developed to help alleviate the regional imbalances and the periodic credit crunches. While the secondary mortgage market had existed for some time in the United States, it was not until the early 1970s that the federal government expanded its involvement in the market. Prior to the formation of national agencies, which serve to control and divert loanable funds in the mortgage markets, the role of buttressing regional imbalances in mortgage credit supply and demand was mainly conducted by mortgage bankers. As opposed to thrifts, the primary role of mortgage bankers is to originate mortgages in geograph-ical areas with high demand for resale to investors in regions where the sup-ply of funds is greater than local mortgage credit demand.

Federal involvement in the secondary mortgage market manifests itself in the activities of the Government National Mortgage Association (GNMA), Federal National Mortgage Association (FNMA), and Federal Home Loan Mortgage Corporation (FHLMC). These entities facilitate the flow of funds into the primary market for mortgage origination by purchas-ing a variety of mortgages from originators; swapping collateral for securi-tized obligations; using MBS to create derivative products, such as collateralized mortgage obligations (CMOs) to satisfy the maturity, invest-ment, and risk management needs of institutional investors; and designing new pooling and purchase programs to support the origination of newer mortgages, such as adjustable-rate loans, mortgages with balloon features, convertible and multi-family mortgages.

Since GNMA is a branch of the Department of Housing and Urban Development, obligations of GNMA are backed by the full faith and credit of the U.S. government. Both FNMA and FHLMC are government-sponsored enterprises, allowing their obligations to be issued with negligible credit risk premiums. The role of these agencies in the market for securitized products began with the issuance of mortgage pass-through certificates, which involves the pooling of relatively homogenous mortgage loans with agency guarantees to increase the investor appeal of these securities, and has expanded in recent years to include the issuance of structured mortgage securities such as CMOs and MBS strips. Under the aegis of these federal agencies, the market for securitizable mortgages continued to expand; for example, the passage of the Secondary Mortgage Market Enhancement Act in 1984 reduced the legal and regulatory hurdles facing non-conforming (private) mortgage securitization.

The success of the securitization vehicle in the mortgage markets as a funding source and the acceptance of the derived securities by the investor base led to the application of this technology to other assets, such as credit cards, home equity loans, automobile loans, lease installment contracts, and manufactured housing loans, to name a few on the ever expanding list of securitizable assets. The first non-mortgage asset-backed security, a computer lease-backed transaction, was issued in March 1985 by Sperry. In that same year, the first auto loan-backed securities were issued by Valley National and Marine Midland banks. Two years later, in 1987, the Republic Bank of Delaware issued the first credit-card backed security. Since then, the asset-backed market has expanded exponentially with the predominance of issuance in credit cards and autos, although other types of assets are being increasingly considered for securitization.

Impediments to the development of markets for non-mortgage assets, such as the lack of federal guarantees, have been solved by a host of credit support mechanisms (such as subordination features, letters of credit, pool insurance policies, and guarantees by private insurers). Simultaneously, with the growth in the breadth and sophistication of the investor base, the market for the purchasers of these securities has also expanded. At the same time, traditional portfolio lenders, such as financial institutions, are increasingly evaluating asset securitization as a means of managing federally mandated capital requirements. This technology has been exported to other parts of the world, such as Europe, Japan, and Latin America, indicating that the concept of asset securitization is truly becoming a global phenomenon. As indicated in Exhibit 1, the asset-backed securitized market (excluding mortgage securitization) has grown exponentially over the years, and is increasingly being considered a permanent sector of the fixed-income market. Additionally, while most of the securitized effort has been concentrated within credit cards and automobiles, other sectors such as manufactured housing and home equity loans have continued to exhibit growth.

Exhibit 1: Issuance Trends (in billions of dollars)

	1993	1994	1995
Agency Collateralized Mortgage Obligations (CMOs)	$319.6	$115.9	$18.6
Corporate Bonds	215.0	115.1	165.2
Asset-Backed Securities	63.1	79.4	109.2

Sources: Corporate Watch, Securities Data Corporation and Prudential Securities Inc. IMPACT database.

In recent years, asset securitization has taken on a truly global character.[1] U.S. based securitization technology has been exported to many countries where regulatory and legal barriers have been lowered. At the same time, the demand for U.S. dollar ABSs has been increasing steadily over the years, especially by foreign institutions with dollar denominated liabilities. This trend has been assisted by innovation in structuring technology by creating specific structures that have wider global appeal. This also has been matched by a growing international acceptance of passive investments, such as mutual funds that invest in collateralized securities. Perhaps the most visible examples of this demand are LIBOR based floating-rate bonds backed by various assets originated in the U.S., including fixed-rate mortgages, home-equity loans, and credit cards. For example, in 1995 65% ($31 billion out of a total of $48 billion) of credit card issuance was predominantly structured as floating rate LIBOR based securities.

The long predicted global spread of securitization is definitely underway, with activity taking place in Europe, Canada, Latin America, Australia, and Asia. After the United States, Europe is by far the leading center for asset securitization. While many legal and regulatory issues have been resolved, especially in the United Kingdom, additional barriers will have to be dismantled before asset securitization becomes widely accepted in Europe. The smaller population base of the separate EEC countries relative to the United States also means that there are fewer companies that originate loans in sufficient volume to justify securitization. This problem is compounded by the fact that securitization regulations vary significantly from country to country within the EEC. Nevertheless, the trend in Europe is toward a broader use of securitization and the number of issuers and transactions has risen steadily over the past several years.

The United Kingdom is the leading country for securitization in Europe. The housing finance industry there has been issuing MBSs since 1987; the mortgage sector represented the dominant collateral class for ABSs in the United Kingdom. However, since 1990, MBS issuance has slipped to less than one-half its earlier levels due to a slump in the housing market and an overall weaker economy. Meanwhile, other asset classes, including unsecured personal loans, auto loans, equipment leases, and trade receivables (with the exception of credit card receivables), have all been used as collateral for securities. With a favorable legal and regulatory environment, the United Kingdom is likely to continue to lead Europe in asset securitization.

France is the second largest issuer of ABSs in Europe. Although the legal framework for securitization became effective in December 1988, it has taken the subsequent passage of several amendments to overcome

---

[1] This discussion draws from various issues of *The Asset Sales Report* and *Securitisation in Europe* published by Duff & Phelps Credit Rating Co, 1994. The next chapter provides a further discussion of securitization in Europe.

the remaining impediments to securitization, including the ability to transfer servicing without obtaining the consent of all debtors. In any event, numerous asset-backed deals have been issued, with the first ever French credit card transaction taking place in December 1994, signifying a decidedly improved atmosphere for securitization. Other European countries that have issued ABSs include Spain, Sweden, and Italy.

In addition to Europe, the usage of asset securitization continues to expand in Canada, Latin America, and Japan. Asset securitization in Canada has grown rapidly from 1992 onwards, benefiting from the proximity of the United States and the presence in Canada of several U.S. companies that are active issuers of ABSs. Major corporations such as Sears Roebuck, IBM, Chrysler, GMAC, and Citibank have all securitized assets from their Canadian operations. Several countries in Latin America, the most important being Mexico, have started using securitization for funding purposes. In Mexico, collateral has included airline receipts, oil trade receivables, toll road receipts, and U.S. dollar receipts for credit cards. Asset securitization has also been used to pierce the sovereign rating by emphasizing the collateralized nature of the transaction.

Securitization in Japan continues to move at a glacial pace. In June 1993, it finally became legal for non-bank Japanese finance companies to securitize and sell certain assets. However, the resulting "divided receivables" do not qualify as securities in Japan and hence cannot be traded in the secondary market. This, plus a reluctance on the part of many Japanese non-bank finance companies to adversely impact their traditional sources of funds, has handicapped the development of an active Japanese market for ABSs. In September 1994, finance companies were given permission to sell ABSs overseas; the first overseas transaction was completed by Japan Leasing Corporation, comprising of a $148 million transaction backed by computer and equipment leases in December 1994. Reportedly, this transaction took an inordinate amount of legal and accounting effort with coordination between the principal agencies that must approve the various aspects of such transactions being a major issue. While some modest steps have been taken, it appears that Japanese participation in asset securitization will continue to develop slowly.

ADVANTAGES OF SECURITIZATION FOR ISSUERS

In view of the current and potential growth of securitization globally, it is important to understand the reasons for the proliferation of this innovative technology. From the issuer perspective, securitization offers several advantages, such as the creation of alternative and often cheaper funding sources, conversion of capital intensive assets to capital economizing assets, generation of servicing fee income, and, in certain instances, reduced exposure to interest rate volatility.

Diversification and Reduced Cost of Funding

The securitization of assets enables asset originators to broaden funding sources and often reduce funding costs. The traditional method of selling whole loans as a funding source is a somewhat cumbersome process, which requires a tremendous degree of due diligence regarding the credit quality of the loan package. More importantly, whole loan sales require the existence of investor groups with investment preferences similar to that of the characteristics of the loan package. In such transactions, more often than not, the risk of default on the loans is usually borne by the investor. However, by using the securitization of assets as a disposition alternative, issuers can take advantage of the risk sharing and transfer mechanism of the capital markets by distributing balance sheet risk to a variety of investor groups. Credit safeguards, which are required by rating agencies to provide investment grade ratings for securitized assets, usually assure wider market appeal of the transformed assets. Due to the fact that the securitized assets are rated and hence less risky than whole loans, the sale of these securities can be achieved at spreads tighter (higher prices) than those required for whole loan execution. Additionally, in the event that the securitization process involves tranching the loans into securities of varying degrees of maturity and default profiles, the specific risks of the loan package are structurally transformed and shared by various investor classes.

To the extent that the proceeds obtained by securitization, after adjusting for the costs of securitization — investment banking fees, distribution costs (e.g., selling concessions), and legal and marketing expenses — are higher than the proceeds obtained by selling the whole loans, the institution can obtain funding at a lower cost. In other instances, the institution may be able to raise funds at a lower rate than that consistent with its unsecured rating by issuing the securities through a special purpose subsidiary. For instance, a corporation with a triple B rating may raise funds by issuing securities in the capital markets at a higher rating (lower cost), say triple A, by issuing collateralized structures with the necessary credit and structural safeguards. As the issuers attain higher unsecured credit ratings, the relative importance of asset securitization as a funding mechanism diminishes. By the same token, issuers whose debt ratings have been subjected to downgrades may attain cheaper financing by using asset based securitization. Additionally, for smaller issuers, securitization serves the dual purpose of liquefying the balance sheet, taking advantage of favorable gain on sale treatment of assets, and improving the earnings stream. For the case of smaller firms, with securitizable assets on the balance sheet, the use of securitization often can be used strategically to familiarize the capital markets with the issuer as a prelude to eventually tapping the capital markets for longer term debt and equity. Notice that the alternative to securitization for most of these issuers without name recognition and unsecured debt raising capacity in the capital markets is frequently higher cost junk bonds.

Management of Regulatory Capital

Securitization of assets can be used as a tool to manage risk-based capital requirements; this is an issue that directly affects U.S. financial institutions such as banks, thrifts, and insurance companies. However, the concept of using asset securitization as a means of attaining optimal capital adequacy standards is also of direct relevance to European financial institutions, for which increased competition due to deregulation and changing regulatory and environmental trends indicates an increased interest in asset securitization in the context of asset/liability management.

While a complete description of mandated risk-based capital guidelines for federal and state regulated financial institutions is beyond the scope of this chapter, several common themes that have direct implications for the strategic importance of asset securitization in the asset/liability management process merit discussion. The main idea behind risk based capital guidelines is the regulatory requirement of a direct association between the capital reserves and the credit risk inherent in assets held by the financial institution. The risk associated with each asset is quantified by assigning a risk weight to each asset category. Upon classifying the assets held by the institution in the various risk categories, the risk weighted value for that category is determined by weighting the book value of the asset classification by the risk weight. The total capital reserves required by the institution are then determined as a percentage of the total risk weighted asset values. While the calculations may be cumbersome, the "take home" lesson is very simple. All things equal, institutions that hold a risky portfolio will have to reserve a higher amount of capital.

The individual risk based guidelines that have been implemented for banks, thrifts, and insurance companies often place a higher risk weight on loans than on securities. This means that frequently an institution can lower its regulatory capital requirements either by buying securitized assets rather than whole loans or by securitizing and holding certain loans that it would normally retain in its whole loan portfolio. For example, insurance company risk based capital guidelines require a risk weight of 3.0% for commercial mortgages versus 0.3% for securitized commercial mortgage backed securities (CMBSs), providing a strong incentive for insurers to purchase CMBSs rather than whole loans. Another example comes from bank risk based guidelines for mortgages. For banks, a single family, residential mortgage loan receives a risk weight of 50%, while a FNMA or FHLMC pass-through receives a weight of 20%, providing a capital conservation motivation for asset securitization. As this regulatory orientation of distinguishing between the higher credit risk of loans and the lower risk of higher grade securitized assets is applied to other asset classes, it is likely that the volume of asset securitization by banks and the purchase of ABSs by those same institutions will increase.[2]

Generation of Servicing Fee Income and the Immediate Recognition of Excess Servicing

The securitization of assets allows the issuer to convert capital intensive assets to a less capital intensive source of servicing fee income, thereby increasing its servicing and origination fees without increasing its capital base. This is done by securitizing and selling the loans while retaining the servicing. The servicing fee that is retained is like an interest only strip of payments, which compensates the servicer for providing the normal clerical, computational, and collection functions involved in receiving payments from loan holders and remitting the proceeds to the paying agent for the securitized assets. Unless the issuer is a capital market conduit, which serves to purchase assets from a variety of sources along with the servicing rights, the issuer of the asset backed structure is usually also the servicer for the issue. In this respect, financial institutions such as banks, thrifts, and finance companies that are also originators of assets are uniquely positioned to take advantage of the growth of securitization since the infrastructure of these institutions includes the human and technical resources required to service assets.

Securitization also serves the dual purpose of allowing the company to recognize into earnings the present value of any excess servicing stream, which otherwise would have been realized over the life of the loan. It is arguable whether the usage of the securitization strategy forces companies that follow the accounting treatment of immediately recognizing the value of any excess servicing as income to rely excessively on asset sales without concern for asset quality (see our discussion below on moral hazard issues associated with asset securitization). Nonetheless, the ability to take advantage of securitization to improve earnings and eventually attain higher price to earnings multiples is a strategic option that can allow companies to maximize shareholder wealth.

---

[2] While risk based capital guidelines have caused many institutions to rely more heavily on securitization, the recently enacted Financial Accounting Standards Board Statement (FAS) 115 has in some instances had the opposite effect. FAS 115 requires institutions to classify as "available for sale" and to mark-to-market, rather than to cost, all securities they might ever sell as part of their normal asset/liability management activities. FAS 115, however, applies only to securities, it does not apply to whole loans. Hence, whole loans need not be marked-to-market and can still be sold at the institution's discretion. In view of this consideration, some banks have acquired whole loans whereas prior to FAS 115 they would have purchased securities.

Management of Interest Rate Volatility

All financial institutions are susceptible to the volatility induced by changes in interest rates unless the institution is duration matched on a continuous basis — a tactical decision that could negatively affect profitability. With respect to the management of interest rate volatility, the securitization of assets fulfills a dual role. The duality stems from the fact that the institution can securitize assets that expose the institution to higher interest rate risk and retain certain customized parts of the securitized structure to attain an improved asset/liability gap management position. In this respect, the financial institution serves the dual role of issuer and investor.

For instance, a bank that originates longer term home equity loans (HELs) funded by short-term floating rate deposits may sell the assets into the capital markets through a multi-class structured transaction. In order to match the re-pricing schedules of the assets to that of the liabilities, the institution could retain a short dated floating rate security. Depending on the rating of the structured security, the institution may be successful in insulating all or most of the credit risk of the HELs. Due to the closer match between the re-pricing frequencies of the asset and the liability, the predictability of the incremental spread income is enhanced while the interest rate risk of the HELs is mitigated. However, the absolute value of the spread income may also be reduced due to the fact that short dated securities usually return a yield lower than longer maturity securities, unless the yield curve is inverted. At the same time, the institution may be exposed to basis risk if the indices for the asset returns and liability costs are different.

INVESTMENT ATTRIBUTES OF ASSET-BACKED SECURITIES

While there are several convincing reasons for originators of assets to consider securitization, the ability of these issuers to securitize assets is heavily dependent upon the investment characteristics of the structured securities. As noted below, ABSs have several appealing investment attributes, such as being defensive in nature due to shorter durations, reduced exposure to embedded options, a low degree of susceptibility to credit downgrades, and increasing liquidity in secondary markets. At the same time, most newer types of ABSs have a certain element of novelty spread due to the lack of liquidity — a feature that provides a degree of total return potential in the event the spread tightens as the asset class becomes more accepted in the capital markets.

The investment characteristics of ABSs may best be exemplified by comparing these securities along several dimensions. The bullet equivalency of ABSs can be assessed by comparing them to non-callable bullet securities such as corporate bonds. At the same time, the exposure of these securities to embedded short call options, such as prepayment risk, can be evaluated by comparing them to other structured securities, such as collateralized mortgage obligations (CMOs). Due to the nature of the collateral underlying most ABS structures, the resultant securities, with notable exceptions such as closed end home equity lines of credit and aircraft leases, are usually short duration securities. As a result, these securities appeal to a variety of investors mainly due to their defensive nature and applicability as "yield enhancers" in structured portfolios. As the ABS market develops, financial engineering technology, which has been used successfully in other structured markets, is increasingly being used to tranche cash flows along various maturity and risk preference attributes. The growth in the aggregate volume and types of assets securitized also has been associated with an increase in the liquidity of these securities as additional investors and market makers become involved with the market.

Using technology pioneered in the maturity and risk tranching of agency and whole loans mortgages, multiple sequentially tranched structures, especially for longer dated collateral such as HELs have been created in the ABS market in order to widen the investor appeal of these securities. Along the same vein, money market tranches, which are structured at conservative prepayment scenarios to ensure payment at maturity have also been utilized primarily in lease and automobile structures. Similarly, zero coupon structures have been used in credit card deals as a means of expanding the product offering and investor base for ABSs. Derivative technology such as the usage of interest only (IO) strips has also been utilized in the ABS market in order to create either discount securities or maximizing issue proceeds. For instance, the usage of Planned Amortization Class IO strips is fairly common in sub-prime automobile deals, with the gross coupon of the collateral is high enough to generate sufficient excess spread, a portion of which can be carved out for sale. However, such deals typically require a higher level of subordination as the entire excess spreads cannot be used for credit enhancement. In the world of adjustable rate collateral, securities which are indexed of broadly accepted indices have been created using collateral indexed off of alternative indices using the available funds structure. In such deals, a host of structural innovations, such as shortfall triggers as well as customized risk management tools, such as caps are used to manage the basis risk between the collateral and security indices.[3]

Despite the fact that ABSs are collateralized securities and not dependent upon the unsecured credit rating of the issuer, these securities are usually priced at wider spreads than comparable debentures. As a result, in recent years the ABS market has attracted a certain amount of

---

[3] We are grateful to Lina Hsu for discussions on several of these structuring methodologies.

"crossover" investment that usually would have been allocated to the corporate bond market. In sharp contrast to both the corporate bond market, for which credit support is the rated general obligation of the issuer, and the MBS market, for which credit support is provided either by an explicit (GNMA) or implicit (FHLMC and FNMA) government guarantee, the credit enhancement in the ABS market is provided by a variety of sources. In this sense, the ABS market is very similar to the structured whole loan market, for which credit enhancement is provided by a combination of a letter of credit, surety wrap, and self-insurance feature, such as subordination of cash flows. Additionally, there may be certain "trigger" conditions that require collateral substitution should certain threshold deterioration levels be realized or cause the structure to early amortize in the event of significant collateral deterioration or bankruptcy of the issuer.

At the same time, the credit risk inherent in these securities has not been significantly greater than the aggregate credit risk associated with the corporate bond market. In fact, as noted by Moody's Investors Services, from 1986 to 1995 the overall rating volatility of the ABS market was less than that of the corporate bond market.[4] Additionally, the downgrades that did occur in the ABS market were mostly caused by downgrades of the credit enhancement providers. At the same time, the rating upgrade activity was also influenced mainly by the replacement or upgrades of credit enhancement providers or by increases in credit enhancement levels and asset performance.

Admittedly, these conclusions are based on the relatively short history of the existence of the ABS market; however, there is a certain degree of comfort in the fact that the downgrades were not caused by collateral related features.[5] At the same time, it must be recognized that due to competitive conditions in the origination of loans, there may be a deterioration of credit standards leading eventually to higher delinquency and foreclosure rates. To the extent such trends develop, asset quality performance is likely to become an important feature in the evaluation of ABSs, despite the existence of external credit enhancement as most of the agreements are associated with limited liability in the event of default

With respect to the prepayment option embedded within most ABSs, it is not as sensitive to interest rates as similar options in first lien mortgages. In general, credit cards and automobile loans are relatively

---

[4]   See "A Historical Review of Rating Changes in the Public Asset-Backed Securities Market, 1986-1995," *Moody's Investor Services*, October 20, 1995.

[5]   The first collateral related downgrade action occurred in December 1995, when Moody's Investors Services placed Mercantile Credit Card Master Trust 1995-1 for possible downgrade due to a doubling of chargeoffs to more than 9% over a period of eight months. However, the rating on the senior bonds (AAA) was affirmed by Moody's. At the same, it was also recognized that the increase in chargeoffs could be related to inconsistencies in reporting periods due to changes in the collection process.

insensitive to changes in interest rates. As a result, these types of ABSs are used increasingly as corporate bond substitutes due to their desirable features, such as rolling down the curve and tight payments. Other types of loans, such as leases, are associated with a "hell or high water" contractual provision which requires the lessor to fulfill the entire payment obligation under the terms of the lease in the event of early termination. Consequently, leases usually have very slow prepayment rates. While higher grade HELs and revolving home equity lines of credit can prepay fast in a low interest rate environment, lower credit HELs are not quite as sensitive. Therefore, as a general rule, the spread compensation demanded by investors for short call prepayment options is not as high as that demanded for MBSs. This feature also serves to increase the corporate bond equivalency of ABSs and thereby the investor appeal of these securities, especially for premium priced securities.

THE MECHANICS OF SECURITIZATION

As an example of asset securitization, consider the case of a financial institution that originates a variety of assets. While the institution can always hold these assets for portfolio purposes, the decision to securitize any of these asset categories involves an interplay of factors. These include the need to economize capital by expunging the balance sheet of higher risk weighted assets; the benefits emanating from securitization, such as off-balance sheet servicing income, gains from the sale of assets, and the recognition into income of excess servicing flows; and a comparison of various execution alternatives, such as selling the loans to a third party, participation in a conduit pool, and private label shelf issuance, which involves an analysis of the costs of securitization such as legal fees, investment banking fees, and distribution and underwriting costs.

The issuing entity in most asset securitized structures is a special purpose entity, such as a trust which is specifically created for the said purpose. The mechanics of asset securitization involve

- the sale of the assets to be securitized by the financial institution to the special purpose trust
- the underwriting of the loans for credit quality and the evaluation of associated credit enhancement costs
- determination of servicing arrangements
- the structuring of various classes of securities consistent with investor needs and preferences and the eventual distribution of these securities in the capital markets.

In order for the "transfer" of the assets to qualify as a sale to the trust, certain conditions, such as the sale of assets for tax and accounting treatment, limited recourse to the issuer, and severance of legal ownership interest by the issuer, have to occur. Another major undertaking in any asset securitization program is the initiation of loan review procedures. In addition to the review of existing systems and files, this process involves a statistical file review to test systems and procedures. Besides descriptive statistics, such as average coupon rate, seasoning, and average maturity of the loans, the actual documentation of the asset pool involves consideration of the underwriting standards, delinquency history, geographical dispersion, and prepayment characteristics of the portfolio. This information is required as part of the due diligence conducted by rating agencies and accounting firms prior to the securitized structure.

The rating process effectively requires consideration of the collateral characteristics and the evaluation of the capabilities of the servicer. An integral element of this process also involves the choice of single versus dual ratings. While ratings add to the cost of issuance, the advantage of incurring this expense is the provision of an added level of comfort to the investors of the securities. The evaluation of the servicing arrangements by the rating agencies is a very important part of securitization and involves consideration of factors such as servicer production volume and systems, delinquency and foreclosure experience, underwriting standards, servicing systems and controls, and quality control procedures.

The other major part of asset securitization involves the choice of the underwriting firm to structure and distribute the securities. An integral part of this selection process involves the negotiation of investment banking fees, legal expenses, and costs of distribution. With the exception of conforming mortgage assets, which are securitized using agency shelves, the decision also involves evaluation of various credit enhancement alternatives. In the case of mortgages underwritten to conform to agency standards, the securitization decision may involve either selling the loans for securitization as pass-through securities or a further conversion of the pass-through securities into derivative securities for resale to investors, using the agency shelf or issuance entity with default risk coverage provided by agency guarantees. Obviously, the execution alternative that provides the highest net proceeds to the originator of the assets is the desired alternative. With other assets, the credit enhancement decision requires an analysis of default risk (special hazard losses occurring due to extraordinary events, such as fire, earthquakes, lightning storms and hurricanes) and any losses due to the bankruptcy of the mortgagor. A variety of devices, such as a letter of credit, pool insurance policies by private insurers, subordination of cash flows, and spread accounts, may be used to cover default risk. Other types of risk may be covered by cash or negotiable securities deposit.

The next major step involves structuring and marketing the securitized assets. This may involve "fine-tuning" the structure several times to accommodate investor yield and maturity preferences. Additionally, the purchase price of the collateral will depend on the ability of the underwriting firm to sell the securities. As noted above, the risk premium in terms of a spread over benchmark Treasury instruments will be a function of market size, liquidity, and investor comfort regarding the cash flow priorities of the engineered securities. Once the final structure has been determined, the collateral is purchased from the originator and the securities sold to the investors.

MACRO-ECONOMIC BENEFITS OF SECURITIZATION

In addition to the firm specific advantages of securitization, a major reason favoring asset securitization is the rising cost of financial intermediation. Other expected macro benefits of the growth of securitization are informational efficiency in the financial markets, allocational and operational efficiencies for financial institutions, and pricing efficiencies in asset valuation.

The concept of securitization directly affects the traditional intermediary functions performed by financial institutions, such as maturity, denomination, and liquidity intermediation. These functions refer to the pooling of funds by fiduciary organizations, such as banks and thrifts from saving units, and providing these funds to borrowers. The intermediary functions improve the efficiency of financial markets by bringing together household units with varying amounts of savings and differing investment preferences, and borrowing units with differing maturity and denominational needs. However, the costs of financial intermediation have been increasing due to higher capital requirements and various regulatory burdens imposed by environmental, public policy, and other legislative initiatives. At the same time, the traditional intermediary domain of domestic financial institutions is being increasingly encroached upon by foreign banks and other non-bank financial intermediaries, such as brokerage houses and insurance companies, which offer many of the same types of services as banks and thrifts. In view of these reasons, the securitizaton of assets can be viewed as an alternative to the intermediary function of financial institutions, where instead of indirectly lending to borrowers, loanable funds are directly advanced to the users of such monies. As the market for asset backed securities matures, it is likely that the costs of securitized lending may be lower across the board than the traditional form of direct lending to borrowers for all categories of assets. This development also portends a de-linkage between the costs of deposits raised in local markets and the contractual rate on assets originated with these funds in a fashion similar to mortgage markets, where rates for primary mortgage origination are more closely correlated with the rates on mortgage-backed securities than the average cost of funds.

Securitization also allows financial institutions to achieve operating economies in certain business areas by leveraging their existing servicing capabilities as a means of increasing profitability. Average operating costs can be reduced when securitization leads to higher loan production and a larger servicing portfolio. In addition to operating efficiencies, a case could be made that securitization of assets enhances the allocational efficiency of financial institutions by expanding the universe of savers and allowing the organization to diversify funding sources. Traditionally, financial institutions have concentrated on borrowing and lending within regional geographic boundaries, and hence are susceptible to the vagaries of local economies. In addition to diversifying funding sources, securitization as an asset disposition vehicle allows the financial institution to diversify credit risk.

The securitization of assets also improves the informational efficiency of the market within which financial institutions operate. As the secondary market for ABSs continues to develop, homogeneity in the packaging and pooling of assets is likely to increase, with attendant developments in the identification of "ideal" risk tolerances, appropriate structuring of cash flow allocations, evaluation of various preferred maturity habitats, and increased synchronization of the securitized structures with desired tax implications. With higher quality information emanating from the secondary market, financial institutions will be provided with better indicators of secondary market pricing of packaged loans, allowing improved "backward induction" for primary market pricing, and overall pricing efficiencies. In the event that the securitized structures also involve a reduction in overall interest rate risk for the originating institution, it is conceivable that these savings will affect primary market prices for originated loans. While segments of the securitized market may currently be characterized by inefficient prices due to a lack of information, it is likely that as these various segments of the market develop with simultaneous links to the primary market the cost savings will ultimately be passed on to the consumer.

CONCERNS RAISED BY SECURITIZATION

Despite the many compelling reasons for issuers to use securitization — the equally appealing investment attributes of the structured securities and the overall macro-economic benefits of asset securitization — the growth of the asset backed securities market has raised several troublesome questions for analysts and regulators. These issues involve the possibility of the adverse selection of assets, "window dressing" of financial statements, moral hazards, agency considerations, and legal and account-ing uncertainties.

Adverse Selection and Risk Shifting

As a variety of assets are increasingly considered for securitization, there is a concern that institutions may tend to securitize lower risk loans, as such structures are associated with reduced credit enhancement costs and lower due diligence expenses. A logical corollary of this development is that institutions may "cherry pick" their portfolios for securitization and leave the existing debtors with an inferior asset base. However, such a development would be a direct contradiction of the traditional fiduciary role played by financial institutions. Nonetheless, while the likelihood of this possibility cannot be ruled out, these instances are likely to be isolated in nature mainly because of the assessment of similar concerns by rating agencies in conducting due diligence. Issues such as the role of securitiza-tion as a continuing funding alternative, the incremental quality of assets in the securitized structure, and the reinvestment strategy of funds obtained through asset securitization are all integral elements of the rating process, which is essential for ensuring investor interest in the securities. It could be argued that it is equally likely that financial institutions will follow a two pronged approach in asset generation. With respect to assets that are easily amenable to securitization, institutions may use "cookie cutter" techniques to generate securitizable loans by following secondary market underwriting standards. However, with respect to assets for which the secondary market does not exist or is underdeveloped, financial insti-tutions are likely to capitalize on their credit underwriting experience, and associated understanding of regional economies, and generate such higher yielding assets for retention in the portfolio.

In contrast to the adverse selection theory, the risk shifting argu-ment suggests that financial institutions will sell only the weakest assets through securitized structures, indicating that investors may find them-selves loaded with lemons. While this argument has academic merit, the practical manifestations of this contention are at best remote, unless the financial institution relies upon this strategy as measure of last resort. Besides impugning the ethical considerations involved in asset generation, this chain of thought also undermines the system of checks and balances involved in asset securitization. Assuming that the concept of asset securi-tization is of strategic importance, the possibility of the existence of moral hazard at the financial institution is a virtual impossibility. Additionally, the due diligence exercised by rating agencies, private insurers, and underwriting firms (such as the evaluation of asset collateral characteris-tics and default risk insurance) are important considerations that negate the "sale of lemons" theory.

The moral hazard and agency issues are somewhat related in that the basis for these contentions is that institutions could disregard care in loan generation and be overly aggressive in generating lower quality assets for securitized structures. However, acceptance of this argument implies that financial institutions will willingly originate loans based on less stringent underwriting standards mainly because the loans are not being held for portfolio purposes.

"Window Dressing" of Financial Statements

The "window dressing" issue refers to the use of securitization by financially distressed companies to create off balance sheet financing and, in the process, improve capitalization, leverage, and profitability ratios. As the argument goes, this improvement in ratios may be interpreted as a signal of improved financial health. A similar argument based on the concept of asymmetric information flows, suggests that corporations or institutions that lack the market receptiveness to issue high rated debt may attempt to obtain a "dubious" higher rating by using a special purpose subsidiary as the issuance vehicle for the securitized structure.

While this argument has some merit for the uninitiated, a closer analysis reveals that it may not be all that important. To the extent that the organization succeeds in improving its capitalization and profitability, the institution has taken advantage of the benefits of securitization. However, from the point of view of investors in the structured securities, it is important to assess the degree of correlation between the credit quality of the issuer and the structural and credit safeguards incorporated in the securitized structure. In the event of issuer default, as long as credit safeguards are a function of the collateral quality and not determined by the ongoing credit worthiness of the issuer, and structural covenants provide for an alternative servicing arrangement, the interests of the investors are protected.

Legal Uncertainties

Most ABS transactions involve the transfer of assets from the originator to a bankruptcy remote issuing entity. In order for this bankruptcy remote status to be maintained, it is important that the transfer of assets fulfill several conditions, such as sale treatment for accounting and tax purposes, a level of recourse less than the anticipated default rates, severance of the originator interest in any appreciation in value of assets, and the legal isolation of assets securing the structure. Developments that followed the Financial Institutions Reform Recovery and Enforcement Act (FIRREA) of 1989 shed some light as to the bankruptcy remote nature of the issuing entities associated with securitized structures.[6] As noted by

---

[6]   The section draws heavily on Neil Baron, "A 10-Year Perspective: How Have MBS and ABS Survived the Thrift Crisis," *The Mortgage-Backed Securities Letter* (February 19, 1990), pp.6-7, 11-14.

Fitch's Investors Service, Inc., during the 1980s approximately 46 ABS transactions issued by various financial institutions which were placed under receivership did not experience payment default after being placed under governmental control. Upon receivership, the payment schedules of these securities were either accelerated or the securities were redeemed in full. With respect to these securities, while the bankruptcy remote nature of the issuing entity appears to have been maintained, the investors lose a certain degree of call protection in the event of early redemption and may suffer losses occurring due to re-investment risk or premium erosion.

Since there is a paucity of case law in the ABS arena due to the developing nature of the market, it is not clear whether the bankruptcy remote status of the issuing entity would be maintained under all circumstances. This issue becomes more "fuzzy" for asset-backed transactions, such as credit card securities, which involve the continual transference of account balances charged by the loan holders. Similar unresolved questions exist with respect to other types of loans for which individual interests can be transferred and the issuer retains a certain degree of default risk by retaining "first loss" liability. There is a chain of thought that suggests that for asset securitizations in which the credit quality of the issuer is important for the ongoing viability of the structure, the securitization of assets does not completely insulate the investor from bankruptcy risk.

CONCLUDING COMMENTS

The once novel concept of securitizing assets has become widely accepted, certainly in the United States and increasingly around the world, with newer assets types being considered for securitization. Issuers and investors alike have adopted this process as a legitimate and proven means of funding and balance sheet management. Investors are attracted to such engineering securities because of features like reduced exposure to embedded short options, higher bullet equivalency, and usually wider spreads than unsecured obligations. Spreads on several of the more common types of ABSs, such as credit cards and autos, that once incorporated a significant "novelty" spread premium have gained acceptance amongst the investment community. This has led to the evaporation of the novelty premium with assets whose credit and prepayment characteristics are understood and to the emergence of the same premium with newer types of assets. Notably, structures with the novelty factor have the most conservative levels of credit enhancement.

Despite issues of moral hazard and window dressing of financial statements, asset securitization is a viable technology that can lead to cheaper costs of funding and an improvement in the earnings stream of the issuer. For smaller issuers with fungible assets, securitization can be used strategically to improve the financial health of the company as a prelude to accessing the capital markets on favorable terms for longer term debt or equity. The fact that many countries outside the United States have changed their laws and regulations to foster the development of this process within their borders is a strong testament to the inherent benefits of securitization, both at the micro level for individual companies and at the macro level for financial systems as a whole. As would be expected, some have adopted these techniques faster than others, but there is no mistaking the overall trend. While there is still room for growth in many countries, and many new types of collateral to be securitized, the process of securitization has become a standard part of the world's capital markets technology.

Chapter 2

Securitization in Europe

Paul Taylor
Senior Vice President
Duff & Phelps Credit Rating Co.

THE DEVELOPMENT OF SECURITIZATION IN EUROPE

Excluding the United States, Europe is the world's largest and most developed securitization market. Although a form of securitization has been in existence in the German and Danish mortgage markets for a long time, securitization in the modern sense only emerged in Europe in the mid 1980s with the issuance of the first UK mortgage-backed securities.

Since 1987, when the first transactions were launched, nearly 186 public, term debt issues have been completed, raising a total of over $50 billion equivalent (all numbers are as at end December 1995). Public, term issues have involved over 75 originators in nine countries. There have also been a number of private transactions, an increasing number of sellers into European commercial paper conduits, a variety of hybrid structures, and significant volumes of debt repackagings which have utilized the same or similar technology to the public securitization issues. By far the most dominant asset category has been UK residential mortgage-backed issues, which represent around 50% (by value) of total issue volumes. (See Exhibit 1.)

Many participants in the market, both existing and potential, have made considerable efforts to understand this new technology, and implement appropriate administrative and systems procedures. The authorities have developed and implemented new legislation and new regulations, and bankers have devoted considerable resources to build and expand the investor base around the world.

However, despite the successful launch of this market, in all its guises, many participants and observers have been disappointed by the relatively slow pace in the growth of issue volumes. There are perhaps two fundamental reasons for the slow, or perhaps perceived slow, growth. (See Exhibit 2.)

The first is that the initial launch of securitization was based largely upon the activities of a small number of centralized, or specialist, lenders in the booming UK residential mortgage market of the late 1980s. The level of activity was unsustainable. The severe recession in the UK housing market and individual problems at some of the most active issuers combined to drastically cut volumes in the dominant part of the European securitization market. The strong growth of the market's first years was therefore something of a false dawn.

Exhibit 1: Transaction Value by Country
Term, Public Debt Issues — U.S.$ Equivalent

Country	Percent
United Kingdom	59
France	22
Sweden	5
Spain	6
Italy	3
Other	5

Exhibit 2: Number of Transactions by Country
Term, Public Debt Issues — U.S.$ Equivalent

	1987	1988	1989	1990	1991	1992	1993	1994	1995
UK	11	13	11	11	20	6	15	18	7
France	0	0	0	3	6	4	5	8	7
Other	0	0	0	2	2	8	6	10	13

In addition to the deep UK housing recession, Europe generally was entering a sharp economic downturn. The resulting lack of loan demand and reduced lending volumes took away much of the underlying pressure on balance sheets, and obvious benefits of securitization as a funding and balance sheet management instrument. Work on the securitization infrastructure in many countries continued, but without the pressure from major institutions, yet to access the market for their own purposes, progress was slow.

There have been other factors that have delayed progress. These include the up-front costs of securitization, which are often seen to be very high. Costs include not only the obvious ones of bond coupon, and legal and other fees, but also less quantifiable costs such as management time and system changes. Also, a number of potential originators have encountered problems, when viewed in the context of securitizations, with the existing management and administration of the proposed assets, such as availability of asset performance information, centralization of files, and asset cash flow collection procedures. But, in general, these problems can and are being resolved over time.

Despite all of the problems and continuing barriers in many countries, securitization has continued to develop steadily as a viable funding alternative for European entities. Duff & Phelps firmly believes that there are good grounds to assume that this steady progress will continue. In particular, from mid 1993, the market's growth foundations have solidified. Since this time, the number of originators has grown (including many substantial and highly rated institutions), along with their underlying reasons for tapping the market, asset types supporting transactions have diversified, the investor base has expanded to easily absorb the increased issuance, costs have fallen, and positive legislative and regulatory changes have been seen in different countries. New public debt issues in 1995, however, were below 1994 levels. The first quarter of 1996 has seen a healthy increase in issue volume. Prospects for the rest of the year look very promising.

The stage of development, positive and negative factors, and the potential for future growth for each of the major European jurisdictions are detailed in the following sections of this chapter. A number of general comments can be made:

- In most countries, regulators have needed to be pushed into becoming familiar with, and receptive to the concept of securitization. Even in countries such as France, Belgium, and Spain, where new regulations were deliberately enacted to allow securitization, amendments to the original laws have been necessary because of shortcomings in the original framework. Regulators are often keen to know what the U.S. regulators are doing, or planning to do, in this field.
- Asset volumes are large in many markets. But often, the suitability of an asset type, or the incentive to securitize, or both, does not exist. The overall size of the "European" asset base is also misleading when looking at the potential for securitization, since in reality, the "European" market is in fact a number of quite different markets, often with fundamentally differing characteristics. It is unlikely that securitization volumes will ever reach those levels seen in the U.S.
- The diversity of market characteristics often makes it difficult to transplant technology from one to another. Apart from causing timing delays for new originators, or new asset classes, this also has adverse cost implications. New legal and tax ground must often be covered for first time issuers and issues. However, much work has already been accomplished. In some markets, such as the UK, precedents have been set in many areas, allowing a more standardized approach to completing transactions. As more and more "firsts" are completed, the problem should continue to diminish going forward.
- Originators have generally underestimated what is involved in successfully completing their first securitization issue. Problems have often resolved around issues such as systems modifications and data availability. Feasibility studies, prior to attempting to launch a transaction, can help identify and resolve such issues in a more efficient (and cost effective) manner. This approach is being adopted by a growing number of potential new originators. The resulting underlying growth in activity suggests a healthy market in the future.
- The market is generally well served by a large number of investment bankers. Given transaction volumes, there will probably be a shake-out over time in the size and/or number of these teams. The trend has already started. However, at present, the considerable effort being exerted by the banks in marketing the concept of securitization has helped spread the idea and introduce a growing number of entities to its advantages.
- Performance of existing transactions has been good, often in the face of highly adverse circumstances. UK mortgage-backed issues

in particular have performed well in the worst UK housing market experienced in decades. Downgrades have been caused by third party supporting ratings being downgraded, not because of asset performance. The Leyland Daf-originated transaction, Truck Funding, tested many (but not all) of the structural mechanisms incorporated into many issues. The procedures, timing, and costs involved in transferring the servicing function are now well understood, allowing appropriate safeguards to be built-in to transactions from the start. No rated securities have missed an interest or principal payment when due.

UNITED KINGDOM

The UK securitization market is the largest such market outside of the United States and is now firmly established as a viable source of funds and balance sheet management tool for many companies. Despite a number of set-backs and continuing frustration amongst many market participants over the pace of development, the UK market has experienced steady, if patchy, growth and is now well positioned for continued steady expansion. The current market fundamentals — type and spread of originators, diversity of asset categories, healthy regulatory environment, good technological knowledge, and strong investor base — all point to a steady increase in new issuance.

Despite a very disappointing couple of years in terms of new issuance volumes, particularly in 1995, DCR expects increased activity in all of the principal asset sectors over the next few years, and believes the UK will continue to be the largest market for securitized transactions in Europe for the foreseeable future.

Securitization Background
Economy The UK economy has finally emerged from a long and very deep recession. The recovery is now broadly based and has been primarily investment and export-driven, rather than through consumer consumption. Of particular interest to the securitization market, was the fact that the recession was particularly harsh in the residential and commercial property markets, where property value declines and default levels reached unprecedented levels. New lending has generally been very slow over the past several years, and only recently shown signs of recovery.

High interest rates over a protracted period and default and delinquencies provided a good test of the strength of residential mortgage-backed securities.

Current debate is focused on the possibility of increased interest rates, since although inflationary pressure does not seem that great at present, spending is trending upwards. Recent tax increases have resulted in continued caution being exercised by the private sector and political uncertainty has added to the length of time it is taking consumers to regain lost confidence.

Although in summary, the economic environment for securitization is looking much brighter than it has for several years, there is one major cloud that continues to overhang the UK market. This is the strong capital position of many of the larger European banks and their general hunger for assets. This has driven-down bank lending margins and created significant price competition to the capital markets.

Activity to Date In terms of both volume and variety of assets, the United Kingdom is the most advanced securitization market outside of the United States. At the end of December 1995, there were approximately £9 billion in outstanding sterling public, term asset-backed securities. Around £21 billion of such securities have been issued since the first transaction was launched by National Home Loans in February 1987. It is interesting that in 1994 and 1995 the actual volume of outstanding paper has declined by around 10%. This is due to a general slow down in new issuance, combined with increased redemption levels on outstanding securities. Increased rates of redemption are due largely to early calls on securities following acquisition of the originator (for example, Household Mortgage Corporation and First National Finance Corporation, both acquired by Abbey National plc).

During the first quarter of 1996, a significant upturn in activity occurred, in particular because of two large transactions (Pendeford Mortgage Securities and Bullet Finance) which together amounted to over £1.5 billion of new securitized paper.

In the 1980s, and early 1990s, the large majority of sterling asset-backed securities were backed by residential mortgage loans originated by centralized lenders. (See Exhibit 3.) Three lenders in particular, National Home Loans, The Mortgage Corporation and Household Mortgage Corporation, were the dominant issuers until late 1991. These originators accounted for over 50% of new issues between 1987 and 1991. New issuance from this source has practically dried up in recent years.

Exhibit 3: Total Number of Public Issues 1987-1995

Area	Percentage
Residential Mortgages	81
Auto Loans	6
Personal Loans/Second Mortgages	8
Leases	3
Commercial Property	7
Other	2
Credit Cards	1

With only a few exceptions, issues have been structured as floating-rate securities, even where the underlying assets generate a fixed-income stream. The typical form of credit enhancement has shifted dramatically since the early 1990s third party insurance policies to less "event risk" susceptible methods such as overcollateralization. Virtually all transactions launched in 1994 and 1995 have included a subordinated tranche of securities, designed to protect the senior notes from losses. Increasingly, the subordinated notes are also covered against losses by the provision of a first loss fund (typically in the form of a spread account). This has allowed the subordinated notes to be rated, usually in the "A" category. As returns on senior tranches have declined, more investors have been devoting the time and effort required to understand the strength of a rated subordinated security.

Although 1995 was a particularly disappointing year for the UK securitization market, with only seven transactions completed, a number of significant developments occurred. These include:

- First securitization of credit-card receivables, originated by MBNA International, Chester Asset Receivables Dealings No.1.
- Increase interest in commercial property-backed securitization. Transactions completed were Acres No.1 (United Bank of Kuwait) and Sonar 2 (Citibank).
- First transaction supported by revolving personal loans, Prospect 2 (HFC Bank).
- First transaction supported by rental receivables generated by housing associations, UK Rents No. 1.

A number of the transactions launched during the first quarter of 1996 continue this trend of innovation, including:

- Bullet Finance B.V. and Train Finance No.1, both involving the securitization of train lease receivables.
- City Mortgage Receivables No.1, the first "B&C" (credit impaired or generally lower credit quality borrower) residential mortgage-backed transaction.

So in spite of a dearth of new issuance, those transactions that did surface were generally innovative, laying the foundations for future activity. The net result of the developments since the market's inception is that the UK market is technically very advanced, particularly in comparison with other non-US markets. The fundamental problem has been lack of new issuance. A number of factors account for the low volumes. These include:

- Collapse of activity in the residential mortgage market. The opportunities for selling mortgage books, attracting premiums of 2% to 5%, have encouraged many centralized lenders to exit the market.

There is at present little or no funding or balance sheet pressure on traditional bank and building society lenders.

- Competition from the banking markets. Banks have largely rebuilt capital bases, and are generally very asset hungry. Margins on alternative financings have fallen considerably.
- Perceived cost, time delays, and general complexity of completing transactions. Given the innovative nature of many transactions completed in the past few years, this concern has been justified to a large extent. It is interesting that those closely involved in the market expect this problem to erode going forward — much of the technology is now in place.

No rated asset-backed security has defaulted in the UK market. A number of transactions have suffered a rating downgrade, but this has been the result of rating downgrades of credit enhancement providers, and in particular, rating action on two companies, Sun Alliance & London Insurance PLC and Eagle Star Insurance Co., who together provide most of the pool insurance cover on earlier mortgage-backed transactions. This strong performance profile has been achieved against a very adverse general economic background in the UK during much of this period, and the worst recession in the UK housing market since records began.

Legal and Tax Framework

Generally, there are very few legal obstacles to completing securitizations in the United Kingdom. Structures have been devised that deal with most potential problems. The flexibility of the UK's common law system has generally benefited the development of a securitization market. As a rating agency, DCR has formed opinions over time (in association with our legal counsel) on the strength of various legal structures having taken account of many different lawyers' views, including leading experts in particular fields. However, it should be highlighted that a fundamental risk is that the voluminous case law on which some structures rely, can be very dated, and decided by courts that, at the time, had not yet envisaged structured financings in their modern form. Little of the legal theory used in many structures has been tested.

While UK structured financings do have an element of uncertainty, due to this lack of definitive case law in some areas, the risk has been mitigated as far as is possible by the rating process. Legal opinions for each transaction, given by the issuer's counsel, explore all aspects of the structure. Where uncertainty exists, an independent expert opinion is usually sort. It should also be remembered, when comparing structured financings and non-structured bonds, that history has shown that even very highly rated companies can, rarely, default due to unforeseen circumstances, for example major legal action, or highly leveraged buy-outs.

Secured Loan Structures A major recent innovation has been the use in some structures of a "secured loan" approach, rather than the traditional "true sale" approach. In a secured loan structure, a loan is made to the asset originator (typically via the purchase of a loan note), payment of which is secured by the cash flow from the relevant assets. DCR will generally assume insolvency of the originator and must gain comfort that such an event will not result in any cash flow timing delay and loss to the transaction.

In many respects, a secured loan structure is stronger than a true sale structure. The key issue is the control by the issuer (via the trustee) over the ability to appoint an administrative receiver to the asset originator upon default (and thus defeat the appointment of an administrator or receiver). This is achieved via the granting by the originator of a floating charge over *all* of its assets. The basic problem with this approach is that most originators would be unwilling or unable to grant such a floating charge.

Appointment of an administrative receiver, who will take charge of all secured assets (that is, all of the originator's assets), by the issuer should allow continued disbursement of cash receipts as collected, without any undue timing delays (as long as the original transaction cannot be set aside as an "antecedent transaction" — essentially preference and undervalue issues).

Tax Tax law has raised a number of difficulties and concerns for UK securitizations. Examples of such difficulties are extracting profit without being assessed to Corporation Tax twice over, preserving MIRAS entitlements, predetermining the tax status of an issuer (investment or trading company status), value added tax, avoidance of stamp duty and the statutory indemnity issuers might have to the Inland Revenue for the tax liabilities of other companies. Most of these difficulties have been addressed in individual transactions, although, inevitably, they rely on the views of the Inland Revenue, which may, of course, change. As a general rule, DCR looks for transactions to be tax neutral for an originator.

Regulatory Framework

While the issuing vehicles are not directly regulated, many originators are regulated, and the relevant regulators thus play a key role in bringing transactions to market. Since most issues are listed (Luxembourg or London typically), there are also listing requirements to meet, for example prospectus requirements.

The most important regulators of securitization are the Bank of England (in respect of U.K. banks), the Building Societies Commission (in respect of building societies) and the Accounting Standards Board (for all U.K. companies, including banks and building societies). All of these regulators have now produced detailed comment and/or regulations on securitization. They basically allow securitization to develop with few restrictions, creating a healthy regulatory environment.

The Bank of England has taken a neutral stance on securitization, neither encouraging, nor discouraging this form of finance. However, it has been very effective in letting banks know where they stand. Guidelines were issued in February 1989 ("Loan Transfers and Securitization") detailing the requirements for obtaining off-balance sheet treatment. A further paper was published in April 1992, which both amended some of the earlier general principles and extended the framework to other asset categories (credit card and other receivables). In September 1995, the Bank of England published a consultative paper on the securitization of revolving credits. This most recent publication from the Bank of England is generally encouraging to banks wishing to securitize revolving credit assets. The most interesting provision is the proposed removal of the 10% limitation (maximum allowed securitization as a proportion of an institutions capital base) set in the Bank of England's 1992 paper, on condition that certain liquidity and early amortization triggers are met. The new framework opens the possibility of securitization of such assets by a wider range of institutions. The first transaction to take advantage of the new provisions was launched in November 1995 — Prospect 2 plc, a £185 million issue supported by a pool of revolving personal loans originated by HFC Bank plc.

Many other European regulators continue to use the Bank of England's general views and guidelines as the basis for their approach to securitization in their domestic market.

The Building Societies Commission (BSC) paper was issued in July 1994. The BSC has been more nervous of the development of securitization, and took a long time to issue a consultation draft of a Prudential Note on securitization. This paper replaced an earlier consultation draft issued in August 1991. The paper does not create insurmountable problems for building societies wishing to access this source of finance. The first true, and only to date, building society securitization was launched in December 1994 — a £150 million commercial mortgage-backed issue called CLIPS, originated by the Bristol & West Building Society.

The UK accounting treatment of securitized assets are detailed in Financial Reporting Standard 5, issued by The Accounting Standards Board in April 1994. FRS 5, which was in preparation for a number of years, aims to spell-out in a company's accounts the substance of a transaction and not the legal form only. Many of the considerable concerns of market practitioners with earlier proposals from the accountancy profession were addressed in FRS 5. In particular, the concept of "linked presentation" was introduced. Linked presentation is allowed where an originator has retained significant benefits and risks relating to the assets, but the downside exposure to loss is limited. In the originator's balance sheet, the amount of assets securitized is shown along with those amounts where there remains no exposure (no matter what happens), and the net balance of the two (i.e. the level of credit enhancement for a transaction provided by the originator). The detailed conditions which support the use of linked presentation are given in the standard.

Securitization Growth Potential

The UK should continue to be the largest securitization market in Europe for the foreseeable future. Conditions are favorable for continued, and accelerated, growth over time. The economy is growing again after a long recession, the regulatory and legal environment are generally positive, the technology exists (although many potential new originators may encounter timing delays due to systems adaptation requirements), asset volumes are large and originators increasingly understand the benefits of this form of financing. Just as importantly, there is a strong demand from international investors for asset-backed paper. Although tighter spreads may offset the current strong demand to a degree, these securities still offer comparatively attractive returns. In addition, growing redemptions from earlier issues should also strengthen demand.

A further interesting development that will increase the level of new issuance going forward is the growing policy for some banks to take assets onto their own balance sheet with a view to using securitization as an exit route. Given that the biggest growth constraint in the UK market to date has been the lack of suitable asset volume available, this new source of issuance may have an increasingly significant impact on activity levels. A couple of major institutions have already been active in this field. An example is the recent Bullet Finance and Train Finance transactions involving passenger train leases, sponsored by Nomura International.

However, for the market as a whole, short term growth constraints remain. In particular, there is competition from the banking markets. Banks have largely rebuilt capital bases, and are generally very asset hungry. Margins on alternative financings have fallen considerably.

The potential for each major asset category are discussed below:

Residential Mortgage Loans The size of this market alone (nearly £400 billion in outstanding loans) makes it extremely important for securitization in the UK. Most new lending is suitable for securitization. The general market has been very quiet following the severe recession experienced in the late 1980s and early 1990s.

The securitization of residential mortgage loans is very well developed and legal documentation is relatively standardized. Over 75% of UK asset-backed issues have been backed by residential mortgage loans. A wide diversity of mortgage types have been included in securitized structures. This includes mortgages in default.

Seventeen different originators have issued mortgage-backed securities (MBS) since 1987. However, new issue volumes and the number of institutions tapping the market declined greatly after 1991, as lending volumes fell and credit concerns arose. Confusion over the capital treatment of MBS holdings and very high spreads required by investors added to the generally depressed state of the market. Only three new originators, Sun Life of Canada, Birmingham Midshires Building Society, and City Mortgage Corporation have tapped the market in the last few years.

Although some large non-centralized lenders, including Barclays Bank and National Westminster Bank, have issued securities, their involvement has been patchy. There are currently no significant repeat-issuers in the market. Further issuance from large, new players, including possibly a few building societies, are expected. A pick-up in issuance from the traditional originators as lending volumes slowly recover is also likely. At the same time, the spread payable on high investment grade MBS securities has fallen to attractive levels for many existing and potential issuers. DCR believes that these factors suggest a healthier volume of new issues going forward than has been the case for the past couple of years. In terms of securities outstanding, this sector will continue to be the largest sector of the European securitization market for the foreseeable future.

A number of interesting developments in the underlying mortgage market will influence the nature of MBS issuance going forward. For example, a high proportion of new lending is currently fixed rate for a period of time. If this trend continues, it may result in the issue of short-term fixed rate MBS. The provision of mortgage finance remains a highly competitive field, largely due to overcapacity amongst lenders. On-going consolidation is likely. This could result in a larger number of private placement MBS derivatives.

A recent trend has been increasing activity with regard to new, specialized lenders established to lend to B and C (that is, lower quality, or credit impaired) borrowers. Such targeted lending is well established in the US market. However, this sector of the UK market appears to have been largely abandoned by the major lenders as they have reacted to their increased problem lending of the late 1980s and early 1990s by tightening credit criteria. A number of the new B and C lenders aim to finance their activities through issuing mortgage-backed securities. This should open a new source of supply to the starved investor community. Higher margins on these loans will compensate lenders for the expected higher default and loss levels.

A jumbo £1 billion mortgage-backed issue, Pendeford Mortgages No.1 plc, a subsidiary of Birmingham Midshires Building Society, was issued in early February 1996. This transaction broke new ground in a number of areas. It represented the largest asset-backed transaction seen in the European market to date, and was the first residential mortgage-backed issue from a building society. This transaction does provide much needed liquidity to the European market. It also showed the healthy investor demand for such securities. However, DCR does not believe this heralds a flood of new residential mortgage-backed issuance from UK building societies. The circumstances behind the issue, funding of Birmingham Midshires purchase of a large mortgage book from Hypo Mortgage Services Ltd, were very specific.

Outstanding UK mortgage-backed transactions have performed very well in the face of a severe recession in the housing market. Some weaknesses in certain structures have been identified, including higher stresses than anticipated on available liquidity (generally due to longer than anticipated repossession and sale periods), and unavailability of some insurance policies in full as and when anticipated (disputes over mortgage indemnity guarantee policy payments being the main issue). However, the availability of mortgage performance data generally during the recent recession, and the resultant impact of this performance on securitized structures, has provided good analytical material to assess future transactions.

Commercial Property While there has been an increasing amount of interest in commercial mortgage securitization and commercial property securitization, only a handful of public commercial property related transactions have been completed:

- BHH International Finance, diversified property portfolio (October 1990)
- 135 Bishopsgate Funding, single property, high quality tenant (December 1991)
- Healthcare Operators Group 1, nursing and residential care homes (December 1993)
- Sonar 1, nursing and residential homes (December 1994)
- CLIPS, diversified mortgage portfolio (December 1994)
- Acres No.1, diversified mortgage portfolio (March 1995)
- Sonar 2, nursing and residential homes (October 1995)

A small number of transactions have been completed in the private market.

The lack of activity in the UK (and Europe generally) is surprising given the size of the asset base available and the incentive for banks, the traditional lenders to this sector, to manage their exposures. The dearth of issues should also be compared to the US market, where for the past couple of years commercial mortgage-backed securities have been one of the fastest growing sectors of the asset-backed market. Much of the US growth has been driven by the Resolution Trust Corporation and its activities in managing the problems of the thrift institutions. It is possible that the deep recession in many European commercial property markets, including the UK, and the resulting problems experienced by many banks will result in the need for a similar move towards new funding sources and methods of managing balance sheet exposures. It is also more capital efficient for banks to securitize 100%-risk weighted commercial property assets rather than 50%-risk weighted residential mortgage assets.

One obvious reason for lack of issuance in this sector is the continuing willingness of a large number of international banks to lend against commercial property. Aggressive bank pricing can leave securitization looking expensive. Also, structuring problems do exist and may be difficult to overcome for many potential originators. For example, although the institutional 25-year fully repairing and insuring lease with five yearly upward only rent reviews can produce a reliable source of cash flow from which to pay down bonds, such leases are unlikely to be used in a fully amortizing bond issue because, for tax purposes, the principal repayment element is generally not deductible from the rental income; thus special purpose companies could face a large unfunded tax assessment in the transaction's later years. While it is possible to structure transactions to avoid this problem, the methods may increase the expense of an issue, or make the highest rating categories difficult to achieve.

Since European investors are active buyers of US commercial mortgage-backed securities, it can be assumed that there will be strong investor interest in European-originated issues. US investors can also be expected to show interest, particularly the large, sophisticated investors active in the US private placement market. But they need to see, or expect to see, sufficient volume before devoting the resources needed to understand the market.

An increase in interest in this asset category does appear to be underway, although it may take some time before structures are developed and transactions come to the public market.

Personal Loans and Credit Cards Personal loans can be further divided among auto loans, credit cards, and general unsecured personal loans.

A limited amount of activity has been seen in this sector. Six originators have issued securities supported by auto loans, credit cards, and unsecured personal loans, although only Chartered Trust and HFC Bank, through their CARS and Prospect transactions, have tapped the market more than once. (First National Bank issued a number of securities prior to its acquisition by Abbey National, but only one was supported by unsecured personal loans.)

Only one UK credit card-backed transaction has been completed — Chester Asset Backed Receivable Dealings No.1 Ltd. (CARDS) originated by MBNA International Bank, and issued in July 1995. In practice, the CARDS transaction largely replicated a US Master Trust structure. With 27 million credit cards in issue in the UK, there is potentially a very large market for debt backed by sterling credit-card receivables.

Excluding auto loan-backed transactions, DCR expects generally increased activity in this sector going forward. A number of factors lead to this conclusion, including:

- Asset volumes are large. For example, there are over £10 billion of consumer credit-card receivables outstanding alone.

- The assets possess characteristics that are well suited to securitization structures. In particular, high margins traditionally achieved on personal loans and credit cards allow a lot of flexibility in structured cash flows, and generally result in low levels of credit enhancement being required "up-front."
- Existing structures can be adopted by new issuers, thus reducing the up-front costs which often act as a barrier. While a number of structuring problems need to be addressed, most issues are well understood.
- The regulatory position is now much clearer for credit-card issuers in particular.
- Many originators already have active securitization programs in the US markets, for example HFC and MBNA. Understanding of the technology therefore exists, and regular issuance should be expected, assuming asset volumes warrant.
- A number of potential originators either do not have unlimited access to bank finance, or are unwilling to rely fully on bank finance, and do not have a high enough rating in their own right to effectively tap the public capital markets. Securitization provides them with greater diversification of funding sources. As lending activity increases, so the requirement for additional funding will increase.
- Those originators who can access capital markets in their own name are increasingly focusing on capital efficiency. The 100% capital adequacy risk weighting applied to personal loans makes this asset category attractive to securitize.

Other Assets Leases, trade receivables, housing association rent receivables, and corporate loans have all been securitized in the UK.

Lease-backed securitization presents a number of opportunities, although few issues have been completed to date, and structuring problems are often large due to taxation. Bullet Finance and Train Finance No. 1, involving leases on passenger rolling stock, were completed in the first quarter of 1996. Anglo Leasing has successfully securitized two portfolios of equipment leases. Many equipment leases in the UK are executory contracts, which create difficulty in structured transactions due to the on-going reliance upon performance by the lessor (since the lessee may be excused from paying were the lessor not to perform its own obligations, e.g., its obligation to provide equipment maintenance). The non-homogeneous nature of many lease portfolios and complex tax issues associated with leases make this a difficult sector to see much increase in the sporadic activity seen to date.

A number of UK companies are active sellers into *trade receivable conduits*. This is a huge market in the US and expectations are for considerable growth in the UK (and Europe generally). However, the pace of this growth may be slower than many people expect due to the inability of potential sellers to administer their receivables, including historic performance data, to the standards required. As economic activity increases and bankers continue to market the benefits of their programs, so interest in this form of finance is likely to grow. The experience of many companies in using US receivable conduits will benefit them in understanding the positives and negatives of the European programs.

The first transaction involving the securitization of *UK housing association rent receivables* was completed in 1995 — UK Rents No.1. This innovative transaction has paved the way for further issuance in this sector. However, the basic problems currently hindering new activity are the aggressive lending competition from banks and building societies, combined with the continuing political uncertainty surrounding certain aspects of housing association activity.

Only one *corporate loan-backed* securitization has been completed to date (Thames Funding Inc., a US$ commercial paper program established by National Westminster Bank). Capital release achievable by banks make this type of transaction potentially attractive. However, structuring problems and sensitivities often associated with selling corporate debt will probably work against development of this sector.

FRANCE

The French market has developed at a much slower pace than expected since the securitization laws were introduced in December 1988. This has been due to a number of factors, including lack of capital and funding pressure amongst the main body of originators, reduced asset generation due to the recession, and difficulties with some provisions of the original law. However, a great deal of progress has been made in the past few years which suggests the obvious potential of this market may finally begin to be realized. The environment is now conducive to increased activity:

- The legal and regulatory framework is clear and generally in favor of the market developing. After a number of amendments, the framework now fits the requirements of most participants.
- Most asset categories have characteristics that are suitable to securitization. Wider margins on residential mortgages have increased the potential in this sector.
- There is a growing level of technical understanding of this form of finance. While many banks still view securitization as overly complex and expensive, the benefits are increasingly understood, and many potential originators are positioning themselves to tap the market if required in the future. The momentum created by the

increased issuance in 1994 will itself generate increased interest and activity.
- The privatization movement in France is gaining momentum. Capital management and return on capital will become increasingly important. Increasing funding pressures are also likely, particularly the ability to maintain cheap retail deposits.

A number of adverse factors still exist — operations and systems are highly decentralized in the French retail banking market, data availability is generally very poor, and securitization is viewed by some as a sign of weakness — but the positive factors now comfortably outweigh these problems. This suggests that increased activity will be seen going forward. Residential mortgages and consumer loans are likely to continue to be the main asset categories supporting new issues.

Securitization Background

Economy The French economy is gradually recovering from the worst recession it has experienced in decades. After very slow growth in the early 1990s, and a contraction of 1.5% in 1993, GDP is likely to grow by over 3% in 1996.

Real interest rates remained very high throughout the recession as France hung on to its policy of protecting the franc, and thus leaving interest rates aligned with those of Germany. The present recovery is driven by exports and investment. An unemployment rate of over 12% has helped to keep domestic consumption at low levels. The demand for consumer loans remains sluggish.

The residential real estate sector appears to have reached its trough in 1993-1994, with the number of transactions and prices now rising. By contrast, activity is likely to remain depressed on the commercial property side, due to the large number of properties overhanging the market.

Activity to Date Transactions to date have either been "FCC" law transactions or off-shore transactions. Total issuance of FCC transactions has been Ffr 54.7 billion (approximately US$10,903 million). (See Exhibit 4.) Thirty-three issues have been launched to the end of December 1995. The data in Exhibit 4 exclude interbank loan-backed transactions. These are sometimes included in commentary on the French "securitization" market. However, this is misleading, since they are not true asset-backed securities. Rather, they involve the repackaging of a bank loan under the securitization law (see below) to provide a bond-type product for individual investors. The bank originator usually guarantees payment to the bondholder. There have been nearly 100 of these transactions amounting to a total issue volume of over Ffr 37 billion.

The jumbo Ffr 9 billion Atlas Capital transaction involving commercial property loans originated by Comptoir des Entrepreneurs (CdE) has also been excluded. This transaction was not a true securitization, but rather relied upon the several guarantee of five major French institutional shareholders of CdE (with a monoline wrap from MBIA Corporation).

Of the 16 consumer loan-backed issues totaling Ffr 22.7 billion (see Exhibit 5), Ffr 12.3 billion were originated by Cetelem, the consumer loans subsidiary of Compagnie Bancaire. Other originators have been Credit Lyonnais, Credit Agricole, Lyonnais de Banque, Casden and Petrofigaz. High margins make this asset generally attractive to securitize. The first transaction to include substitution provisions was launched in May 94 (Noria 1), and the first credit-card-backed transaction was launched in December 1994 (Titricarte 12-94). Only one other credit card issue has been launched (EOS 1 in November 1995).

Residential mortgage-backed originators have included Credit Foncier, Credit Lyonnais, Comptoir des Entrepreneurs, UCB, and Credit Martiniquais. Many of these players are likely to use the structured markets again going forward. Nine of the ten transactions completed to date were issued in 1994 and 1995. A number of factors explain this:

- The fall in interest rates in 1993 enabled originators to securitize loans that were issued at very tight or negative net margins, and not suffer an accounting loss on transfer.
- A change in the treatment of subordinated notes (see below) effective from July 1, 1994 brought forward some issues.
- The amendments to the securitization laws allowed transfer of the servicing function. This opened the market to a greater variety of originators.

Exhibit 4: Total Value of FCC Transactions in France
Ffr Millions

	Pre-1990	1991	1992	1993	1994	1995
Consumer Loans	2,471	4,215	5,178	3,880	13,252	1,834
Residential Mortgages	0	1,000	0	0	7,275	4,968
Loans (excluding interbank)	1,557	2,058	0	1,391	1,700	634
Credit Cards	0	0	0	0	10,016	3,000

Exhibit 5: Total Number of FCC Transactions

Area	Number
Consumer Loans	16
Residential Mortgages	10
Local Regional Loans	2
Credit Cards	2
Corporate Loans	2
Other	1

Loan-backed transactions have involved local authority debt, stockbroker debt, and long-term bank debts.

Off-Shore Transactions It is difficult to get an accurate picture of this market since much of it is private. Reasons for continued activity in this market include the fact that FCC vehicles cannot acquire trade receivables or debt in arrears. It can also be easier to access other capital markets for some issuers.

There are a number of French companies who sell receivables into European commercial paper conduits.

Improvements to the domestic securitization laws should reduce the need for off-shore structures for most originators going forward.

Legal and Tax Framework

A specific legal framework for securitization, Law No.88-1201, was introduced in France in December 1988. This initial law has been further supplemented by numerous additional amendments.

The absence of the concept of trust under French law resulted in the creation of a special purpose vehicle to facilitate securitization, called Fonds Commun de Creances (FCC). An FCC is not a legal entity, but rather a co-ownership which owns a pool of receivables and issues certificates to investors. An FCC is set up jointly by the custodian of its assets (the depositary bank) and the company that manages it (the management company). Securitized receivables must not be in arrears upon transfer to the FCC.

Management company operations are restricted to managing FCCs. They must be approved by the Commission des Operations de Bourse (COB), and no more than one third of their shares can be held by any of the entities that have sold assets to the FCCs they manage.

The initial government-driven framework has been amended over time, as shortcomings of the original framework became apparent. Amendments have included:

- Relaxation of restrictions on asset types that can be acquired by an FCC. Under the initial legislation, an FCC could only acquire debts with an original term of over two years. This restriction was in line with the initial objectives of the government to facilitate the refinancing of housing loans.
- Allowance of substitution provisions in transactions. This is important, since it allows originators utilize one transaction for a greater amount of assets and amortize start-up costs over a longer period.
- Eligible assets were extended to include insurance company assets, although it should be noted that corporate assets are still excluded.
- The original law did not allow a change of servicer for the securitized assets without first obtaining debtor consent. This provision basically restricted the domestic market to originators of the high-

est credit quality. From January 1994, an amendment to the law enabled the servicing function to be transferred to another financial institution (the borrower must be notified by letter).

Despite the detailed securitization provisions, including the various amendments, some grey areas still exist under French law. For example,

- In the event that bankruptcy proceedings are initiated against one of the parties to the transaction, it may not be possible to legally isolate sums held by that party, but due to the FCC. Credit and liquidity cover would need to be sized to allow for this.
- The law of December 23, 1988 did not contain specific information on the nature of assets that could be securitized. It is not clear if, for example, leases can be securitized.

Withholding tax on interest payments to overseas investors presents a problem to some potential investors in the French market.

Regulatory Framework

After a hesitant start, the French regulatory authorities are now demonstrate a much more positive attitude towards the concept of securitization.

Management companies (Societes de Gestion) are regulated by the COB. A decree was published on July 1, 1994, increasing the requirements for these companies, in terms of human resources, systems capacity, and capital.

Each transaction must receive COB approval before a public offer can be made. This system of approval is found frustrating by many market participants since it often interferes with transaction timing. As market volumes expand, the pre-approval procedures of the COB will need to be enhanced if disruptions are to be avoided. A credit assessment provided by an authorized rating agency is required by the COB as part of the approval process.

Until June 30, 1994, the Commission Bancaire ruled that banks using senior/subordinated structures and retaining the subordinated debt need only count that subordinated debt as a risk asset for capital purposes (even though the bulk of the credit risk for the entire transaction asset pool was vested in that subordinated piece). Not surprisingly, all senior/subordinated transactions (with one exception) are thought to have involved placement of subordinated debt with the originator. From July 1, 1994, this practice ceased as the capital adequacy treatment moved into line with international practice.

Securitization Growth Potential

There are good grounds for believing that the French securitization market will continue to expand at a steady, and more consistent, rate going forward. Residential mortgages and consumer loans are likely to continue to be the main asset categories supporting new issues.

While total *residential mortgage loans* volumes are large at over Ffr 2,000 billion (approximately US$370 million), this does not give a true picture of the potential for the development of the mortgage-backed market. There are a number of limiting factors to the market's growth in the short-term. Much of the outstanding stock, and certain mortgage types in particular, including prêts conventionnés (regulated mortgages), plans épargne logement (a scheme involving a period of savings followed by the mortgage loan), and prêts aides à l'accession à la propriété (subsidized (PAP) loans, carry either very narrow, or negative, spreads to market rates of interest. Even some non-regulated loans provide negative returns to lenders — the lenders having used them as a loss-leader in developing long-term banking relationships with customers. Lack of centralized data and systems ability to administer securitization issues are also a major medium-term constraint.

However, the environment is changing. Spreads are rising as banks focus on the need to raise profitability and improve capital returns. Capital itself is also more of an issue in the French banking system than before. These pressures will only increase as privatization gathers momentum. A number of existing and potential issuers are known to be looking at the market as an on-going financing mechanism. Steady issuance can be expected.

There is a large and diversified *commercial property* market in France. The motivation to securitize almost certainly exists, since many institutions would be glad of the opportunity to reduce balance sheet exposure to this sector. However, the practical ability to do so at cost effective levels may be more elusive. The recent recession has impacted particularly hard in the commercial property sector. The resulting glut of property on the market, and many problem properties on bank balance sheets, will take many years to unwind. DCR does expect to see some activity in this sector going forward.

Transactions backed by unsecured *consumer loans*, including *auto loans* and *credit-card receivables*, are likely to be a major component of the French asset-backed market in the future. As shown above, this sector currently accounts for the largest number and value of issues to date. Although growth in new lending has slowed considerably since 1991 due to the recent recession, the market remains substantial.

In general, the high margins on these loans, centralization of the lender's operations, and strong investor demand for short-term paper, should encourage healthy growth of this sector. A significant part of the market is held by specialized finance institutions, and finance subsidiaries of retailers and auto manufacturers. These entities tend to have strong origination capacity, but limited balance sheet capacity and/or ability to hold the assets. As the economy recovers from recession and loan demand picks up, the number and variety of issues and issuers should expand. Regulatory changes, discussed above, should also encourage expansion in this sector.

The potential size of the *trade receivable* market is very large, given the size of the French economy. Limited progress has been made to date, with only a few French corporates actively selling receivables to European conduit funding programs. Considerable effort is being expended by bankers active in this market to sell the benefits of this funding technique. Increased interest reflects the success of these efforts, although lack of appropriate data and administrative system constraints and problems are common amongst potential sellers, both problems that will take time to resolve. These structures must go off-shore under the current legal and regulatory environment.

There may be some limited activity involving other asset types, for example, leases, and corporate loans, but volumes are likely to be small with no regular supply.

SPAIN

Spain is one of the most promising countries in Europe for the development of a sizable residential mortgage securitization market. The regulatory and legislative environment are favorable to increased activity, asset volumes are large, and there is healthy interest amongst existing and potential originators. However, explosive growth should not be expected since there are still a number of negative factors that will hamper the market's growth. These include the lack of real motivation at present to securitize amongst the major mortgage lenders (there are no significant capital or funding needs, and lending volumes are not high), and the need to expand the investor base internationally and away from over-reliance on domestic investors, where the market may not be that deep if volumes expand.

Non-mortgage securitization should expand slowly, but structural issues in the short-term (e.g., ability to transfer the servicing function) pending new legislation, and lack of suitable asset volumes in the longer-term may inhibit growth. Nonetheless, a handful of non-mortgage-backed transactions, from both domestic and off-shore issuers, can be expected.

The long awaited Nuclear Moratorium transaction involving electricity surcharge receivables is expected to be launched in the second half of 1996. The $1.8 billion equivalent transaction should provide a filip to the Spanish asset-backed sector.

Securitization Background

Economy Spain has recently emerged from the clutches of economic recession. It has suffered similar problems to other countries in the European community, but exacerbated by additional factors, such as a rigid labor market, generous welfare benefits, and a high cost of capital, that further weakened Spanish industry. Spanish unemployment levels are one of the highest in Europe, at over 20%.

Recovery has been driven by increases in export sales which have been aided by the devaluation of the peseta in 1994 and 1995. Increasing exports will be largely dependent upon the economies of Spain's major European export markets. Interest rates are at historically low levels, encouraging companies to issue new debt. This should lead to increased activity in both domestic and international capital markets for Spanish issuers.

Activity to Date The 16 issues as of early 1996 total Pts244 billion (US$1.93 billion), as shown in Exhibit 6. Many originators have little immediate need to access the securitization market. However, some of the above issues have reflected strategic planning by the originator, that is, they want to know that they have the ability to tap this funding source if required at reasonably short notice. The size of some of the transactions reflects this point.

The first Spanish asset-backed transaction was an unrated, Ptas 7 billion, auto loan-backed private placement issued in late 1990. The assets were originated by Citibank's Spanish subsidiary.

Much of the above paper has been placed with domestic institutional investors, although increasing international placement is being achieved. It is likely that future transactions will increasingly need to tap the international investor base. The domestic investor base is limited in part due to the high yields on Spanish government securities.

Exhibit 6: Public, Rated Transactions Launched as of Early 1996

Issue	Type	Date	Size
Citibank Espana *	Mtges	1991	Pts7bn
Sociedad Espanole de Titulization 1	Mtges	11/91	Pts12.75bn
Spanish Asset-Backed Finance	Loans	1/93	US$1bn
Fondo de Titulization Hipotecaria	Mtges	8/93	Pts3.5bn
Hipotecario 1	Mtges	9/93	Pts11.5bn
TDA 1	Mtges	12/93	Pts12bn
AIG Finanzes 1	Mtges	12/93	Pts3bn
Hipotebansa 2	Mtges	3/94	Pts16bn
Hipotebansa 3	Mtges	6/94	Pts45bn
UCI 1	Mtges	11/94	Pts10.45bn
TDA 2	Mtges	12/94	Pts10bn
TDA 3	Mtges	1/95	Pts14bn
Hipotebansa 4	Mtges	4/95	Pts60bn
UCI 2	Mtges	7/95	Pts20bn
AIG Finanzes 2	Mtges	12/95	Pts3bn
BBV -MBS 1	Mtges	2/96	Pts15bn

* This transaction was a sub-participation structure and was not a "true" securitization.

Legal and Tax Framework

A formal legal structure for mortgage securitization (titulizacion hipotecaria) was established on July 7, 1992. This allows the establishment of independent funds, Fundos de Titulizacion Hipotecaria (Fundos), which are only allowed to invest in Participacion Hipotecarias (PHs). A PH is a certificate backed by an individual mortgage loan. Thus the new law allowed the grouping of these individual PHs together to form collateral for a mortgage securitization. Additionally the new law ensured that these assets would be excluded from the bankrupt estate of the issuer. A fundo must be managed by a Sociedad Gestoras de Fundos de Titulizacion Hipotecaria (Gestoras). These management companies currently have to be run by five separate partners which has not proved popular with the Spanish banks as it precludes the possibility of individual control. The authorities have indicated their willingness to review this. One further requirement of this law is that every issue must be rated by an independent, authorized agency.

The Treasury announced in late 1993 that it intends to pass new legislation that will allow Spanish entities to securitize other asset types using a similar structure as that designed for mortgages. Primary legislation along these lines was passed on March 10, 1994. The regulations have still not been fully implemented and further regulations may well be required before the appearance of asset-backed issues through the domestic framework. In the meantime, off-shore structures can be used by issuers, although Treasury approval is required. Specific legislation for the forthcoming Nuclear Moratorium transaction has been enacted.

Investors in bonds issued by a Spanish special purpose company have to certify that they are resident in a European Union country otherwise they are liable for withholding tax on payments of interest on the bonds.

Regulatory Framework

The regulators have generally encouraged the market's development, although without being seen to be too positive. The main supervisory bodies are the Bank of Spain, Banco de Espana; the securities market regulator, Comision Nacional del Mercado de Valores; and the Ministry of Finance financial policy unit, Direccion General del Tesoro y Politica Financier. The Bank of Spain produced "Circular 4" on June 14, 1991 which allowed PHs to be classified as asset transfers and thus they would qualify for off-balance sheet treatment. The off-balance sheets treatment of securitization was further clarified by the Bank of Spain in "Circular 7" of November 13, 1992.

Securitization Growth Potential

Spain is one of the most promising countries in Europe for the development of a sizable securitization market. Activity in the last couple of years has been relatively high, following resolution of various outstanding regulatory, legislative and taxation issues. After much work, and a long lead time, a number of originators are now in a position to effectively securitise their mortgage assets. This has involved a lot of administrative work, including systems changes. Most existing and prospectIve originators intend a securitization program, as opposed to one-off transactions. This is encouraging for the market's development.

It is certain that *residential mortgages* will continue to dominate as the asset type most common in transactions. The residential mortgage market is substantial. Mortgage lenders fall into five main categories:

- Savings and loans institutions (cajas de ahorros) who are the main providers, accounting for a little under 50% of the market.
- Commercial banks are the next largest lending group accounting for around 32% of outstanding loans.
- Banco Hipotacaio de Espana (BE), the state-owned mortgage bank accounted for around 14% of outstanding loans. This had dropped from over 25% in the early 1980s.
- Specialist mortgage lending companies (sociedades de credito hipotecario) accounting for around 5% of outstanding loans. They are typically owned by the commercial banks.
- A small amount of lending is undertaken by non-banking institutions such as insurance companies and pension funds but they account for a very small part of the market.

It is encouraging that both of the main categories of lender, savings and loan institutions and commercial banks, have been active in the securitization market to date. Also, the increasingly difficult availability and rising cost of traditional retail funding sources for the main lenders will act as a fillip for the off-balance sheet market. The current Spanish government has encouraged the expansion of housing finance.

The potential for transactions involving *non-mortgage* assets is limited at present, although a handful of transactions are likely in the near future. As mentioned above, one auto loan-backed sub-participation issue was launched in 1990 by Citibank, and a Banesto originated loan-backed deal was issued early in 1993 (Spanish Asset Baked Finance BV). These have been the only non-mortgage transactions to date although there are a number of transactions at varying stages of development involving a variety of asset categories. Regulatory and legislative changes are being worked on which will encourage development and expedite the process, but large issuance in this area is not likely in the near future. One of the major problems to non-mortgage securitization in Spain is the simple lack of suitable assets in terms of volume and homogeneity. Such assets may exist, but identification and isolation for securitization purposes is often not possible with current systems and procedures in use.

The long awaited Nuclear Moratorium transaction involving electricity surcharge receivables, is expected to be launched in the second half of 1996. The$1.8 billion equivalent transaction should provide a fillip to the Spanish asset-backed sector.

SWEDEN

Sweden is a relatively small economy with a population of less than 9 million. As such, "securitizable" asset volumes are not large. However, there are a number of sectors with the potential for reasonable volumes and there is a good basis for assuming the securitization market can develop broadly over time. The positive factors suggest long-term growth factors are present. However, the negatives are going to hamper and delay this development. A key factor for future growth will be the entry of a wider variety of originators into this market.

Securitization Background

Economy Sweden is slowly recovering from three years of deep recession. Devaluation of the krona has resulted in lower interest rates. GDP growth of around 2.4% is anticipated in 1996. The export sector is leading this recovery.

However, recovery, particularly in the banking sector (a significant part of which collapsed into government ownership during the recent recession) and the commercial property market is taking longer than expected by many observers. Historically high unemployment rates are also placing a lot of strain on the country's very generous social welfare system. Changes will likely be made going forward, with adverse effects on overall personal credit quality compared to previous experience. The generous welfare system has probably disguised the true credit quality of Swedish consumer assets in the past.

The government introduced a support package for the banking sector in December 1992, following a crisis of confidence in the country's major banks. This package costs around $9 billion. While lower interest rates have eased the burden, asset quality problems remain, particularly in commercial property, and will take many years to resolve.

Activity to Date There has been limited activity to date, as shown in Exhibit 7. With the exception of St. Erik Securities, the originator for all of the transactions shown in Exhibit 7 has been Svensk Fastigetskredit, a wholly-owned subsidiary of Skandinviska Enskilda Banken, one of Sweden's largest commercial banks. St. Erik Securities involved loans to municipal housing companies owned by the City of Stockholm, secured by interests in a portfolio of multi-family residential properties.

Exhibit 7: Swedish Securitization

Issue	Asset Type	Issue Date	Size(Mn)	Lead Mger.
Osprey 1	res. mtges	Nov. 90	$159.5	CSFB
Osprey 2-6	res. mges	Jul. 92	Sk2,58	Nomura
Osprey 7	res. mtges	Sep. 92	$363.9	G/Sachs
(sub.notes)			$22 .0	
Osprey 8	res. mtges	Jan. 93	$280.3	G/Sachs
(sub.notes)			$27.1	
Fulmar No	multi-family	Mh. 94	$332.4	M/Stanley
	mtges		Sk1,004	
(sub.notes)			Sk319.6	
St Eri No1	com. mtges	May 95	$160	ABN MRO
			Sk1,000	

Fulmar was the first European transaction to be backed by multi-family mortgages. Around 40% of the securities were sold into the US market under the 144a private placement rule.

A few Swedish companies are sellers into European trade receivable conduit programs. Other lenders have undertaken feasibility studies into securitization of a variety of asset types, although none have yet decided to proceed. It is believed that one or two have been very close to launching a transaction, but cancelled primarily because of cost considerations, general market slow down, regulatory issues, and commercial property sector problems.

Legal and Tax Framework

There are no Swedish laws that prohibit securitization. However, there are also no laws that encourage its development. A number of characteristics of the Swedish legal system require individual structures and analytical approach to be tailored to the market. For example the "pantbrev" system whereby a property will often provide security for a number of mortgages. Some specific points to note are:

- Debtors must be notified to achieve a true sale of receivables, otherwise they can discharge their obligations by paying the (potentially insolvent) originator.
- There is no "trust" concept within Swedish law. This is one of the reasons transactions to date have used off-shore SPVs (the other main reason is that an on-shore, i.e., Swedish, SPV, will be treated, and regulated, as a financial institution).
- There is no stamp duty on receivable transfer, or withholding taxes on payments to an off-shore SPV.

- It is essential that collections from the securitized assets are segregated from other originator funds, and easily identifiable. If not, the issuer is likely to have only an unsecured claim against the bankruptcy estate of the originator.
- General preference rules apply.

The transactions completed to date provide a good framework for the analysis of new transactions. The market generally believes that the legal system does not create insoluble problems for potential issuers.

The secured loan structure (as opposed to a "true sale" structure) utilized by St.Erik Securities set new precedents for the Swedish securitization market. The structure was possible due to the mechanics of Swedish insolvency law. However, substantial liquidity support was required to achieve the desired rating on the transaction.

Regulatory Framework

There are currently no published regulatory guidelines. The Finance Inspection Board and the Bank of Sweden have not encouraged the market's development to date, and may have actually discouraged some potential issuers. However, this attitude seems to be changing. There appears to be a number of reasons for this change of heart, including:

- The development of securitization elsewhere in Europe.
- Increasing pressure from domestic institutions to be allowed to look at this form of finance.
- The regulators' increasing understanding of securitization, following SE Banken's issues.
- Change of personnel at the Finance Inspection Board.

The regulators are currently reviewing what legal and regulatory treatment changes may be necessary to facilitate growth of the market. In particular, they are looking at implementing changes to allow the establishment of on-shore SPVs, following recommendations from a member of the Swedish supreme court who was asked to investigate the issue. But progress continues to be slow.

There are also no specific accounting guidelines for achieving off-balance sheet treatment. It appears at present that the authorities are following the lead of the UK Accounting Standards Board in deciding what criteria should be applied.

Securitization Growth Potential

The general level of interest in securitization remains high in Sweden. Many potential issuers are commercial real estate companies. However, a flood of issues should not be expected from this source in the near term, given the problems in this market. The deep recession in Swedish commercial property has resulted in a lack of liquidity and a large stock of repossessed property overhanging the market. This situation will take many years to resolve itself. Any transaction requiring the sale or refinancing of commercial property at a given point in time, or over a certain period, will provide a difficult challenge to structure economically.

There are likely to be more *residential mortgage-backed* transactions over time, particularly *multi-family-backed* issues, although short-term factors are delaying issuance. The market is relatively large, with around $100 billion equivalent of outstanding mortgages, 50% of which are on multi-family residences. A major restraint on the growth potential is the large and active unsecured mortgage bond market that finances a significant proportion (up to 75%) of outstanding loans. There may also be some problems structuring a transaction due to lack of centralized asset information and documentation.

As a fully industrialized economy, trade activity, particularly in the export sector, is high. Substantial *trade receivables* are generated in the ordinary course of business. This is an area that should see greater activity going forward. Lack of historic performance data may be a problem in the short term.

There is a much lower likelihood of transactions involving *other consumer assets*, such as unsecured personal loans and credit cards, due primarily to low volumes. However, the high margins on these assets and general characteristics suitable to securitization may facilitate some limited activity in the medium term as asset volumes expand.

In general terms, there are the positive and negative factors affecting the Swedish market balance. The conflicting forces should result in steady, but unspectacular development of this market. The positive factors are:

- A few transactions have been completed, creating the framework for future issues.
- Legislation does not preclude securitization.
- Major asset categories have suitable characteristics (although commercial property may be difficult).
- An upturn in economic activity generally over the next few years could lead to more funding pressure and the need for new funding sources to be investigated.
- Interest in this subject amongst Swedish institutions remains strong.

The negative factors are:

- There are no formal regulatory guidelines. However, this situation appears to be improving. Formal guidelines may be seen later this year.

- There remains a desire to achieve a "AAA" rating on issues placed internationally. Sweden's sovereign ceiling causes problems here and transactions generally require a "AAA" swap counterparty. These are very limited, and expensive. Development of a domestic krona market may take a long time.
- The severity of the recession, and subsequent government support of the banking system has removed much of the short-term motivation for players looking at securitization.
- Most domestic investors (of whom there are few of any size), are at early stages of understanding these instruments.
- With the exception of residential mortgages, and possibly trade receivables, "securitizable" asset volumes are small. There exists a large (unrated) on-balance sheet domestic mortgage bond market.

ITALY

A number of factors are holding back the development of securitization in Italy. These include:

- Lack of formal regulatory guidelines.
- Sovereign ceiling problems, and the need to achieve a high investment grade, often "AAA," rating, resulting in the need for swaps from highly rated counterparties.
- High structuring costs due to the complexities of the Italian legal and tax system with regards to securitization.
- Asset administration issues, including processing delays, lack of centralized documentation and historic performance data.

The development of technological knowledge amongst market participants and investor awareness will also take time.

But there are reasons why the market will develop going forward. For example, the major structural reforms occurring to the Italian banking system will enhance the benefits of securitization as a capital and funding management tool. Also, regulators appear to generally be in favor of a market developing. But these are longer term forces. In the shorter term, new transactions are expected, albeit on an infrequent basis, and much of this activity may be in the private commercial paper conduit market.

Securitization Background

Economy Italy has a fully industrialized and diversified economy. It also has a highly volatile political system, although the recent election results may finally see a more stable government. The country has very high levels of public debt and a large budget deficit. One of the major objectives of the authorities is to contain expenditure and ease the fiscal deficit.

Much of the recent political turmoil has related to the concerted attempt by special magistrates to expose and purge the system of bribes and criminal influence in political and economic life. A number of high profile and successful prosecutions of powerful individuals have occurred, and are continuing.

The economic outlook is stable with steady growth predicted. Rising unemployment and high real interest rates are also expected. The lira's devaluation following the currency's suspension in 1992 from the Exchange Rate Mechanism is benefiting the terms of trade.

Activity to Date There has been limited activity to date. Ten public transactions have been launched, totalling approximately US$1,513 million equivalent, as shown in Exhibit 8.

The limited number of transactions completed to date have involved a surprising variety of terms and structure. Transactions have been both onshore and off-shore, on and off-balance sheet, and supported by a variety of enhancement methods. Most of the leases involved in these transactions have been auto-related, although leases on ships, aircraft, and general office equipment have also been included.

In addition to the above public transactions, there have been a couple of private transactions completed and a number of Italian corporates sell trade receivables into European commercial paper conduits.

New transaction enquiries and general interest in securitization are currently high in Italy. Although, in the past, similar activity has not resulted in as many transactions as expected. Structural concerns, cost considerations, and information provision problems have been amongst the problems.

Exhibit 8: Italian Securitization

Issue	Asset Type	Date	Size	Lead Manager
Chariots 1	car loans	Mch. 90	L r.220bn	Citi/BCI
Auriga	leases	Mch. 91	Lr.140bn	BCI
Osiris	leases	Apr. 92	FF.584mm	Paribas
Car P Ifim	leases	Jun. 92	Lr.150bn	Chemical
Iris No1 Ltd	leases	Apr. 94	Lr.100bn	Paribas
Iris No2 Ltd	leases	Oct. 94	Lr.420bn	Paribas
Crystal Castle	trade receivables	Dec. 94	US$150m	Swiss Bank
Novara	personal loans	Sept. 95	Lr.140bn	Chemical
Iris No3 Ltd	leases	Dec. 95	Lr450bn	Paribas
Parma	receivables	Dec. 95	US$222m	SBC Warburg

Legal and Tax Framework

There are no laws that specifically address securitization in Italy. Existing securitization structures have been designed to address particular Italian legal and tax issues, and provide a good set of guidelines for future transactions.

In general, debtors must be notified to achieve a true sale under the Italian Civil Code (Articles 1260 through 1267). The Auriga and Osiris rated structures used an old law called "publico proclame" to achieve this which involved the issuing of three public notices: an official gazette, local court tribune, and a nominated national daily. There is a possibility that a debtor could argue successfully that he had not been notified. Law 52 was introduced in 1991 as a modification to parts of the Civil Code in an attempt to simplify assignment binding a liquidator. Law 52/1991 applies to "factoring" companies, and allows asset transfer without notice to the debtors. The later Italian transactions have utilized Law 52/1991. Effective from January 1, 1994, the new Banking Law seeks to further clarify some inconsistencies in existing legislation, including Law 52/1991.

Executory contracts, where there is residual risk on the originator, are widely used in Italy and have been the subject of a lot of interest regarding securitization. However, under Italian law, a liquidator or trustee in bankruptcy is entitled to reject executory contracts (Italian Bankruptcy Law 1942 Royal Decree No 267). This asset category thus presents difficult structuring problems.

Italian tax law generally provides for a range of withholding taxes on interest and other payments. Transactions have used off-shore withholding tax-exempt conduits (Italian bank branches, typically the London branch) to get around this problem.

Registration tax (stamp duty) is payable on asset transfer. However, execution of the transfer outside of Italy can avoid this cost. An exchange of letters (offer letter and acceptance letter) can also be used.

Regulatory Framework

There are currently no published regulatory guidelines with respect to securitization. The Bank of Italy is actively seeking to familiarize itself with the securitization process with a view to producing guidelines, although timing of any announcement is uncertain at present. Transactions completed to date have been dealt with on a case-by-case basis by the regulators.

A number of changes have recently been enacted, designed primarily to bring Italy into line with EEC directives, but none specifically address securitization.

Given some of the legal and tax difficulties faced by potential issuers, any significant expansion of the Italian securitization market will require a positive attitude from the regulators, and the implementation of clear regulatory and accounting guidelines. As interest continues to grow, this situation should be resolved in the medium term.

Securitization Growth Potential

There are plenty of "raw materials" for the development of a substantial securitization market in Italy. The suitability of some asset categories, due both to asset characteristics and lending practices, does however reduce this large base in practice.

In particular, residential mortgage securitization may take time to develop. The assets themselves generally have characteristics that suit securitization, including low loan-to-value levels and good margins. The asset pool is large — over Lire 200,000 billion ($130 billion). However, other aspects of mortgage lending may create significant barriers. For example, repossession procedures are lengthy, interest rate assumptions will be high in stress scenarios, availability of performance data and documentation may be lacking, and payment collection procedures may present problems for some issuers. Property transfer tax issues must also be addressed. On balance, therefore, development of this sector will likely be slow.

The leasing market presents more immediate opportunities for securitization activity. This sector is where most activity has been seen to date, and continues to be an area of interest from potential new originators. There are a large number of leasing companies in Italy — in excess of 1,200 — although six banks and affiliate groups represent about 95% of the market, which in 1993 totalled around Lire 40,600 billion (US$25bn).

The activities of leasing companies have only recently come under the supervision of the Bank of Italy. Leasing companies are now required to report monthly or quarterly to the Bank of Italy and meet minimum capital ratios. This increased focus on capital, combined with a need for new and additional funding sources and the general suitability of the assets (although not in all cases — as mentioned above, problems exist with executory contracts for example) to structured transactions suggest this sector has good potential to develop.

Personal loans, including auto loans, represent another area of possible activity. Much of the personal loan market represents finance to purchase autos. Banks hold approximately 50% of the Italian auto loan market, with auto manufacturer's captive finance companies 28%, and finance subsidiaries of foreign and domestic banks 16%. Limited activity has already been seen.

A few Italian corporates are already actively involved in selling trade receivables to commercial paper (and medium term note) funding conduits. A number of others are investigating the possibilities this form of funding represents. It is likely that this sector of the asset-backed market will expand in the future. However, given that sellers into conduit programs are generally not identified to investors buying the paper or other observers (with the exception of the rating agencies assigning a rating to the program), it will be difficult to monitor this growth.

GERMANY

All current indications are that securitization in Germany will be very slow to develop. This is due to a variety of factors, including already long-established financing methods, adverse sentiment from regulators (most banks will be very reluctant to rock the regulatory boat in order to access a source of funding they do not currently require), and no pressing capital or cost needs. The long-standing and very close banking relationships traditional in Germany present another considerable barrier.

The sale of trade receivables by German companies to conduit programs appears to be the one exception to this general observation. There is also likely to be limited activity from bank and non-bank finance companies over the next few years.

It is worth noting that highly rated German banks are increasingly active overseas in providing liquidity and credit support facilities to securitization structures. The technological knowledge of the major banks in this area will not therefore reflect the shortage of domestic issuance.

Securitization Background

Economy Germany is one of the world's largest, most robust and diversified economies. Recent past recessionary pressures (common across Europe), compounded by the continuing pressures from the integration of the former East Germany, caused a slowdown in industrial activity during 1993 and early 1994, but GDP growth of close to 3% has been experienced in the past couple of years. The country's strong net creditor position and the government's cautious monetary policy will allow the country to bear the medium-term economic and financial costs imposed by the reunification of the German state.

Inflationary pressures have been largely held back by a prudent monetary policy that has kept German interest rates high. This has resulted in pressure on the currencies of other European Monetary System members.

Activity to Date There have been just three public securitizations in Germany. These were:

- A DM 230 million issue launched in December 1990 by Consumer Loan Finance No.1 Ltd. The transaction was backed by consumer loans originated by KKB Bank AG, a 97% owned subsidiary of Citibank. Citibank guaranteed KKB's obligations and privately placed the bonds with a limited number of investors.

- GEMS Mortgage Securities issued in April 1995, a DM522 million (US$350 million) issue supported by the junior portion of real estate loans. Loans were originated by Rheinhyp, a subsidiary of Commerzbank.
- Volkswagon Car Lease No.1 Ltd. issued in February 1996, a DM 500 million auto lease-backed transaction.

German trade receivables have been sold by German corporates to a number of European conduit programs. Deutsche Bank established its Rhein-Main securitization program in September 1993. Rhein-Main is a Cayman Islands company. Deutsche Bank has also established a Delaware-based conduit program called Twin Towers.

Other than the transactions just cited, activity has been very limited. A couple of private transactions have been completed, including a dealer floor plan transaction, and some work has been undertaken in looking into lease securitization, and commercial property-backed issues, but progress has been very slow for a variety of reasons.

Legal and Tax Framework

Securitization is feasible within the German legal system. However, the system does not necessarily encourage its development.

The legal and beneficial ownership interest in a receivable may be assigned without notice to the debtor and the assignment can be evidenced by computer records. However, notice is required to be given to debtors to avoid them obtaining a good discharge for payments to the originator. Exceptions to assignment exist where there is a contractual prohibition on assignment (e.g., German auto manufacturers prohibit assignment of their obligations), where the assignment would change the nature of the obligation or where there is a judicial attachment.

It is likely that SPV's will be incorporated off-shore. This is for a number of reasons, including:

- So as not to be regulated as a financial institutions.
- To avoid trade tax (Gewerbestauer), which is currently charged on companies' long-term debt (and short-term debt that is constantly rolled-over).
- There is no "trust" law in Germany.
- Withholding tax is payable on payments from a German-domiciled SPV.

It is possible that future legislation may include provisions that complicate the ability to securitize assets. For example, the introduction of automatic stay provisions to help prevent or delay liquidation of insolvent companies, and servicer (originator) insolvency may become an unenforceable termination event under a servicing agreement.

It is uncertain at present (due to lack of transaction precedent) to what extent commingling problems will exist for German transactions. Much will depend upon a transaction's specific structure. However, it is possible that the originator's bankruptcy may cause sever collection problems.

There is no stamp duty payable on the sale of receivables.

Regulatory Environment

The Bundesaufsichamt (bank supervisory authority, BAK) and the Bundesbank have generally not favored the development of securitization to date. The main concerns are similar to those shown by many regulators at the prospect of a securitization market developing, and include:

- Issuing institutions may select only their best quality assets to include in transactions, thus reducing the overall quality of a balance sheet ("cherry picking").
- Loss of control over the institution's customers; for example, the treatment of delinquent accounts may be directly affected by terms of transaction documentation.
- The complexity of issue documentation, often combined with use of untested legal structures.
- Securitization may be seen as a sign of weakness at an institution.

None of the above issues need be a concern as the market develops. However, it takes time for understanding to grow. In the meantime, progress will be slow, as the regulators seek to control any development closely.

While the BAK has no direct powers to prevent a bank selling assets, it is possible the supervisory treatment of the institution generally could be influenced by the regulator's negative views on securitization.

Securitization Growth Potential

There is certainly no shortage of assets in Germany that could be included in securitized structures. However, the incentive to securitize does not currently exist for most potential participants.

Lack of incentive is true for residential mortgage-backed securities. A substantial and active domestic mortgage bond market exists. Pfandbriefe are fully match-funded securities, issued by mortgage institutions at spreads (which can vary widely) over government securities. Although unrated and on-balance sheet structures, they are viewed as very safe by (primarily domestic) investors. Pfandbriefe also carry a zero capital weighting in Germany. Other mortgage lenders fund their lending from retail deposits and wholesale money. There is some potential for transactions backed by second mortgages, or mortgages with LTVs in excess of 60% (excluded from Pfand-briefes) or mortgages originated by insurance and other companies. How-ever, the mainstream mortgage market will continue to be dominated by the Pfandbriefe system.

It is possible that the recent recession and the Schneider collapse will boost interest in commercial mortgage securitization. Particularly if finance in this area becomes harder to attract and/or more expensive. But any progress will probably be slow. The close banking relationships enjoyed by German companies, although likely to gradually weaken in the longterm, acts as a strong counterforce to any need to change the current system. Commercial mortgages can also be included in Pfandbriefe.

Trade receivables securitization is an already active market, and one that offers good growth opportunities. The presence of Deutsche Bank as one of the major players is helping to increase momentum in the development of this sector. It is likely that other funding programs will be established by other major German banks going forward. Some are familiar with the tech-nology due to their activities in the US market and as credit and liquidity pro-viders to existing European programs. The potential asset base is huge, given the size of the German economy and the importance of the export sector. Fac-toring is already well established and the technology exists for selling receiv-ables. In addition, securitization enjoys a key advantage over factoring — no notice to debtors is required (versus factoring where notice is required and such financing is sometimes interpreted as distressed finance).

Lease finance, and auto lease finance in particular, is a growth busi-ness in Germany. Leasing companies that are not bank subsidiaries and not regulated, for example the finance subsidiaries of the major auto manufactur-ers, may have an incentive to look at the benefits of securitization. However, the law governing the insolvency of leasing companies is currently being amended in a manner which will make rating lease-backed transactions diffi-cult. The amendment gives a receiver (or other insolvency practitioner) the ability to either terminate a lease or continue to perform it. If the lease is ter-minated then the SPV would be relying on the value of the assets alone and not the lease cash flow. If the lease is performed then effectively a "new" lease is created going forward (although the lessee sees no change) the payments from which are not included in the original assignment and therefore the pay-ments would flow through the receiver who could deduct costs and possibly delay payments. Structures will need to be designed to remove this concern (perhaps originate direct to an SPV subsidiary of the originator).

Unsecured personal loans and credit-card receivables present only limited opportunities for securitization. Most finance is provided by the main banks, where regulatory problems exist, and incentives for securitization are not strong. In addition, asset volumes are generally not that large, for exam-ple, credit card balances are typically repaid on a monthly basis.

OTHER COUNTRIES

Beyond those transactions involving assets from the major European economies, only a few issues have been seen to date (although sellers into European conduits are located in a variety of countries).

Considerable progress has been made and continues to be made in a number of countries in developing a viable securitization infrastructure. The usual array of legal, tax, and regulatory issues need to be addressed, and the complexity of these possible barriers varies widely between jurisdictions. On a more positive note, the main domestic institutions are often familiar with the mechanics of securitization through investment activities, US structured market operations, and the provision of credit and liquidity support to European and other issues. However, it is unlikely that more than a dozen securitization transactions from a handful of originators will be seen over the next couple of years from European countries other than those detailed earlier in this chapter.

Very brief summaries of some other countries are given below. The focus is on new issue activity, and thus some important countries in the context of the overall market are excluded on this basis. For example, Switzerland is an important center for investors in structured paper, and the big Swiss banks are major players in arranging transactions and providing various enhancements. However, the possibility of new issues involving domestic Swiss assets appears remote.

The potential for trade receivable securitization exists in all of these markets to varying degrees. References to a "shortage of suitable assets" therefore excludes normal trade receivables.

Belgium

Some major domestic institutions have been active in lobbying the authorities to implement changes to the Belgium Civil Law Code that will allow them to use securitization if required, and the regulators have been generally receptive and helpful in creating a suitable securitization framework. The historic problem under Belgian legislation is the need to notify debtors of any asset transfer (Article 1690 of the Civil Code). There are also potential structuring difficulties with set-off issues, withholding taxes, and registration tax. The position with regard to achieving off-balance sheet treatment is also unclear at present.

A new law was enacted in August 1992 to create a legal framework for establishing special purpose vehicles. The law takes its lead from the French "titrisation" law of December 1988. A further new law is scheduled to be put before Parliament in the near future making additional changes to the securitization framework, involving the creation of private investment firms with reduced involvement of the Belgian Banking and Finance Commission (who will play a lead role in supervising domestic issuers under existing legislation).

The interest of potential originators is encouraging, and once the necessary changes are made, they should facilitate some activity during 1996, probably involving personal loans, and residential mortgages. A couple of transactions are predicted.

The size of the overall market will be limited by the relatively small size of the suitable asset base. Also, the traditional supply of attractive retail funding to the banks, although likely to change over time, is a factor against the need to tap new funding sources. Capital management is likely to be more of a motivation for originators. Lack of standard underwriting criteria for residential mortgages, and generally limited asset performance data, may also delay progress.

Denmark

Given the success and depth of the existing domestic Danish on-balance sheet mortgage bond market, and the short supply of other assets, it is easy to assume that there is no need for a securitization market in the modern sense in Denmark. This is probably true in the primary market. However, it ignores the possibility of a market developing in derivatives of the underlying mortgage bonds — similar to collateralized mortgage obligations seen in the US markets, for example.

Tranching of bonds may attract new investors and increase the international investor base. To the extent that the underlying mortgage finance market expands from the depressed levels of recent years, this increase in bond distribution may be necessary. Given the size of the domestic bond market (approximately US$130 billion equivalent), the opportunities for such a market to develop over time are large. Since it is likely that activity will be offshore, the usual regulatory and legislative concerns may not be as significant. In spite of the potential however, only one transaction has been completed to date — a Dkr2.5 billion issue sponsored by Unibank Securities in July 1995.

Finland

There was a time, in the second half of 1992 and into 1993, when Finland was a major marketing focus of the main European securitization bankers. The intense interest was generated by the problems experienced by the country's banking system and the urgent need to access a new funding source and conserve capital. Most of the major domestic banks were actively looking at the prospects of issuing asset and mortgage-backed securities. However, the problems of the system were such that the authorities were forced to explicitly support the system. This action took away much of the short-term pressure from the banks, and the immediate need to securitize.

Some longer-term benefits from this period of activity exist. This includes the work undertaken by a working party under the Ministry of the Environment into all aspects of Finnish securitization (one of the conclusions was that no specific changes are needed to Finnish law to facilitate securitization), and the systems and procedural work undertaken by the individual banks.

The only public securitization in Finland to date was the US$350 million Fennica No.1 p.l.c. transaction launched in November 1995. This was an unusual transaction in that the originator and servicer was the Finnish state itself. The assets involved were housing loans advanced by the Housing Fund of Finland (ARA). Further issuance under the Fennica program are expected.

A well publicized Postipankki residential mortgage-backed transaction was pulled by the originator at a very late stage following difficulties in completing formalities with the currency and interest rate swap provider (Merrill Lynch Derivative Products). Over the long gestation period of this transaction, the pressures faced by Postipankki were reduced, taking away many of the immediate reasons for accessing the securitization markets. As the Finnish banking markets settle down over the coming years, some of the longer-term strategic benefits of securitization will reassert themselves, and wider interest is likely to grow again.

Republic of Ireland

Two transactions were completed in Ireland during 1995, heralding the opening of this market:

- Ireland Residential Securitized Home Mortgages, a US$63 million equivalent residential mortgage-backed transaction launched in October 1995. The originator was Irish Life Homeloans.
- Ulysses securitization plc, a US$88 million equivalent transaction supported by Irish local authority loans, launched in December 1995.

The two Aircraft Lease Portfolio securitization (ALPS) issues, which have raised over US$1 billion, and the jumbo US$4 billion Airplanes Pass Through Trust have also involved an Irish originator in Guinness Peat Aviation. Although given the nature of the assets, the number of jurisdictions involved, and the general structure of these three issues, they effectively represent a true international securitization. A large proportion of these securities were placed with US investors.

The regulatory framework is clear, following a 1992 publication from the Central Bank of Ireland. The paper takes its lead from the Bank of England paper on securitization, and details conditions to be satisfied for transferred assets to be exempted from the calculation of an institution's capital position.

Given the small size of the asset base (the residential mortgage market totals less than $10 billion equivalent), it is unlikely there will ever be more than a maximum of a few issues a year involving Irish assets. However, the general securitization environment is positive and more activity is likely in the medium term.

Part II: Product Areas

Chapter 3

Credit-Card Receivables

Robert Karr
First Vice President
ABS Trading
Prudential Securities Inc.

Greg Richter
Senior Vice President
Head, ABS Trading
Prudential Securities Inc.

R. J. Shook
Vice President
Prudential Securities Inc.

Lirenn Tsai
Vice President
Fixed Income Research
Prudential Securities Inc.

INTRODUCTION

The credit-card sector has grown tremendously since its inception and has become a widely accepted sector of the fixed-income market. The spread between credit-card securities and the Treasury curve continues to tighten toward levels in the triple-A corporate market. This is a testament to the fact that credit-card securities are increasingly sought after by traditional fixed-income investors as well as new investors. The cash flows of credit-card securities differ significantly from other structured securities, such as mortgage-backed securities (MBSs). In fact, the cash flows associated with credit-card securities, particularly bullet-payment structures, are more akin to those of corporate bonds. Because credit-card securities have a more attractive convexity profile than MBSs, and are less dependent on market perceptions of the issuer than corporates, they offer an attractive alternative to these securities.

As the credit-card market continues to evolve, its scope of investors broadens as investors in structured securities grow to appreciate the relatively stable cash flow associated with credit-card securities and non-structured investors realize the benefits of structured product. The growth of the market also has led to greater efficiency in execution, enabling issuers to lower their cost of funds on a relative basis and providing a permanent financing alternative.

PROFILE OF ISSUERS AND INVESTORS

Primary Issuers

The primary issuers of credit-card-backed securities include: banks, such as Citibank and First Chicago; retailers, such as Sears and JC Penney; and "non-bank banks" controlled by financial institutions, such as ADVANTA and Household Finance. Exhibit 1 shows the top five issuers of credit-card-backed securities with the total amount issued by that company (from January 1987 to June 1995). Total issuance for 1994 reached approximately $32 billion through 59 new issues. Credit cards continue to rank as a top profit center for large banks.

As the structuring and marketing of revolving receivables continues to evolve and develop, a larger number of issuers are attracted to the market for the following reasons:

Competitive Financing Costs Receivables owed to a company can be structured into a security of higher credit quality than that of the issuing company. As a result, the securitization of the receivables can provide a less expensive financing alternative (compared to issuing corporate debt).

Exhibit 1: Top Five Credit-Card Issuers to Date

Company	Dollar amount (in billions)	Percentage
Citibank	36.1	23
MBNA	17.2	11
Discover	12.8	8
First Chicago	12.6	8
Sears	12.5	8
Other	—	42

Access New Source of Funds Issuers now have a more diverse means of raising capital.

Enhance Equity Ratios Securitization of assets, when executed as a sale of assets for accounting purposes, liberates costly equity capital.

Increase Fee Income A securitization can transform net-interest income into fee income during the life of the securitization.

Improve Asset/Liability Management Issuers can structure ABSs to match specific funding needs.

Primary Investors

The growth and evolution of the credit-card-backed security market is due to its appeal to both mortgage participants and corporate participants, including thrifts, pension funds, insurance companies, commercial banks, international investors, investment funds and dedicated portfolios. MBS investors consider credit-card securities a safe haven in times of high prepayment volatility in the MBS marketplace. Corporate bond investors also are natural buyers of credit-card securities as the cash flows can be structured to resemble corporate securities. These investors increasingly are attracted to the benefits of structured securities over unsecured corporate securities. Overall, investors find value in credit-card securities for the following reasons:

- Triple-A credit ratings and wider spreads than comparable corporate securities.
- Reduced risk from issuer downgrading.
- Low prepayment risk.
- Short stated maturities.
- Tight principal-payment windows.

In general, the credit-card-backed security market has expanded the range of investors in structured securities because it is, in many ways, a hybrid of the corporate and mortgage securities markets. Credit-card securities offer investors the same credit quality and yield advantages inherent in structured securities, while offering a modified form of call protection, which helps to avoid some of the prepayment risk normally associated with mortgage pass-throughs. Generally, these securities trade approximately 20 to 25 basis points wider than comparable average-life triple-A corporate issues and 15 to 25 basis points less than PAC CMOs.

OVERVIEW OF CREDIT-CARD RECEIVABLES

Collateral: Credit-Card Accounts

Credit cards can be originated by banks (such as MasterCard and Visa), travel and entertainment companies (such as American Express, with its Optima Card) or retailers (such as Sears and JC Penney). These pools of assets fluctuate as card holders pay off their balances in varying amounts (from the minimum payment amount up to its entirety). The pools also can grow as new charges occur.

In accordance with a card holder's contractual agreement, minimum monthly payments are computed based on new purchases, prior balances, cash advances, finance charges, and annual fees. Under many card programs, if an account has no outstanding balance at the beginning of a billing cycle, and if the entire balance has been paid off prior to the payment due date, a finance charge will not accrue (except for cash advances, which usually are subject to finance charges from the date of the advance). This is known as the grace period. If a balance is maintained, finance charges generally accrue to the average daily balance during the billing cycle. If the minimum payment is not made by the due date, a delinquency will result.

Convenience users are those who do not incur finance charges. These credit-card holders utilize the cards for payments, then repay prior to the payment due date, thus eliminating all finance charges. Approximately 5% to 20% of all credit-card holders are convenience users; the remainder carry revolving balances. Issuers of credit cards that offer low annual percentage rates (APRs) may not offer a grace period since it lowers the overall yield of the portfolio.

Characteristics of the Credit-Card Portfolio

In order to properly evaluate a credit-card security, the monthly payment rate, the portfolio yield, and credit quality of the underlying accounts must be considered.

Monthly Payment Rate (MPR) Credit-card portfolios experience repayments, not prepayments (as found in mortgage- and auto-backed securities). The

MPR is the total payment amount that credit-card holders pay (principal and finance charges) each month as a percentage of the total outstanding balance.

To illustrate, suppose a portfolio contains $100 million of credit-card receivables. And suppose $15 million in principal payments and finance charges were received in a given month. The MPR is 15%. However, since some portion of the $15 million is attributable to finance charges, the actual reduction in principal balance will be less than $15 million. Since the portfolio consists of revolving accounts, it is likely that new balances will be generated even as existing balances are paying down.

Portfolio Yield Portfolio yield is closely monitored as a key indicator of the performance of any trust. Portfolio yield is the gross yield of the portfolio, or that portion of monthly payments attributable to finance charges and fees (e.g., annual fees and late fees). In addition, portfolio yield may include interchange, a portion of the merchant's discount that general-purpose card programs share with their member banks.

Many factors influence portfolio yield and cause it to fluctuate. Portfolio yield may decrease (assuming new balances have not been generated) as a result of:

- A decrease in the APR.
- An increase in convenience usage or lower-rate borrowers.
- Higher delinquency rates.

All things being equal, the yield on a portfolio of credit-card receivables (for a typical credit card) will increase for the following reasons:

- An increase in account balances.
- A reduction in convenience usage.
- An increase in the APR.
- An increase in cash advances.

It is important to note that portfolio yield is also cyclical. Because purchases are stronger during December's holiday season, and consumers tend to float these balances, portfolio yield is at its highest shortly thereafter.

Credit Quality/Credit Losses The credit quality of the collateral is the most fundamental issue when evaluating a credit-card portfolio. Since credit-card receivables generally represent unsecured loans, recoveries on defaulted receivables are typically low, and charge-offs are high relative to other asset types. However, portfolio yields are high enough to provide a significant amount of cushion against these losses.[1] Currently, losses on a typical

---

[1] See the discussion on excess servicing later in this chapter when credit enhancements are explained.

credit-card portfolio range from 3% to 5% and generally are higher for many portfolios of retail-card programs. The charge-off rate, or recognized losses, of a credit-card portfolio is a key indicator of credit quality. Usually, 180 days are given before a delinquent account is charged off.

Factors influencing the credit quality of the portfolio include account-solicitation methods, credit-scoring methods used in evaluating applicants, collection procedures on delinquent accounts, and servicing-system capabilities.

Although profit margins are likely to continue to diminish as competition for market share increases in the credit-card market, we expect the profit margins to be supported by technical advances in collections and more efficient operations. Additionally, tighter underwriting standards for credit-card users, following a spike in default rates in 1991, reduced default rates significantly.

There is a correlation between the portfolio yield and the charge-off rate assessed on a portfolio of credit-card receivables. If portfolio yield is increased through aggressive underwriting (during which standards tend to be relaxed), the gross charge-off rate tends to be higher.

OTHER COLLATERAL: RETAIL CARDS

Retail credit-card programs often are securitized in a structure similar to that used for general-purpose cards (such as Visa / MasterCard and Discover). However, there are special concerns associated with retail-card structures. The first concern is that, while general-purpose credit-card programs are designed to operate at a profit, retailers' credit-card programs are often used as a marketing tool. For example, more lenient underwriting standards may be employed, monthly payments are often lower (though in some programs they are designed to be higher to keep existing credit lines available for new purchases) and "payment holidays" (offers to skip payments, sometimes without accruing any finance charges) are more frequent.

STRUCTURES OF CREDIT-CARD TRANSACTIONS

A credit-card trust is created via the transfer and sale of assets to a bankruptcy remote subsidiary, which deposits the assets into a trust. The structure of the transaction protects the investor from the insolvency or bankruptcy of the seller. The property of the trust includes the following:

- A portfolio of credit-card receivables that arise from time to time pursuant to a group of designated accounts.

- Certain cash balances.
- Credit enhancements (to cover losses).

Certificates subsequently are issued to represent interests in the trust. These interests are divided into seller certificates and investor certificates.

The seller certificate represents an interest in the receivables pool equal to the difference between the total amount of receivables deposited into the bankruptcy-remote subsidiary and the investor certificate amount. The seller certificate is unrated and is designed to absorb fluctuations in the total outstanding principal amount of the card portfolio in the trust. Continued ownership of a pro-rata share of the trust provides an incentive for the issuer to properly service the entire pool.

Investor certificates represent an undivided interest in a portion of the trust. These certificates have the benefit of credit enhancement to cover expected losses. The investor certificates are sold to the public.

Each time a trust is established, a trustee is assigned to represent the interest of the certificate holders by monitoring reports required to be presented to ensure proper distribution of funds and compliance with the documents.

Exhibit 2 shows a sample credit-card structure. Exhibit 3 is a glossary of collateral terms. Exhibit 4 is a glossary of certificate terms.

Revolving and Amortization Periods

Credit-card securities are structured to have two phases, the revolving period and principal-amortization period.

Revolving Period During the revolving period, interest is paid to investors periodically, e.g., monthly, semiannually, etc., at the corresponding certificate coupon rate. Interest payments are funded from the finance charges on the receivables and any discount option funds[2] collected during the preceding month and, if necessary, from a draw on a credit enhancement. During the revolving period, principal that otherwise would be allocated to investors is used to purchase additional receivables. The purchase of additional receivables during the revolving period is used to maintain the investor certificate amount at a constant level for the duration of the revolving period. The revolving period typically lasts from 18 to 48 months. The length of the revolving period, as well as the length and structure of the principal-amortization period, determine the weighted-average life (WAL) of the security and can be chosen at issuance to take advantage of different investor appetites and issuer objectives.

---

[2] See the discussion on discount options later in this chapter.

Exhibit 2: Sample Credit-Card Structure

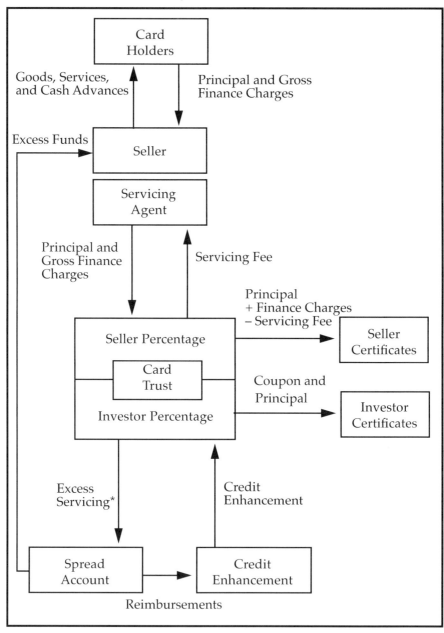

* Excess Servicing = Portfolio Yield – Finance Charges – Trust Expenses – Coupon – LOC
Fee – Losses

Exhibit 3: Glossary of Collateral Terms

Charge-Off Rate: Losses measured as a percentage of the average receivables outstanding.

Convenience Use: The outstanding principal balance is paid in full each month, thus no finance charges are levied.

Interchange: A portion of the merchant's discount in VISA/MasterCard programs that is rebated to member banks. Frequently included as a component of portfolio yield.

Merchant's Discount: The percentage fee that is collected by the merchant's bank for each card-holder transaction.

Monthly Payment Rate: The total amount credit-card holders pay each month, including finance charges, as a percentage of the total outstanding balance. The monthly payment rate is one of the primary determinants used to measure how fast a portfolio is paid down.

Portfolio Yield: The realized current annualized periodic finance charge on a credit-card portfolio. The portfolio yield should be sufficient to pay the certificate coupon, servicing fees, charge-offs and the spread account.

Repurchase Rate: Measures the card-holder rate of reborrowing. The repurchase rate is expressed as the ratio of new charges to the previous month's principal balance.

Principal-Amortization Period The principal-amortization period follows the revolving period and generally lasts for a period of 12 months or less. During the principal-amortization period, principal is paid to the investors according to a specific amortization structure.

Amortization Structures
Several amortization structures have been used in the securitization of credit-card receivables, namely the pass-through structure, the controlled-amortization structure, and the bullet-payment structure.

Pass-Through Structure As shown in Exhibit 5, during the principal-amortization period, principal cash flows from the underlying credit-card accounts are taken from the trust estate and paid to the certificate holders. This payment is in an amount equal to the ratio of the invested investor-certificate amount to the aggregate amount of principal receivables in the trust estate on the last day of the revolving period. The investor ratio is set on the last day of the revolving period and remains fixed for the duration of the amortization period. However, if the amount of principal received from the underlying credit-card accounts increases (decreases), the amount of principal distributed in any month to bond holders also will increase (decrease). Therefore, any substantial portfolio growth (shrinkage) causes the amount of monthly principal paid to investors to increase (decrease) resulting in a faster/slower liquidation of the investors' proportionate share of principal.

Exhibit 4: Glossary of Certificate Terms

Accumulation Period: The period during which principal receivables from the underlying collateral are deposited into a principal-funding account prior to making a bullet payment. During the accumulation period, investors receive only interest payments.

Controlled-Amortization Amount: A predetermined sinking-fund amount to be distributed to certificate holders each month during the principal-amortization period. The controlled-amortization amount is calculated by dividing the total original certificate amount by the length of the controlled-amortization period.

Early Amortization Event: An event that results in the discontinuation of the revolving period and in the commencement of the principal-amortization period. A pay-out event is caused by the bankruptcy, insolvency or receivership of the seller, a servicer default, excessive charge-offs or delinquencies or significant declines in portfolio yield, growth or payment rate.

Hard Bullet Payment: When the issuer purchases a maturity guarantee to ensure payment of principal to certificate holders at maturity should the aggregate amount on deposit in the principal-funding account be insufficient to cover the investor certificates.

Principal-Amortization Period: The period following the revolving period during which certificate holders receive allocations of principal received on the underlying collateral pool. The principal-amortization period is also known as the liquidation period.

Revolving Period: The period during which the principal arising from the underlying receivables is reinvested in additional receivables. Investors receive interest-only payments during the revolving period.

Soft Bullet Payment: When investors rely solely on the payment speed of the portfolio for full payment of principal on the maturity date.

Titanium Bullet: Permits the principal funding account to collect principal, during its accumulation phase, from all the series in the master trust that are in the revolving period.

Exhibit 5: Pass-Through Structure

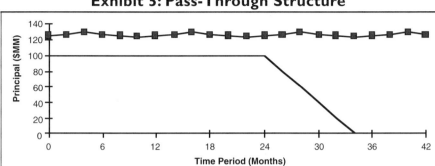

Exhibit 6: Controlled-Amortization Structure

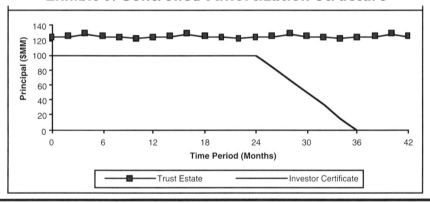

Controlled-Amortization Structure Exhibit 6 shows the controlled amortization structure. Under the controlled-amortization structure, investors are paid the lesser of the allocable percentage amount or the controlled-amortization amount. The controlled-amortization amount is set low enough so that the schedule can be met even under certain stress scenarios, traditionally one-twelfth the original certificate amount. All principal due to investors in excess of the controlled-amortization amount is taken from the trust and is paid to the seller for the purpose of purchasing additional receivables.

Bullet-Payment Structure In contrast to the controlled-amortization and pass-through structures, the bullet-payment structure (shown in Exhibit 7) does not employ a principal-amortization period. Similar to corporate bonds, principal arising from the accounts is paid on a specified maturity date. Because sufficient principal cannot be generated in one month to pay off investors, a principal-accumulation period is employed. Principal generated by the underlying receivables is deposited into a principal-funding account, generally in equal monthly installments. Similar to a controlled-amortization structure, one-twelfth of all principal will be available for distribution. Those monies are invested pursuant to a guaranteed-rate agreement to ensure that sufficient income will be generated to pay investors interest during the principal-accumulation period, as well as principal on the maturity date (at the end of the accumulation period).

In a "hard" bullet payment (common in earlier structures), the issuer purchases a maturity guarantee to ensure payment of principal to certificate holders at maturity should sufficient funds not be generated during the accumulation period. In a "soft" bullet payment, investors rely solely on the payment speed of the portfolio for full payment of principal on the maturity date. The accumulation schedules are structured so that this is highly likely. A "titanium" bullet payment permits the investor to collect principal with respect to other receivables in the trust during its accumulation phase.[3] This principal-reallocation feature also allows for compensation in the event of a reduction in the MPR.

MEASURES OF MATURITY

Several measures of maturity can be given for credit-card securities: stated maturity, expected maturity, and average life.

Stated maturity is the final date on which a credit-card security can still be outstanding. It assumes an extreme stress scenario (slow prepayment rates established by the rating agencies). It is stated for legal and regulatory reasons and has little relevance for investment analysis. *Expected maturity* is the final date on which a bond will be outstanding at the projected payment rate. *Average life* is the average time to receipt of principal, weighted by the amount of principal, at the assumed payment rate or according to the specified payment schedule.

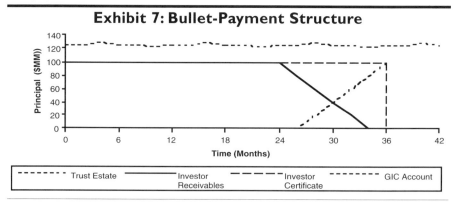

Exhibit 7: Bullet-Payment Structure

---
[3] This is discussed later in this chapter.

While the following events are possible, extension risk is highly remote and would occur only under unique and relatively unlikely scenarios:

- A dramatic slowdown in payment rates.
- Issuer bankruptcy.
- Interruption in servicing.
- Lower APRs.
- Decrease in the minimum monthly payment.

Cleanup provisions exist to retire securities when the outstanding principal balance decreases to a given percentage (such as 5%) of the original face amount. This feature reduces the possibility of a long "tail" (small amounts of principal that remain outstanding). The issuer's incentive to utilize the cleanup provision is to reduce servicing and administrative costs when only a small balance remains.

Credit-card securities are priced at a spread over "comparable-maturity" Treasuries, i.e., a Treasury with a maturity close to the average life of the credit-card security. The spreads over Treasuries are dictated by the market and change over time. Securities that are perceived to have greater risk, such as lower-rated subordinated classes, have wider spreads to Treasuries. Other factors affecting spreads include supply, changes in the Treasury yield curve, dollar prices, and perceived risk of early amortization.

CREDIT ENHANCEMENTS

Issuers of securities backed by credit-card receivables usually obtain triple-A ratings from independent rating agencies. The rating agencies review the historical-delinquency experience and loss performance of the issuer's portfolio and the quality of the servicer to determine the amount of credit support required for the security to achieve the issuer's desired rating.

The amount of credit support required to achieve a triple-A rating is determined by using a presumed worst-case-scenario analysis. In this scenario, the payment rate, the portfolio yield and the repurchase rate are lowered such that no excess cash is available to fund the spread account during the revolving period. During the principal-amortization period, the charge-off rate is increased to three to five times that of historical levels. From this scenario, the amount of credit support required for the transaction structure is determined.

The four primary sources of credit enhancement used in credit-card-receivable securitization are described below.[4]

---

[4] Monoline-surety providers, such as Capital Markets Assurance Corporation (Cap Mac), Municipal Bond Investors Assurance Corporation (MBIA), Financial Guaranty Insurance Company (FGIC) and Financial Security Association (FSA), have not enhanced any credit-card transactions in the public markets.

Excess Servicing

In all structures, current excess servicing is the first source available to cushion investors from losses on defaulted receivables. Excess servicing is made up of income earned on the investor share of the credit-card portfolio, less the expense of the debt service on the investor certificates (interest payments), the servicing fee and other trust expenses. The remaining finance charges are first employed to fund any charge-offs in the current period. Any remaining excess servicing is deposited into a spread account up to a specified balance, which is maintained to provide a first-loss buffer for the credit enhancer.

Cash-Collateral Loans (CCLs)

This credit enhancement was introduced in early 1991 and became the enhancement of choice for issuers who could not retain subordinated classes. The cash collateral represents an evolution from letters of credit (see below). It is a loan from a bank to the trust with the loan proceeds often invested in the short-term deposits of the lending institution if the institution has a sufficiently high short-term rating to qualify. The loan amount is reduced by repayment from excess spread. The trust is charged a fixed spread over the deposit interest rate on the outstanding loan amount. If shortfalls in interest or principal occur, the classes covered by the cash-collateral loan will be reimbursed.

Subordination

In a subordination structure an originator issues two classes of securities: a senior class (class A) and a subordinated class (class B). The B class is designed to absorb default losses for the A class. The size of the B class is based on the amount required by the rating agencies to achieve the desired rating.

While bank issuers must sell B-pieces to achieve regulatory-sale treatment on the assets, even though they still may obtain a GAAP-sale without taking such action, corporations, while still receiving GAAP sale, will still be subject to 88-11 exceptions. B-pieces sold to the public may be supported either by a third-party enhancement or by a retained C class. In cases where the B-piece is sold, these structures are almost always sequential-pay in that all of the principal payments first go toward the retirement of the A class; the B class receives no principal until the A class has been retired. If a subordinated class is retained, it is likely to pay on a pro-rata basis with the sold class(es). Otherwise, it might prevent a GAAP sale.

Letter of Credit (LOC)

The triple-A letter of credit is rarely used today. This enhancement represents a limited obligation of a third party to assure timely payment of principal and interest to the extent required by the rating agencies. The biggest disadvantage of a LOC is that the security cannot be rated higher than the credit enhancer in most cases. With the recent downgradings of so many triple-A-rated banks (the traditional providers of LOCs), investors penalize structures for event risk of enhancement downgrade.

Collateral Investment Amount (CIA) A relatively new form of credit enhancement, the Collateral Investment Amount (CIA) is the evolution of the cash collateral, senior subordinate and LOC forms of credit enhancement. Traditional senior/subordinate structures contain only A and B securities. The structure that contains A, B and C credit tranching is referred to as the CIA structure, with the CIA being the triple-B rated C bond.

The B-piece in a traditional A/B structure is often supported by a CCL and/or excess interest while, in the CIA structure, the B bond is supported by the C tranche and a combination of the CCL and/or excess interest.

As the CIA structure has developed, funding costs associated with it have become generally lower than those of traditional structures. In this structure, the difference between the portfolio yield and bond coupon (excess spread) may be used by the issuer to generate more credit-card receivables after being applied to charge-offs, effectively allowing for reinvestment in the portfolio yield. Conversely, in the CCL structure, excess spread must first be used to pay down the loan provided by the third party credit enhancer and therefore can only earn yields of eligible short term reinvestments such as LIBOR.

EARLY AMORTIZATION

While the revolving period of a credit-card security occurs for a specified period of time, early amortization, or the commencement of amortization ahead of the assigned schedule, is implemented as a means of safeguarding the quality of the security.

All credit-card securities have provisions to begin amortization early should the trust fail to generate sufficient income to cover its expenses (investor coupon and servicing fee) over a predetermined period of time. This provision is usually referred to as early amortization or rapid amortization.

The market price of a credit-card security is a major factor in determining the effect early amortization could have on the yield to maturity of the security. Early amortization is bearish, for example, for a premium security in a positively shaped yield-curve environment. Conversely, a shortened average life is bullish for a discount security.

An early amortization event may be triggered by one or more of the following events:

Exhibit 8: Breakdown of Excess Spread

Portfolio Yield	18.28%	Coupon	9.50%
+ Interchange	+1.00%	+ Servicing	+2.20%
Gross Portfolio Yield	19.28%	Base Rate	11.70%

Gross Porfolio Yield	19.28%
− Charge Offs	−6.00%
− Base Rate	−11.70%
Excess Spread	1.58%

- Excess spread disappears from the issue (due to either reduced portfolio yield or increased loss rates).
- MPR falls below a specified minimum.
- Credit-support balance falls below a specified minimum.
- Issuer violates pooling and servicing agreement.
- If the issuer is a bank, an FDIC conservatorship may be a triggering event.
- Representations or warranties are found to be invalid.
- Servicer default.

If any of these events occurs, the trustee will trigger the early amortization event. At this juncture, principal payments no longer are reinvested in new receivables, but instead are passed through to the security holders proportionately. For example, if total receivables equal $1 billion and the investor share is $500 million, then 50% of all incoming principal payments will be directed toward paying down investor securities.

Analyzing portfolio yield is critical to determining the performance of a credit-card portfolio. The portfolio yield will provide clues as to the potential of an early amortization event. When portfolio yield is high, a greater cushion is provided to impede this possibility. An example of the breakdown of portfolio yield is shown in Exhibit 8.

Consequently, excess spread is viewed as protection against early payout. Alternatively, if a lower portfolio yield leads to less excess spread, protection is uncertain.

When determining the likelihood of an early amortization event, an investor must consider the actions an issuer might voluntarily take to avoid such an occurrence. If the securities are trading above par, an issuer, for example, with the consent of the certificate holders, might add high-quality credit-card accounts to a portfolio or enhance excess spread by implementing a discount option.[5] This is most likely to occur with frequent, large issu-

---

[5] Discount option is explained later in this chapter.

ers versus smaller, infrequent issuers. Frequent issuers have the greatest incentive to maintain a reputation in the marketplace.

TOTAL RETURN

Some investors may shy away from premium credit-card securities due to fear of early amortization. In this section, it is demonstrated that even with aggressive early amortization assumptions, premium credit-card securities are expected to perform at least as well as Treasuries.

Total return is the overall return received on an investment when factoring in interest and principal payments, reinvestment income and any gain or loss of capital.

In a steep yield-curve environment (assuming constant rates), credit-card securities, during their revolving periods, tend to perform well on a total-return basis as they quickly "roll down" the yield curve. This occurs because, since they are not currently paying principal, the average life declines one-for-one with the passage of time. As a result, the security is priced off a lower point on the curve and, assuming a constant yield curve and spread, prices increase. Also, the spread may tighten as the security rolls down the curve, resulting in further price appreciation.

Oftentimes, total-return analysis is used to determine the fair value of a security in the event amortization does occur. Since total return takes into account any capital gain or loss, a security that amortizes early can be viewed as being sold at par at the weighted-average-maturity date.[6]

CURRENT MARKET TRENDS

Floating-Rate Securities

In recent years there has been a sharp increase in the issuance of credit-card floaters. Prior to 1993, few credit-card ABSs were issued as floating-rate securities. In contrast, in 1994, over 62% of credit-card securities came in the form of floaters. This shift was caused in part by some issuers switching from a fixed- to a floating-rate index, such as prime. With floating-rate collateral, a floating-rate coupon on the securities is preferred because it lowers the risk of a mismatch between the cash flows from the collateral and the payments to the securities holders. More importantly, however, is the growing number of investors, especially those overseas, who prefer to buy floating-rate paper. Many of these institutions are LIBOR funded and hence

[6] It is important to note that early amortization has occurred for only one public issuer in the history of credit-card securities (as of the writing of this publication). Southeast Bank Credit Card Trust A and B experienced early amortization in July 1991.

prefer LIBOR-based investments. About 90% of the credit-card floaters issued in 1994 were LIBOR based. To facilitate this demand, issuers have turned to the swap market, which allows them to issue either fixed- or floating-rate depending on which execution provides the cheapest funding and which sector exhibits the strongest demand. Hence, the percentage of credit-card securities issued as floating- or fixed-rate is now more a reflection of investor demand and swap spreads than an indication of the type of collateral supporting the transaction.

The performance of floating-rate securities is affected by the level and behavior of the relevant short-term index (which determines the coupon rate on the bond).

Like other floating-rate instruments, floating-rate credit-card securities are bearish: when short-term rates rise, the rates on the securities increase.

Master Trust

The master trust has been the preferred structure in recent times. This type of structure makes it easier for sellers to prepare for future series issuances. There are two types of master trusts:

- A dynamic master trust, in which an issuer has the option to commence with a large pool of accounts in the trust or to add accounts continuously, and
- A discrete master trust, in which lump-sum additions may occur at a later date.

The biggest advantage of a master trust to an issuer is that it cuts down on the preparation necessary to launch a new issue and it facilitates ongoing trust administration. Dynamic master trusts offer investors pool diversification, because receivables are constantly added, thus stabilizing their performance. When securitized pools consist primarily of newer accounts, the accounts will tend to experience their highest loss rates all at the same time, since they will all travel through the seasoning/loss curve together.

A key advantage to investors in either a dynamic or discrete master trust is the ease of analysis these trusts afford. The trust allows investors and rating agencies the ability to track and monitor all of the receivables as one pool. However, some investors prefer individual discrete trusts to master trusts because the specific accounts designated at issuance represent the vast majority of collateral. Since very few additional accounts will be added, the investors are not exposed to changes in underwriting standards when generating new accounts.

Discount Option

In contrast to revolving credit-plan products, which do not require payments in full every month, debit cards, as well as many trade receivables, require payment in full when billed. This generates a high turnover rate, or MPR, as card holders cannot finance their purchases. For this reason, assets of trusts generated by receivables that do not pay interest often are set up with discount mechanisms.

To provide yield to the trust on these receivables, a portion (usually a factor of 3 to 5%) of the collections on the receivables are designated as yield collections, while the remaining amount is designated as principal. The yield is calculated by multiplying the factor, say 3%, to the receivables collected over a given period of time. This number is divided by charge volume and fees for the same period. The result is the computed yield for the portfolio. (A formula and example are given later.)

Even if the collateral is interest bearing, a discount option may allow issuers to sell receivables into the trust at a discount rate whenever the trust's net portfolio yield falls close to the base rate. The use of the discount option is basically a method of boosting portfolio yield. The discount rate will be accounted for as finance-charge revenue and will affect portfolio yield. The value of the discount option to the issuer is that it is an inexpensive way to address possible losses in portfolio yield, thus increasing demand for the securities. From the investor's perspective, the discount option reduces early amortization concerns with the result being that securities utilizing this option currently are in high demand.

CASH-FLOW ANALYSES

Investor Cash-Flow Analysis

The amount of principal and interest available for distribution to certificate holders, given the following collateral and certificate characteristics, is computed here.

Trust Estate:	$150,000,000
Invested Amount:	$100,000,000
Certificate Coupon Rate:	8.25%
Monthly Payment Rate:	20.00%
Portfolio Yield:	19.80%
Annual Charge-Off Rate:	4.50%
Servicing Fee:	3.00%
Debt Service:	3.00%
Revolving Period:	18 Months
Principal-Amortization Period:	12 Months

Pass-Through Investor Cash Flow

In the pass-through structure, the amount paid to each certificate holder is dependent on the investor's fixed allocation percentage, equal to the original certificate amount divided by the total trust estate amount. The amount of interest and principal available for distribution to certificate holders is computed as follows:

$$
\begin{aligned}
\text{Investor \%} &= \text{Original Certificate Amount / Trust Estate} \\
&= \$100{,}000{,}000 \ / \ \$150{,}000{,}000 \\
&= 0.666667
\end{aligned}
$$

$$
\begin{aligned}
\text{Total Payment} &= \text{Monthly Payment Rate} \times \text{Trust Estate} \\
&= 20\% \times \$150{,}000{,}000 \\
&= \$30{,}000{,}000
\end{aligned}
$$

$$
\begin{aligned}
\text{Finance Charges and Fees} &= \text{Trust Estate} \times \text{Portfolio Yield} \\
&= \$150{,}000{,}000 \times 19.8\% \ / \ 12 \\
&= \$2{,}475{,}000
\end{aligned}
$$

$$
\begin{aligned}
\text{Investor Coupon} &= \text{Original Certificate Amount} \times \text{Coupon \%} \ / \ 12 \\
&= \$100{,}000{,}000 \times 8.25\% \ / \ 12 \\
&= \$687{,}500
\end{aligned}
$$

$$
\begin{aligned}
\text{Investor Principal} &= \text{Investor \%} \times (\text{Total Payment} \\
&\quad - \text{Finance Charges and Fees}) \\
&= 0.666667 \times (\$30{,}000{,}000 - \$2{,}475{,}000) \\
&= \$18{,}350{,}000
\end{aligned}
$$

Controlled-Amortization Investor Cash Flow

In the controlled-amortization structure, principal received on the underlying receivables during the liquidation period is distributed to certificate holders at the controlled-amortization amount, equal to 1/12 the total beginning balance. This method of principal allocation resembles a corporate sinking fund or a CMO PAC bond. The total amount of interest and principal available for distribution is calculated as follows:

$$
\begin{aligned}
\text{Investor Interest} &= \text{Original Certificate Amount} \times \text{Coupon \%} \ / \ 12 \\
&= \$100{,}000{,}000 \times 8.25\% \ / \ 12 \\
&= \$687{,}500
\end{aligned}
$$

The amount of interest distributed each period is calculated based on the beginning balance for that period.

$$
\begin{aligned}
\text{Investor Principal} &= \text{Original Certificate Amount} \times 1/12 \\
&= \$100{,}000{,}000 \times 1/12 \\
&= \$8{,}333{,}333
\end{aligned}
$$

Bullet-Payment Investor Cash Flow

In the bullet-payment structure, principal is paid in full to certificate holders on the scheduled maturity date. During the accumulation period, principal is deposited into the principal-funding account at $1/12$ the original certificate amount. As a result, the total amount of principal available for distribution to certificate holders at maturity is equal to the original certificate amount.

$$
\begin{aligned}
\text{Principal-Funding Amount} &= \text{Original Certificate Amount} \times 1/12 \\
&= \$100,000,000 \times 1/12 \\
&= \$8,333,333
\end{aligned}
$$

$$
\begin{aligned}
\text{Investor Interest} &= \text{Original Certificate Amount} \times \text{Coupon} \% \ / \ 12 \\
&= \$100,000,000 \times 8.25\% \ / \ 12 \\
&= \$687,500
\end{aligned}
$$

The amount of interest distributed each period is calculated based on the beginning balance for that particular period.

$$
\begin{aligned}
\text{Principal} &= \text{Original Certificate Amount} \\
&= \$100,000,000
\end{aligned}
$$

Excess Spread

Excess spread is deposited into a spread account. It consists of the finance charges earned on the investor certificate share of the card less the servicing fee, the debt service on the investor certificates and any charge-offs. After the investor certificates mature, the balance of the spread account reverts to the issuer.

For non-revolving consumer receivables, the merchants' discount fee constitutes the bulk of the finance charges.

$$
\begin{aligned}
\text{Excess Spread} &= \text{Portfolio Yield} - \text{Servicing Fee} - \text{Debt Service} \\
&\quad - \text{Charge-offs} \\
&= 19.8\% - 3.0\% - 3.0\% - 4.5\% \\
&= 8.3\%
\end{aligned}
$$

Chapter 4

Auto Loan-Backed Securities

Thomas Zimmerman
First Vice President
Fixed Income Research
Prudential Securities Inc.

Leo Burrell
Analyst
Investment Banking
Prudential Securities Inc.

INTRODUCTION

Auto-loan-backed securities represent one of the largest and most mature sectors of the ABS market. The first auto-loan deal was issued in May 1985, a scant two months after the first ABS securitization — the Sperry computer-lease issue of March 1985. Auto loans were a natural follow-up to the large-scale securitization that was already under way in the mortgage market at the time. Like home mortgages, auto loans are an amortizing consumer asset, but they have virtually none of the negative prepayment characteristics of mortgages. As such, auto ABSs compete with credit cards and Treasuries as stable, short average-life investments for banks, money managers and other investors. Because of their straightforward structure, they are often one of the first securities investors turn to when they contemplate entering the ABS market. Issuance in the early years of the ABS auto market was dominated by commercial banks and the captive-finance subsidiaries of the Big Three U.S. auto makers. In recent years, independent finance companies have become equally important in terms of issuance.

Some major changes underway in the auto-finance industry are having a significant impact on the auto ABS market. For example, leasing continues to grow in importance and now accounts for about 30% of new-car financing. While it is likely that auto-lease backed securities eventually will become a major part of the auto ABS market, only a few auto lease-backed deals have been completed to date. Hence, so far, at least, the growth of leasing has acted to restrain the volume of auto ABS issuance, not expand it. Also, the sub-prime sector has grown rapidly in recent years. However, the sub-prime sector differs from the prime sector in that its high level of defaults make it a totally separate product category. Because both auto-lease-backed securities and sub-prime auto securities have their own unique characteristics they will not be discussed in this chapter.

The Auto-Finance Industry

The amount of auto financing originated each year is a function of new- and used-car sales, new- and used-car prices, and the percent of the purchase price that is financed. As shown in Exhibit 1, sales of new cars and light trucks in the U.S. run around 14.5 to 15.0 million units per year. A noteworthy trend is that the share accounted for by light trucks, which typically are more expensive than cars, has increased from 32.9% in 1990 to 41.3% in 1995.

Exhibit 2 shows the trend in average new-car prices from 1985 to 1995. The average price increased from $12,022 in 1985 to around $19,750 in 1995, an annual increase of 5.09% — a rate substantially greater than the increase in median family income during that period. Because of this, fewer families can afford to buy new cars and a growing percentage are buying used ones. Abetting this trend has been a large number of "almost" new cars coming off of lease. These developments have caused an increase in the sale of used cars, and today the dollar value of used-car sales is about 33% of the dollar value of new-car sales.

These sales and price trends can be used to estimate the annual volume of auto financing in the United States. Sales of 15 million units and an average sales price of $20,000 mean that around $300 billion is spent each year on new cars and light trucks. Furthermore, with about 90% of new sales financed and the average amount financed around 100% (including taxes, financing fees, preparation charges, etc.) new-car financing accounts for approximately $270 billion. Adding another 33% to that estimate for used cars yields a total new and used-car financing requirement of around $360 billion. This estimate agrees with the data compiled by CNW Marketing/Research, which puts total auto financing in 1995 at $369 billion. CNW breaks down the total as $226 for new and used prime loans, $67 billion for prime leasing, and $76 billion for sub-prime loans. According to the Federal Reserve Board, commercial banks control 43.8% of the auto-finance market, followed by finance companies at 31.0% and others, mainly credit unions, at 25%.

Exhibit 1: Unit Sales of New Cars and Light Trucks, 1990 to 1995

| | Units ($ MM) | | | | | |
	1990	1991	1992	1993	1994	1995
Cars	9,300	8,175	8,214	8,518	8,990	8,635
Lt. Trucks	4,556	4,133	4,642	5,366	6,052	6,081
Total	13,856	12,308	12,856	13,884	15,043	14,716
% Trucks	32.9	33.6	36.1	38.6	40.2	41.3

Source: Ward's Automotive Reports

Exhibit 2: New Car Prices

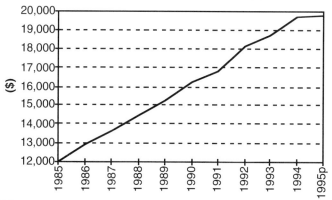

P = Preliminary.

Source: U.S. Department of Commerce Bureau of Economic Analysis

Exhibit 3: Typical Terms on Auto-Installment Loans

	1991	1992	1993	1994	1995
Interest Rates (%)					
Comm. Banks (New)	11.14	9.29	8.09	8.12	9.57
Finance Cos. (New)	12.41	9.93	9.48	9.79	11.19
(Used)	15.60	13.80	12.79	13.49	14.48
Maturity (Mos.)					
Finance Cos. (New)	55.1	54.0	54.5	54.0	54.1
(Used)	47.2	47.9	48.8	50.2	52.2

Source: Federal Reserve Board

Auto-Loan Terms

Auto receivables take two forms: (1) installment-sales contracts and (2) consumer loans, made or purchased by banks, captive finance subsidiaries of the major auto manufacturers, and independent finance companies. The typical maturity ranges from three to six years, with most loans written for four or five years. As shown in Exhibit 3, the average maturity of a new-car loan at finance companies has stayed in a narrow range of 55.1 months to 54.0 months from 1991 to 1995. During that period, the average maturity of a used-car loan increased from 47.2 months to 52.2 months. The exhibit also shows that the average auto loan at finance companies had an interest rate of around 150 basis points greater than the rate at commercial banks, and that used-car loan rates averaged 300 to 350 basis points greater than new-car loan rates.

AUTO-LOAN SECURITIES

The first auto-loan securities were issued by Valley National Bank and Marine Midland in May 1985. From then to mid-June 1996, 355 deals representing $162 billion of auto securities have been issued. On a year-to-year basis, this sector has been either the largest or second largest sector of the ABS market. However, as shown in Exhibit 4, auto-security issuance has fluctuated a fair amount in recent years, rising to $26 billion in 1993, falling to $16 billion in 1994, and then recovering to $25.8 billion in 1995.

Major Issuers

The fluctuations in annual issuance reflect the varying degrees to which the major originators of auto loans have chosen to utilize the ABS market. For example, following the 1990/1991 recession — which severely impacted earnings and balance sheets — the long-term debt of all Big Three auto makers was downgraded. In the next two years, 1992 and 1993, GMAC found it beneficial to securitize a large number of their auto receivables. However, the strong expansion in the economy in recent years, coupled with major productivity improvements and other restructurings have led to rating upgrades for all of the Big Three. Chrysler Financial's rating fell to Ba3 and has recovered to A3, GMAC bottomed out at Baa1 and is now rated A3, and Ford Motor Credit fell to A2 and is now rated A1.

As GMAC's fortunes recovered in 1994 and 1995 and their ratings improved, they reduced their reliance on term securitization and turned to other funding mechanisms, including asset-backed commercial paper. In recent years, they have been only marginal participants in the auto ABS market, but they continue to issue a deal or two per year to maintain their access to the ABS market. The impact of GMAC's changing use of the ABS market is illustrated in Exhibit 5, which shows auto ABS issuance by major sector since 1990. Chrysler and Ford made more consistent use of securitization during those years.

Note in Exhibit 5 that the commercial banks also have been variable issuers of auto ABSs. After a three-year period of little issuance, 1992 to 1994, commercial banks issued $6.3 billion in 1995. In part, this was a result of balance-sheet adjustments that accompanied several large-scale bank mergers, but it also reflected the emergence of several new bank issuers, such as NationsBank and Banc One, and a decision by Chase Manhattan to securitize a major portion of its auto portfolio.

Exhibit 4: ABS Auto Issuance

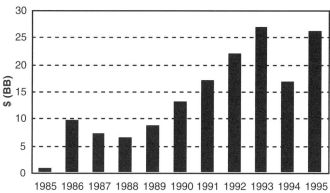

Source: Prudential Securities' IMPACT data base

Exhibit 5: Annual Auto ABS Issuance by Sector

	GMAC $ (BB)	Ford and Chrysler $ (BB)	Comm. Banks $ (BB)	Other $ (BB)	Total $ (BB)	% Big 3	% Comm. Banks &Other
1990	1.2	6.4	2.8	2.5	12.9	58.9	41.1
1991	3.2	7.8	2.1	3.7	16.8	65.5	34.5
1992	12.0	4.0	0.4	5.3	21.7	73.7	26.3
1993	10.2	9.3	0.7	6.3	26.5	73.6	26.4
1994	1.2	8.6	0.1	6.5	16.4	59.8	40.2
1995	1.1	8.3	6.2	10.3	25.9	36.3	63.7

Source: Prudential Securities IMPACT data base

Exhibit 6: Auto ABS Structure

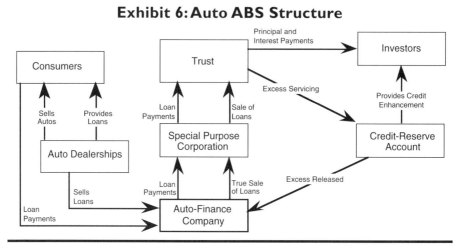

The third major sector of the auto ABS market, and the fastest growing, consists of the independent finance companies and small financial institutions that specialize in auto loans. These include such companies as Olympic Financial, Western Financial, and Union Acceptance Corporation. These firms differ from commercial banks and the captive finance subsidiaries in that they do not look upon the ABS market as an alternative source of funding, but rather they literally exist because of the ABS market. Because of securitization, these smaller capitalized institutions can create triple-A securities and fund themselves at much lower rates than if they had to rely on traditional funding sources.

Structure

Exhibit 6 contains the structural elements common to most auto-loan securitizations. As indicated, the receivables are purchased by a finance company from dealerships and then transferred to a bankruptcy-remote special-purpose corporation (SPC) through a true sale. The receivables are then sold to a trust that issues asset-backed securities to investors.

Auto securities are structured both as pass-throughs and pay-throughs. In the pass-through structure, payments of principal and interest flow through the trust to certificate holders on a pro-rata basis. In the pay-through structure, the SPC allocates cash flows to note holders and certificate holders.

Most auto structures are pass-throughs in which a grantor trust retains legal title to the assets. The trust is a passive entity that holds the self-liquidating receivables for the benefit of the certificate holders. The grantor trust is not taxed on the entity level. This tax status is a result of the fixed nature of the trust. The only allocations of cash flows permitted in a grantor trust are credit-tranching and into senior and subordinate classes. Maturity tranching is not permitted. The pass-through grantor-trust structure is appropriate for most auto-loan securities because auto-loan maturities range from four to five years and the average life of a pool of auto loans is usually two years or less. Unlike the mortgage market, where asset maturities stretch to 30 years, there is less of an incentive to tranche auto-backed cash flows.

The early 1990s saw an increase in both the size and quantity of auto-backed security issuance. With the flood of pass-through paper, issuers began to tailor their bonds' cash flows to investor demand. They achieved tighter execution by issuing pay-through securities that allow for varied payment characteristics. Pay-through securities generally are issued in multiple tranches by an owner trust. The owner trust is structured for tax purposes as a partnership. The SPC retains a 1% interest in the owner trust to maintain its characterization as a partnership for tax purposes while the remaining 99% is sold to outside investors. Unlike the grantor trust, the owners trust issues both debt and equity securities (in the form of partnership interest). The owners of the "equity certificates" are taxed as partnership holders and the owners of the notes, which are issued under an indenture, are taxed as creditors.

Typically, more deals are issued as pass-throughs than as tranched deals, but since tranched deals are often larger than the average pass-through deal, about 35% to 45% of each year's issuance comes in the form of tranched securities. Exhibit 7 shows the typical structure of a tranched auto and a pass-through auto.

The Financial Asset Securitization Investment Trust (FASIT) legislation that currently is before Congress at the time of this writing would simplify the structuring of auto-loan securities in the same way that the Real Estate Mortgage Investment Conduit (REMIC) provided greater tax certainty in the structuring of mortgage-backed securities.

Credit Support

Most auto securities use a senior/subordinate structure for credit enhancement, often coupled with one or more other types of enhancement, such as overcollateralization or a cash-reserve account. Total support usually runs in the 8% to 12% range, with the lower enhancement levels reserved for the larger, more secure issuers. Some of the new and smaller issuers have chosen to use a super-senior structure. This type of credit support utilizes subordination to bring the senior tranches to a triple-A level and then the entire deal, including the subordinate bonds, is wrapped by a monoline insurer. In the unlikely event of an insurer default the senior bonds would be protected by the support bonds.

Exhibit 7: Pass-Through versus Tranched Structure

| | ———Pass-Throughs——— | | | | ———Tranched——— | | |
Class	Amount ($)	Avg. Life (Yrs.)	Spread (BPs.)	Class	Amount ($)	Avg. Life (Yrs.)	Spread (BPs.)
A	187,050,000	1.87	52	A1	250,000,000	0.2	Pvt.
B	18,499,000	1.87	60	A2	545,000,000	0.8	1-Mo. L+7
IO	6,000,000	1.46	84	A3	400,000,000	1.9	34
				A4	248,760,000	3.0	35
				B	56,240	3.3	53

Source: Prudential Securities' IMPACT data base

Exhibit 8: Net Portfolio Losses for Major Auto-Loan ABS Issuers
(As Percent of Outstanding Receivables at Year-End)

	1988	1989	1990	1991	1992	1993	1994
Chrysler	0.57	0.83	0.98	1.21	0.97	0.75	0.73p
GMAC	0.93	1.13	1.11	1.08	0.89	0.64	0.57p
Ford	1.40	1.57	1.31	1.29	0.90	0.69	0.59p
Daimler Benz		0.30	0.54	0.55	0.90	0.46	
Volvo	0.12	0.06	0.19	0.51	0.26p		
Honda		0.24	0.43	0.51	0.40	0.41	
Nissan	1.18	2.42	3.19	1.99	2.40	2.78	0.99p
Toyota	1.30	1.33	1.01	0.85	0.69	0.49p	
World Omni	1.60	1.82	1.68	1.87	1.22	0.93	
Olympic					0.22	0.52	0.66
UFSB	0.63	1.29	0.80	0.71	0.64	0.69	1.08
RCSB	1.19	1.29	1.02	0.95	1.33p		
Western Fin.			1.21	1.40	1.73	1.53	1.09

P = preliminary.

Source: Moody's Asset Credit Evaluations

CREDIT PERFORMANCE

In general, cumulative losses over the life of most auto issues average about 1% to 2%, but there is a good deal of variation from company to company depending on underwriting and servicing standards. Exhibit 8 shows annual portfolio loss data for several of the major ABS auto-loan issuers. The data was taken from company prospectuses and shows a fairly wide variation. The Big Three U.S. auto companies have fairly comparable loss rates, running roughly between 0.5% and 1.5%. In contrast, some of the foreign-car companies, such as Volvo and Daimler Benz have much lower loss experiences. This appears to reflect the higher credit characteristics of the typical buyer of those upscale cars. However, even though Honda, Toyota, and Nissan all have similar customer profiles, they have very different average loss rates, which suggests their underwriting and collection standards vary considerably. Auto-loan losses also are sensitive to economic cycles. As shown in Exhibit 8, losses mounted during the last recession only to decline in recent years as the economy recovered.

Exhibit 9: Cumulative Losses for Selected Auto-Loan Deals as a Percent of Original Balances

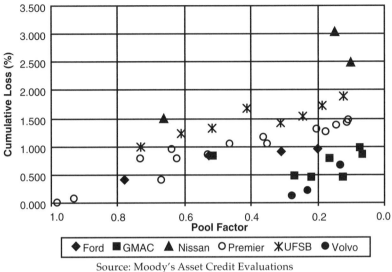

Source: Moody's Asset Credit Evaluations

While portfolio data can give a general picture of overall losses it is also important to look at losses on individual pools of auto loans. Exhibit 9 shows cumulative losses for a number of individual auto-loan pools through the third quarter of 1995. The pools range in age from a few months (pool factors greater than 0.800) to nearly three years (pool factors less than 0.200).

The pool data in Exhibit 9 show a slightly different picture than the portfolio data in Exhibit 8. The portfolio data show that the Big Three have roughly the same level of losses, but the cumulative pool data show that Chrysler pools have had larger losses than Ford pools and GMAC pools have had the smallest losses of the Big Three. It should be noted, however, that the relatively low loss experience on the GMAC pools is due, in part, to GMAC using more seasoned loans in some of their securitizations. Since the largest loss rates occur on auto loans in the second year, a pool made up largely of loans seasoned for two years or more will show a lower loss rate than a pool of mainly new loans.

It is important to understand that loss rates are driven by company-specific underwriting and servicing standards, as well as by the overall economy, and that these factors change over time. Historical data, such as the data shown in Exhibits 8 and 9, can give only a rough estimate of likely losses. Developing a sound projection of losses for a particular deal requires a careful examination of the latest information available with respect to the issuer, the industry, and the general economy.

PREPAYMENTS

Prepayments are much less of a concern in auto securities than in mortgage related securities. However, speed is still an issue — i.e., pools from certain issuers or with certain characteristics will prepay faster than others, but auto ABSs have virtually no prepayment response to changes in interest rates. In other words, these securities have no discernible negative convexity.

There are several reasons for this lack of response to changes in interest rates. Since autos are a depreciating asset, after a short time, the amount of the loan oftentimes is more than the value of the auto, so a refinancing of the loan would mean putting up cash to pay off the old loan. Also, used-car loans have much higher rates than do new-car loans, as much as 300 basis points or more. Interest rates would have to fall a great deal before refinancing into a used loan would make economic sense. Finally, the size of the average car loan, at around $20,000, is far less than the average home-mortgage loan. This means a reduced interest rate will not make a great difference in monthly payments. For all of these reasons auto prepayments are largely interest-rate insensitive.

Non-interest sensitive prepayments occur for several reasons, including theft, accidents, and the desire to trade up to a newer car. Prepayments from theft and accidents do not vary significantly with the age of the loan, but the desire to trade up increases as the loan seasons. Hence, prepayments on autos, measured in CPR terms, show a rising trend as the loans age. This is illustrated in Exhibit 10, which plots average prepayment speeds for 15 auto deals originated in 1993. The top half of the exhibit shows speeds in terms of CPR, the traditional speed measure for MBSs. However, because there is no one CPR speed that adequately describes this pattern of prepayments, a new measure of prepayment speed, called ABS, was developed for auto-loan securities.

ABS versus CPR as Speed Measures

The ABS measure calculates prepayments by comparing actual prepayments each month with the original outstanding balance in the pool. CPR, the traditional prepayment measure in the mortgage market, is calculated by comparing actual prepayments each month with the remaining balance in the pool. A constant ABS curve translates into a continuously rising CPR curve. Exhibit 11 shows the CPR equivalent to a 1.5% ABS speed. In reality, auto-loan prepayment speeds do not increase continually in CPR terms as a constant ABS implies, but rather level off after three or so years and then turn down. Hence, in ABS terms speeds do not remain constant but, after holding stable for several years, decline in the last years of a pool's life. However, there is very little principal remaining by then, so the use of a constant ABS does not lead to any significant error in calculating yields or average lives. The speeds for the 1993 auto deals in ABS terms are shown in the bottom half of Exhibit 10.

Exhibit 10: Average Prepayment Speeds on 1993 Auto Deals

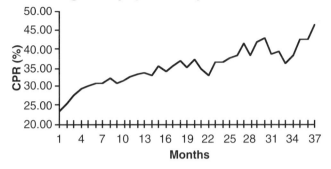

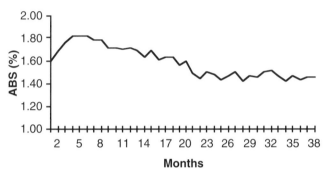

Source: Prudential Securities' IMPACT data base and Bloomberg

Exhibit 11: CPR Equivalent of 1.5% ABS

Source: Prudential Securities' IMPACT data base

Historical Prepayment Speeds

While prepayment speeds vary slightly from issuer to issuer and also vary slightly with weighted-average coupon (WAC), weighted-average maturity (WAM), and percentage of used cars, these influences have only a minor impact. Prepayments on most auto-loan-backed ABSs are quite similar. This is shown in Exhibit 12, which presents the pricing speeds and actual lifetime speeds for a number of auto issues originated in 1992 and 1993. Those issuance years were chosen because the deals from those years have either recently paid down fully or will in the near future, so the lifetime speeds for the entire life, or almost the entire life, of each deal are available.

As the data in Exhibit 12 show, actual speeds for issues from both 1992 and 1993 fell in a fairly narrow range of 1.47% ABS to 1.90% ABS. The actual average speeds for 1992 and 1993 were 1.57% ABS and 1.64% ABS, respectively. The standard deviations in those years were 0.08% ABS and 0.13% ABS, respectively. If we use an average speed of 1.60% ABS and a standard deviation of 0.10% ABS to represent the overall population of auto loans, then 95% of all auto speeds would be expected to fall within a range of 1.40% ABS to 1.80% ABS. A prepayment variation of 1.4% ABS to 1.8% ABS would cause the average life of a typical auto-loan security to shift from 1.6 years to 1.9 years. For a 95% confidence range this is relatively small and because of this, prepayment speed on autos is not a major concern for most investors.

Having said that, however, the data in the exhibit also show that, in 1992 and 1993, most issuers used pricing speeds that proved to be slower than actual speeds. For the 1992 issues in Exhibit 12, the average pricing speed was 1.35% ABS, compared with an actual speed of 1.57% ABS; for 1993, the average pricing speed was 1.41% ABS compared with an actual average of 1.64% ABS. In response to this underestimation, issuers have begun to use slightly faster pricing speeds. In the first five months of 1996, more 1.5% ABS and 1.6% ABS speeds were used in pricing than in prior years and the average climbed to 1.51%, not far from the average actual speeds recorded for the 1992 and 1993 origination-year deals.

SPREADS — AUTOS VERSUS OTHER ABS

In the ABS market, auto securities, next to credit cards, have the simplest structure. As noted earlier, they are amortizing securities but they have virtually no negative convexity. Hence, they trade only slightly behind credit cards, but tighter than mortgage related products, such as manufactured-housing and home-equity-loan (HELs) securities. Exhibit 13 shows the typical spread relationship between autos and other ABSs. Most pass-through autos have average lives of 1.8 to 2.2 years — with 4- to 5-year windows. Tranched deals include bonds with average lives that range from 1 to 5 years, with the majority having average lives of 1 to 3 years. Only a small percentage of the tranched bonds have average lives as long as 4 or 5 years. Windows on tranched deals run from 1 to 3 years.

Exhibit 12: Actual Auto Prepayment Speeds Versus Pricing

1992 Issuance

		Pricing ABS (%)	Actual Lifetime ABS (%) *	Diff. (%)
UAC	1992-A	1.40	1.51	+0.11
	1992-B	1.40	1.53	+0.13
	1992-C	1.40	1.52	+0.12
GMAC	1992-A	1.30	1.49	+0.19
	1992-C	1.30	1.60	+0.30
	1992-D	1.30	1.60	+0.30
	1992-E	1.30	1.56	+0.26
	1992-F	1.30	1.79	+0.49
CARAT	1992-1	1.30	1.66	+0.36
Nissan	1992-A	1.30	1.48	+0.18
	1992-B	1.30	1.63	+0.33
Volvo	1992-A	1.30	1.49	+0.19
	1992-B	1.30	1.60	+0.30
World Omni	1992-A	1.30	1.56	+0.26

1993 Issuance

		Pricing ABS (%)	Actual Lifetime ABS (%) *	Diff. (%)
GMAC	1993-A	1.50	1.71	+0.21
	1993-B	1.50	1.78	+0.28
Ford	1993-A	1.30	1.63	+0.33
	1993-B	1.30	1.47	+0.17
UAC	1993-A	1.40	1.52	+0.12
	1993-B	1.50	1.48	- 0.02
	1993-C	1.50	1.53	+0.03
Olympic	1993-A	1.30	1.90	+0.60
	1993-B	1.50	1.86	+0.36
	1993-C	1.50	1.73	+0.23
	1993-D	1.50	1.64	+0.14
Toyota	1993-A	1.40	1.56	+0.16
Hyundai	1993-A	1.30	1.52	+0.22
World Omni	1993-A	1.30	1.60	+0.30

Summary Statistics

Issues	#	Pricing ABS (%) Range	Avg.	Actual ABS (%) Range	Avg.	Std. Dev.
1992	14	1.30-1.50	1.35	1.48-1.79	1.57	0.08
1993	14	1.30-1.50	1.41	1.47-1.90	1.64	0.13
1996 **	11	1.30-1.80	1.51			

* Most deals in Exhibit 11 have been paid down fully or will be paid down fully in the near future.
** For the first six months of 1996.

Source: Prudential Securities IMPACT data base and Bloomberg

Exhibit 13: Auto Spreads versus Other ABS Spreads*

Spread	2-Year	3-Year
Credit Cards	26	28
Autos — Tranched	34	36
Autos — PTs	40	
Manufactured Housing	45	47
HELs	68	75

* As of 5/8/96.

Source: Prudential Securities' IMPACT data base

Exhibit 14: Spread Comparison — 2-Year Auto versus 2-Year HEL and Credit-Card Bullet

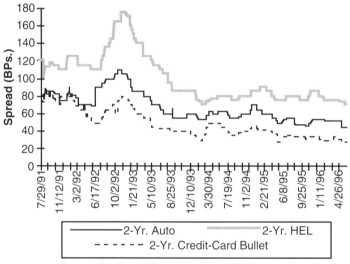

Source: Prudential Securities' IMPACT data base

Exhibit 14 shows historical spreads on 2-year autos compared with 2-year credit cards and HELs. In late-1991/early-1992, auto spreads and credit-card spreads were virtually the same. In part, this reflected the credit concerns of the 1990/1991 recession and the fear that increasing defaults on credit cards would lead to early amortization events. Since then, auto spreads have fluctuated in a more typical range of 10 to 25 basis points wider than cards. The current difference of around 15 basis points in mid-June 1996 is roughly in the middle of that historical range.

Finance-Company Spreads

One pricing aspect of the auto market that investors should be aware of is that issues from the independent finance companies and smaller issuers such as Olympic and Union Acceptance Corporation (UAC) typically trade 5 to 10 basis points wider than the issues from the Big Three or the major commercial banks. This is illustrated in Exhibit 15, which shows spreads on a group of auto deals issued in February/March 1996. In the tranched section, the 2-year bonds from Olympic 1996-A and Western Financial 1996-A were priced 6 and 8 basis points, respectively, wider than the 2-year from the Premier 1996-1. In a like manner, the UAC 1996-A pass-through was priced 6 to 8 basis points wider than the auto pass-throughs from the three major commercial banks shown in the exhibit.

The wider spreads exist because of liquidity and credit concerns. However, since the bonds from the finance companies are rated triple-A just as are the bonds from the Big Three, there seems little reason to view the securities from the finance companies as any less credit worthy. There is a question of liquidity because the finance companies typically have smaller issues than the Big Three, but this does not seem to be worth the 6 to 8 basis-point differential, especially for buy-and-hold investors. Hence, we believe that the wide spreads on the independent finance-company auto ABSs often represent an opportunity for investors.

RELATIVE VALUE AND THE SHAPE OF THE YIELD CURVE

Autos, as amortizing assets, have wider payment windows than many competing securities, such as credit cards and Treasuries. Because of this, the relative value of autos versus credit cards and other short-term securities can be impacted significantly by the shape of the yield curve. In general, bullet-like securities, such as cards, perform better with a steep yield curve because they roll down the curve faster than wide-window bonds. This can be seen by comparing autos to cards under two scenarios, one when the curve is flat and another when the curve is relatively steep. The first quarter 1996 was an excellent period to make this comparison because the short end of the curve went from slightly inverted to steeply positive in a few weeks between mid-February and the end of March.

Exhibit 15: Recent Auto ABS Issues

Tranched	Date	Amt. (MM)	Avg. Life (yrs.)	Spread (BPs)
Premier 1996-1	3/21/96	1,250	2.0	34
Olympic 1996-A	3/7/96	600	2.0	40
Western Fin 1996-A	3/21/96	484	2.0	42
Pass-Throughs				
Chase 1996-A	2/14/96	1,474	1.6	41
Banc One 1996-A	3/15/96	537	1.6	42
Fifth Third 1996-A	3/19/96	408	1.7	43
UAC 1996-A	2/9/96	203	1.9	49

Source: Prudential Securities' IMPACT data base

Exhibit 16: The Impact of Curve Steepening on Total Return

————————2/14/96————————

Type	Pass-Through Auto	Credit Card
Issue	UAC 1995-C	Advanta 1992-3
Class	A	A
Price (32nds)	101-09+	101-08
Average Life (Yrs.)	1.49	1.40
Yield (%)	5.43	5.08
Spread/Coupon (BPs.)	50	28
Spread/WAL (BPs.)	62	28
6-Mo. Total Return (%)	5.45	5.08
Total-Return Advantage (BPs.)	37	

————————3/28/96————————

Type	Pass-Through Auto	Credit Card
Issue	UAC 1995-C	Advanta 1992-3
Class	A	A
Price (32nds)	100-04	100-05
Average Life (Yrs.)	1.49	1.40
Yield (%)	6.28	5.91
Spread/Coupon (BPs.)	50	28
Spread/WAL (BPs.)	62	28
6-Mo. Total Return (%)	6.38	6.26
Total-Return Advantage (BPs.)	12	

Source: Prudential Securities' IMPACT data base

Exhibit 16 shows how the steepening of the curve impacted the total return on a pass-through auto (UAC 1996-C) and a controlled-amortization credit card (Advanta 1992-3). Prior to the curve steepening, the auto had a spread advantage of 34 basis points (62 versus 28) and all of that advantage was passed on in its total-return advantage of 37 basis points (5.45% versus 5.08%). That is, the auto was not penalized for having a wide window and rolling down the curve at a slower speed than the card. However, after the front end of the curve steepened, the total-return advantage of the auto declined to 12 basis points, even though its nominal spread advantage remained at 34 basis points.

During this period, a similar change took place with the Z-spreads on auto issues. A Z-spread calculation differs from the traditional yield-spread calculation in that it uses the entire curve to discount a bond's cash flows rather than just one point. Because of this, a Z-spread gives a more accurate representation of value when the yield curve is sloped than does yield spread. The impact of the February/March 1996 steepening on auto and credit-card Z-spreads is shown in Exhibit 17. The Z-spreads on the shortest autos, Olympic 1995-E and USFB 1994-C, tightened by 8 and 11 basis points, respectively, even though nominal spreads were unchanged. On the cards, the Z-spreads tightened by only 2 to 4 basis points. For the Z-spread buyer, the autos suddenly had become 6 to 7 basis points more expensive.

Exhibit 17: Impact of Curve Steepening on Z-Spreads

Tranched Autos	Window* (Yrs.)	Averge Life (Yrs.)	Price (32nds)	Spread to Cpn. (BPs.)	Spread to WAL (BPS.)	Z-Spread (BPs.)	Diff. (BPs.)	Date
Olympic 1995-E A2	0.2-1.3	0.66	100-09+	46	57	56	1	2/14/96
			100-01	46	57	48	9	3/12/96
Pass-Through Autos								
UFSB 1994-C 1A	0.1-2.4c	1.11	101-10+	50	59	55	4	2/14/96
			100-21	50	59	44	15	3/12/96
UAC 1995-D A	0.1-3.5c	1.74	100-29+	49	59	51	8	2/14/96
			99-19	49	59	48	11	3/12/96
Cards								
Discover 1992-B A	1.3-2.2	1.78	102-19+	28	35	35	0	2/14/96
			101-06+	28	35	31	4	3/12/96
Standard 1993-1 A	2.6	2.60	100-05+	28	31	31	0	2/14/96
			97-31	28	31	29	2	3/12/96

* The UFSB 1994-C and UAC 1995-D autos are priced to their cleanup calls.

Source: Prudential Securities' IMPACT data base

SUMMARY

Auto-loan securities have long played a leading role in the ABS market and occasionally have vied with credit cards for the largest ABS issuance sector. Like most other ABS securities, autos typically carry a triple-A rating based on expected losses, structure, and credit support. They are either structured as pass-throughs, with a single senior class, or as an owners' trust, when they are tranched into different average-life securities. Their prepayment seasoning pattern shows an ever increasing speed in CPR terms but, when translated to ABS — the speed metric for autos — they show roughly a constant speed, with slightly faster ABSs in the first two years. Prepayment speeds vary little from issuer to issuer or over the economic cycle and generally fall within a small range of 1.4% ABS to 1.8% ABS. The stable prepayments and short average lives make auto ABSs attractive to short-term investors. Spreads usually run 10 to 25 basis points wider than credit cards.

Chapter 5

Manufactured Housing Securities

Thomas Zimmerman
First Vice President
Fixed Income Research
Prudential Securities Inc.

Inna Koren
First Vice President
Fixed Income Research
Prudential Securities Inc.

The manufactured housing (MH) securities market and the manufactured housing industry have both gone through major transformations over the past decade. Historically, manufactured homes were associated with low-income housing and MH financing was viewed as a high risk form of lending. The image of the industry probably hit bottom in the mid-1980s, when delinquencies and losses on MH loans in Texas soared to record levels. Today, manufactured housing units and communities are evolving into a far better housing alternative. The size and quality of the average unit has increased and the financing options have expanded greatly.

At the same time, the MH securities market has shifted from a largely FHA/VA backed GNMA product to a conventional product securitized and distributed as a part of the ABS market. In the mid-1980s, annual issuance of GNMA mobile home securities ranged from $500 million to $1,200 million and the first conventional MH security had yet to be issued. Today, GNMA mobile home issuance has slipped to around $100 million while conventional issuance has grown to $5.8 billion. (See Exhibit 1.)

Conventional MH securities have emerged as an attractive alternative to other ABSs and corporate securities due to their high yield, high credit quality and relatively stable prepayment characteristics. Currently, manufactured housing is the fourth-largest sector of the ABS market behind credit cards, autos and home-equity loans. To date, over 100 MH issues have been brought to market, totaling over $22 billion. The $5.8 billion of MH bonds issued in 1995 reflected a large increase in manufactured housing shipments in recent years and an increased reliance on securitization by manufactured housing lenders.

MANUFACTURED HOUSING INDUSTRY

History

The manufactured housing industry evolved after World War II to help meet the pent up demand for housing in the United States. At first, growth was modest, but it accelerated sharply in the 1960s, a decade that saw a two-fold increase in manufactured housing shipments. In those years, manufactured homes became known as an inexpensive type of housing and trailer parks, often located in the less desirable parts of a community, became associated with housing for low-income families. That reputation lingered for many years but has recently begun to change, a trend that has important implications for the future of the industry.

Mobile home shipments soared during the late 1960s and early 1970s when site-built housing costs began to spiral upward. During this period, however, concern increased about the quality of the units some manufacturers were producing. In order to ensure that manufactured homes were produced in a safe, reliable manner, Congress passed the

National Manufactured Housing Construction and Safety Standards Act in 1974. This landmark legislation was a major turning point in the MH indus-try. Many low-cost producers left the industry, the average cost of a manu-factured home increased and shipments plunged to 200,000 in 1975 from 550,000 in 1972 . Since then, manufactured housing shipments have fluctu-ated in a range between 200,000 and 300,000 units per year. The recent low in annual shipments occurred during the recession of 1991 when shipments hit 171,00 units. Shipments have since trended steadily upward with growth accelerating to a double-digit rate in recent years. (See Exhibit 2.)

Exhibit 1: Issuance of Manufactured-Housing Securities, GNMA and Conventional

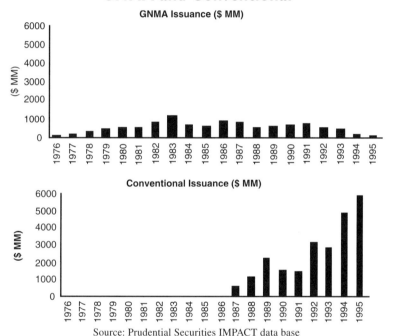

Source: Prudential Securities IMPACT data base

Exhibit 2: Annual Shipments of Manufactured Housing

Source: Manufactured Housing Institute

Production and Sales Growth

The manufactured housing industry shows few signs of concentration from a production standpoint. With no engine and few high tolerance parts, the production process is much less complicated than that of an automobile or a recreational vehicle. Consequently, start-up costs are relatively small and a large number of companies — approximately 100 — are involved in the production of manufactured homes. The largest manufacturers are Fleet and Clayton Homes. Distribution and sales are made through thousands of independent dealers across the country, although some manufacturers, such as Clayton, also own dealerships.

The steep growth in manufactured housing shipments since 1991 has been driven by a number of factors. One important element is the changing perception of the industry. Beginning with the 1974 law and continuing with recent improvements in the quality of construction and the number of amenities available, the average manufactured home is much higher quality housing than it was several decades ago. Low interest rates have also helped drive the sale of manufactured homes but, unlike site-built housing, which has experienced sharp swings during the past several years as mortgage rates have fluctuated, the trend in manufactured housing sales has been uniformly upward. In the final analysis, the economics of manufactured homes as an alternative form of housing have pushed sales higher. Compared to renting or buying a site-built home, manufactured homes are still the least expensive form of housing. In an economy noted for its slow increase in wages, especially for middle and low-income families, manufactured homes have become an increasingly attractive alternative. The economic advantage of manufactured homes combined with their improved image has created the environment for the recent surge in manufactured home ownership.

Manufactured housing currently represents around 7% of the housing stock in the U.S., or, in other words, roughly 1 in 16 Americans live in manufactured homes. However, in recent years, almost one out of every five new single-family homes purchased was a manufactured home. If this trend continues, as appears likely, manufactured homes will become an even more significant part of the housing industry.

MANUFACTURED HOUSING CHARACTERISTICS

Manufactured homes, as opposed to trailers, are built at a factory and then transported on a wheeled chassis to a site to be attached to either a concrete pad or a permanent foundation. The home site can be either a manufactured home community or private land. Manufactured homes can be either single-section (built in one unit) or multi-section (built in several units that are shipped separately and attached at the home site). Single-section units average about 1,000 square feet and multi-section homes average 1,500 to 2,000 square feet. Multi-section homes are not only larger but they often contain more amenities and often have superior construction. Because of this the average price of a single-wide home averages around $20,000, while a multi-section unit averages around $37,000. Some recent upscale manufactured housing communities in Florida have been built around golf courses, are virtually all multi-section units and sell for $70,000 to $80,000. This is a far cry from the typical mobile home of only a few years ago.

The percentages of single and multi-section units has changed dramatically over the past ten years. As shown in Exhibit 3, about 28.5% of all manufactured housing units were multi-section units in 1984; today the ratio is 46.9%. This trend strongly supports the contention that today the average manufactured home is a larger, better equipped and higher quality dwelling than the manufactured home of the past.

Demographics

As one would expect, demographics of the single-section home borrower vary substantially from those of multi-section borrowers. Exhibit 4 demonstrates that multi-section borrowers tend to be older and more affluent; 76.5% of multi-section borrowers are at least 35 years old. In comparison, 71% of single-section borrowers are in the 18- to 34-year old category. The average family gross income for the majority of multi-section borrowers is in the $25,000 to $50,000 range while 64.7% of single-section borrowers have incomes of less than $25,000. These data reflect the fact that the two largest categories of MH borrowers are newly married couples who cannot afford a site-built home and choose a less expensive single-unit manufactured home as their first home, and retired, older couples who can afford a larger multi-unit manufactured home and probably no longer need nor want to care for a large house.

Exhibit 3: Multi-Section Units as a Percent of Total Manufactured-Housing Shipments

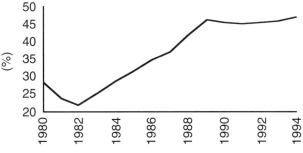

Source: U.S. Bureau of Census

Exhibit 4: Demographics: Single- versus Multi-Section Manufactured Housing

	Single (%)	Multi (%)
Average age:		
18-34	71.0	23.5
35-54	24.2	67.9
55 or over	4.8	8.6
Average years on the same job:		
Less than 5	72.3	29.1
5-10	24.4	59.5
More than 10	3.4	11.4
Average family gross income:		
Less than $25,000	64.7	12.8
$25,000 to $50,000	34.5	84.6
More than $50,000	0.8	2.6

Exhibit 5: Prices for Mobile and Site-Built Single Family Homes

	1987 ($)	1994 ($)	Increase (%)
Mobile	23,700	35,500	+49.8
Site-Built	127,200	154,000	+21.1

Manufactured Homes versus Site-Built Homes and Rentals

The average sales price for a mobile home in 1994 was around $33,500 per unit. In contrast, the average price of a new site-built single family home was $154,500.

Since 1987, the average price of a manufactured home has increased over 49%, while the average price of a site-built home went up only 21.1% (see Exhibit 5). The larger relative price increase for mobile homes can be partly attributed to the fact that the quality of manufactured housing has improved over the years and the percentage of multi-unit homes has increased. However, even with the relative increase in price the average cost of a manufactured home is still only 50% of that of a site-built home when measured in terms of dollars per square foot.

Another housing variable important to the manufactured housing market is the relative cost of renting versus home purchase. There is a strong relationship between rental rates and the purchase of manufactured homes.[1] That is, the choice for many young couples or low income families

---

[1] This was pointed out by Lawrence Horan, Prudential Securities housing analyst.

is between renting and the purchase of a manufactured home. In recent years, marked by a near absence of multi-family construction, rental rates have remained relatively high and vacancy rates relatively low. This makes the purchase of a manufactured home attractive versus renting an apartment. If multifamily construction picks up and vacancy rates begin to increase, it would be a signal for rents to stabilize or possibly decline, a trend that might slow the growth of manufactured housing shipments. However, no such change is on the horizon and manufactured housing shipments continue to grow at a healthy pace.

GEOGRAPHIC LOCATION

Mobile homes are usually located in rural or suburban areas, and are not actually as mobile as their name suggests. According to a study reported in Housing Economics magazine, at least 56% of the units were still at their original sites. Manufactured homes are found nationwide, however; over 60% are located in the southern part of the U.S. This is explained in large part by the fact that a sizeable number of manufactured home owners are retired couples who have moved to the sun belt to escape the northern winters. (See Exhibit 6.)

FINANCING

The typical MH loan is a 15- or 20-year fully amortizing retail installment loan. Most single-section units have loan maturities of 15-year, while most multi-section units are financed with 20-year loans. The vast majority (90%) of MH loans are made as consumer retail installment loans. Only about 10% are written as mortgage loans and these typically include both the land and the mobile home. Hence, most MH loans carry interest rates 2% to 3% higher than loans for conventional home financing. Manufactured homes destined for a mobile-home park are not eligible for mortgage financing and most retail MH dealerships (where the majority of MH lending is done) are not equipped to handle mortgage lending. If consumer loan criteria is used, a sale can be closed in a few days, prior to the manufactured home being placed on its permanent site, which is not possible if real estate lending is used. However, the percentage of MHs financed by real estate loans may increase in the future. A 1994 report from the National Commission on Manufactured Housing recommends that the industry move more in the direction of mortgage lending, especially since the federal government views MHs as an affordable housing alternative.

Exhibit 6: Manufactured Home-Shipments by Region

Region	Percentage
Northeast	5.3
East North Central	11.2
West North Central	6.4
South Atlantic	30.7
South Central	30.2
Mountain	8.5
Pacific	6.3
Destination Pending	1.4

Annual sales of new manufactured homes reached around 335,000 units, or $12 billion in 1995. Including sales of used units, which typically average about 25% of new sales, total sales of manufactured homes approached $15 billion last year. It is common for finance companies to finance about 90% to 95% of a manufactured home's sales value (banks typically will finance only about 85%). Making allowance for those units sold on a cash basis, we estimate total MH financing requirements at around $12 billion per year. According to the 1994 annual survey from the Manufactured Housing Institute, financing for the MH industry is provided mainly by finance companies (84.6%), followed by commercial banks (9.6%), thrifts (5.6%) and credit unions (0.1%).

Several of the finance companies are captive finance subsidiaries of the major manufactured housing manufacturers, such as Vanderbilt, which finances the manufactured homes produced and sold by Clayton Homes. With 196 company-owned and 467 independent dealers, Clayton is one of the largest manufacturers and retailers of mobile homes in the country. Green Tree Financial is the largest of the specialty finance companies providing financing to the manufactured housing industry. Green Tree has 2,800 dealers in its nationwide network and accounts for approximately 28% of total MH loan originations each year.

According to the Manufactured Housing Institute, most of the MH loans originated in 1994 by banks, saving institutions, and credit unions were kept in portfolios, while finance companies sold 35.1% of their loans. Many of these were securitized and sold in the secondary markets.

MANUFACTURED-HOUSING SECURITIES

Like mortgage-backed securities, there are two types of MH securities, those backed by loans guaranteed by the FHA or VA and packaged as GNMA securities and the rest that are backed by conventional MH loans. In recent years, the conventional MH securities market has become very liquid and diversified with respect to structure, average life and credit protection. The market has grown rapidly over the years, with issuance reaching $5.8 billion in 1995 compared to $4.8 billion in 1994 and $2.7 billion in 1993. In 1992, the RTC issued approximately $560 million, or 22% of that year's volume. This represented the MH loans held by the thrifts which were taken over by the RTC. The largest issuer of MH securities in 1995 was Green Tree Financial, with a 75.0% market share, followed by Vanderbilt and Oakwood with a 6.5% and 5.8% market share, respectively.

Structure and Credit Support

With an average prepayment speed of around 8%-10% CPR, the average life of a pool of MH loans with 15- and 20-year loans is around five to seven years. As with other long window mortgage-like collateral, the structure of MH securities transactions has evolved over the years. Initially, they were structured as single-class pass-throughs with third-party protection. Today, MHs utilize a multi-class, senior-subordinate structure with various principal lockout mechanisms and credit-enhancement provisions.

The majority of MH transactions now use subordinate securities and excess servicing for credit protection. The excess servicing is equal to the weighted average annual percentage rate on the underlying contracts, less servicing fees and the weighted average certificate rate paid on the certificates. The excess servicing rate varies, but typically is between 200 and 300 basis points.

In most structures the combination of excess servicing and a corporate guarantee provided by the issuer acts as credit protection to the most junior bond, which generally has a rating equal to that of the issuer. A typical MH issue contains four to five triple-A tranches with average lives of between one and ten years, one or two single- or double-A support tranches with average lives of eight to ten years, and one or two triple-B support tranches with average lives of eight to ten-plus years. This range of average lives and credit ratings provides investors with one of the widest selection of securities in the ABS market.

Credit Performance

Historically, delinquencies and defaults have tended to be higher on MHs than on other types of consumer loans. For example, the American Bankers Association reports that 30-day delinquencies on MH loans at commercial banks in mid-1995 were running at around 3% of outstandings compared to 1% to 1.5% for autos, recreation vehicles and marine loans. One reason for the higher delinquencies on MHs is the demographics discussed earlier. The home owner who chooses a manufactured home typically has a less secure credit history than the average American consumer. Also, defaults are a function of the equity the home owner has in the property and the ability to make the contractual payments. Unlike site-built homes, the price of a manufactured home typically declines after the initial purchase, making it a depreciating asset. Hence, a mobile home owner usually has less equity to protect than does the owner of a site-built home.

In addition to the amount of equity in the MH, the most important loan characteristics that determine the number and severity of defaults include: unit size, loan term, new versus used units, site location, land and home contracts versus a loan on just the MH and the loan-origination year.

Unit-Size: Single-section versus Multi-section

• Multi-section owners are better credit quality borrowers.
• Multi-section contracts have lower repossession frequency and loss severity.
• Multi-sections retain their value better in the resale market.

Loan term

• Since most 15-year loans are for single-section MHs, the credit performance is usually worse than for the 20-year loans, which are typically made on multi-section MHs.

New versus Used Manufactured Houses

• Borrowers for new manufactured homes tend to be more creditworthy than those for used manufactured homes.
• Repossession frequency and loss severity for used units is higher than those for new units.
• The value of used units more difficult to ascertain.

Site location: MH Community versus Private Land

• Manufactured homes located on private land generally have lower repossession rates and loss severity.

Land and Home Contracts versus Retail Installment Contract

• Land and home contracts are conservatively underwritten.
• Land does not depreciate, while a manufactured housing unit does.

Loan origination year

• After heavy losses following the last recession, many MH lenders have stiffened their underwriting terms.
• MH securities from 1992 onward should have fewer delinquencies and losses than pre-1992 issues.

Exhibit 7: Net Portfolio Losses for Major MH ABS Issuers
(As a Percent of Outstanding Receivables at Year-End)

	Percent (%)						
	1989	1990	1991	1992	1993	1994	1995
Greentree	0.98	1.37	1.41	1.60	0.92	0.60	0.41(9)
Security Pacific	0.98	0.97	1.17				
Oakwood		0.81	0.80	0.97	0.63	0.66	0.75(9)
Vanderbilt:							
— Company Orig.	0.35	0.42	0.32	0.41	0.17	0.07	0.04(6)
— Total	0.53	0.59	0.89	1.10	0.64	0.30	0.20(6)

Parentheses indicate latest month data was reported.

Although delinquencies are higher, net losses on MH portfolios are similar to those on autos and HELs. As the data in Exhibit 7 show, the trend in portfolio losses, especially on Green Tree portfolios, is at much lower levels in the last two years. As Moody's Investors mentioned in a January 1995 report, Green Tree and other MH lenders have taken steps to improve their underwriting after suffering sizeable losses during the 1990 to 1991 recession. Green Tree pools from 1992 to 1994 are showing about 50% of the losses of the pools originated in the 1987 to 1992 period.

The improving consumer credit climate of recent years is reflected in MH delinquencies. As shown in Exhibit 8, MH delinquencies reported by the Manufacturing Housing Institute are running well below the levels of 1990 to 1992. However, we expect to see some of the recent gains reversed in all consumer loan areas as the economy slows. While we expect the credit performance in the MH industry to slip along with other consumer credit sectors, the changes in the industry as far as quality of product and quality of underwriting are concerned, are likely to keep the industry's actual credit performance above the level of previous years.

MHP Prepayment Curve

MH loans, like those on single family mortgages, experience a seasoning curve, with few prepayments in the first months and an increasing level of prepayments for about two-years. A common prepayment curve used in the industry is the Manufactured Housing Prepayment (MHP) curve which is illustrated in Exhibit 9. The base, or 100% MHP curve begins at 3.7% CPR in month one and increases 0.1% CPR each month until the month 24, at which time it remains constant at 6.0% CPR for the life of the pool. An MHP of 150% is simply the 100% MHP curve multiplied by 1.5. MH securities are typically priced using speeds of from 100% MHP to 175% MHP, i.e., with long term speeds of 6% to 10% CPR.

Exhibit 8: Year-End Delinquencies on Manufactured-Home Loans

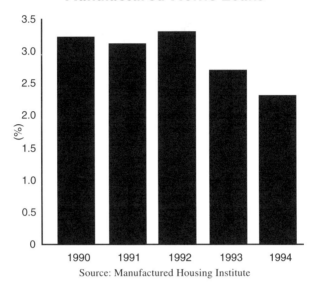

Source: Manufactured Housing Institute

Exhibit 9: Manufactured Housing (MHP) Curve

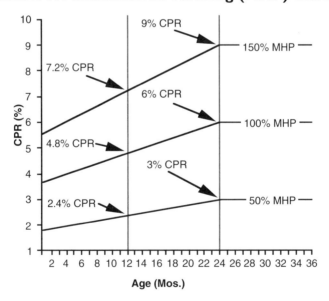

Exhibit 10: Prepayment Speed Comparison: Manufactured-Housing Versus 15-Year Pass-Throughs

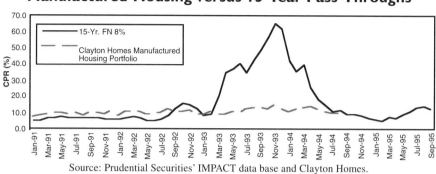

Source: Prudential Securities' IMPACT data base and Clayton Homes.

Prepayment Stability

One of the most important investment characteristics of MHs are their stable prepayments. This is demonstrated in Exhibit 10, which compares the prepayment volatility of MH securities with that of 15-year agency pass-throughs.

The exhibit shows that MH prepayments responded much less to the refinancing waves of 1992 and 1993 than did pass-throughs. The following is a list of factors that contribute to the prepayment stability of manufactured housing loans.

- *Small Loan Balance.* Changes in interest rates have a minimal dollar impact on monthly payments because the average loan balance is small compare to loans for site-built homes.

- *Depreciation.* MHs, like autos but unlike site-built homes, depreciate over time. In the early years of a MH loan, depreciation may exceed amortization, leaving the borrower with lower equity and a reduced ability to refinance.

- *Few Refinancing Options.* Relatively few refinancing programs exist for used mobile homes.

- *Low Credit Rating.* The lower credit-quality borrowers that typically purchase manufactured housing may not qualify for alternative financing.

For these reasons, manufactured home owners are much less prone to refinance than owners of traditional housing, and it is the refinancing component of prepayments that are the most volatile. The stability of MH prepayments is also illustrated in Exhibit 11, which shows that prepayment speeds are similar for the three major issuers of MH securities. The stable prepayment characteristics of manufactured housing result in stable average-life profiles and contribute to the attractiveness of MH securities.

Spreads

MH securities can be viewed as filling the position between autos and home equity loans in the ABS spectrum. Their stable prepayments give them less negative convexity than home equity loans but more prepayment uncertainty than auto loans. Spreads on MHs reflect this. Short MHs trade 5 to 15 basis points wider than autos and 15 to 30 basis points tighter than home equities. Longer tranched MHs trade 30 to 40 basis points tighter than similar average life home equities. Exhibit 12 compares the spreads of a typical MH issue to those of an auto and a home equity issue, all priced near the end of August 1995.

SUMMARY

Manufactured housing, although one of the smaller sectors of the ABS market, is one of the more dynamic. It has well established, seasoned issuers and a sufficient history of prepayments and losses for investors to feel comfortable with the performance characteristics of these securities. A strong upward trend in shipments, the movement to larger, more upscale units, an improving image as a mainstream type of housing and the economics of MH home ownership, all suggest this sector will become an increasingly important part of the ABS market.

Exhibit 11: Historical Prepayment Speeds on Manufactured-Housing ABSs

Series	Gross WAC (%)	Life MHP (%)	Series	Gross WAC (%)	Life MHP (%)
Merrill Lynch			Vanderbilt		
1987-B	14.51	202	1994-A	11.38	179
1987-C	13.68	209	1994-A	12.56	183
1988-E	13.56	188	1995-B	12.93	169
1988-H	12.99	188			
1988-J	13.42	171			
1988-P	13.33	180			
1988-Q	13.64	201	Series		
1988-R	13.48	197	Green Tree		
1988-U	13.66	197	1992-1	11.89	186
1988-X	13.76	218	1992-2	11.28	174
1989-A	13.92	207	1993-1	11.36	169
1989-B	14.16	233	1993-2	10.65	151
1989-C	13.83	200	1993-3	10.23	148
1989-D	14.39	243	1993-4	9.71	141
1989-E	13.03	177	1994-1	9.78	143
1989-F	13.93	223	1994-2	10.27	143
1989-G	13.14	189	1994-3	10.65	133
1989-H	13.74	235	1994-4	11.02	149
1990-A	13.45	199	1994-5	11.14	144
1990-B	13.98	247	1994-6	11.45	140
1990-C	13.59	201	1994-7	11.42	153
1990-D	14.25	244	1994-8	11.53	150
1990-G	14.21	250	1995-1	11.85	166
1990-H	13.80	228	1995-2	12.04	169
1990-I	14.07	255	1995-3	11.60	122
1991-A	13.55	216			
1991-B	14.09	252			
1991-C	13.33	207	Series		
1991-D	14.25	239	Security Pacific		
1991-G	13.49	242	1991-2	13.23	210
1991-H	14.03	202	1991-3	12.80	213
1991-I	13.07	227	1992-1	12.13	192
1992-E	13.34	210	1992-2	12.18	183
1993-A	12.88	212	1992-3	11.57	173
1993-G	11.66	170			
1994-E	11.23	147			
1994-G	11.27	149			

As of December 1995. 100% MHP prepayment rates are equal to 3.7% per annum in the first month with an additional 0.1% per annum in each month until month 24 and 6.0% per annum in month 24 and each month thereafter.

Source: Bloomberg Financial Markets

Exhibit 12: Spreads on Manufactured Housing Securities Compared to Spreads on Autos and HELs

Autos Olympic 1995-D

Class	Average Life (Years)	Spread (BPs)
A2	1.0	40
A4	3.0	41
A6	4.8	45

MHs Vanderbilt 1995-B

Class	Average Life (Years)	Spread (BPs)
A1	1.1	47
A2	3.1	50
A3	5.1	58
A4	7.2	73
A5	9.8	92
A6	12.9	125
B1	6.7	135
B2	12.6	167

HELs United Companies 1995-C

Class	Average Life (Years)	Spread (BPs)
A1	1.0	63
A2	3.0	73
A3	5.4	88
A4	7.2	100
A5	10.7	130

Chapter 6

Analysis of Manufactured Housing-Backed Securities

John N. Dunlevy, CFA, CPA
Director and Senior Portfolio Manager
Hyperion Capital Management, Inc.

Andrew Shook
Senior Securities Analyst
Hyperion Capital Management, Inc.

INTRODUCTION

Manufactured housing, also referred to as mobile homes, are single-family detached homes constructed off-site and transported to a plot of land or to a manufactured housing community (park). Currently, manufactured housing is the fourth-largest sector of the asset-backed market (behind credit cards, automobiles and home equities), with over 100 deals outstanding totaling over $22 billion. In the previous chapter, the fundamentals of the manufactured housing market were presented. In this chapter we look at how to analyze manufactured housing-backed securities.

MANUFACTURED HOUSING ABS — OVERVIEW

There are two types of manufactured housing units: (1) single-section (also known as "single-wides") and; (2) multi-sections. Single-wide units, which are transported to their site in one piece, average 1,065 square feet. Multi-section units, on the other hand, are assembled at the site after being transported in pieces, and average 1,525 square feet. Exhibit 1 summarizes the manufactured housing loan characteristics.

The typical manufactured housing loan is a 15- to 20-year fully amortizing retail installment loan. Single-section units are usually financed over 15-year terms at rates between 300 bps and 350 bps above conventional 30-year rates. Multi-section units are usually financed over 20-year terms at rates between 250 bps and 300 bps over conventional 30-year rates. Currently, only 10% of all units financed are written as mortgage loans (i.e., financed with the unit's land).

Green Tree Financial continues to dominate the issuance of securities backed by Manufactured Housing loans. For example, during 1995 Green Tree issued $4 billion of the $5.8 billion MH securities issued. As shown in Exhibit 2, Green Tree is dominant in both number of issues outstanding as well as dollar value of securities outstanding.

Exhibit 1: Manufactured Housing Loan Characteristics

	Single-Wide	Multi/Double-Wide	U.S. Average Site-Built
Average Home Size	1,065 Sq. Ft.	1,525 Sq. Ft.	1,945 Sq. Ft.
Average Sales Price	$26,000	$50,000	$143,000
Loan Rate vs. Conventional	+338 bps	+288 bps	—
Average Loan Term	200 mo.	240 mo.	360 mo.
Average Monthly Payment	$260	$406	$831

Source: Green Tree Financial

Exhibit 2: Total MH Issuance 1987-1995

Issuer	Number of Issues Outstanding	Percent	Dollar Value ($000) Issues Outstanding	Percent
Green Tree Financial	66	77%	15,735	82%
Security Pacific	6	7	919	5
Vanderbilt	3	4	539	3
RTC	3	4	616	3
Oakwood	3	4	468	3
Others	4	4	799	4
Total	85	100%	19,076	100%

Exhibit 3: Manufactured Housing Refinancing Incentive

	MH	Single-Family
Loan Balance	35,000	150,000
Term	200 mo.	360 mo.
Current Rate	11%	8%
Monthly Payment	$382	$1,100
-100 b.p.		
New Rate	10%	7%
New Payment	$360	$998
Savings	$22	$102
-200 b.p.		
New Rate	9%	6%
New Payment	$338	$899
Savings	$44	$201

Manufactured Housing Prepayment Experience

Manufactured housing has proven to be a market which is largely interest rate insensitive. We believe that this is the case due to four reasons. First, MH loans have small balances resulting in minimal saving from refinancings. (See Exhibit 3.) Even a decline of 200 basis points for a typical $35,000 MH loan would result in only a $44 monthly savings.

Second, manufacturing housing units, like cars, are subject to depreciation. In the early years of a loan's life, depreciation exceeds amortization leaving the borrower with little equity which is needed to refinance. Third, few refinancing options are currently available for used manufactured housing units. This is another reason why MH loans are insensitive to interest rate movements. Finally, MH borrowers may not qualify for alternative financings because of their limited financial resources.

Exhibit 4: Prepayment Sensitivity to Rate Movements (CPR)

	+300	+200	+100	0	-100	-200	-300	+300 BP range (CPR)
Mfd Housing ABS	6.0	6.0	6.0	6.0	11.3	13.4	15.8	9.8
Home Equity ABS	9.0	12.0	17.0	22.0	27.0	31.0	35.0	26.0
1994 FNMA 6.5	5.0	5.9	7.0	8.6	20.6	49.1	63.1	58.1

Source: Lehman Brothers

Exhibit 5: Green Tree MH Static Pool Losses

Year	Orig. Pool Size ($ billion)	Pool Factor	Loss % of Orig. Pool
1991	$0.6	0.47	4.55%
1992	1.4	0.58	2.16
1993	2.1	0.80	0.67
1994	3.2	0.90	0.16
1995	4.0	0.98	0.02

Exhibit 4 shows the interest rate sensitivity of manufacturing housing prepayments to interest rate movements. Manufactured housing have a CPR prepayment range (+300 to -300) of 9.8% CPR which was substantially lower than the 26.0 CPR and 58.1 CPR range for home-equity ABS and 30-year FNMAs, 6.5s, respectively.

Manufactured Housing ABS Credit Performance

In evaluating the credit performance of manufactured housing-backed ABS it is important to consider delinquencies, loss statistics, and rating agency upgrade/downgrade data.

In terms of delinquencies, the American Bankers Association (ABA) statistics show that total delinquencies were running at around 3% during 1995 (slightly higher than single-family mortgages) but higher than the 1% to 1.5% delinquency rates for automobiles, recreational vehicles, and boat loans. According to the Manufactured Housing Institute, delinquency levels since 1990 have ranged between 2.25% and 3.50%. Based on Green Tree static pool data, losses by cohort year are reported in Exhibit 5.

The default curve for manufactured housing starts off at a very low rate and peaks by year three. After year three the default rate will decline gradually until leveling off at about 50% of its peak level in year ten. Historical experience shows that loss severity ranges between 30% and 60% (double-wide units have the highest recovery rates).

Finally, the credit record for the manufactured housing sector has been excellent. For example, as shown in Exhibit 6, manufactured housing-backed securities has had more upgrades than any other ABS sector. As shown in the exhibit, the rating agency criteria for ABS appears very conservative. No single-rated ABS has ever defaulted due to performance problems. The downgrades shown above reflect third party credit-enhancement deterioration.

MH DEAL STRUCTURES

A typical structure, which is representative of late 1995 and 1996 deals is shown in Exhibit 7. The deal outlined in the exhibit was priced at a prepayment assumption of 100 MHP. MHP is a prepayment curve used for manufactured housing collateral, which assumes that prepayments start in month one at 3.7% CPR and rise 0.1% CPR per month until they reach 6% CPR in month 24, then stay constant at 6% CPR. Therefore, if a deal is priced at a 125 MHP assumption it is simply 1.25 times the 100 MHP vector (as just described).

Exhibit 6: ABS Rating Changes

Asset Type	Number Upgrades	Number Downgrades	Upgrade / Downgrade Ratio
Automobiles	17	27	0.63
Credit Cards	7	14	0.50
Home Equity	4	7	0.57
Manufactured Housing	38	2	19.00
Other	4	6	0.67
Total	70	56	1.25

Exhibit 7: Green Tree 1995-10 MH Structure

Class	Size ($MM)	% Deal	Rating	A/L	Window (Months)	Spread
A1	48.0	11.9%	AAA	1.05	1-24	+47
A2	63.0	15.5%	AAA	3.06	24-57	+48
A3	41.0	10.1%	AAA	5.07	41-73	+55
A4	33.0	8-1%	AAA	7.09	73-98	+71
A5	59.0	14.6%	AAA	10.25	98-152	+94
A6	92.0	22.7%	AAA	17.24	152-241	+145
M1	37.0	9.1%	AA-	12.57	63-241	+145
B1	16.0	4.0%	BBB+	8.30	63-143	+145
B2	16.0	4.0%	BBB+	17.20	143-241	+177
Total	405.0			9.25		

Collateral

No. Loans	11,805	New Unit %	83%
Avg. Size	$34,134	Non-Park Unit %	72%
WAC	10.05%	WA LTV%	76%
WAM	280 M	Geographics: 10% North Carolina, 8% Michigan, 7% Texas	

Exhibit 8: Typical Green Tree MH Payment Priority

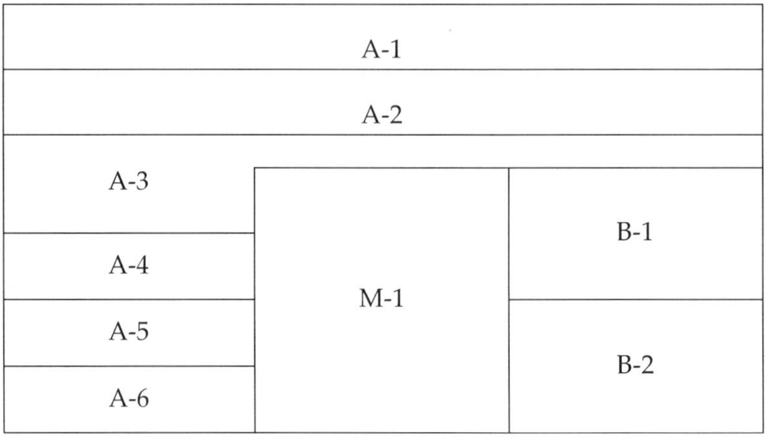

A-1		
A-2		
A-3		B-1
A-4	M-1	
A-5		B-2
A-6		

Exhibit 9: Typical Green Tree MH Loss Allocation

Loss Priority	Tranche	Credit Source	Credit
5th	A1–A6	Subordination	16%
4th	M1	Subordination	8%
3rd	B1	Subordination	4%
2nd	B2	Green Tree Guarantee	4%
1st	—	Excess Spread	349 bps

The deal shown in Exhibit 7 also assumes a 10% cleanup call. This is the same assumption used in non-agency CMOs as well as many other ABS sectors. The investor must be sure to understand that for the longer tranches, whether the tranche is priced to maturity or to the call provision.

Third, it is important for the investor to understand the deal's waterfall or cash flow priorities. The deal in the exhibit has sequential-pay priorities for classes A1 through A5 until the first crossover date. The crossover date refers to the date when the lockout period ends and the subordinated tranches (M and B1) begin to receive their pro-rate share of principal payments. Exhibit 8 shows the payment priority for Green Tree 1995-10.

As previously noted, the senior bonds pay sequentially until the crossover date, which is the latter month of 49 or when the deal's "step-down" tests (discussed below) are met. Exhibit 9 shows how losses are allocated within the structure. If losses were to exceed the first four loss priorities, then a pro-rata principal write-off would occur among the A1 to A6 tranches.

Exhibit 10: Green Tree 1996-1

Tranche	Size ($MM)	A/L	Window Months	Spread	Z-Spread	Option Cost	OAS
A1	120	2.1	1-48	50	42	7	35
A2	50	5.2	48-78	54	40	10	30
A3	35	7.5	78-95	71	70	18	52
A4	50	11.6	95-145	93	79	17	62
A5	76	17.5	145-309	145	101	11	90

SENIOR BOND RELATIVE VALUE ANALYSIS

The structure, pricing details, Z-spreads, and OAS data for a recent deal -- Green Tree 1996-1 are in Exhibit 10.

Based on nominal spreads, Z-spreads, and OAS analysis, the longer bonds in the senior structure seem to offer the best risk/return profile. The A4 bond, for example, at +93 versus the 10-year Treasury given the sectors stable prepayment profile is attractive versus the following alternative products:

Type	Spread	Z-Spread	OAS
MH	+93	79	62
Credit Cards	53	53	53
Corporate Industrial	35	35	35
Agency PAC	90	71	56

Finally, the senior bonds of manufactured housing ABS are both SMMEA and ERISA eligible.

Mezzanine and Subordinated Bond Analysis

Before analyzing the lower rated tranches on manufactured housing ABS, the investor must be sure to understand the priorities of cash flow which flow to these bonds. For example, the step-down tests used for the Green Tree 1995-10 deal is given in Exhibit 11. Likewise, the B1 and B2 tranches have to pass a similar series of tests in order to begin to receive principal.

The investor should know when the expected crossover date will occur. For example, Green Tree 1995-10 M1, although locked out for 48 months is not scheduled to receive any principal until month 63. This 100 MHP pricing assumption (138 MHP is needed to accelerate the principal date on M1 to month 49) is too slow to achieve step-down in month 49.

It is therefore necessary to evaluate these tranches on an OAS basis in order to capture the extension risk in the structure. Exhibit 12 shows this evaluation for the subordinated tranches of Green Tree 1996-1.

Exhibit 11: Green Tree 1995-10 Step-Down Tests

M-1

Principal lockout until 12/99 (48 months)
Then must pass the following five tests:
1. Average 60-day delinquency ratio <3.5% of orig. pool balance
2. Average 30-day delinquency ratio <5.5% of orig. pool balance
3. Current losses <2.25% of orig pool balance
4. Cumulative losses must be less than:

48-59 months	<5.5% of orig. pool balance
60-71 months	<6.5% of orig. pool balance
72-83 months	<8.5% of orig. pool balance
84+ months	<9.5% of orig. pool balance

5. De-leveraging test
   M1 + B principal   >25.5% of orig. pool balance

Exhibit 12: Evaluation of Subordinated Tranches of Green Tree 1996-1

Tranche	Size ($MM)	A/L	Window Months	Spread	Z-Spread	Option Cost	OAS
M1	36	11.9	49-309	145	124	13	111
B1	16	7.4	49-123	145	142	14	128
B2	16	20.0	123-309	175	130	13	117

Among the subordinated tranches shown above, we find the M1 bond is attractive versus the following alternative products:

AA Product	Spread	OAS
MH ABS	+145	111
Subordinated CMO	+150	135
CMBS	+115	90
Industrials	+50	50

Although AA-rated subordinated CMOs appear more attractive in the comparison above, MH ABS are publicly traded, increasing more liquid, and available in bigger block sizes than subordinated CMOs. However, the intermediate duration B1 tranche as shown below, does not appear attractive versus the following alternative BBB-rated products:

BBB Product	Spread	OAS
MH ABS	145	128
Subordinated CMO	230	215
CMBS	175	135
Industrials	75	75

Finally, the current attractiveness of the AA-rated M1 tranche is a relatively recent phenomenon. That is, through the end of January 1996 only five deals have been structured with this 11- to 12-year average life AA mezzanine structure. Prior to Green Tree 1995-7, the M1 tranche was a much longer bond (i.e., 17- to 19-year average life) due to a much longer principal lockout (crossover date).

SUMMARY

Manufactured housing ABS deals offer an intriguing combination of spread, prepayment stability, and growing liquidity. This chapter explains how to evaluate the relative attractiveness of manufactured housing ABS tranches.

Chapter 7

Introduction to the B&C Home-Equity Loan Market

Morton Dear
Executive Vice President and
Chief Financial Officer
The Money Store Inc.

Len Blum
Managing Director
Head, Asset-Backed Banking Group
Prudential Securities Inc.

INTRODUCTION

A home-equity loan allows a homeowner to tap their embedded home equity and grants an originator a lien on that borrower's home. Home-equity loans can be either home-equity lines of credit (HELOC) or closed-end home-equity loans (HEL). Within these broad groupings, loans have a wide variety of credit, prepayment, and contractual characteristics, as well as enjoy first-, second-, or other lien positions. This chapter reviews the various features of home-equity loans and explores the characteristics of one of the fastest growing areas of the HEL market, namely the non-prime (B&C) sector.

Generally, the common uses of an HEL's proceeds are home improvement, education, debt consolidation, medical expense, business use, and other major purchases. The use of proceeds can provide insight into the performance of a loan. For example, home improvement loans often have stronger credit characteristics because the use of proceeds increases the value of the collateral. These loans are also likely to prepay more slowly in the early years of origination as a borrower is much less likely to sell a home that was recently improved.

With respect to debt consolidation, repayment of existing debt may not be the borrower's initial goal. Instead, it may be suggested by the originator, especially in the case of B&C loans where the originator may serve the dual function of credit counselor and lender. HELs usually are tax deductible with lower rates than other forms of consumer credit (such as credit cards) allowing the consumer to economize on debt service charges. Additionally, if the borrower's aggregate payment does not increase dramatically, the probability of default can be reduced. Note, however, that critics of debt consolidation argue that this type of activity can increase the consumer's ability to access additional credit. Once consumers have repaid debts, the potential to draw upon credit lines is increased, thereby potentially increasing aggregate debt service and the likelihood of default.

HELs are also increasingly being used to consolidate existing mortgage debt. For obvious reasons, this type of activity is likely to occur with greater frequency in a low interest-rate environment. Nonetheless, mortgage debt consolidation not only increases loan size, but also potentially benefits consumers by consolidating at a lower interest rate. At the same time, from the lender's perspective, potential loss severity is also reduced as the consolidated first lien position is not subordinated to other lenders. A larger loan also increases income from interest, points, and servicing.

CONTRACTUAL CHARACTERISTICS

Open-End Loans

A HELOC grants the homeowner a line of credit against the embedded equity in the home. The consumer generally accesses this line by writing checks. The borrower generally draws part of the balance at closing and makes additional draws during a "revolving" period. This revolving period may last from 10 to 15 years, following which there is either an amortization period or a balloon payment. Some HELOCs do not have revolving periods; instead, each drawn balance is amortized over a set period. Additional draws adjust the monthly payment in an amount sufficient to amortize the then-outstanding balance over the loan's term.

Closed-End Loans

HELs are closed-end loans, which can have fixed or floating rates of interest. These mortgages generally fully amortize over 10- to 30-year periods, and may have balloon payments due in 5, 10, or 15 years. HELs generally are level-payment loans, where the consumer generally makes a fixed payment each month. In the early years of a loan, a larger percentage of this payment is allocated towards interest, whereas in the later years, a larger percentage is allocated towards principal.

In contrast to mortgages that amortize on an actuarial basis (as is the case with agency-conforming mortgages), HELs generally use the simple-interest method. With an actuarial loan, the borrower pays a pre-computed amount of interest in a given month as long as the payment is received before a certain date. If the payment is received after that date, the lender assesses a late charge. Conversely, in a simple interest loan, the amount of interest due varies based on the number of days since the last receipt of payment.

Adjustable-rate HELs (ARMs[1]) bear interest relative to an index, which is often the London interbank offered rate (LIBOR).[2] Generally, LIBOR ARMs are teasered. A teasered loan has an initial rate of interest that is lower than its margin plus its index. These loans also have life and periodic caps. Life caps limit the maximum interest rate the borrower will pay in any given period during the life of the loan (life caps often are set at 6% over the teaser). Periodic caps limit the maximum amount the rate can change at a given reset date (periodic caps are often set at 2% per year). Some of these loans also have floors; in some cases the floor is set at or near the teaser.

---

[1] Not all ARMs are HELs. Purchase money mortgages also are originated as ARMs.
[2] Many established originators have begun including this product in their securitizations. Several California originators specialize in this type of loan, a home-equity product that has traditionally flourished in that state.

Lien Position

Historically, the HEL market was known as the "second mortgage industry." Recently, however, industry and economic trends have changed the mix of originations to be predominantly first-lien; hence the "second mortgage" designation is no longer appropriate.[3] This trend is due to two major factors. First, with recent low interest rates, many borrowers have found it advantageous to refinance their existing mortgages when taking out equity. In traditional mortgage parlance, this is referred to as a "cash-out refinance" loan. Second, lenders are aware of the superior credit quality of first-lien collateral. Many of these lenders have encouraged borrowers to "roll" their existing mortgage into the home-equity loan (which also benefits the lender by providing a potentially more profitable larger loan amount).[4]

MAJOR ORIGINATORS OF HELS

The majority of HELs are originated by banks and finance companies, although credit unions as well as individuals are participants in this market. Major bank originators include CoreStates, NationsBank, Chase, and Chemical. Generally, banks originate to highly creditworthy borrowers. Cross-selling is often a marketing strategy. Major finance company originators include The Money Store, United Companies Financial, Aames, First Alliance, Champion Mortgage, and Delta Funding. Finance companies often focus on borrowers that have at least minor credit blemishes; these borrowers frequently are referred to as B&C credits.

THE B&C HEL MARKET

As noted above, finance companies market to B&C credits. They are able to do this profitably for several reasons. First, the security provided by the borrower's home may allow the lender to lend to a borrower to which the lender may not otherwise extend credit. Since these loans often have low loan-to-value ratios and lenders focus carefully on LTV adequacy and appraisal accuracy, the risk inherent in lending to this group of borrowers is significantly reduced. Second, many finance companies carefully analyze

---

[3] Interestingly, the National Second Mortgage Association, a leading industry group, has changed its name to the National Home Equity Mortgage Association.

[4] As a result of this development, many recently securitized HEL deals may contain up to 90% first-lien loans. While certain investors have used this development to question prepayment stability of non-prime HELs, it can be argued that the inclusion of a higher percentage of first liens in the pool does not dramatically alter the prepayment propensity of such borrowers as they still are more sensitive to the amount of the payment and other factors rather than the level of interest rates.

borrower credit and often use effective subjective underwriting that allows them to identify borrowers that have a high probability of satisfying a loan. Yet, the same borrower may not pass strict, formulaic underwriting evaluations. Also, the higher rates charged to these borrowers compensate lenders for the increased risk and the more intense origination, servicing, and collection procedures inherent with these loans.

Even within the finance company universe, there is a wide range of borrowers that can be called B&C credits. Some borrowers may have steady sources of income and only modestly blemished credit. Other borrowers have weak credit, but have significant home equity to secure the loan. Some finance companies specialize in a given homeowner demographic/credit sector, whereas others balance their underwriting guidelines and loan pricing to accommodate a wide diversity of borrower profiles.

Finance companies focus on this population for a number of reasons. First, finance companies often have relatively high weighted-average costs of capital; they cannot accept deposits or operate at high leverage ratios similar to a bank. As a result, their business orientation is focused on high return opportunities. It is for this reason that many finance companies simply are not interested in making low-rate, conforming loans. Also, the entrepreneurial culture of many finance companies has encouraged loan portfolio analysis, with an emphasis on predictable, after-loss net yield. The philosophy of some (but not all) banks, on the other hand, is to underwrite to a zero loss, which can sometimes result in a lower risk-adjusted portfolio yield.[5] Furthermore, B&C borrowers often "self select," choosing to do business with target-marketing finance companies, which some of these borrowers may perceive as less intimidating (although many banks are attempting to rectify this).

Origination

B&C originators gather loans through various channels. The largest distinctions are direct and indirect originations. Direct origination occurs when the lender markets directly to the borrower or directly originates through correspondent brokers. Indirect origination occurs when the lender purchases loans from others. Indirect origination can be stratified along correspondent, flow-purchase, or bulk purchase bases. Loans are purchased from brokers or lenders. Typical direct marketing channels include newspapers, radio, direct mail, and television. Larger originators enjoy significant advertising economies of scale, and often can truly exploit mixed media campaigns causing such entities to build market share at rapid rates.

Some lenders purchase third-party loans to supplement their existing business. Others originate exclusively through indirect channels. Experienced originators perform careful due diligence to ascertain the quality of

---

[5] Interestingly, banks have often purchased whole-loan B&C product from finance companies.

third-party originations and examine not only the broker's business practices, but also the homeowner's credit and the quality of the collateral. When properly administered, an indirect lending operation can be a strong supplement to an originator's retail flow or a logical general business strategy in general.

Underwriting

Finance company home-equity lending is sometimes misunderstood by those familiar with traditional mortgage origination. Many non-finance-company originators underwrite with formulaic methods. These methods use minimum borrower requirements, such as strong credit records and low debt-to-income ratios. HEL origination, conversely, is more flexible; credit-impaired borrowers often have complex credit profiles. The experienced underwriter understands how to "look through the numbers" and assess the borrower's ability to repay. For obvious reasons, the flexible origination criteria of finance companies make the underwriting function critical. Nonetheless, in underwriting loans to credit-impaired borrowers, controlled delinquency levels should be expected. Yet these losses generally are low, especially given the aggregate portfolio yield and have hovered below 1% for the industry.

B&C borrowers have credit blemishes that range from minor delinquencies to bankruptcies. Also, their debt-to-income ratios may be high. Some borrowers may be strong credits, yet they may have suffered a temporary setback. For example, they may have been displaced in an economic contraction, and may have found re-employment at a lower salary level. To mitigate the risks of lending to B&C borrowers, lenders require LTV ratios that are significantly lower than those found with loans made to conforming borrowers. Also, as discussed, B&C lenders generally charge more points and/or higher yields, which significantly compensate for the additional cash-flow risk. For example, many home-equity originators shun making loans with LTVs of 80% or more. Yet 80% LTVs are commonplace in the conforming market. While the average LTV for a "typical" B&C pool may be from 65% to 70%, conforming loans average 70% to 75%. These mitigating factors have allowed finance companies to fulfill an important social function by providing credit to a vastly underserved market as only a minority of the American public has unblemished credit histories.

When underwriting a loan, the originator generally focuses on both the ability of the borrower to repay and the adequacy of the borrower's collateral. Although most originators prefer to have both factors present, some will focus more on one factor than the other. For example, some lenders originate loans with very low loan-to-value ratios, and may focus less on the borrower's credit history or the ratio of the borrower's gross debt service to income. Yet they still may not make the loan if the subjective evaluation suggests that the borrower may be unable to repay the loan and foreclosure would be expected. Other lenders focus primarily on borrower credit and may make loans with loan-to-value ratios in excess of 70% or even 80%. It is the lower LTV ratio that allows a lender to underwrite a credit-impaired borrower. In fact, many lenders will only extend loans with higher LTV ratios to their most creditworthy borrowers. These low LTVs account for low expected loss severities in the event of default (as well as mitigated foreclosure frequency), as well as the low net losses experienced by the industry as a whole. The lower LTVs also mitigate the lack of transactional verification of value. With purchase-money mortgages, the "value" component (the denominator) of LTV is the lesser of the purchase price or the appraised value.

When assessing credit quality, originators often view mortgage delinquencies differently than other delinquencies, such as credit card or automobile loan delinquencies. Some originators will tolerate significantly higher levels of non-mortgage than mortgage delinquency history. Originators will study the borrower's credit over specific time periods (e.g., one or two years). They will require that, for a specific grade of loan, the borrower's frequency and severity of delinquency on specific debt has not exceeded certain limitations. Finance companies also review the borrower's previous judgements, foreclosures, and bankruptcies. Other considerations include level of documentation (full documentation versus limited documentation), property types (e.g., high-rise condominiums versus low-rise condominiums or single-family-detached homes), and occupancy status (e.g., second homes and investor properties versus primary residences).

Grading

Originators commonly grade their loans. They use designations such as "A," "B," "C," or "D" (sometimes with pluses and minuses within grades). One confusing feature, however, is the lack of standardization among originators. One originator's A- could be another lender's B. Hopefully, the standards used by the rating agencies, the sureties, and the large originators will standardize this diversity over time. As the lender moves from "A" to "D," maximum allowable LTVs decline, while debt-to-income ratios increase and credit histories deteriorate. Many originators will further limit their LTVs if alternate verifications of income are used or the property type is perceived as risky. Regardless of the originator's philosophy, it is important that an originator be consistent in limiting LTV as other perceived risks increase.

Due to the reliance on LTVs, appraisal procedures and quality control programs are important. Obviously, an LTV is meaningful only if the appraisal is accurate. Although many originators use outside appraisers, they generally have strict review policies. For example, strict approval processes for new appraisers generally apply. Originators carefully monitor appraisers through reviews and reappraisals. Appraisers with significant adjustments are removed from approved status. Low LTV ratios and strong appraisal controls are the cornerstone of several home-equity programs. Credit underwriting decisions also are often carefully re-underwritten. Experience by broker is often tracked. Finance companies also monitor performance by in-house personnel. Re-review of delinquent and defaulted loans is commonplace.

Servicing

B&C borrowers may be more likely to become delinquent than A borrowers. Notably, these borrowers are far more sensitive to the quality and intensity of servicing than their conforming quality counterparts are. Generally, the lower grade the borrower, the more intense the servicing procedures should be. Because of the higher incidence of delinquency relative to conforming borrowers, lenders contact B&C homeowners early and often. Finance companies maintain intense contact throughout a delinquency cycle. As a delinquency progresses, the frequency and intensity of calls increase. Lenders realize that, because of their high debt loads and lack of financial resources, many borrowers will find it difficult to recover if they miss a payment.

SUMMARY

The majority of American borrowers have some credit blemish. Yet traditional lenders have been hesitant to lend to these borrowers. Lenders increasingly are providing loans to credit-impaired borrowers. As a result, they are providing credit to a previously underserved market and performing a valuable social function. Although loan terms generally compensate lenders for the additional credit risk in this sector, lenders have developed policies and procedures to control risk. Because of the benefits to both borrower and lender alike, we expect continued growth in this sector.

Chapter 8

Evolution of the B&C Home-Equity Loan Securities Market

Henry C. McCall III
Senior Vice President
United Companies Financial Corporation

Len Blum
Managing Director
Head, Asset-Backed Banking Group
Prudential Securities Inc.

INTRODUCTION

Modern home-equity lending has its roots in consumer credit. In the 1970s, several consumer credit companies started lending to a niche mortgage market, which has been labelled as the B&C market and is characterized by borrowers with blemished credit histories. The success of this market is based upon the reality that, although such borrowers have financial needs, they often do not have access to credit. However, these borrowers have built a "savings" account in the form of equity in their homes, which can be tapped efficiently as collateral for credit. And, with a properly structured and serviced loan, these borrowers can be expected to perform. With the growth of this market, several originators have efficiently utilized asset securitization as a funding mechanism, which has facilitated rapid growth. This chapter explores the growth of the B&C home-equity loan market and critically evaluates the attendant role of securitization in contributing to this growth.

ROOTS OF THE INDUSTRY

In the 1960s, home-equity lending by finance companies was virtually non-existent. Lending by such entities was usually for a specific purpose, such as the purchase of a consumer durable. Over time, such lenders realized that consumers had additional borrowing needs. At the same time, due to some degree of blemished credit histories, consumers had limited funding resources. Yet, these consumers did own homes, which could serve as collateral for loans. Lenders also recognized from experience that these consumers were generally creditworthy, even if they were occasionally delinquent. In the 1970s, a group of "ma and pa" lenders — small, family-owned lending companies — (and some finance companies) got involved in what has been since labelled as the B&C market and began to originate home equity loans. Some of the early finance companies included institutions such as Aames, United Companies, The Money Store, and Advanta.

In its early stages, the industry was extremely fragmented due to a lack of capital. Often, lenders funded themselves with retained earnings and loan sales. In these early days, non-warehouse, direct institutional equity and debt were generally unavailable to such lenders. As a result, the ability of lenders to make loans was limited. A typical strategy involved gradually building a loan portfolio and using the cash flow from this portfolio to make additional loans. Over time, borrowers had additional financing needs and could be refinanced. In many ways, in this environment, a company's portfolio represented the franchise value of its business. Often the customer base was built from referrals from friends and family.

As discussed, in this market environment, finance companies had limited access to warehouse lines. Yet, advance rates were low (usually 80% to 85% of principal balance, but sometimes as high as 90%), which stretched precious capital. At the same time, these warehouse loans had high interest rates (prime rate plus 100 basis points or more). Still, there were few banks extending credit to finance companies in the 1970s and 1980s, and the outstanding lines generally were small. In general, capital was tight even for the better finance companies. Daily cash management was an art. Yet, because these lines had recourse and low advance rates, lenders could originate and warehouse loans with a wide variety of characteristics. For example, lenders made church and multipurpose loans, broadly serving their communities.

Finance companies sold whole loans on both recourse and non-recourse bases as a financing source. Sometimes, the recourse was limited. For example, it could be restricted in aggregate to one investor or a specific loan pool. Early investors included banks and wealthy individuals, and many loans were sold servicing-retained. Many of the loans sold to individuals were hard-money loans (i.e., low loan-to-value (LTV) loans made to less creditworthy borrowers). Because of the low LTVs, net losses associated with such loans was usually low. In the mid 1980s, the whole-loan market broadened, and finance companies began selling loans to banks, insurance companies and savings and loan associations.

TURNING POINTS IN THE INDUSTRY

During the 1980s, the HEL industry enjoyed several watershed events. The Tax Reform Act of 1986 created an impetus for the growth of the primary and securitized markets. First, the Act created the Real Estate Mortgage Investment Conduit ("REMIC") rules which allowed the tax-efficient structuring of multi-class HEL securitizations. Second, tax legislation phased out the deductibility of most non-mortgage consumer debt. Since interest on HELs generally is deductible, this form of debt became relatively more attractive to the consumer.[1] At the same time, participants in the market realized the potential of asset securitization as a means to funding growth. As a result, originators started securitizing HELs. These early securitizations, notably by The Money Store, were small private placements, structured as single-class, surety-wrapped issues.[2] These transactions, which occurred in the late 1980s, paved the way for providing home-equity originators direct access to the institutional capital markets.

---

[1] However much B&C borrowing is not tax driven. We suspect that many borrowers focus more on the pre-tax monthly payment.
[2] Although separate, subordinate classes often were retained by the originator.

REASONS FOR THE RAPID GROWTH IN B&C HELS

In general, finance companies have been more active than banks in the HEL securitization market. This is generally a result of the capital structures of the two types of entities. Banks fund loans on their balance sheets with low-cost deposits. As a group, banks typically operate with high leverage ratios. Finance companies, conversely, generally have more expensive debt-funding costs, less access to non-warehouse funds, and operate with lower leverage ratios.[3] Also, finance companies are more active securitizers of B&C HELs because they are more active than many banks in this sector. Banks and finance companies often target different borrower groups, and have since the early days of the industry. Banks generally focus on the minority of the American population: the top 20% of borrowers that use 80% of the available credit. Conversely, finance companies focus on non-prime borrowers. This type of segmentation exists for several reasons. First, non-prime borrowers often are intimidated by banks. Market-driven finance companies, on the other hand, stress user-friendliness. Second, the lending culture at banks historically has favored low-risk loans; conversely, finance companies often are willing to originate an accordingly priced, riskier loan. Incidentally, many finance companies considered this origination schism odd, as banks had been large buyers of their secondary market whole-loan pools.

Prior to the development of asset securitization, the constraint for most originators was limited capital. For experienced entities with developed origination, underwriting and servicing infrastructures, securitization has permitted dramatic growth as such organizations now can sell loans efficiently. They enjoy improved access to capital without excessive reliance on piecemeal sales at high implied rates. The following reasons have contributed to the rapid growth of the securitized HEL market:

- Since loans are legally sold to an issuing trust, investors have minimal credit exposure to the originator. Therefore, sold loan pools can be structured to a higher credit grade than the credit rating of the originator. This has allowed non-investment grade and unrated originators (the majority of the market) to create investment-grade transactions.
- The liquidity of the securities market has enhanced cost efficiencies. Although early transactions were private placements, a public market has developed and the investor base has broadened, which has further reduced issuance cost.
- The availability of credit enhancement has streamlined securitization. Most transactions have been 100% principal and interest

[3] Obviously, it is difficult to conclude whether the capital structure created the operating strategy or visa-versa.

guaranteed by a monoline surety. This has "genericized" the securities and broadened the investor audience.

- The transactions generally are accounted for as accounting sales. This allows finance companies to increase their return on equity and utilize capital more efficiently.
- Although the originator remains effectively at risk for credit losses, certain risks (including asset/liability mismatch) are transferred to third parties.
- As the investor base for ABSs has expanded, originators haven been able to diversify funding risk. Increasingly, originators are less vulnerable to the risk of large investors leaving the market. The capital markets are made up of a diverse group of participants, which promotes stability.

BENEFITS OF ASSET SECURITIZATION

As a result of the growth of the securitized HEL market, originators have been able to accomplish several strategic objectives as described below.

Improved Asset/Liability Management

Asset securitization allows an originator to "match fund" assets and liabilities. This benefit is particularly important with fixed-rate HELs. By selling fixed-rate "liabilities," the originator has partially, but not completely, transferred interest-rate risk. Nonetheless, some degree of risk still remains on the balance sheet in the form of capitalized excess servicing. If rates fall, a modest pick up in prepayments should occur, which would reduce the value of the retained asset. Note, however, that B&C borrowers have demonstrated significantly less sensitivity to changes in interest rates; prepayments on these loans have remained relatively stable through interest-rate swings. Also, in the case of LIBOR ARMs funded with floating-rate ABSs, the cash flows on the underlying asset are defined by periodic and lifetime caps, whereas the securities pay interest based on a floating index and limited to "available funds" (funds that are available after covering certain trust expenses). Because the originator's excess servicing (ongoing interest in the trust) is represented by the difference between payments on the assets and the securities, this cash flow could deteriorate in certain rate scenarios. This risk can be transferred to investors if the securities are structured as pass-throughs. Yet, this generally raises the originator's funding costs; obviously, investors demand a higher return for taking on this incremental risk.

Improved Velocity of Capital

Securitization has allowed finance companies to increase the velocity of their capital. By selling loans and using the capital markets to transfer interest rate and funding risks, the finance company can focus its capital on the areas of the business that it knows best: marketing, originating, and servicing loans, not funding them.

Improved Credit Discipline

The securitization market has imposed credit discipline. Portfolios are scrutinized by investment bankers, investors, sureties, and rating agencies; each incremental risk explicitly adds cost. This allows the originator to understand the cost of a loan's attributes and to either (i) charge the homeowner a different rate; (ii) restructure the loan; or (iii) not make the loan.

Control of Leverage

As discussed, under generally-accepted accounting principles, securitization is treated as a sale of assets. This allows the finance company to grow its market share without increasing accounting leverage (or bumping up against loan covenants).

Acceleration of Earnings

Securitization enhances the revenue stream of a finance company. When the finance company securitizes, it recognizes a gain on sale based on the present value of its retained interest in the securitization plus its net proceeds. Yet this benefit also brings a drawback: it potentially increases the volatility of earnings and public finance companies are put under constant growth pressure by the capital markets.

SECURITIZATION VERSUS WHOLE-LOAN SALES

When a finance company securitizes loans, it sells a "par-coupon" security and retains "excess servicing." Excess servicing is the interest component of the loans in excess of the investor rate. The sum of the net cash proceeds from the securitization and the non-cash present value of the retained excess servicing generally is greater than the cash proceeds the originator would receive if it had sold the loans in a servicing-retained sale.

- A finance company will have a higher present value if it securitizes than if it had sold whole loans. This generally is because its retained excess servicing is greater than the premium it would have received in a whole-loan sale.
- Compared to a whole-loan sale, the cash proceeds at closing are lower in a securitization. This is an important consideration for many smaller, "cash-strapped" originators, who may not have sufficient access to capital to fund their excess servicing.

- When a finance company securitizes loans, it receives cash flow equal to the net proceeds at closing. Yet it must pay origination costs and taxes on its gain on sale. Some of this cash outlay is financed by the points it charges borrowers. Still, for most finance companies, securitization, although superior from a present-value perspective, can cause negative cash flow, especially in a fast-growth scenario.
- Compared with a whole-loan sale, the originator generally retains more risk in a securitization. This is because the originator often retains prepayment and credit risk in the form of its excess servicing asset.
- A hybrid form of sale/securitization is to securitize and then sell some of the excess servicing. Depending on the specifics of such a transaction, the economic outcome will be between a whole loan sale and a securitization.

STANDARDIZATION OF THE MARKET

Securitization has increased the standardization of originations by finance companies. Prior to the advent of securitization, lenders made loans in their community secured by a variety of collateral types. Church loans, mixed-use multifamily loans, and other real estate loans were not uncommon. The advent of securitization also led to a higher degree of homogeneity in loan pools for a variety of reasons, although other collateral types are still sometimes securitized as a separate tranche of a HEL transaction. Sureties and rating agencies either required high levels of subordination for non-homogeneous or high-risk pools or rejected them outright. Investors prefer homogenous pools. As many lenders originate for sale into the secondary market, they have either (1) discontinued originating loans that are unacceptable for securitization or costly to securitize; (2) retained their non-securitizable originations in their portfolio and charged a higher rate on these loans than otherwise would be the case;[4] or (3) sold these loans in whole-loan form, while securitizing their other originations.

Despite a higher degree of standardization and homogeneity, the use of securitization as a strategic tool is associated with certain risks. These risks may be broadly stated as follows.

- The availability of surety or other guarantees could become limited or prohibitively costly. Also, guarantors could be downgraded.

[4] It is interesting to note that these borrowers still have access to credit from family-run and/or non-securitizing finance companies; yet, their rates are still at historic high rates — the same rates as the pre-securitization world.

This most likely would occur if a surety took a large loss, which is improbable, given their practice of requiring underlying investment grade risk and diversifying their assumed risks. Furthermore, in such a scenario, the surety potentially could raise additional capital, thereby protecting its market position.

- A general widening of spreads or an increase in rates could occur. This is a normal risk of any fixed-income market; any profit diminution caused by such increases could be mitigated by increases in borrower rates.
- A credit downgrade of the originator could cause access loss. Although this potentially could raise the issuer's cost (for example, by necessitating a master servicer), it is unlikely that an originator would be precluded from issuing ABSs due to a *reasonable* credit deterioration as ABSs are designed to be credit-remote from the issuer.[5]

MARKET CHALLENGES

As the industry develops, the influx of new industry participants is a challenge to the industry's stability. We identify some of the contemporary challenges in the industry below:

- Conforming lenders are entering the HEL market. Yet, the HEL market is distinct and requires different skills. Underwriting is subjective, not formulaic, and servicing is intense, not passive. No doubt, some will be successful; yet, others may face challenges in adapting.
- Experienced participants understand risk/reward pricing. Through years of experience, such entities have developed a "feel" for the foreclosure frequency, loss severity, and risk-adjusted price of a loan. As competition intensifies in the industry causing a greater degree of price competitiveness, the value of originated loans and hence, their ability to be securitized, may suffer.
- Loan terms have been formulated carefully by experienced lenders based upon years of experience with their borrowers. As new lenders adjust these terms, the borrower and the investor both could suffer should the terms make the loan difficult to repay. For example, extended maturities and high LTV's without compensating credit factors, and poor "financial consulting" with borrowers could make a loan difficult to repay.

[5] In the case of a large credit deterioration, the previously securitization-eligible issuer may still be able to sell whole loans, or securitize through a conduit on a servicing-released basis.

- Efficient servicing is the key to a successful securitization. Servicing should be intense, fair, and disciplined. A good loan can be ruined through bad servicing. A bad loan can be repaired through the efficiency of the servicing mechanism. While servicing expertise has grown over time, there is a limited supply of knowledgeable servicers in this sector.

INVESTOR CONSIDERATIONS

In view of these considerations, investors should increasingly incorporate the following in their evaluation of securitized HELs in addition to the relative value analysis of the securities.
- How long has the originator been in business?
- Is the management team stable and experienced in consumer (not conforming mortgage) credit?
- Why is the issuer in business? Is it a long-term plan or merely a strategy to finance downturns in other markets?
- Is the originator investing side-by-side with the investor? Has the originator retained or sold the excess servicing in the transaction?
- Does the originator have a lending philosophy? Do they stick to that philosophy, even at the cost of slower growth?
- What is the originator's servicing experience?

SUMMARY

Securitization has allowed the HEL industry to grow dramatically. Yet, it also has standardized HEL lending and imposed a higher degree of credit discipline. These developments have benefited borrowers and investors alike. Borrowers have gained increased access to funds at competitive rates. Investors have found a low-risk vehicle, which can be tailored to meet their demands. We expect continued market growth, although it should occur at a slower rate than in the past.

Chapter 9

Equipment Lease-Backed Securities

John Lucas[*]

Thomas Zimmerman
First Vice President
Fixed Income Research
Prudential Securities Inc.

---

[*] This chapter was written when John Lucas was in the Mortgage and Asset Finance Group, Prudential Securities Inc.

INTRODUCTION

The rapidly expanding market for lease backed securities represents an important new opportunity for fixed-income investors. With annual origination volume exceeding $150 billion, equipment leases play a major role in the U.S. industrial economy and constitute one of the most important financing mechanisms for industrial corporations worldwide.

Characterized by low defaults and delinquencies and few prepayments, equipment leases make ideal collateral for asset-backed securities (ABSs). As compared to obligors in most other ABSs, lessees are typically corporations rather than individuals; due to the structure and prepayment disincentives of most leases, there are few refinance driven prepayments. Furthermore, because of their comparative novelty, lease backed securities currently trade at more generous spreads than other types of ABSs.

This chapter explores the characteristics of equipment leases and the securities structured from them. It discusses the fundamentals and mechanics of a lease agreement, the lease pooling process, and the structure and credit enhancement of lease backed securities. Finally, lease backed securities are examined within the context of the larger fixed-income market.

OVERVIEW OF THE EQUIPMENT LEASING INDUSTRY

According to the U.S. Department of Commerce, U.S. companies placed around $522 billion of new industrial equipment into service in 1994. This was a dramatic 17% increase over 1993 and a steep recovery from the slow and no growth years of 1991 and 1992. Roughly 30% to 35% of equipment acquired each year is financed via leasing, which means that perhaps as much as $150 billion of equipment leases were written in 1994. As these figures show, equipment leases represent a very large pool of potential collateral for securitization, of which only a small portion has been tapped to date.

Exhibit 1 presents recent annual leasing volumes and a breakdown by equipment type as reported by the Equipment Leasing Association of America. For the period examined, transportation equipment, such as aircraft, railcars and trucks, accounts for 25% to 30% of the total. Computers and software account for another 23%, while other office equipment represents roughly 10%. The remainder is spread over a variety of industrial, agricultural, construction and medical sectors.

Advantages of Leasing

Lessees of capital and other equipment find leasing advantageous for a variety of reasons, including service needs and accounting and funding benefits.

Exhibit 1: Annual Equipment Leasing Volume

	1991	1992	1993
Agriculture	0.9	0.9	1.0
Aircraft	22.9	15.3	12.2
Computers & software	21.1	22.9	22.7
Construction	4.4	5.0	6.6
Containers	1.2	3.0	2.0
Electrical power	0.7	1.1	0.4
Fresh & salt water transportation	0.7	1.1	1.3
Office furnishings	1.9	3.8	4.2
Industrial & manufacturing	11.1	8.9	8.7
Materials handling	1.0	1.6	1.6
Medical	3.5	5.1	6.1
Office machines	6.8	7.6	10.7
"Turnkey" industrial plants	1.8	1.2	0.3
Railroad	2.4	3.6	4.8
Telecommunications	5.8	6.2	5.9
Trucks & trailers	6.0	7.4	8.7
Other	7.8	5.2	2.8
Total (%)	100.0	100.0	100.0
Total ($ billion)	120.0	121.7	130.5

Source: U.S. Commerce Department; Equipment Leasing Association of America

Equipment and Service Needs Because of the sheer volume and cost of equipment purchases, the "lease-or-buy" decision is an important one for corporate finance managers. Corporations often choose to lease for several reasons. First, ownership remains with the lessor, so the lessee receives built-in protection against the risk of obsolescence. Second, the lease format may provide the lessee with additional leverage to ensure that the equipment functions properly and is adequately maintained. Third, technical and maintenance services can be bundled with leased equipment. Fourth, a leasing company can provide added clout in obtaining priority delivery for equipment in short supply. Finally, short-term needs can be matched to the lease term.

Accounting There are two accounting advantages of leasing. First, in the early years of an operating lease, payments are often smaller than the depreciation and interest expenses associated with a purchase, improving reported earnings. Second, leases often can be taken out of a manager's operating budget, circumventing the more elaborate justification typically required for inclusion in a capital budget.

Exhibit 2: Volume of Public Equipment-Lease-Backed Securities Transactions

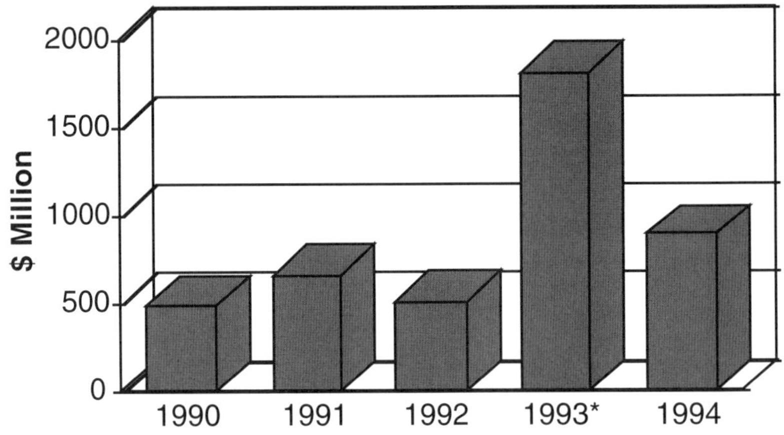

* Includes a $1.2 billion transaction by IBM.
Source: Prudential Securities' IMPACT data base

Funding Flexibility There are funding flexibility advantages of leasing. Unlike bank loans, lease agreements rarely contain restrictive covenants. Leasing permits lessees to diversify their funding sources. Leases generally require smaller down payments than loans, conserving cash. Payments can be tailored to suit the lessee's cash flow; step-up, step-down, seasonal, skipped-payment and other structures are possible. Leases are often simpler and quicker to arrange than other financing forms.

Types of Leasing Companies

Lease originators fall into four major categories: (1) "captives" or subsidiaries of industrial corporations, (2) banks, (3) independent leasing companies, and (4) financial-service companies.

The Increasing Role of Securitization

Exhibit 2 illustrates the growth of the lease-backed securities market during the 1990s and Exhibit 3 lists all public lease-backed securitizations for the nine years ending 1994.

The growth of lease-backed securitization has been motivated by balance-sheet considerations to a much lesser extent than securitization in other sectors. Rather, the primary motivation for securitization has been funding cost.

Exhibit 3: Public Equipment-Lease Backed Securities Transactions
As of Year-End 1994

Deal Date	Issue	Types of leases	Amount ($ MM)	S&P's/Moody's Rating	Underwriter
12/19/94	Japan Leasing Corp 1994-1	Office & Industrial Equipment	148.4	AAA/Aaa	CITI
12/16/94	Pruential Securities Secured Funding 1994-3	Misc.	77.2	AAA	PSI
12/8/94	Leasing Solutions 1994-2	Computers/Telecom Equip	37.5	AAA/Aaa	PSI
10/31/94	Copelco Captal Funding 1994-A	Medical Equipment	153.0	AAA	PSI
10/11/94	Charter Financial Corp 1994-1	Video & Medical Equip	57.1	AAA/Aaa	PSI
8/1/94	Pruential Securities Secured Funding 1994-2	Office & Manufacturing Equipment	18.5	A	PSI
7/29/94	Pruential Securities Secured Funding 1994-1	Medical Equipment	49.5	AAA	PSI
6/28/94	DVI Receivables 1994-1 A1	Medical Equipment	85.0	AAA/Aaa	PSI
6/28/94	IBM Credit Receivables 1994-A A1	Computers	103.4	AA+/Aa1	FBC
6/28/94	IBM Credit Receivables 1994-A A2	Computers	116.6	AAA/Aaa	FBC
4/5/94	Leasing Soltions 1994-1	Computers/Telecom Equip	36.7	AAA/Aaa	PSI
12/16/93	Copelco Lease Funding 1993-A	Medical Equipment	94.7	AAA/Aaa	PSI
11/23/93	IBM Credit 1993-1	Computers	1176.5	AAA/Aaa	FBC
2/17/93	Unisys 1993-1	Computers	125.0	AAA/Aaa	ML
2/8/93	Comdisco 1993-A A2	Computers	185.3	AAA/Aaa	SAL
2/8/93	Comdisco 1993-A A1	Computers	83.0	A/Aa1	SAL

Exhibit 3 (Concluded)

Deal Date	Issue	Types of leases	Amount ($ MM)	S&P's/Moody's Rating	Underwriter
9/23/92	IBM Tax-Exempt 1992-A&B	Computers	105.3		FBC
5/22/92	Comdisco 1992-A1	Computers	85.0	A/Aa1	SAL
5/22/92	Comdisco 1992-A2	Computers	158.0	AAA/Aaa	SAL
4/24/92	USLIC Grantor Trust 1992-AB and C	Misc.	94.4	AAA	ML
11/21/91	General Elec. CPF Tax-Exempt 1991-3 A thru C	Telecom & Computers	79.1	AAA	KP
10/24/91	IBM Tax-Exempt 1991-ABC	Computers	124.9	AAA/Aaa	FBC
5/24/91	Comdisco Receivables 1991-A	Computers	332.2		SAL
5/16/91	General Elec. CPF Tax-Exempt 1991-2 A-thru D	Telecom & Computers	115.3	AAA	KP
11/27/90	IBM Tax-Exempt 1990-A B C & D	Computers	302.8	AAA/Aaa	FBC
11/21/90	General Elec.CPF 1990-1	Computer, Medical, etc.	137.5	AAA/Aaa	KP
7/19/90	CFC-9 Tax Exempt Guarantor Trust 1990-9	Office Equio.	34.9	AAA	ML
12/20/88	Chase Manhattan Grantor Trust 1988-A	Computers & Printing	100.1	AAA/Aaa	GS
12/17/86	Sperr Lease Finance Corp C	Computers	174.5	AAA	FBC
12/5/86	Goldome Guarantor Trust	Misc.	205.7	AAA	FBC
9/12/85	Sperry Lease Finance Corp B	Computers	145.8	AAA	FBC
3/7/85	Sperry Lease Finance Corp A	Computers	192.5	AAA	FBC

Several leasing industry trends have favored the use of this funding tool. The increasing standardization of lease documentation has made the available collateral pool of leasing product more uniform. Industry consolidation has concentrated the supply of leases available for securitization. Widespread availability of analytical technology for evaluating leases has forced originators to compete on price. Narrowing profit margins have heightened the importance of low-cost funding. Increased acceptance of equipment-lease securitization has permitted originators to diversify and stabilize their sources of funds, which has allowed them to expand origination volume. With no sign that these trends will end soon, the expectation is that the volume of lease securitizations to expand rapidly during the remainder of the decade.

BASICS OF LEASING[1]

Lessors and Lessees

A lease is a contract between two parties, the *lessor* and the *lessee*. The lessor obtains the equipment at the start of the lease term, usually by purchasing it from the manufacturer. The lessor then agrees to make it available to the lessee for a stated period of time in exchange for a specified schedule of payments. Often, the lease may contain provisions that give the lessee an option to purchase the equipment outright from the lessor on pre-specified terms when the lease expires; this option is one element that determines the classification of the lease, as described below.

Finance and Operating Leases

Understanding the type of lease in a lease backed security is important for two major reasons. First, the Uniform Commercial Code filings required to perfect a security interest in underlying equipment depend on the type of lease in the transaction (see "Legal Structure," discussed below) and second, the amount of residual realizations that may be available for additional credit support will be affected by the lease type.

In the ABS market, primarily two types of leases have been securitized: finance and operating leases.

Finance Lease A finance lease, also called a capital lease, is essentially a secured loan. The lessee rents the equipment for its substantial economic life, and has the obligations and benefits of ownership of the equipment during the term of the lease. At the end of the lease term, the lessee has the option to purchase the equipment, usually for a nominal amount.

---

[1] For an in-depth discussion of leasing, see Peter K. Nevitt and Frank J. Fabozzi, *Equipment Leasing* (Homewood, IL: Dow-Jones Irwin, 1988).

Exhibit 4: Finance Lease Classification Tests

At least one of the following four statements must be true for a lease to be classified as a finance lease:

1. The lease transfers title and ownership of the equipment under lease to the lessee by the end of the lease term;

2. The lease contains a bargain price option;

3. The lease term at inception is at least 75%[*] of the estimated life of the equipment leased; or

4. The present value of the minimum lease payments is at least 90%[*] of the fair market value of the equipment at the inception of the lease.

[*] Note that these percentages apply speifically to new equipment; the criteria differ slightly if applied to leases on used equipment.

Operating Lease An operating lease provides the lessee with the use of the equipment for a period of time, while the obligations and benefits of ownership remain with the lessor. The purchase option, if present, is for a more substantial sum than that for a finance lease.

The key distinction between finance and operating leases is whether the lessor or the lessee bears the substantial economic risks and rewards of owning the equipment. A brief summary of the tests that generally are used to distinguish between the two lease types are highlighted in Exhibit 4. A lease is classified as an operating lease unless at least one of the items numbered one through four in Exhibit 4 is true. Additional information on lease classification may be obtained from FASB 13 and related statements.

Operating leases tend to have shorter terms and lower payments (for the same term) than finance leases, which can benefit both parties. The shorter term protects the lessee against technological obsolescence; for this reason, operating leases can be especially well suited to high-technology equipment. For example, when an operating lease on high-technology equipment matures, the equipment may be leased again to a business with less sophisticated needs.

The *leveraged lease*, in which an outside equity investor borrows money to purchase equipment that is subsequently leased to the user in order to obtain certain tax advantages, is another kind of operating lease. Most leases of transportation equipment, such as aircraft or railcars, are leveraged leases. Because their credit profiles and structures differ significantly from those of typical equipment-lease transactions, leveraged leases will not be discussed further in this chapter and are not included in the list of securitized lease transactions in Exhibit 3 or in the data on equipment-lease securitization volumes.

Municipal leases are leases issued to municipalities. The interest income received from securities backed by municipal leases may be exempt from federal income taxes, provided that the structure of the securitization meets certain criteria. In addition, municipal leases generally provide that the lease may be canceled at some future date if the municipality fails to appropriate the necessary funds; addressing this possibility introduces additional complexities. Because of their unique characteristics, municipal leases will not be covered in this chapter. *Automobile leases*, which have special properties in common with other types of consumer obligations, also will not be covered.

Residuals

At the end of the lease term, the lessee may have the option to purchase the equipment either at a price specified in the contract or at prevailing fair market value. If the lessee declines to exercise this option or it is not offered, the lessor may re-lease the used equipment to the same lessee, another lessee or sell the equipment to a third party.

Residuals are the proceeds realized from the sale or re-lease of equipment at the end of a lease term. The lessor may attribute a book residual value to the equipment when the lease is originated by estimating its value at termination. For operating leases, the lessor can choose to follow a depreciation schedule, which leaves an implied residual when the lease expires.

UNDERSTANDING LEASE-BACKED SECURITIES

Determining Principal and Interest

Unlike loans, leases generally do not specify an interest rate, although the lessor may use one to calculate the lease payments. Instead, the contract calls for the lessee to make a specified stream of payments over some fixed time period.

To create fixed-income securities, we construct an interest rate, or *discount rate*, which is used to separate the cash flows into principal and interest components. Typically, this rate is chosen so that it exactly supports the transaction's ongoing expenses, which include (1) the coupon on the securities, (2) servicing fees, (3) trustee payments, and (4) credit-enhancement fees, if any. Any required excess spread also is included in the discount rate.

For each lease, payments are allocated to principal and interest so that the remaining notional principal balance of the leases always equals the net present value of the remaining payments (see Exhibit 5). For a lease paid in equal monthly installments, the amortization schedule is identical to that of any other level-payment, fixed-rate obligation.

Exhibit 5: Discounting Leases for a Securitization

Transaction Expenses

Coupon	8.75%
Servicing	0.75%
Trustee	0.05%
Credit Enhancement	0.45%
Total (Discount Rate)	10.00%

Lease Cash Flow

Month 0	—
Month 1	100
Month 2	100
Month 3	200
Gross Cash Flow	$400

Lease Implicit Contract Balance (LICB)

$$\text{LICB} = \frac{\$100}{(1+(0.10/12))^1} + \frac{\$100}{(1+(0.10/12))^2} + \frac{\$200}{(1+(0.10/12))^3} = \$392.61$$

Bond Cash Flow

	Bond Principal ($)	Interest and Expenses ($)	Total ($)	Bond Balance ($)
Month 0	—	—	—	392.61
Month 1	96.73	3.27	100	295.89
Month 2	97.54	2.46	100	198.35
Month 3	198.35	1.65	200	0.00
Totals	392.61	7.39	400	

Note: The sum of the LICBs for all leases in a portfolio is equal to the amount of supportable principal in a lease backed transaction and also is equal to the principal balance of the issue, assuming no subordination.

The exact face amount of securities cannot be determined until investor demand is gauged and the transaction is priced. Therefore, lease-backed securities typically are marketed with a preliminary discount rate and approximate face amount.

Unlike loans, many leases feature payment schedules customized to the lessee's needs. As a result, they may pay quarterly, semi-annually or annually instead of monthly. Alternatively, they may not feature regular periodic payments at all, but rather, seasonal payments or payments that step up over time. Because stepped-payment contracts often have back-ended cash flows, they typically amortize more slowly than level-pay leases of similar present value. Most lease-backed securities pay on a monthly basis, however.

Since irregular and/or stepped payment schedules may constitute a significant proportion of some securitized pools, it is important for the rating agencies or credit enhancer to verify that there is sufficient liquidity in the structure to pay interest on a regular basis. Generally, however, there is a sufficient proportion of level-pay contracts in a transaction to satisfy this condition.

Credit Enhancement

Equipment-lease transactions make use of many of the same credit enhancement mechanisms seen elsewhere in the ABS market, including excess spread, subordination, monoline insurance policies and trigger events. In addition, these transactions make use of residuals as a form of credit enhancement.

Excess Spread In some leasing structures, a portion of the payment stream is earmarked as *excess spread*. These funds are available to cover potential losses and, in some cases, may accumulate in a spread account which can provide protection at a later date. In addition, because all the leases in a pool typically are amortized at the same interest rate, any excess spread in a lease securitization is generally more predictable than in a loan pool with varying coupons.

A more common form of excess cash flows in leasing transactions is *residual realizations*, which will be discussed later in this chapter.

Subordination Senior/subordinated structures are common in the lease backed securities market, with the originator typically retaining a small interest in the lease pool, usually in the form of the residuals or a subordinated payment stream. Senior/mezzanine/subordinate structures, in which both senior and mezzanine securities are sold, while the originator retains a subordinated interest, also are employed in the equipment-lease market. Subordinate tranches may be paid pro-rata or sequentially, depending on rating agency requirements and the issuer's objectives.

Monoline Insurance Policies Third-party credit enhancements often are utilized in the lease-backed securities market. The most common vehicle is the "wrap" or monoline surety bond that guarantees 100% of the principal and interest on the senior securities. The surety bond also may be supported by a subordinated security, cash collateral account or some combination thereof.

Trigger Events A trigger event changes the direction of cash flow, increasing the amounts available to the most senior securities, either by directing additional cash flow to such securities directly or by increasing the amounts retained in the spread account. Trigger events may occur if pool performance deteriorates due to higher than anticipated defaults or delinquencies or if the servicer falters, for example by declaring bankruptcy or relinquishing the servicing function. Sometimes, a senior/subordinate structure will have a trigger event if the subordinate security balance reaches a specified minimum level.

Some triggers are reversible: If pool performance improves sufficiently or a servicing transfer is completed successfully, the cash flow allocation will revert to its original pattern. Other trigger events are non-reversible and may require acceleration of the securities with the increased cash flow that is available.

Because there is additional uncertainty about the exact level of excess cash available to the structure in any given period, lease-backed structures tend to rely on more stringent trigger events than do transactions backed by loans. Rating agencies and insurers also tend to be exceptionally cautious when dealing with a new asset type and use triggers to provide additional protection to investors.

Residual Realizations Residuals, the proceeds received from the sale or re-lease of the equipment when the lease expires, typically are not sold to investors as part of their principal balance, but more often are used for credit enhancement. Leases expire continuously in most transactions, resulting in an intermittent stream of cash flows. Like excess spread, residuals generally flow through the structure as current credit enhancement for losses. Sometimes they are trapped in a spread account, but usually this occurs only when certain trigger conditions are met.

As a credit-enhancement mechanism, residuals have several advantages over excess spread. By nature, residuals are back-ended and thus likely to be available to the security, if needed, in its later stages, while excess spread may flow out of the securitization early in the transaction's life rather than remaining available for loss coverage. However, the full benefit of this back-loading depends on the shape of the loss curve for a particular transaction's collateral. In addition, residuals for prepaid leases remain dedicated to the transaction and collateral, although they may flow through sooner than if a prepayment had not occurred, while excess spread is limited to those assets still generating coupon income.

The timing of residual payments cannot be fixed with the same precision as that of excess spread, since residual payments depend on the secondary purchase and lease markets for the equipment. However, there are strong incentives for both lessor and lessee to resolve equipment disposition quickly.

Based on an originator's historical record of value and timing of residual realizations, some fraction of the booked residual amount may be credited toward the required enhancement target level.

Legal Structure

As with other asset types, certain legal issues must be addressed in order to ensure the integrity of a leasing transaction and to fulfill rating agency requirements. In addition to the normal corporate and securities law opinions and concerns, the following requirements should be noted.

True-Sale Back-Up Security Interest Opinion A reputable law firm must opine that the equipment-lease collateral has been conveyed irrevocably by the lease originator to the special-purpose corporation or trust that issues the securities. Thus the leases would not be consolidated with the seller's estate in the event of the originator's corporate bankruptcy. While the true-sale opinion itself does not provide a guaranty as to bankruptcy-remote status, it provides investors with the comfort that reputable parties are confident that collateral is properly insulated from potential bankruptcy proceedings of the lease originator. In addition, the rating agencies will require an opinion that, in the event that a court were to hold that the transfer by the lease originator to the issuing entity is not a "true" sale, that the lease originator has granted to such issuing entity a first priority perfected security interest in the leases.

Perfected Security Interest or Ownership of Underlying Asset A finance lease is essentially a secured loan, in which the lessor can look to a security interest in the underlying equipment if the contract should default. Thus, in order to protect investors, the lessor must transfer a first perfected security interest in the equipment to the issuing entity. In order to effect this, the issuer must make a filing under the Uniform Commercial Code (U.C.C.) granting the interest to the trustee. For an operating lease, the issuer owns the equipment, as well as an associated rental contract; both are conveyed to the trust. Perfection of this sale also requires filings under the U.C.C. Depending on rating agency requirements, U.C.C. filings may not be completed for all equipment in a transaction, but merely for some specified "threshold" amount.

Accounting Considerations

The complex tax implications associated with ownership of operating leases make it essential to insulate investors from the administrative burdens of ownership. In addition, there may be tax benefits to the seller in retaining ownership of the leases. As a result, many transactions that are backed in part or full by operating leases have been structured as secured debt, rather than as equity participations, such as pass-through certificates.

However, some finance-lease transactions have been structured as grantor trusts, which give the seller sales treatment for accounting and tax purposes. In such structures, it is unusual to achieve off-balance-sheet treatment.

Secured debt transactions receive financing treatment for tax purposes, but grantor trusts receive sale treatment for tax purposes.

EVALUATING LEASE-BACKED SECURITIES

An evaluation of any ABS begins with an understanding of the credit and prepayment characteristics of the underlying collateral. With respect to both prepayment and credit risk, equipment leases have less uncertainty than most other assets used for securitization.

Prepayment Risk

Leases generally are structured without the prepayment option found in most loans. While a typical borrower may repay an outstanding loan balance at any time, if a lessee has a prepayment option, it must comply with a "hell or high water" provision that obligates it to make all contractual payments upon early termination. This economic disincentive to prepay results in a very stable average-life expectation, virtually eliminating refinancing driven lease prepayments.

The courts have held that these "hell or high water" clauses are enforceable even in extreme circumstances, such as the bankruptcy of the manufacturer or the failure of the equipment. Recent decisions have specifically acknowledged that the lessor's ability to rely on these provisions is crucial to the functioning of the leasing industry. This body of law and judicial interpretation have created a second powerful barrier against prepayment risk.

Even given these disincentives, there are still lease prepayments that may affect investors; they come from three primary sources: equipment upgrades, outright prepayments, and lessee defaults.

Equipment Upgrades Upgrades account for the majority of early terminations. Under an upgrade, the lessee takes out a lease for new equipment and is permitted to prepay the old lease, sometimes on liberal terms. Many lessors have a policy that permits or even encourages lessees to upgrade to new equipment. Such upgrades are actually to the lessor's advantage because they maintain the quality of the lease collateral.

Outright Prepayments These are infrequent, but if a lessee decides to exit a business line or to purchase equipment earlier than the stated lease term, the lessee may prepay the lease and curtail the cash flow stream, despite the cost of doing so.

Lessee Defaults A lessee may default on its lease payments. An originator's portfolio history is the best indicator of how a particular pool will perform over time and, with respect to principal protection, the extent to which any defaults will be covered by a transaction's credit enhancement. Typically, however, lease-backed transactions require the amount of prepayments and defaults to be included in the principal paid to investors on the payment date after the month in which such prepayment or default occurs.

Many lease securitizations give the lessor the option to replace a prepaid or defaulted lease with one that is of equal or extended terms and has equal or larger payments and residual value. This replacement feature is allowed provided that the lease rental stream from the substitute lease does not extend beyond the expected maturity of the transaction. A substitution provision, which usually applies to all types of lease prepayments, can minimize the effect of prepayments on investors.

The substitution feature is an option of the seller/originator rather than a requirement because an obligation to continue to sell collateral to the entity issuing the securities would provide the issuing entity with ongoing recourse to the seller. Such a recourse relationship would violate the "substantive non-consolidation" condition essential to protecting investors in the event of a corporate bankruptcy of the originator.

Although legal and practical considerations generally mandate that the substitution feature be structured as an option rather than as an obligation and limited to 10% of the original pool, lessors often opt to substitute to the extent permissible because it mitigates the effects of prepayments and thus helps to maintain good investor relations.

Since substituted leases may terminate later than the leases they replace, substitution provisions pose some extension risk. However, this risk tends to be balanced by increased cash prepayments toward the end of the life of a transaction, since as the transaction approaches its maturity date it becomes less practical to substitute leases that expire before that date.

The economic disincentives to prepay and the substitution provisions, taken together, mean that the effect of prepayments on leasing transactions is generally minimal.

Credit Risk

Industry surveys have consistently shown a net loss rate for the leasing industry as a whole of 1% to 2% in each year since 1990, according to the Equipment Leasing Association of America. However, there is considerable variation among individual issuers; most seem to fall in the range of 1% to 4% annually. The issuer's historical loss rates, particularly if they are provided for equipment and lessees similar to those included in the transaction being considered, are probably the best single indicator of expected future losses.

In general, the factors discussed below should be considered in examining the credit risk associated with a leasing transaction.

Borrower Credit Quality The most important determinant of loss rates is the creditworthiness of the borrowers. Indeed, much of the variation in loss rates among lessors can be explained by the differing credit profiles of their customers. For example, Fortune 500 companies can be expected to default on their leases much less frequently than small companies or individual professionals.

Lessee Concentration A collateral pool with many lessees spreads the risk of default and decreases event risk.

Lease Size Generally, the larger the average lease size as a proportion of the total collateral pool, the greater the impact any single default will have on the transaction as a whole. Transactions for high-ticket items such as aircraft generally trade at wider spreads because of this risk.

Geographic Concentration Smaller lessees are most apt to be affected by regional economic cycles. A heavy concentration of small companies in a single industry and in a single geographic region could increase event risk.

Technological Obsolescence If the leased equipment becomes so outdated as to be worthless, the disincentives to default weaken.

The following factors can mitigate credit risk from the underlying lessees in a transaction.

Default Disincentives Because leased equipment is often an integral part of the lessee's business operations and because the obligation provides both a security interest in the equipment and recourse to the borrower, there are generally strong disincentives to default. Smaller entities often are required to provide a personal guaranty, which strengthens this disincentive.

Upgrade Policy A policy that permits lessees to replace outdated equipment with a new lease for an upgraded model, under liberal prepayment terms, provides leases with a means of avoiding the prospect of obsolete equipment. Furthermore, even though equipment may be obsolete compared to newer models, it may still be useful to the lessee, thereby mitigating obsolescence risk.

Service Industry The presence of well established third-party service companies to maintain and service equipment allows lessees to continue to make active use of leased equipment even in the event of a manufacturer's bankruptcy. For example, Memorex Telex Corporation (MTC) has filed for and emerged from bankruptcy twice since February 1992. Nevertheless, their equipment has been included in securitizations without a problem, and in one instance (Leasing Solutions Receivables, Inc. 1994-1), MTC equipment constituted approximately 75% of the equipment in the pool by original equipment cost.

Maturity of Securities Leasing transactions generally have two- to three-year average lives. In some cases, payments are directed so that the final maturity of the securities is shorter than that of the collateral. A pool of leases extending to seven years, for example, might be structured into securities with a five-year expected maturity. In general, the shorter the security, the less the likelihood of credit problems related to changes in economic conditions.

Should lessee defaults occur in lease-backed transactions, the following features of their typical structure limit the effect of the default on investors.

Credit Enhancement The protection afforded by a transaction's credit enhancement generally can be characterized by a maximum sustainable loss rate, both annually and over the transaction's lifetime. One common measure of the adequacy of credit support is the ratio of this maximum sustainable annual rate to the estimated loss rate (usually the issuer's historical loss rate, preferably for similar lessees and equipment). Credit agencies generally set a target value for this ratio, known as the *loss coverage ratio*. The ratio target is typically three to five (for a triple-A rating) but can vary depending on the agency and such factors as the amount and quality of loss history available.[2]

Substitution Policy A policy on the issuer's part to substitute performing leases for those that default substantially mitigates the effect of defaults, particularly for subordinated securities. (Substitutions are discussed more fully in the *Prepayment Risk* section.) In addition, because leases are considered to be in default after a specified delinquency period (typically 120 days), this feature effectively maintains the quality of the transaction's cash flow.

The creditworthiness of a leasing transaction also can be affected by the reliability of projected residual values, which are an important form of credit enhancement.

Residual Values

At origination, a lessor books a residual amount for each piece of equipment based on its anticipated recovery. (For operating leases, the lessor may choose instead to compute the residual based on a depreciation schedule.) The booked residuals and the originator's residual realization history are presented to rating agencies for use in their evaluation of a transaction's credit strength.

As with loss rates, the most important measure of the accuracy of residual estimates is the consistency with which recoveries equal or exceed projected values. The leasing industry as a whole is quite conservative in its forecasts of residuals. Industry surveys indicate that actual recoveries for finance leases have come in consistently at 1.1 to 1.5 times book value, and ratios less than one are quite uncommon, according to the Equipment Leasing Association of America.

However, because realizations are options rather than contractual obligations, rating agencies rarely give more than 50% credit to book residuals and very often much less. Thus, if there is reason to believe that the lessor's estimates are justified, residuals can provide an additional layer of credit support beyond that acknowledged by the rating agencies.

As with loss rates, the most important indicator of the reliability of residual values is the originator's historical experience, particularly if data are supplied for similar collateral and lessees. Other factors that may support residual realization estimates follow.

---

[2] The presence of a surety wrap, which introduces an additional measure of credit protection, reduces the importance of the loss coverage provided by other elements of the transaction structure.

Access to Marketing Channels These channels may include used-equipment markets and the market in which the equipment is located. For example, some lessors have a direct sales force that sells into a specialized marketplace.

Vendor Participation This includes vendor incentives and exclusivity. An example of the former is an agreement with the vendor to share any resale proceeds above an agreed-upon target level. Such arrangements typically provide access to the vendor's sales force, contacts and other resources. Vendors also may be motivated to participate in such arrangements in order to preserve the value of their trademark and the integrity of their marketing channels.

Exclusivity is an agreement with the vendor that the lessor is the only marketer of the vendor's used equipment to protect the lessor's investment in a remarketing operation.

Leasing Experience First, this is the lessor's level of experience with the industry to which the equipment belongs and with the remarketing process. Second is the historical proportion of comparable equipment that is purchased or re-leased by the original lessee. This cuts remarketing costs, tends to produce higher proceeds more quickly than remarketing to a third party and avoids any concerns about the quality of the used equipment.

Following are factors that may increase the risk of lower than expected residual recoveries.

Technological Obsolescence If product cycles for the type of equipment under lease are very short (in comparison to the lease term), there is likely to be greater risk that used equipment will decline in value more rapidly than expected.

Equipment and Geographic Concentration The concentration of leases in a specific type of equipment or geographic region tends to amplify the effects of other risks, such as technological obsolescence or shifts in the equipment market.

INVESTMENT CHARACTERISTICS

The characteristics of lease-backed securities examined in earlier sections will affect the securities' cash flows. In particular, the stability and simplicity of lease-backed securities make their behavior relatively simple to predict. In addition, the novelty of these securities may provide incremental yield to investors compared to other ABSs.

Summary of Cash Flow Characteristics

Typically, equipment leases are written for a term of three to seven years. Lease-backed securities generally have a two- to three-year average life and are structured so that their expected maturity is five years or less. Because prepayments are infrequent, the cash flows tend to be highly stable and predictable. In fact, the month-by-month payment stream resembles that of any amortizing security, such as a pool of automobile loans.

As discussed earlier, early terminations may result in substitutions or in the one-time payment of the net present value of the remaining contractual lease payments. The replacement of a new lease by one that matures later may extend the securities' average life somewhat. However, extension risk is often counterbalanced by increased cash prepayments toward the end of a transaction. In addition, such factors as the commonplace "hell or high water" provision inhibit voluntary prepayments.

Comparison to Other Asset-Backed Investments

Lease-backed securities offer the following advantages when compared to other ABSs.

- The underlying collateral is of high quality. Leases have one of the lowest loss levels of any securitized asset. As mentioned earlier, the Equipment Leasing Association's annual surveys have shown net loss rates of between 1% and 2% for each year since 1990.
- The "effective" credit support on lease transactions is greater than on other ABSs. As noted, residuals effectively provide lease securitizations with an extra layer of credit support beyond that acknowledged by the credit-rating agencies. These cash flows, coupled with the stringent trigger conditions built into transaction structures, can provide lease securitizations with unusually strong credit protection in comparison to other asset types.
- Equipment-lease backed securities, unlike many other ABSs and mortgage-backed securities, have relatively little extension risk because they are typically priced at 0% ABS. Although infrequent, there is one circumstance that could extend the average life of a lease-backed security. In some transactions, the surety provider is not required to pass through defaulted principal payments to the investor until the deal matures. If such a provision is present and a default occurs, the defaulted principal may be paid later than scheduled, thereby extending the average life of the security.
- The low prepayment sensitivity of leases to interest-rate changes means that they lack the negative convexity of mortgage securities and, to a lesser extent, home-equity loans.

- In a flattening yield curve, lease-backed securities are not penalized for rolling down the curve at a slower rate than bullet securities, such as credit cards.
- Lease-backed securities offer a "novelty" spread that is likely to diminish as issuance climbs and their familiarity increases among investors. They currently trade five to ten basis points wider than auto spreads but offer the same or better credit quality and prepayment characteristics.

CONCLUSION

The equipment-leasing sector is growing rapidly and is expected to continue to do so for the remainder of the decade. Key to its growth is a continuation of existing trends, such as the standardization of lease documentation and industry consolidation. Exhibit 6 summarizes the key points to consider in evaluating a lease-backed securities transaction.

Exhibit 6: An Evaluation Checklist for
Lease-Backed Securities

CREDIT RISK

Reliance on lessees
- What is the general credit quality of the lessees?
- Is the equipment likely to be integrally important to the lessee's business operations?

Concentration
- Are leases concentrated with just a single lessee or a few lessees?
- What sizes are the leases and would individual defaults significantly affect the transaction as a whole?

OBSOLESCENCE RISK
- Is the lease term matched with the estimated useful life?
- Is the risk of obsolescence offset by lessee credit quality?
- Does the lessor permit lessees to upgrade to new equipment models?

RESIDUAL VALUES
- Are residual realizations paid out to investors as part of the sold cash flows or are they used for credit enhancement only?
- What are the historical realized residual values?
- How conservatively has the originator historically estimated recovered residual values?

PREPAYMENTS
- What are the originator's historical prepayment rates?
- Is the issuer's policy to substitute new leases for those that have prepaid?
- Are there other factors that might serve to inhibit prepayments?
- Are all leases "hell or high water"?

CREDIT ENHANCEMENT
- What are the issuer's historical loss rates?
- What level of losses will be borne by the subordinated securities (if any)?
- Will residual realizations be available as credit enhancement? If so, what credit was given for residual recoveries by the rating agencies?
- Is there any indication that the issuer's policy is to substitute new leases for those that have defaulted? Is the issuer both motivated and financially able to continue this policy?
- Is an insurance wrap provided? What is the rating of the insurer?

Chapter 10

SBA Loan-Backed Securities

Donna Faulk
Vice President
ABS Trading
Prudential Securities Inc.

INTRODUCTION

The Small Business Administration (SBA), an agency of the federal government, was created in 1953 to assist, advise and safeguard the interests of small businesses. To facilitate the flow of funds to the small-business sector, the SBA is empowered to guarantee loans made by approved SBA lenders to qualified borrowers.

SBA guaranteed-loan pools, backed by the full faith and credit of the U.S. government, offer the advantage of excellent credit quality, while allowing investors to earn high yields indexed off of the prime rate. Variable-rate SBA pools are responsive to changing interest-rate environments as their coupons adjust every 30 or 90 days based on the current prime rate.

SBA SECONDARY MARKET

The SBA has been guaranteeing loans made by lenders to small businesses since 1958. A secondary market in SBA-guaranteed loans emerged in 1975 when a group of bankers, traders, and SBA officials worked together to allow for the sale of the guaranteed portions of SBA loans. Under the aegis of this program, the lender of an SBA loan retained the unguaranteed portion and servicing of the loan and sold the guaranteed portion to a secondary party. In most cases, the secondary party (a dealer) subsequently sold the SBA-guaranteed loan to an investor and, as a result, transferred full rights of the government guarantee. The liquidity provided by the secondary market served to free the lender's capital for creation of subsequent small-business loans, thereby giving such businesses access to more capital.

In 1984, Congress passed the Small Business Secondary Market Improvement Act. It provided for the central registration and servicing of loans sold in the secondary market by a single fiscal and transfer agent (FTA). More importantly, the legislation allowed for the pooling of SBA loans. The intent of the act was to provide increased efficiency and better liquidity, as well as to establish an improved SBA product in the secondary market. Allowing single-guaranteed SBA loans to be pooled was an important step toward attracting institutional investors to this product.

SBA POOL INVESTMENT CHARACTERISTICS

Coupon

The majority of the loans sold in the secondary market are variable-rate loans that are tied to the prime rate. The prime rate, a leveling rate set by commercial banks, is the highest index used on any variable-rate security in today's marketplace and has always produced a wide margin above banks' cost-of-funds rates (see Exhibit 1).

Exhibit 1: Prime Rate versus One-Month LIBOR

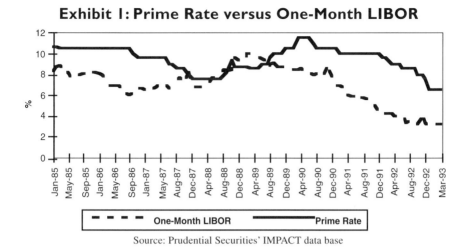

Source: Prudential Securities' IMPACT data base

Variable-rate loans reset monthly on the first of the month or quarterly on the first of January, April, July and October. Coupons on these securities are usually quoted in terms of their spread to the prime-rate index rather than by current coupon. The maximum coupon allowable in the secondary market under present SBA regulations (as of 1988) equals prime plus 1.625%. Most SBA pools do not have caps or floors on their rates, so investors should recognize the benefit of a fully adjustable coupon in the event of increases or decreases in interest rates over the life of the investment. SBA-pool owners are assured of a positive spread in relation to other short-term yields, regardless of the actual rates that exist in a given market climate.

Maturities

The terms on new issues range from 7 to 25 years. Remaining maturities of less than seven years are available through investment in seasoned SBA pools. SBA loans must have similar terms and features in order to be pooled with one another. Thus certain maturities have become more or less standard for SBA pools. These maturities are 7-year maturities, 10-year maturities, 15-year maturities, 20-year maturities, and 25-year maturities.

Payment Schedules

Almost all SBA loans and pools make monthly payments of principal and interest based on a level-debt service, or "mortgage-type" amortization schedule. Like similar mortgage-backed securities, yields on SBA pools are quoted on a "bond-equivalent" basis, which allows investors to compare this monthly paying security with other debt instruments that pay semi-annually. SBA loans are not simply pass-through securities. While borrower payments are applied to the pool payments, some important differences exist between

SBA pool payments and the underlying cash flows on the loans. These differences include:

- Timely remittances of principal and interest are guaranteed on SBA pools and are issued on the 25th of each month by the FTA.
- Payment schedules are re-amortized to accommodate coupon changes every time rates are adjusted.
- There is a pass-through delay of 85 days on variable-rate pools.
- Amortization schedules are based on the final maturities of SBA pools and on the net-pool rate.

The features of the payment method for SBA pools give investors the benefit of receiving precisely the correct amount of principal and interest to account for variable rates. Significantly, the payment schedule for SBA pools precludes any possibility of negative amortization. All SBA pools are fully amortized by their maturity dates.

SBA Standard Pooling Requirements

The following are the required parameters for assembling a pool of SBA loans:

- Minimum pool size of $1 million.
- Minimum of four loans in a pool.
- No single loan can comprise more than 25% of a pool.
- All loans in a pool must be either fixed or variable rate.
- All loans in a pool must have the same repayment term.
- Variable-rate pools must be comprised of loans having the same adjustment dates.
- For variable-rate pools that contain loans with interest-rate caps, the pool will reflect the lowest cap on any of the loans in the pool.
- The maximum difference in borrower-note rates in a given pool must be 2%.
- The maturity dates of the loans underlying a pool all must be within 30% of one another. In other words, the maturity on the shortest loan in the pool must be no less than 70% of the maturity on the longest loan in the pool.
- The loan having the longest maturity date will determine the maturity date of the entire pool.
- The minimum pool-certificate amount is $25,000, with $5,000 increments thereafter.

SBA Pool Assemblers

To obtain approval from the SBA to assemble SBA loans into a pool for sale in the secondary market, SBA-pool assemblers must conform to the following criteria:

- Assemblers must meet SBA regulations (or those of a regulatory agency) or be a member of the NASD.
- Assemblers must meet a minimum capital requirement and obtain good standing with the SBA (as determined by the SBA administrator).

In the competitive marketplace for SBA loans and pools, market makers, usually dealers or dealer banks, generally assume the role of SBA-pool assemblers.

SBA-approved pool assemblers purchase the guaranteed portions of SBA loans from lenders across the country, usually in competition with other SBA dealers. Loans having similar terms and features are grouped together to form pools that conform to the SBA's standard pooling requirements. The SBA loans to be placed in a pool are sent to the FTA, which issues a pool certificate in lieu of the single-loan certificates. Registered participation certificates can then be issued to investors.

Whether they create the pools themselves or if other dealers create the pools, most SBA dealers make an active secondary market in existing SBA pools. Detailed information is available to every SBA dealer concerning all SBA pools issued, thereby allowing market makers to determine a pool's market value based on its characteristics and performance.

The Role of the FTA

An integral factor of the enhanced SBA secondary market is the role of the government-appointed central FTA, presently Colson Services Corp., based in New York.

The FTA handles all clearing, transfers, and ongoing servicing for every SBA-guaranteed loan and pool sold in the secondary market. The FTA collects payments from the lenders and remits those payments to the registered holders of single loans. When loans have been placed in pools, remittances are incorporated into the monthly payments made to the holders of pool participations. In addition to regular collection and servicing duties, the FTA administers all default claims and any prepayments.

Colson Services Corp. issues certificates for single loans and for pools, and is responsible for the registration and transfer of these certificates when SBA loans and pools are traded in the secondary market. Accurate records are kept by the FTA for each transaction and on every payment. Finally, the FTA issues monthly factor tables for SBA pools used by SBA dealers and pool assemblers. For its services, the FTA retains an ongoing servicing fee of one eighth of a point on every SBA loan and pool.

Investors

Among institutional investors, particularly financial institutions, the popularity of asset-backed securities has increased along with the demand for

SBA pools. Banks and thrifts purchase SBA pools to enhance their asset/liability management because the frequently adjusted rate on SBA pools tends to produce a positive spread to fluctuating cost-of-funds rates. Historically, the spread relationship between the prime rate and other short-term interest rates has proven to be wide. While adjustments in the prime rate lag money-market-rate fluctuations, the prime rate tends to adjust upward more quickly than it adjusts downward.

Banks and thrifts are not the only institutions that have found SBA pools to be attractive investments. While SBA pools can have final maturities as long as 25 years, the 90-day or 30-day rate adjustments make SBA pools a high-yielding alternative to money-market securities for mutual funds, pension funds, and credit unions.

Changes in regulatory guidelines imposed by the Federal government have made SBA pools even more attractive to banks and thrifts; SBA pools can be held with zero risk-weighted capital and effective GAP management can be achieved with investments in SBA pools. While regulatory treatment may vary, generally speaking, pool certificates are treated as investments and may be pledged as collateral for public funds, Federal Reserve and Federal Home Loan Bank advances, and Treasury tax and loan accounts.

INVESTING IN SBA-POOL SECURITIES

Liquidity

Although SBA pools have been available since August 1984, they are still relatively new to the marketplace. Due to the increased participation from the traditional fixed-income investor base and improved research on the behavior of SBA loan-backed securities, SBA pools are now traded in an efficient and competitive marketplace. The upshot is that investors can now enjoy the benefits of improved pricing efficiency and liquidity equal to that associated with larger markets. The increased participation and demand insures an increasingly competitive marketplace, as well as liquidity for investors going forward.

Credit-Risk Quality

SBA pools provide excellent credit quality because they are backed by the full faith and credit of the U.S. government and, as a result, are implicitly triple A-rated securities. The investor in an SBA loan or pool has an unconditional guarantee as to the repayment of 100% of the principal and accrued interest outstanding on a timely basis.

Interest-Rate Risk

Variable-rate SBA pools are relatively free from interest-rate risk. Since these investments are indexed to the prime rate, they are adjusted monthly or quarterly and are mainly non-capped; in turn, the investor's coupon and yield adjust to changing interest-rate environments.

Prepayment

Qualifying guaranteed loans for SBA pools may be prepaid without penalties by the small-business borrower at any time during their term, at the borrower's option. Moreover, SBA loans may occasionally default. In the event of either prepayment or default, the Federal government will advance 100% of the outstanding principal and interest to the FTA, who, in turn, passes it through to the holders of pool participations on a pro-rata basis. Investors receive principal at the 100% outstanding par balances of accelerated-SBA loans. Like comparable mortgage-backed securities, SBA pools generate monthly cash flows, which may include proceeds of accelerated principal.

Prepayment rates on SBA pools include all events of early principal redemption, whether an actual borrower prepayment or default has occurred. Because SBA-pool yields are calculated on the basis of their cash flows, it is critical to assume a reasonable prepayment rate for accurately generating a proper cash-flow yield and average-life forecast. Prepayment rates on SBA loans are expressed as an annual constant prepayment rate (CPR) based on historical performance.

In conjunction with the Congressional passing of the Secondary Market Improvements Act of 1984, allowing for the creation of the pooling process, the Public Securities Association (PSA) undertook a prepayment study of more than 10,000 SBA-guaranteed loans with originations ranging from 1972 through 1984. The results of the prepayment study established standard benchmark prepayment rates (CPRs) for fixed- and variable-rate SBA loans and pools, i.e., one prepayment rate was assigned to all fixed-rate SBA loans and pools, and one prepayment rate was assigned to all variable-rate SBA loans and pools. These CPR recommendations were adopted by the SBA and quoted until April 1990. Today, based on ongoing prepayment studies, prepayment rates vary according to each individual loan and pool. As such, the onus is on the seller of an SBA pool to provide investors with yield quotations based on the individual prepayment assumptions for the loans or pools in question. More accurate prepayment assumptions, combined with data supplied by the FTA on all SBA pools, provide market participants with a better understanding of the performance of qualifying SBA-guaranteed loans.

What Have We Learned About Prepayments?

We now know that variable-rate SBA loans and pools, depending on their maturity dates, are subject to prepayment at different speeds. The underlying SBA-guaranteed-loan maturity is determined by the purpose of the financing. Loans made for working capital, for example, will not perform the same way as loans made to finance real-estate purchases or construction. Regardless of the coupons on SBA pools, almost all variable-rate SBA loans are originated at interest rates between prime plus 2.25% to the maximum rate of prime plus 2.75%. For these reasons, the maturity dates on variable-rate SBA pools are the significant factor in prepayment analysis, rather than the coupon rates on the pools.

The highest prepayment rates on SBA loans and pools exist on shorter-maturity product. Ten-year and shorter-term SBA pools, with underlying loans made for working capital, prepay at the highest rate. Conversely, long-term, real-estate-backed SBA pools prepay much more slowly. The lowest prepayment rates tend to be on variable-rate SBA pools with interest-rate caps, all of which are long term and comprised of loans made with the most competitive terms to the best-quality credit borrowers.

Whether investors purchase SBA pools at a premium, at par or at a discount, prepayment rates are paramount to anticipated yields. As with most debt instruments, the "risk/reward" factor is an element of pricing. Risk on any product guaranteed by the Federal government begins with securities priced above par. SBA pools offered to investors at premium prices will carry higher yields than pools offered at par or at a discount. Keep in mind, regardless of the coupon or the price paid, every SBA variable-rate pool with a stated-maturity date can be expected to prepay at close to the same rate. Once investors determine the amount of acceptable risk, offerings on SBA pools can be found to match investor objectives.

SUMMARY OF INVESTMENT ADVANTAGES AND DISADVANTAGES OF SBA POOLS

Variable-rate SBA loan pools represent diversification through ownership in assembled pools of small-business loans guaranteed by the SBA. SBA pools are a safe investment that offer high yields versus comparable money-market instruments and enhance the overall performance of well-managed portfolios.

There are two disadvantages of investing in SBA pools. First, they are often issued at a premium, unlike other securities that are issued at par. Second, they require physical delivery of certificate as opposed to book entry.

The advantages of SBA pools as an investment outlet are summarized below:

- Full faith and credit guarantee by the U.S. government.
- Timely remittance of monthly principal and interest payments.
- A wide variety of maturities and coupons.
- Investment in intermediate to long-term maturities with yields in excess of short-term fixed-rate alternatives.

- Adjustable rates indexed to the prime rate provide price stability and sensitivity from interest-rate risk.
- Collateral eligibility.
- Zero-percent risk weight for banks and thrifts.

Chapter 11

The Securitization of Health-Care Receivables

Vincent T. Pica

President
Capital Finance Division
Prudential Securities Inc.

Anand K. Bhattacharya

Senior Vice President
Director of Fixed Income Research
Prudential Securities Inc.

INTRODUCTION

With the success of asset securitization as a funding mechanism in generic consumer receivables, the application of this technology is being increasingly considered in other areas, such as health-care receivables. Historically, following the initial focus on consumer assets, the securitization of commercial receivables was the next frontier to be conquered. For instance, lease-rental payments were positioned as analogous to the cash flow from a pool of automobile loans, while trade receivables were likened to credit-card debt. In the early 1980s, the securitization of trade receivables became an accepted financing option in a variety of industries. Securities backed by trade receivables were priced using newly issued credit-card securities as benchmarks. In 1992, the trade receivables of health-care-service providers, representing receivables due from insurers (Medicare, Medicaid, Blue Cross and commercial carriers) for medical services rendered were incorporated into the public market for asset-backed securities (ABS), prior to which most transactions were structured as private placements.[1]

As noted by Moody's Investors Services, health-care providers in the face of shrinking revenue, rising costs, and increasing frequency of rating downgrades of hospitals are increasingly considering the securitization of receivables as an alternative funding source.[2] While this sector of the ABS market may still be labeled as an "emerging" asset class, it merits individual discussion mainly because of the unique nature of the receivables and the attendant issues and risks associated with securitized health care receivables.

Securitization provides a remarkable means for health-care providers to borrow at a better rate than they can obtain on their own, especially for those borrowers with senior unsecured corporate-debt ratings of single-A or lower. While the cost of debt may be the motivating factor, there are other benefits, both tangible and intangible. The limited-recourse nature of the financing is preferential to recourse debt, which can involve the personal guaranty of the borrower's principals. Securitization represents off-balance-sheet financing, which improves leverage and certain other balance-sheet ratios. Additionally, it provides diversification of financing

---

[1] This transaction, NPF III Health Care Receivables Program Notes involved the securitization of a pool of receivables sold by approximately 14 health care service providers. In January 1994, Jersey City Medical Center became the first health-care provider to securitize its receivables in a stand-alone program with the issuance of five-year single-A rated medium-term notes. Although there previously had been three stand-alone securitizations of receivables by health-care providers, those transactions involved the use of commercial paper, while the Jersey City Medical Center transaction innovated the use of medium-term notes as a more efficient financing option than commercial paper.

[2] See *Healthcare Receivables Securitization: An Outline of the Issues*, October 1993 and *An Anatomy of Issues Associated with Healthcare Receivables Securitization*, May 19, 1995, Moody's Investors Services.

sources. An increase in available cash enables the borrower to take advantage of prompt-pay vendor discounts. The ability to plan ahead for projects and investments is enhanced. Finally, the requirement that the seller of the receivables track payments and that abnormally high delinquencies would trigger a wind-down of the financing, is a disciplinary mechanism for the borrower to be vigilant in monitoring the quality of receivables, ensuring the timeliness of reimbursement by individual payers, and being proactive in improving the efficiency of the collection process. In view of such considerations, receivables-days outstanding, a measure of collection efficiency, is invariably improved following a securitization.[3]

From a corporate finance perspective, securitization can be both a means and an end to the consolidation process currently underway in the health-care-services industry. For many providers, securitizing their own or the receivables of the target company can generate part of the proceeds needed to finance an acquisition. In other instances, when the merger is effected through a stock swap, the issuance of additional stock often creates under leverage. When considering post-merger financing, if the consolidated entity is rated less than single-A, securitization should be the most cost-efficient form of raising capital on an ongoing basis (including equity financing) for the entity.

As noted above, while there are many benefits emanating from the securitization of health-care receivables, not all health-care providers may qualify as candidates for securitization. It is worth noting that from the standpoint of the Internal Revenue Service, receivables securitization needs to be in the form of taxable debt, rather than tax-exempt debt, in order not to violate the useful life test, which maintains that the useful life of an asset being financed with tax-exempt debt should be at least as long as the average life of the debt security. Thus, for many borrowers who have unconstrained access to tax-exempt borrowing, securitization may not be the most inexpensive financing option. Receivables that are considered eligible for securitization are those for which a medical service has been provided and those that are covered by a valid primary insurance or by a secondary insurer only after the primary insurer has paid in full. In general, Medicare, Medicaid, commercial-insurance, managed care relating to fee-for-service receivables and Blue Cross and Blue Shield plans are considered eligible payers. The eligible-receivable amount must be net of any contractual allowances or the amount

---

[3] The Jersey City Medical Center transaction, part of a relatively cash-rich system, disproved the myth that receivables are sold only by the cash starved. The LIBOR +90-basis-point pricing for the single-A rated security, with a 79% advance rate against the receivables, was an incentive for the Medical Center to gain additional liquidity at a lower rate than that offered by other available sources. The Medical Center was able to invest the proceeds of the issuance and earn a positive carry, benefit from prompt-pay vendor discounts and increase its flexibility with respect to project planning.

of the charges that will not be reimbursed by the insurer. Self-pay receivables, co-payments and deductibles, which collectively represent amounts due directly from the patient, have not yet been securitized.

Given the diversity and complexity of health-care receivables, one of the critical issues in the securitization of these assets is the determination of eligible assets and the purchase price for these receivables, which is known as the advance rate. There is a trade-off between the advance rate and the eligibility criteria; stringent inclusion requirements are likely to result in a high advance rate. Due to low collectibility rates, the "co-pay" component of receivables is usually excluded from securitizations. As noted recently by Duff and Phelps, the continuing consolidation among health-care providers and the trend towards managed care as a result of cost containment efforts, is likely to affect to affect advance rates as historical performance may overstate future collection efforts.[4]

STRUCTURES OF HEALTH-CARE TRANSACTIONS

The exact nature of health-care receivables transactions has run the gamut from medium-term notes, collateralized commercial paper, and commercial paper conduits. However, in the evaluation of these transactions, it is important to realize the nature of the receivables. Health-care receivables are created by a variety of health-care providers. However, due to the fact that most health care services are rendered under the aegis of some form of public or private insurance, the payers of the receivables are third-party entities. Public insurance refers to Medicare, which is administered by the Federal government, and Medicaid, which is administered by states under stated Federal guidelines. Private medical insurance refers to policies provided by insurance companies, Blue Cross and Blue Shield and a variety of managed care providers, such as health maintenance organizations (HMOs).

While health-care receivables have been described as being akin to other receivables, such as credit cards, it is important to note that there are significant valuation differences. First, the exact amount of the receivable is never known with a high degree of certainty. In most "fee for service" arrangements, which are characteristic of private insurance plans, the insurance company pays only the "usual and customary charges" for the service with the remainder being the responsibility of the insured. Therefore, in medical receivables, the uncertainty arises in the event the insurer considers certain charges over and above the normal and customary charges, as well as in situations when the patient's portion is not paid in a complete and timely fashion. In managed health care systems, such as HMOs, a flat fee

---

[4] See *Asset-Backed News*, Duff and Phelps Rating Co., September 1995, p. 2.

per member, known as a capitation arrangement, is paid irrespective of services rendered. Medicare payments to hospitals are made at a pre-determined rate by assigning each type of hospitalization stay to a diagnosis related group (DRG), regardless of the amount and type of actual services performed. Similarly, Medicare payments to physicians involve caps on the types of services rendered. These inherent differences in the type of receivable are further complicated by the fact that the actual billed amount may change due to classification related disagreements, errors, and, in the case of Medicare and Medicaid, audit related offsets. As a result, it is important to examine the actual type of receivables included in the structured transaction due to the high degree of heterogeneity in this generic asset class.

Issuing Entity

As with any securitization, a bankruptcy remote entity must be established as the securitization vehicle. This structure insulates the investor from any corporate risk of the seller of the cash-flow stream. Once the cash flow or the asset is transferred, a legal opinion concludes that it cannot become the property of the transferrer, not even in a bankruptcy of the transferrer when the bankruptcy court has distinctive authority with respect to the assets and liabilities of the bankrupt entity. Certain conditions need to be satisfied to achieve a bankruptcy remote or true sale of assets. A critical condition is the transfer of the assets to a special-purpose corporation, created for the sole purpose of buying assets and issuing debt. The receivables must be recorded as a sale to the special-purpose corporation; the seller records the transfer of assets as a FAS 77 sale for GAAP-accounting purposes. Limited recourse to the seller is permitted for purposes of providing a credit enhancement for the receivables.

In order to obtain the desired rating, the security also must be structured in a manner that provides ample protection for anticipated losses. The tenet that history predicts the future is implicit in rating and structuring the security, which require extensive historical analysis of the bad-debt experience for the assets. Since direct recourse to the seller for losses can be very limited (to ensure a bankruptcy remote transfer), the protection for losses usually takes the form of credit support from a highly rated entity, such as a bank or a monoline insurer, or what has become increasingly popular, a subordinated security held by the special-purpose corporation. The subordinated security represents the residual cash flow of the transferred assets after the debt service of the senior securities, taking into account any losses. The subordinated securities are accounted for by the seller as a capital investment in the special-purpose corporation, described above.

Securities backed by health-care receivables usually take the form of medium-term notes issued by the special-purpose corporation, with the term ranging from three to ten years. The life of the receivable and the corresponding cash flow and debt-service profile are similar to the more familiar securities that are backed by credit-card debt. In consideration of the short-term nature of the asset relative to the term of the debt, the notes pay interest only for a stated term, then retire the principal at the end of the interest-only period. During the interest-only (or revolving) period, collections from purchased receivables are used to purchase new receivables weekly. Therefore, from the borrowers perspective, the securities are analogous to a term working-capital line of credit. It is for this reason that for issuers actively considering securitization, the ability to continue to generate similar medical receivables is important. In the absence of continued growth, the securitized deals are likely to suffer from dilution of assets.

Perfection of Security Interest

The securitization of health-care receivables requires that the receivables must be sold free and clear of any prior liens. If negative pledges cannot be removed (e.g., for those providers with tax-exempt debt) whose indentures specifically prohibit the issuance of additional debt collateralized by gross receipts (receivables), securitization may not be an option. With respect to both Medicare and Medicaid receivables, the ability of the provider of services to assign the rights of payment are prohibited except for assignments to a government entity, by order of court or to a billing agent.   In other words, payments for services rendered under Medicare and Medicaid cannot be made to persons other than the provider of the services. Therefore, in securitized structures, the provider must collect the payment even if it is contractually bound to immediately transfer it to the third parties that have purchased the receivables, as opposed to collection through lockbox arrangements as part of the securitization structure. In such financings, arrangements must be made to transfer such receivables to the securitization vehicle on a daily basis to adequately meet the requirement for perfection of security interest in Medicare and Medicaid receivables. The perfection of security interest in commercial-insurance claims is achieved through notification of the carriers that the receivables have been assigned.

Rating Considerations

As noted earlier, the rating process used to determine the size of the credit support necessary for the desired rating of the securities revolves around an analysis of the historical loss experience. Losses may occur due to the receivables aging beyond a definitional write-off period (typically 180 days), the bankruptcy of a payer or offsets due to the statutory right of Medicare and Medicaid programs to withhold specific amounts that were overbilled in previous years from current payments to the provider. It is not surprising that consumer assets were the first to be securitized, as substantial empirical data on defaults has long been available on mortgages, auto loans, and credit cards. With health-care receivables, recent experience dictates a write-off period of 180 days past the date of billing (or patient discharge), with recoveries or collections of 50% attributable to defaulted receivables occurring within six months of default. The issuer should be able to supply, by payer category, aging (30 to 210 days) information in the format of a subsequent-receipt test on monthly billings going back at least 12 consecutive months. This information can be illuminating with respect to the quality of the providers billing system, the Medicare/Medicaid intermediary and the reimbursement pattern of specific types of payers.

The health-care provider also should provide accounting information regarding the contractual allowances of various payer categories and the variability of these contractual allowance, as measured by actual reimbursement versus anticipated reimbursement To avoid the concentration of lowly rated insurance carriers, the transaction should limit the amount of receivables due from any one carrier having a rating less than the rating of the securities. Credit support to size the offset risk is based on historical Medicare/Medicaid cost-report-settlement information (due to and due from Medicare and Medicaid resulting from cost-report audits). Securitization assumes that the seller of the receivables will continue to bill and collect the receivables as normal. It is important then that the candidate should have satisfactory billing, collection and tracking systems. In its servicing capacity, the health-care provider should be able to monitor the payments, reconcile sold receivables and cash collections and provide monthly aging reports for the sold receivables. Due to the complexity of the receivables and the associated issues regarding collection, which may dilute the value and increase the aging of these accounts, the servicing capability of the issuer is subject to an added degree of scrutiny in health-care securitization transactions.[5]

THE IMPACT OF REFORM

Securitization of receivables in the health-care services industry is an area of growth in the ABS market. While health care reform will continue to be a major legislative and public policy concern and the exact form of the legislation may be shaped over the years, it is almost certain that any reform will include measures to contain health care costs. This may translate into pres-

---

[5] Additionally, the servicing capability of the health care issuer may also be scrutinized due to historical evidence of seller servicer fraud in such securitizations, as evidenced by the Towers Financial Corporation incident, that involved the issuance of five structured transactions collateralized by health care receivables, with a total of approximately $200 million. In 1993, the issuing entities in these transactions filed for Chapter 11 bankruptcy due to deficiencies in cash flows arising from the failure to purchase the required collateral for the deals and defective legal documents for perfecting the security interest in these receivables.

sure on insurers, growth in capitated reimbursement (not eligible for securi-tization) and, perhaps, reduced paperwork through standardization in accounting and collection procedures, which are likely to be beneficial for the securitization process. Cost control will cause health-care providers to seek new financing options and consider asset securitization as a possible financing alternative. At the same time, the need to contain costs has resulted in a trend among hospitals to contract out many ancillary services, such as laboratory, X-ray and anesthetic services; this has led to the growth of companies specializing in such auxiliary services. This trend is likely to spur on continued growth and perhaps, add a different set of medical receivables eligible for securitization.

Chapter 12

The Commercial Property Market and Underwriting Criteria for Commercial Mortgages

Jonathan Adams
Vice President
Fixed Income Research
Prudential Securities Inc.

INTRODUCTION

Among the wide variety of asset-backed securities (ABS), commercial mortgage-backed securities (CMBSs) stand out due to the diversity and complexity of the commercial mortgage market. As a result, analyzing the underlying collateral of a transaction is the most important component of CMBS relative value analysis. Prepayment options are also a consideration, when available, but the values of such options are much less than in the residential MBS market. This chapter presents an overview of the commercial mortgage market, a review of the three major property types present in CMBSs and an analysis of the underwriting requirements employed in the origination of commercial mortgages.

Although it is common to speak of commercial property as a uniform class of assets, many differences may be found in the variety of property types in this market. Rating agencies and investors recognize these distinctions by assigning different underwriting standards and risk weightings to each of the five major property types, consisting of office, retail, industrial, multi-family, and hotel. Of these five, office space, retail property and multi-family housing have most often been employed as collateral for CMBSs.

Exhibit 1 shows 1994 and 1995 CMBS issuance categorized by the type of property representing the underlying mortgage collateral. Many diversified pools have incorporated miscellaneous property types such as nursing homes, mini-warehouse facilities, recreational sites, etc. Nevertheless, for transactions in which property level information was available, approximately 80% of CMBS collateral fell into one of the three categories of retail, office, or multi-family during 1994 and 1995. These major property types are analyzed in greater detail in the sections that follow.

Exhibit 1: 1994 and 1995 CMBS Issuance Categorized by Property Type (Dollars in millions)

Property Type	1994 Issuance	1995 Issuance
Multi-family	$5,974.4	$6,517.0
Retail	5,390.3	4,507.9
Office	2,249.8	2,412.7
Industrial	967.0	773.7
Hotel	299.8	1,236.6
Other	1,654.2	1,336.3
Not Available	3,439.6	1,248.0
Total	$19,975.1	$18,032.2

Source: Prudential Securities Inc., based on data from *Commercial Mortgage Alert*.

THE OFFICE MARKET

Office space represents approximately 25% of the aggregate value of commercial buildings. Within this sector, real estate practitioners recognize three different building types and two unique markets in which office buildings compete. The most fundamental distinction in the office market is one of building quality. Office buildings are grouped and marketed according to their overall quality within the local economy they serve, ranging from class A space (the most desirable) to class C space (the least desirable). Each class is described below and an outline of their evaluation criteria is shown in Exhibit 2.

Class A consists of properties of above-average location that are equipped with state-of-the art mechanical systems. Class A properties usually have 24-hour access, contain large or flexible floor plates, and are free of asbestos or other environmental problems. "Trophy" properties of historic or architectural significance also fall into this category, but landmark status is not sufficient to be considered a class A property. Amenities usually offered in class A buildings include special dining services and high-quality retail shops. Typically, rent levels meet or exceed the rents obtainable from new construction and tenants are of very high credit quality.

Properties in class B must be in a good location and retain professional management for smooth operation of the building. Mechanical systems are adequate but may be outdated or possess some other limitation. Class B buildings often lack distinction in their design and contain fewer amenities than class A property. This type of building also tends to cater to mid-sized or smaller firms, often taking away from the building's prestige. Asbestos may be present in this type of building, but only if adequately contained. Rental rates in class B buildings usually approximate the average for the market and will fall short of the amount needed to justify new construction.

Class C buildings are usually located at the edge of the central business district or have poor accessibility to transportation. Mechanical systems are deficient in some form and are in need of an upgrade. For example, elevator systems may be unable to serve the building's traffic efficiently, or heating and cooling systems may not provide uniform or consistent temperature control, etc. These buildings are typically older and also require some type of upgrade to the building facade. Often, floor plates are small and columns are not conveniently spaced for a modern office. Class C building tenants are smaller; many are start-up firms and less credit worthy. Tenant turnover and vacancy rates are comparatively high. Rents are at the bottom tier. Often, aspects of the building fail to meet existing building code requirements and maintenance or building services are poor.

Exhibit 2: Office-Market Segmentation

Building Feature	Class A	Class B	Class C
Location	Excellent; near center of CBD or adjacent to major transportation routes	Good; within CBD or easy access to highways	Poor; edge of CBD, facing side street or poor access to highways
Age	New or renovated within 10 years	More than 10 years since renovation	More than 10 years since renovation
Floor Plates	Expansive and unhindered by columns, usually 20,000 square feet or more per floor	Functional, but may include space constraints and excessive columns; Usually 10,000 square feet or more per floor	Poor quality; usually leading to inefficient work space; often less than 10,000 square feet per floor
Mechanical Systems	State of the art or modern, including: –Central heating/cooling –Back-up generator –Heavy-load wiring –Large, efficient elevators	Functional, meets building code, but may not be state of the art, including: –Limitations on electrical usage –No back-up power	Outdated, deficiencies may include: –Code violations –Need of retrofitting –General deterioration
Physical Condition	Excellent, no need of repair	Good, may need repair or renovation in the near future	Poor, often requiring immediate upgrade of facade, mechanical system or building structure
Architectural Style	Distinct or "trophy" property	Attractive, well preserved	Usually non-descript

Exhibit 2 (Continued)

Building Feature	Class A	Class B	Class C
Environmental Problems	None	Asbestos may be present, but must be contained	Asbestos/lead paint often present and in need of mitigation
Access	Full lobby personnel, security, and 24-hour access	Lobby personel on duty 24 hours or surveillance through professional management	Poor security and access after business hours
Special Amenities	Usually consist of several, including: –Dining services –Retail shops –Banking/other special services –Health facilities	May or may not be present	None
Rent Levels	High, usually meeting or exceeding rent levels available from new construction	"Market" rents, hovering one-third above or below market average	Bottom tier of the market – at times insufficient for proper building maintenance

A small portion of the building stock may fail to meet any of the standards of an adequate office facility. These "functionally obsolete" buildings have serious structural flaws, fail to meet building-code requirements, and usually reflect substantive deferred maintenance. They are candidates for demolition and typically are not included in surveys of the total office stock. Nevertheless, these buildings serve a role in the market. If market rents accelerate, a functionally obsolete building may become part of an assemblage for future construction or it may be profitable to renovate such buildings to capture tenants priced out of the class-C market.

Distinguishing Properties by Location

In addition to building quality, office properties are typically grouped according to whether they are located in a suburban area or central business district (CBD). Suburban office space tends to use extensive tracts of land within a "campus" setting, while CBD office space is usually distinguished by taller, tightly grouped buildings. Despite these significant architectural differences, tenants in both types of buildings require adequate access to other firms, clients or suppliers. Consequently, many suburban office parks have evolved into a new form of business district outside of the traditional urban center.

The extent of this transformation is evident from the level of new construction in each market over the past 15 years. From 1980 to 1993 approximately two-thirds of the country's new office space was built in suburban markets. As a result, over one-half of the total office supply is now located outside of the traditional downtown of large metropolitan areas.

The high level of new construction in suburban areas partly reflects the lower cost of suburban land and the greater availability of developable space under local zoning regulations. After the 1980's construction boom ended and office values began to decline, intense competition developed between the newer suburban markets and traditional CBDs. This competition is likely to continue, but it is unlikely that values in one type of location will significantly improve at the expense of the other. Rather, our analysis indicates that centralization within a CBD continues to attract some industries, but that other firms (or divisions within firms) are able to serve customers more efficiently in a decentralized and less expensive (i.e., suburban) market.

Supply and Demand Characteristics

Office property values are particularly volatile, due to the unique supply and demand characteristics for this property type. In particular, shortages in office supply are often met with several large, new projects, each of which attempt to take advantage of favorable market conditions by locking in long-term leases.

As the available supply expands, often increasing by 500,000 to 1 million square feet as each new building is completed, the demand for new space is eventually overwhelmed and the market steadily shifts from an owner's market to a renter's market. Inevitably, these market conditions are corrected, but only after depressing rents significantly.

THE RETAIL PROPERTY MARKET

In contrast to the office market, large retail centers are perceived as a comparatively stable property investment, despite the fact that regional and super-regional malls add significantly to the level of retail space in a local market. The important distinction between office and retail property lies in the more restricted competition among the largest retail centers and the unique market dynamics among mid-tier shopping centers. Shopping centers are categorized as either neighborhood, community, regional, or super regional.

Neighborhood Centers

As the name implies, neighborhood centers usually serve a small geographic area and its tenants cater to daily shopping needs such as food items and common, personal services. This type of shopping center is the smallest, seldom exceeding 100,000 square feet of gross leasable area (GLA). Often, a supermarket serves as the anchor tenant, but on occasion (as in the case of small strip centers), a neighborhood center will operate without an anchor.

Since there is very little product differentiation for common, everyday goods, neighborhood centers are particularly susceptible to competitors unless they are well located and easily accessible. By the same logic, developers of new neighborhood centers must calculate their trade area carefully, since it is difficult to draw consumers from existing, convenient shopping patterns. However, a recent and important exception to this rule has been the discount chain store, for which existing rather than new markets have been a critical source of growth.

Community Centers

Community shopping centers are essentially an elaborate version of the neighborhood center. They provide additional products such as limited lines of clothing, a greater selection of housewares, and services such as banks and restaurants that cater to a broader community. Ranging from 100,000 square feet to 450,000 square feet in size, a community center may host one or two anchor tenants, almost always including a supermarket or discount retailer such as K-mart or Walmart. The quality of the anchor tenant is particularly important to the economics of the community center, since the property typically does not have the presence and inherent draw of a multi-tenanted mall. At the same time, its size requires a greater volume of traffic than the typical neighborhood center.

Regional Malls

The regional mall or shopping center usually becomes a destination only when a wider selection of goods and services is desired, such as household furnishings, clothing, and large appliances. Regional malls also provide a host of community services, offering restaurants, entertainment, movie theaters, and special events and displays.

To draw from a wider geographic base, the atmosphere and services of regional malls must accommodate customers who wish to shop for several hours. Thus, appropriate food services and a variety of stores are important to the regional center's survival. Attracting high-quality anchor tenants is equally important since many customers define a mall by reference to such tenants. Anchor tenants typically represent at least one and often two highly regarded department stores. The size of most regional centers falls in the range of 450,000 square feet to 850,000 square feet, with the anchor tenants typically occupying 100,000 square feet to 250,000 square feet of this space.

Super-Regional Malls

Super-regional centers are similar to the shopping districts of central cities, offering at least two department stores and as many as several hundred smaller stores. To generate sufficient sales, these centers must draw from an entire metropolitan area and at times from neighboring areas or states. This goal is routinely accomplished by developing theme parks or similar entertainment facilities to create a unique attraction to customers that would normally be considered outside of the shopping center's trade area. The gross leasable area (GLA) of super-regional centers ranges from 850,000 square feet to well beyond 1 million square feet. The largest such center contains approximately 3.0 million square feet of GLA and hosts close to 400 stores.

The Landlord/Tenant Relationship

For most non-retail property types, there is little immediate connection between the success of the tenant and the viability of the property. Tenants are primarily seen as customers who may or may not rent space in a building. Given this relationship, developers compete under the hope that new and better space will attract a quality tenant from other buildings. If this strategy saturates the market and owners are forced to lower rents, tenants receive significant cost savings from such competition.

In the shopping center market, however, the tenant, as well as the owner, will face direct competition from additional stores. From the retailer's perspective, an overbuilt market leads to an over-served market. Hence, both tenant and property owner have a strong incentive to avoid projects that may unnecessarily add to the market's capacity. Such incentives are most effective in limiting the over-supply of larger store sites because the level of sales needed to justify new construction is the most difficult to achieve. Conversely, smaller properties are more susceptible to changes in merchandising, so retailers are more willing to occupy or partly fund the construction of new properties in the hope of ousting existing rivals.

The common interest shared by property owners and merchants is most clearly reflected in tenant leases. Most retail leases capture a portion of tenant sales as rent, along with a guaranteed base rent. At times, such "percentage rent" may reach as much as 12% of gross sales, depending upon the importance of the shopping center to the tenant's sales volume. The greater franchise value represented by larger centers will command higher rent levels. Similarly, tenants most dependent on consumer traffic — fast food stands, specialty gift stores and kiosks — tend to pay higher percentage rents than department stores or other anchor tenants.

By a similar principle, retail leases also reflect the value of the tenant to the success of the shopping center. Larger tenants, especially anchor tenants, pay the least rent per square foot in recognition of their larger contribution to the center's total cash flow. Such tenants also tend to sign longer leases, thereby offering income stability to the landlord while gaining a predictable market base.

A common financial structure in regional shopping centers is to relinquish the ownership of the anchor store site to the retail tenant. This arrangement strengthens the financial commitment of the anchor tenant, but also diminishes the owner's management authority. As a result, the agreement to sell an anchor store site will typically include covenants regarding its use. Covenants usually commit the retailer to use the site in a specific fashion that is beneficial to the shopping center. By attracting shoppers, a prominent, owner-occupied anchor store is able to bolster the center's overall operations although it will not directly add to the center's cash flow. Department stores and large, discount chain stores are the most common users of this type of structure.

When not purchased outright, another way a tenant may obtain full operational control of a retail site is through a triple-net lease, so called because the lease payment to the property owner is net of operating costs, taxes, and insurance payments. These expenses are paid directly by the tenant to the appropriate recipients. In shopping centers, triple-net leases often accompany a sale-leaseback arrangement, in which the retailer sells a store site (at times to a related entity) and subsequently leases back the site under a long-term, net lease. The triple-net lease and sale-leaseback strategy give retailers greater control in site management without carrying the asset on the company's balance sheet.

The Shopping Center Inventory and Sales Performance

According to the National Research Bureau, the supply of shopping centers expanded to 4.9 trillion square feet of GLA in 1994. Exhibit 3 shows the growth rates for the components of this inventory from 1986 to 1994. Similar to other types of investment property, retail properties experienced a steady expansion from 1986 through 1990, but the average growth rate has slowed considerably since then. From 1986 to 1990, total GLA grew at an average annual compound rate of 5.7%. From 1990 to 1993, this growth rate fell to 2.8% and from 1993 to 1994 the rate of growth declined further to 1.9%.

Analyzed by size, community shopping centers with 200,000 to 400,000 square feet grew most rapidly from 1986 to 1994, expanding at an annual compound rate of 5.1%, while super-regional centers grew the least, expanding at an annual rate of 2.3%. The lower growth rates of regional and super-regional malls are partly due to the unique tenant/landlord relationship discussed previously. In addition, the tremendous cost required to assemble and develop land as a regional or super-regional center eliminates all but the most experienced developers from this type of construction. These inherent restraints on new construction directly reduce the risks in this area of real property investment.

As shown in Exhibit 4, a direct correlation exists between the level of expansion in the mid- to late-1980s and the level of sales within each type of shopping center. At one extreme, community centers added space well beyond the level of new demand generated through retail sales. On the other side of the spectrum, the expansion of regional and super-regional centers failed to meet new levels of demand, thereby allowing these centers to strengthen their position in the market. From 1986 to 1994, the compound growth rate in sales per square foot ranged between 0.4% for community centers to 3.0% for super-regional malls.

It should be noted that many specialized retailers have prospered since 1986 regardless of store size. Price clubs, discount chains and category killers expanded by building and operating new stores within existing, well served markets. These new stores prospered because the lower cost of operation and distribution more than offset the lower margins earned on sales. As already noted, these extremely competitive store types will continue to threaten smaller community centers anchored by less competitive tenants.

Exhibit 3: Total Gross Leasable Area of Shopping Centers
(Millions of Square Feet)

Category of Shopping Center	1986-1994 Compound Annual Growth Rate (%)	1986-1994 Growth Rate (%)
Neighborhood	4.1	37.4
Community	5.1	49.4
Regional	3.3	29.3
Super Regional	2.3	19.6
Total	4.1	38.0

Source: National Research Bureau, 150 N. Wacher Drive, Suite 2222, Chicago, IL 60606.

Exhibit 4: Average Sales in Various Types of Shopping Centers
(Dollars Per Square Foot)

Category of Shopping Center	1986-1994 Compound Annual Growth Rate (%)	1986-1994 Growth Rate (%)
Neighborhood	1.5	12.3
Community	0.4	2.9
Regional	1.8	15.5
Super Regional	3.0	27.1
Total	1.3	10.9

Source: National Research Bureau, 150 N. Wacher Drive, Suite 2222, Chicago, IL 60606.

THE MULTI-FAMILY MARKET

Multi-family housing holds a unique position in the realm of mortgage-backed securities. As an essential component in financing the country's housing stock, the purchase and securitization of multi-family mortgages is clearly included in the mandate given to GNMA, FNMA, and FHLMC. At the same time, multi-family housing is largely income-producing property, thereby falling into the category of commercial property rather than the traditional type of residential real estate.

Multi-family housing may take the form of owner occupied or rental housing. Owner occupied housing may be further distinguished between a condominium and cooperative form of ownership. Condominiums are units wholly owned by the resident, but incorporated into a larger community through joint ownership of the land on which the units are built. Condominiums (and a related form of ownership and construction known as townhouse projects) are financed in a manner similar to single-family housing and have not played a role in the CMBS market.

Multi-family cooperative housing provides joint ownership of both the dwelling unit as well as the land and any common facilities serving the community, such as laundry rooms or recreational space. Residents own a portion of these assets through shares in a private housing corporation. In turn, the corporation owns each of the housing units and rents them to its shareholders through a long-term proprietary lease. In the limited cases in which cooperative loans have been securitized, only mortgage loans granted to the corporation and backed by the corporation's fee simple interest in the property is an eligible form of CMBS collateral. This is because the "mortgages" made to individual shareholders are really personal loans secured by the residents' shares and proprietary lease.

Similar to the single-family housing market, apartment buildings may be financed through private lenders or with some form of government assistance. For the mortgagor, government assistance usually takes the form of Federal Housing Administration (FHA) mortgage insurance to help meet the cost of rehabilitation, construction, or acquisition. In addition, Section 8 or other forms of rental assistance may be granted to the various forms of eligible housing.

Agency Participation in the Multi-Family Market

GNMA's activity in the multi-family MBS market has focused on the securitization of FHA insured project loans. These loans are issued individually as pass-through securities, annually adding between $0.8 billion and $2.6 billion to the multi-family MBS market since 1985. The analysis of government assisted mortgage loans is complicated by the various components of each type of program. However, because GNMA project loans reflect GNMA's guarantee of the timely payment of principal and interest, the credit analysis of project loans is limited to projecting the possibility of a prepayment should the loan default. Such a detailed discussion is beyond the scope of the present analysis.

FNMA and FHLMC participation in the multi-family market has varied considerably between 1985 and 1994. Each agency's participation is illustrated in Exhibit 5 as measured by mortgage purchases and the sale of FHLMC Participation Certificates (PCs). In the case of FHLMC, MBS issuance in the form of PCs constituted a central portion of the multi-family MBS market until 1990, at which time a severe downturn in multi-family values triggered losses for the agency and a dramatic reduction in the purchase of multi-family mortgages.

Exhibit 5: Government Related Multi-family Mortgage Activity (Dollars in millions)

Year	GNMA Project and Construction MBSs	FNMA Loan Purchases/MBSs	FHLMC Loan Purchases/PC Sales
1985	$810.0	$693.3	$1,602.8
1986	2,141.4	1,327.5	3,393.3
1987	2,385.3	321.2	2,120.4
1988	2,498.8	421.2	1,191.3
1989	1,711.5	1,561.0	1,823.9
1990	2,618.5	2,492.0	1,338.2
1991	1,141.6	1,789.0	236.0
1992	933.7	2,106.0	26.5
1993	2,084.2	4,135.0	191.2
1994	2,024.5	4,940.0	1,056.0

Source: The Mortgage Market Statistical Annual for 1995.

FNMA's participation in multi-family MBSs has grown notably during the past four years. Most recently, securitization activity has centered around its Alternative Credit Enhancement Structure (ACES) Program and Delegated Underwriting and Servicing (DUS) Program. Under the ACES program, FNMA adds its guarantee to a pool of loans originated in the private sector. The credit quality of the loans may vary, but must meet certain FNMA guidelines. FNMA's guarantee is applied to a transaction's senior securities for a negotiated fee. As part of the ACES structure, FNMA also requires the subordination of securities equal to approximately 10% of the pool's original principal balance. The subordinate CMBSs do not receive FNMA's guarantee and may be offered separately or together with the guaranteed CMBSs.

Under the DUS program, eligible lenders originate loans consistent with specific underwriting standards established by Fannie Mae. These mortgages then are purchased by Fannie Mae, although the original lender continues to service the loan and must retain a specified level of exposure against any loss experienced by the loan.

Fannie Mae has purchased over $16 billion of DUS loans since the program started in 1988. In August of 1994, Fannie Mae began offering these loans as pass-through securities, most of which are backed by one or two loans, although pools of up to five loans may be assembled under this type of securitization.

Evaluation Criteria for Multi-Family Housing

To evaluate the quality of a multi-family mortgage, investors must follow guidelines applicable to other forms of income-producing property in terms of property condition, location, and ability to attract tenants. Similar to office space or retail property, multi-family housing is a tiered market. In order to receive the highest rents on a consistent basis, modern mechanical systems must be in place and the building must offer accessibility to adequate shopping, transportation, etc.

An important point of departure from other forms of commercial real estate is the typical lease term for multi-family tenants. Unlike the 10-year term common to high-quality office, retail, or industrial space, multi-family leases are usually written for one year at a time, although on occasion two-year leases may also be granted. As a result, multi-family properties are more susceptible to short-term changes in market conditions. At the same time, the large number of leases in a typical multi-family building is often an advantage over property types that rely on a few large tenants because many tenants would have to leave an apartment building before it suffered a large drain in cash flow.

When all the attributes of multi-family properties are considered, most investors consider it one of the most stable types of collateral available in the CMBS market. While the persistent demand for rental housing may support this conclusion, it is important to realize that poorly managed or improperly maintained properties are not immune from financial stress, particularly if they are not centrally located.

UNDERWRITING CRITERIA FOR COMMERCIAL MORTGAGES

The credit quality of CMBSs largely depends on the ability of a pool of properties to generate income over an extended period of time — often ten or more years. During this time, each property's cash flow may change dramatically due to changes in the property's tenant mix, position in the market, or physical condition. For investors in CMBSs, these risks are addressed primarily through careful underwriting at the time of loan origination.

Debt-Service Coverage

When a commercial mortgage is underwritten, several financial ratios are calculated to summarize the strength of the property's cash flow. The most important of these is the debt-service coverage (DSC) ratio, which compares the property's net operating income with the necessary debt-service payments. For this purpose, net operating income (NOI) is defined as all property income (rents, fees, reimbursements, etc.) less all operating expenses (utility costs, management expenses, property taxes, etc.) and an allowance for replacement reserves. NOI is usually calculated after accounting for the amortized cost of leasing commissions and tenant improvement work, but never reflects depreciation.

DSC is usually calculated with financial data from the most recent complete year of the property's operation. However, the latest annual data may not accurately reflect the property's income potential, making it necessary to annualize data from a more recent period of less than one year. The latter situation occurs when a property recently has been acquired and/or subject to a period of vacancy due to renovations, etc. When applied selectively, an annualized income supports the goal of reflecting an accurate cash flow for underwriting purposes.

Conversely, some properties may generate one or two years of NOI that overstates the property's prospective income. This situation may occur for several reasons, including the presence of above-market leases, lower than average capital expenditures, or other nonrecurring adjustments to building management and operation.

To account for these fluctuations, DSC is calculated with a "stabilized" NOI, incorporating conservative assumptions as to nonrecurring shifts in cash flow. For example, if capital expenditures are significantly below average in the year under consideration, this line item would be adjusted to reflect the higher average figure for the property. As a general rule, stabilized NOI should reflect the property's minimum expected cash flow over an extended time period.

What constitutes a prudent DSC ratio varies by property type and location. In general, a property should be able to generate cash flow of 1.25 times the required debt service, although some lenders accept a DSC as low as 1.15 for properties with a very stable financial outlook. These levels are slightly below those employed by the rating agencies as appropriate benchmarks for a diversified pool of commercial mortgages. Subordination (i.e., credit enhancement) levels of most pools are generally predicated upon mortgages with DSC between 1.30 and 1.40, although property types that have displayed some volatility with regard to prior NOI might be required to maintain DSC as high as 1.70. Even then, such properties would be allowed to comprise only a small portion of a diversified pool without significantly adding to the level of credit enhancement required in the transaction.

For a single-asset securitization, the concentration of risk in a single loan pushes DSC requirements even higher. To grant a rating of double-A or higher, it would not be uncommon for a rating agency to require DSC of 2.0 for comparatively stable property types such as retail or multi-family. However, these levels could be adjusted downward if another form of credit support was present, such as a reserve fund or a tenant guarantee of debt service payments.

Property types for which cash flow is comparatively stable include multi-family, retail and, in some markets, certain generic warehouse facilities. Property types that are more likely to experience some volatility in cash flow include hotels, office buildings, specialized industrial facilities, and property types catering to specialized markets such as nursing homes, resort areas, etc. Property types such as hotels and health facilities are particularly dependent on high-quality management and service to residents in order to succeed, thereby adding one more risk factor to the underwriting process.

Loan-to-Value Ratios

The second essential financial ratio used by underwriters is the ratio between the loan amount and the property's value, or loan-to-value (LTV) ratio. Lenders establish maximum LTV ratios in order to maintain an incentive for the borrower to continue debt-service payments even in the event of diminished cash flow from the property. An LTV ratio greater than one would imply that the asset is not worth the debt owed to the lender, in which case a default would be very likely.

Acceptable LTV ratios generally range from 65% to 75%, depending on the property type, quality and other factors regarding the loan. As with the DSC ratio, retail and multi-family loans are generally allowed more lenient underwriting standards (i.e., higher LTVs), while office properties, hotels and any single-asset CMBS require lower, more conservative LTVs.

Not only must the LTV fall within a certain range, but the property's value must be able to be realized in the case of default. In particular, lenders must be aware of any conditions that create a claim senior to the mortgage or complicate the process of foreclosure. For example, encumbrances due to environmental liability, tax liens, or mechanics liens are often senior to the claim of a mortgagor.

Alternatively, the presence of a second mortgage could trigger a foreclosure and interrupt or reduce the income available for the holder of the first mortgage. Similarly, resolving claims against an owner subject to a ground lease is more complicated than resolving claims against the owner of a fee simple interest on commercial property. Since each of these conditions could reduce the property's net value or complicate foreclosure proceedings, they are rarely allowed within a CMBS transaction.

Capitalization Rates

In order to estimate a property's value, most appraisers and real estate investors capitalize its stabilized NOI by an appropriate capitalization rate. The basic form of this calculation is:

$$\text{Property Value} = \frac{\text{Net Operating Income}}{\text{Capitalization Rate}}$$

An appraiser typically deduces the appropriate capitalization rate based on recent property sales or other investments in real property.

A capitalization rate reflects the perceived risk of maintaining the property's stabilized stream of income, as well as the riskless cost of capital. However, capitalization rates do not reflect the entire return expected on the property. Often excluded from the estimate of value provided by capitalization rates are capital appreciation, expected returns on property improvements, and higher cash flow due to superior management expertise.

In essence, selecting the correct capitalization rate is equivalent to estimating the rate of return that would be demanded from the property considering its current stream of income and its likelihood of continuation. A property with a large number of lease expirations in an unstable market would therefore be valued using a comparatively high capitalization rate and vice versa.

Exhibit 6 presents the results of a survey designed to identify average capitalization rates for various types of income producing property. The exhibit illustrates that investors view strip shopping centers, which tend to be poorly anchored and easy to replicate, as one of the riskiest property types. Regional malls, however, which are anchored with credit tenants and very difficult to reproduce, are considered much less risky. These two property types would not have the same risk profile, even if they had the same DSC ratio. Capitalization rates are therefore an important indicator of the perceived level of risk borne by different property types in a diversified pool.

Exhibit 6: Fourth-Quarter 1995 Capitalization Rates for Various Types of Income Producing Property

Property Type	Range of Equity Cap. Rates (%)	Average Equity Cap. Rates (%)
Regional Malls	6.25 - 11.00	7.86
Strip Shopping Centers	8.25 - 12.50	9.74
CBD Office Space	7.50 - 12.50	9.52
Suburban Office Space	8.00 - 11.50	9.57
Industrial Space	7.25 - 13.00	9.36
Apartments	7.50 - 10.50	8.99

Note: All rates refer to an initial "cash-on-cash" rate of return for free and clear equity holdings of property.

Source: Korpacz Real Estate Investor Survey.

Borrower Motivation and Other Requirements

Underwriters of commercial mortgages must be confident that borrowers are economically motivated and committed to servicing the property's debt. Requiring adequate LTV and DSC ratios are just two ways of establishing this condition. Lenders also must consider a property's history and the borrower's motivation for obtaining the loan (i.e., the use of the loan proceeds). These measures become especially important if a property's value ever falls close to its remaining loan balance.

One measure of borrower motivation is the level of cash equity invested in a property. When investor equity is not at risk, the level of long-term commitment to a marginal property may decline considerably. For purposes of this judgment, it is important to realize that a borrower's cash equity does not include unrealized appreciation in a property.

For example, real estate entrepreneurs often search for troubled properties to buy at a significant discount to their potential value. If these entrepreneurs are successful in stabilizing the property's cash flow, it is common to refinance the property with long-term debt, possibly allowing the entrepreneur to remove the initial equity and "cash out" of the property. Cashing out does not imply an inadequate risk profile in terms of LTV or DSC, but it could imply a lower level of owner commitment. Owners of commercial property who continue to have their own funds at stake tend to be more committed to making the property profitable over the long term.

In addition to reviewing the use of funds, lenders typically require a full review of the property's financial history and current physical condition. Documents that are assembled during this process include:

- Title report
- Environmental and engineering reports
- Property appraisals

- Financial statements
- Proof of insurance
- Current rent roll, and
- Major leases

Refinancing Risk

Most mixed pools of commercial mortgages consist of loans with a variety of amortization schedules, usually ranging from a 10-year, interest-only balloon to a 15-year, fully amortizing loan. The most common type of commercial mortgage structure incorporates a 20- to 30-year amortization schedule but requires a balloon payment in year 10 or 15.

The ability to refinance a mortgage at the end of a loan's term is an important element in the risk profile of CMBSs. If refinancing is not feasible, the loan must either be foreclosed or extended, thereby leading to a principal shortfall or extension of the average life of the CMBSs. A common measure of this risk is the loan's balloon LTV. A balloon LTV compares the remaining principal balance at the maturity of the loan to the value of the property at the time the loan was originated. In general, loans with a balloon LTV between 50% and 55% have minimal refinancing risk.

For example, a $1 million loan paying a 10% interest rate and amortizing over 25 years would require a $845,614 balloon payment if the loan matured at the end of the tenth year. If the original LTV of the loan was 65%, the balloon LTV in this example would be 55%. At the time of the loan's balloon payment in the tenth year, the remaining debt could be refinanced at an LTV of 65% even if the property lost as much as 15.4% of its initial value over the term of the loan.

In the case of a single-asset CMBS, the security is often structured to mitigate the risk that a loan is unable to be refinanced. The most common form of risk mitigation is to assign a maturity date to the security that is several years after the maturity date of the mortgage debt. If the mortgage is unable to be refinanced, the time between the loan's maturity and the security's maturity should be sufficient to foreclose and liquidate the property, thereby raising the necessary funds to pay down the principal balance of the security. Furthermore, as long as the property continues to generate sufficient income to pay debt service, the bond's coupon payments should remain current during this lag or "tail" between the maturity dates of the loan and the security.

Monitoring Commercial Mortgages and CMBSs

As previously mentioned, properties must generate income over an extended period of time in order to repay CMBS investors in full. It is therefore essential that accurate and timely information be distributed regarding the performance of the properties in the loan pool. For CMBSs, the transaction's Pooling and Servicing Agreement requires the loan servicer to distribute summary statements of pool performance each month, including the total funds collected from the loan pool, payments made to each class of security holder, the outstanding principal balance of each certificate and the status of any delinquent loans.

At times, the loan servicing function is divided between a special servicer and a master servicer. The master servicer issues pool performance reports, collects loan payments, and administers the transfer of loan proceeds to the transaction's trust fund. Should a loan enter an extended period of delinquency, the special servicer provides a more thorough level of loan monitoring, administration and possibly a loan workout.

In addition, loan documents usually require borrowers to submit financial statements to the servicer on a periodic basis, providing a summary of the property's performance. In some cases, the servicer's duties will include site inspections of each property, adding one more dimension to the degree of information about each property's status. Obtaining the relevant material from these records is particularly important for investors in subordinate CMBSs. Annual statements indicate whether the property's performance is consistent with the covenants of the loan. In addition, if the property enters a period of financial stress, annual statements may provide the first warning signs and subsequently offer an important record of capital improvements, expenses, leases in place, etc. Such information is critical to developing an appropriate stabilization plan or, alternatively, to confirm the need for immediate loan acceleration and foreclosure.

As the CMBS market develops, loan monitoring systems are offering increasingly sophisticated forms of analysis for investors. As an example, Midland Loan Services, a major servicer of CMBS pools, recently premiered its Loan Portfolio Analysis System (LPAS). This on-line monitoring program allows CMBS investors immediate access to performance records for each property in a specific loan pool. LPAS was first applied to CMBSs issued by the Prudential Securities Secured Financing Corporation, Series 1995-C1. LPAS offers a varying level of detail with regard to the loan pool, depending on the needs of each investor. Investors in subordinate securities receive the highest level of detail, including information on rent rolls, NOI and vacancy rates. As the loans season, updates on appraisals and other property-specific information are also available.

Working Out Problem Loans

As the financial conditions of a property change, fiscal stress may arise from a number of causes, including lease turnover, heightened market competition or deterioration of the local economy. Should a default occur, the transaction's Pooling and Servicing Agreement details the specific responsibilities and authority of the servicer with regard to foreclosure or loan modifications. Recent trends in the structure of CMBSs have allowed greater servicer control in this area, as long as its actions maximize proceeds on behalf of all bondholders.

If the actions of the servicer are considered unsatisfactory, CMBS investors may be provided limited authority to appoint a new servicer or to act in place of the servicer. Such actions usually require a vote by the holders of outstanding certificates as well as confirmation by the agency that rated the transaction that such action will not result in a downgrade.

Chapter 13

CMBS Structures and Relative Value Analysis

Jonathan Adams
Vice President
Fixed Income Research
Prudential Securities Inc.

ORIGINS AND GROWTH OF THE CMBS MARKET

Prior to 1990, commercial mortgage securitization represented a comparatively minor technique in real estate finance, contributing several hundred million dollars of securities to the market in an average year. Most of the early offerings between 1985 and 1990 were single-asset transactions with a close resemblance to a traditional mortgage syndication. Since 1990, the CMBS market has grown rapidly because it offered a solution to two distinct problems afflicting the real estate capital markets. First, commercial mortgage securitization provided the liquidity that allowed institutions to clear their balance sheets of unwanted assets. Second, and equally important, the CMBS market filled a financing void by providing funds for owners and operators of real estate unable to access other forms of capital.

In the period 1990-1993, the commercial property markets suffered a severe recession, thereby discouraging the extension of credit to this sector of the economy. According to the NCREIF Property Index, capital returns for all types of income producing property fell by 28% during this three-year period. In addition, lower values undermined the pace of new construction, triggering an extraordinary collapse in the real estate development industry.

As property values declined, mortgage defaults increased sharply, forcing lenders to work out and reserve against an unprecedented level of commercial property. Exhibit 1 shows commercial mortgage defaults from 1988 through the third-quarter of 1995. As shown in the exhibit, delinquency and foreclosure rates reached their peak in the second quarter of 1992, although they did not decline meaningfully until the second quarter of 1993.

During this period, lenders began to divest their commercial mortgage holdings rather than originate new loans. As shown in Exhibit 2, commercial mortgage debt outstanding peaked between 1990 and 1991 before falling steadily through 1994. Since then, outstanding balances have risen slightly, reflecting a turnaround in commercial lending.

The first substantial surge in commercial mortgage securitization may be traced to the Resolution Trust Corporation (RTC) and its decision to use the CMBS market to liquidate the assets of insolvent thrifts. Between 1991 and 1993, the RTC issued an extraordinary $13.8 billion of CMBS, consisting of $4.4 billion of securities backed by multifamily properties (the RTC "M" series) and $9.3 billion backed by nonresidential income-producing properties (the RTC "C" series). During the same period, insurance companies, banks and pension funds added $5.8 billion of securities to this total, the vast majority of which represented asset liquidations. In sum, at least $19.6 billion of capital was raised through the CMBS market to restructure the real estate portfolios of institutional lenders and investors during the real estate recession of the early 1990s.

Exhibit 1: Commercial-Mortgage Delinquency Rates* by Major Property Type, From 1988 to Third Quarter, 1995
(In Percentage Terms)

Period	Apartment	Retail	Office	Industrial	Total
1988					
1st Qtr.	4.52	1.46	2.43	2.13	2.80
2nd Qtr.	4.46	1.48	2.81	2.16	2.86
3rd Qtr.	4.42	1.55	2.48	2.17	2.72
4th Qtr.	4.11	1.35	2.35	1.23	2.49
1989					
1st Qtr.	4.47	1.93	2.36	1.64	2.69
2nd Qtr.	4.42	1.81	2.87	1.73	2.82
3rd Qtr.	4.10	1.75	3.05	1.57	2.79
4th Qtr.	3.07	1.65	2.64	1.68	2.42
1990					
1st Qtr.	3.18	2.46	3.34	1.89	3.04
2nd Qtr.	3.68	1.78	3.58	2.09	3.00
3rd Qtr.	3.53	2.16	4.05	2.07	3.36
4th Qtr.	3.20	2.24	4.57	2.26	3.69
1991					
1st Qtr.	4.32	3.84	5.46	2.96	4.77
2nd Qtr.	5.57	4.03	6.22	3.32	5.41
3rd Qtr.	6.18	4.30	6.76	3.10	5.75
4th Qtr.	7.12	3.88	7.03	3.21	5.93
1992					
1st Qtr.	6.33	4.14	8.05	3.90	6.42
2nd Qtr.	6.45	5.75	9.49	3.96	7.53
3rd Qtr.	6.12	5.73	9.50	3.65	7.37
4th Qtr.	4.78	5.36	8.52	3.65	6.62
1993					
1st Qtr.	5.35	5.60	8.49	4.58	7.11
2nd Qtr.	4.27	5.32	7.89	5.17	6.35
3rd Qtr.	3.51	5.22	7.50	4.87	5.98
4th Qtr.	2.33	3.79	5.73	3.92	4.54
1994					
1st Qtr.	2.52	4.22	6.51	4.66	5.24
2nd Qtr.	2.15	3.98	6.49	5.07	5.07
3rd Qtr.	1.81	3.43	5.48	4.10	4.21
4th Qtr.	1.28	2.23	4.48	3.94	3.38
1995					
1st Qtr.	2.02	2.11	4.86	4.67	3.68
2nd Qtr.	1.78	2.27	4.61	4.31	3.58
3rd Qtr.	1.80	1.95	4.32	3.96	3.22

* Includes loans in foreclosure

Source: American Council of Life Insurance, "Quarterly Survey of Mortgage Loan Delinquence," *Investment Bulletin* (various issues), Washington, D.C. Reprinted by permission.

Exhibit 2: Commercial Mortgage Debt Outstanding
($ Billions)

Year:	1989	1990	1991	1992	1993	1994	1995-Q1	1995-Q2(P)
Commercial Mortgages:	$754.0	758.3	759.0	713.9	704.1	701.8	709.9	710.3
Multifamily Mortgages:	306.5	309.3	306.6	295.4	292.0	295.5	298.2	300.6

P = Preliminary
Source: Federal Reserve Bulletin

Exhibit 3: Total CMBS Issuance From 1990 to 1995

Year	Amount Issued ($Millions)	Number of Transactions
1990	$5,996.4	41
1991	8,196.7	51
1992	13,927.2	54
1993	17,627.0	125
1994	20,335.4	123
1995	18,556.6	96

Source: Commercial Mortgage Alert

Exhibit 3 illustrates total CMBS issuance from 1990 to 1995. Although asset liquidation was an important foundation for the CMBS market, RTC and similar activity represents only a portion of the total picture. In addition to balance sheet restructuring, the CMBS market allowed real estate professionals to access capital for the fundamental business of acquiring and operating commercial property. From 1991 through 1994, direct funding of developers, owners and operators of commercial property accounted for at least $15.7 billion of new CMBSs, an amount comparable to new issuance by the RTC. This total excludes all indirect financing such as conduit or investment fund activity.

A New Financing Regime

Beginning in 1994, commercial property values finally stabilized in most regional markets. Hitting this perceived "market bottom" gave lenders and investors greater confidence in commercial property, particularly as the economy strengthened throughout 1994.

Due to this recovery, the role of the CMBS market changed. Rather than providing borrowers direct access to capital for real estate operations, the public markets began to be used more frequently as a means to recapitalize conduits, banks, and other institutional lenders. The commercial mortgage conduit is the model for the flow of capital taking place under this structure. Conduits are entities that purchase loans with the intent to securitize them at some future date. The relationship between the loan originator and the funding source varies considerably according to the expertise and resources of each entity.

For example, in some cases, an investment bank may be willing to purchase loans from a conduit upon origination, while in other cases loans will be purchased only when a pool of sufficient size has been generated. Similarly, some conduits have considerable discretion in the type of loans that are contributed to the pool, while others operate under narrow restrictions of property type, loan size, and underwriting standards. Whatever standards are adopted, the conduit will not succeed if the mortgage originator is not mindful of the ultimate need to structure and market the resultant pool of mortgages. On the other hand, investment banks must allow the necessary flexibility in loan terms to permit the conduit to compete effectively with alternative sources of financing.

Although a large number of commercial mortgage conduits were established in 1993 and 1994, these funding sources have only recently generated sizable pools for securitization. According to an industry survey conducted by *Commercial Mortgage Alert*, approximately 75 originators now have a conduit relationship with one or more of approximately 21 funding sources, including all of the major New York City investment banks. Conduit activity represented just $741 million (4%) of 1993's $17.6 billion of CMBS issuance. In 1994, however, conduit activity grew to approximately $2.4 billion (12% of total volume), while in 1995 approximately $4.4 billion (25% of total volume) of conduit generated CMBSs were issued.

The slow start for conduits was in part due to competition from other lenders. In addition, the necessary time to market, document, approve, and fund a pool of loans meeting specific rating and/or market criteria is significant, particularly within the framework of a new form of real estate finance. However, as lenders and dealers become more familiar with this process, conduit lending should develop greater efficiencies in both loan origination and securitization.

The Senior/Subordinate Payment Structure

When commercial loans are securitized, the set of terms and conditions guiding the flow of funds to each class of bonds is the payment structure of the transaction. Most commercial-mortgage pools have been securitized under a senior/subordinate payment structure as a form of credit enhancement for investors of the senior securities. In a senior/subordinate structure, the pool's monthly cash flow must be used to satisfy the principal and interest payments of senior securities before payments are made to subordinate securities. This payment hierarchy enhances the credit quality of the senior securities by transferring the marginal risk of a payment shortfall to a more subordinate class of bonds.

Exhibit 4: Sample Structure for $69.74 Million of Hypothetical CMBSs backed by a Diversified Pool of Loans

Face Value of Bonds ($ MM)	Priority of Claim to Cash Flow	Cumulative Level of Subordination (%)	Rating	Industry Designation
48.82	First	30	AAA	Senior Securities (Investment grade)
4.18	Second	24	AA	Mezzanine Securities (Investment grade)
3.49	Third	19	A	
2.79	Fourth	15	BBB	
4.18	Fifth	9	BB	Subordinate Securities or "B" Pieces (Non-investment grade)
3.49	Sixth	4	B	
2.79	Seventh	NA	Unrated	First Loss

Exhibit 4 illustrates the various classes of securities that might be structured from a small, diversified pool of commercial mortgages. The exhibit also illustrates typical subordination levels, expressed as a percentage of the transaction's initial principal balance. Subordination levels reflect the amount of additional mortgage principal available to each class of security to absorb any losses sustained by the pool of loans. As shown in Exhibit 4, triple-A rated, senior securities backed by a diversified pool of loans are likely to enjoy a 30% level of subordination, while approximately 15% of CMBSs in a senior/subordinate structure will be considered non-investment grade debt.

Allocation of Available Funds

In addition to understanding the payment priorities of a transaction, it is important to clarify the different types of payments collected in the transaction's trust fund and how they are allocated to each class of CMBS. On each distribution date, the servicer of a securitized loan pool calculates the total funds available for distribution to the bondholders. In most transactions, available funds include:

- scheduled principal and interest paid in accordance with the mortgage notes,
- servicer advances,
- net income from real estate owned (REO) by the trust due to any defaults and subsequent foreclosure,
- liquidation proceeds, and
- principal prepayments.

Available funds do not include servicing fees, reimbursements for servicing advances, or principal and interest received for a loan's subsequent due date. The treatment of prepayment penalties tends to differ with each transaction and is discussed in more detail in a later section.

Reflecting a senior/subordinate structure, available funds are typically provided first to senior securities and subsequently to each level of subordinated debt. Within this framework, the obligations to each class of CMBSs are usually met in the following order:

- interest payments,
- previously missed interest payments,
- principal distributions, and
- previously missed principal (i.e., realized losses) and any relevant interest penalties.

One of the fundamental ratios in a CMBS structure is the relationship between the principal balance of the certificates and the principal balance of the assets dedicated to repaying the certificates. In order to maintain a favorable ratio between these measures, "principal distributions" are broadly defined to include any portion of a payment that represents a reduction in the principal balance of the underlying loans.

In this context, the repayment of principal would include prepayments, principal payments made in default, liquidation proceeds or any other payment that could be identified as a recovery of principal by the loan servicer. These funds would be passed through to the most senior certificate holder to reduce the outstanding balance of such certificates.

Excess Interest

In most cases, CMBSs are structured such that the highest coupon on the securities does not exceed the lowest coupon of the underlying mortgages. This policy insures that every performing loan in the pool will generate sufficient interest payments to meet the interest due on the outstanding securities with a comparable principal balance.

Such structure leads to a higher level of cash flow from the mortgage pool than is necessary to satisfy the principal and interest payments of the CMBSs. This extra cash flow, referred to as *excess interest*, is often used to create a separate interest only (IO) security or, on occasion, may be used to pay down the principal of subordinate bonds.

When excess interest is used to pay down a security's principal, the outstanding principal balance of the loans gradually exceeds the balance of the CMBSs. The subsequent overcollateralization then serves as a buffer to absorb losses from the loan pool, over time adding a modest level of credit support to the remaining securities.

When a CMBS IO is created, it receives no principal payments throughout the life of the security. As a result, its coupon is usually calculated as a percentage of the remaining principal (i.e., the notional balance) of an associated class. Often, the associated class is the senior class of bonds because the lower coupon on the senior debt leaves the greatest amount of excess interest with which to create an IO. Alternatively, IO payments may be stripped from the coupon payments in excess of the weighted average coupon (WAC) reflected by the entire mortgage pool. In this case, payments to the IO will fluctuate according to both the scheduled and unscheduled principal payments experienced by the pool and the investor's income will change accordingly.

DEVELOPING SCENARIO ANALYSIS FOR CMBSs

Structuring a Hypothetical Mortgage Pool

To illustrate certain principles of CMBS cash flow, we will review a hypothetical securitization using loans that would be typical of conduit generated CMBSs. A summary of the structure of this transaction is shown in Exhibit 5. Since loans in a diversified pool are likely to mature throughout the term of the CMBSs, they create a unique, uneven principal paydown for most of the securities.

For the transaction shown in Exhibit 5, aggregate monthly payments available to certificate holders range from $77,397 for the next-to-last payment to $6,276,690 for payment 143, about 80% of the way through the 15-year life of the loan pool. As a point of comparison, if the loans represented level payments for debt amortizing over 15 years, the average payment would equal $731,000. The irregular payment schedule typical of a commercial mortgage pool occurs regardless of prepayment or default activity, thereby leading to structures which employ both premium and discount bonds with a wide range of average lives and durations.

Consistent with a senior/subordinate structure, all principal loan payments in the hypothetical transaction are applied sequentially to the principal balance of the securities, beginning with the senior debt. Exhibit 6 presents the timing of the first and final principal payments for each class of securities in the hypothetical transaction.

Class A1 receives principal on a somewhat regular schedule, similar to fully amortizing debt, although several bullet loans cause the principal payment in year 10 to jump to over 50% of the initial principal balance. Class D, alternatively, is structured to resemble that of a non-amortizing corporate bond. Class E lies between the two, receiving 12 years of interest payments and then receiving principal payments over the course of 2.5 years.

Class F securities immediately receive small principal payments from the excess mortgage interest not allocated to the A2 IO or B2 IO. However, the amount of principal reduction is minor until payment 164 (in year 14), at which time the outstanding principal balance still exceeds 75% of the original balance. These different patterns of principal paydown are important factors in determining each security's final yield under various default scenarios.

Exhibit 5: Summary Data for the Securitization of a Hypothetical Commercial-Mortgage Pool

Total Value of Loans ($ MM)	69.74
Number of Loans	40
Average Loan Size ($ MM)	1.74
Range of Loan Size ($ MM)	0.56 to 4.25
Weighted Average Coupon (%)	10.55
Coupon Range (%)	10.00 to 11.39
Weighted Average Life (Years)	9.63
Balloon Terms (Years)	10 to 15

Class	A1	A2 (IO)	B1	B2(IO)	C	D	E	F	G
Rating	AAA	AAA	AA	AA	A	BBB	BB	B	Unrated
Size ($ MM)	48.82	NA	4.18	NA	3.49	2.79	4.18	3.49	2.79
Percent of Total	70.0	NA	6.0	NA	5.0	4.0	6.0	5.0	4.0
Coupon (%)	8.34	1.24	8.60	0.98	8.81	9.44	9.57	9.57	9.57
Price ($)	101.00	6.28	101.00	6.14	100.02	100.02	86.58	79.64	25.00
Yield (%)	8.20	11.80	8.53	12.04	8.88	9.53	11.78	13.13	40.80
Average Life (Years)	8.26	8.26	11.78	11.78	11.88	11.90	12.51	12.92	14.97
Spread to Trsy. (BPs)	120	479	145	495	180	245	469	603	3,367
Duration (Years)	5.88	3.69	7.47	4.61	7.41	7.20	6.93	6.50	2.85

Exhibit 6: Schedule of First and Final Principal Payments for Hypothetical CMBSs Backed by a Diversified Loan Pool

Rating	Security Class	First Principal Payment (Month)	Final Principal Payment (Month)
Investment Grade	A1	1	138
	B1	138	142
	C	142	143
	D	143	143
Non-Investment Grade	E	143	174
	F	1	178
	G	178	180

CMBS Default Scenarios

Should a borrower default on one of the loans in the pool and the available funds be insufficient to meet the interest and principal payments on the securities, the servicer of the loan pool is generally obligated to advance payments to certificate holders up to the amount deemed to be recoverable from the underlying property. As soon as the property is liquidated, proceeds (net of servicer expenses and advances) are passed through to the senior certificates to reduce their principal balance and then sequentially to other classes (or tranches). While servicer advancing does not add to the net funds available to bondholders, it does ensure timely payment of principal and interest until proceeds from the collateral can be realized.

To illustrate the sensitivity of each bond's yield to different mortgage default rates, three default patterns were applied against the hypothetical transaction outlined in Exhibit 5. The effects of these changes in cash flow are shown in Exhibit 7. The analysis employs a cumulative default rate equal to 17.2% of the original principal balance of the pool. This level of stress approximates the cumulative default rates identified in an in-depth empirical study of commercial-mortgage defaults. Defaults were assumed to occur periodically between months 18 and 60 of the 15-year life of the loan pool and, after an 18-month delay, loss rates were applied equal to 30%, 40% or 50% of the loan balance at the time of default. Loss rates include all transaction costs associated with foreclosure, including lost interest payments on the underlying loans.[1]

The changes in yield due to defaulting loans are summarized in scenarios 1, 2 and 3 in Exhibit 7. Despite the broad range of loss severity, only classes A2, F and G suffer a notable change in yield. The effect on all other classes is minimal, including the double-B rated class E, for which the most severe loss rate generates a comparatively modest 16-basis-point reduction in yield.

In the case of the class A2 IO, the drop in yield in the first scenario, to 9.50% from 11.80%, may be attributed to the early retirement of principal and subsequent reduction in the average life of the senior securities, to 7.44 years from 8.26 years. However, the amount of prepaid principal is based on the amount recovered from the defaulted loans. As the recovery rate progressively falls in scenarios 2 and 3, the average life of the senior securities extends beyond that of scenario 1 and generates a correspondingly higher yield on the IO. These dynamics illustrate the way in which an IO may be used as a partial hedge against large losses in a commercial loan pool.

With regard to the performance of the subordinate securities, it is essential to recognize the disparate effects of default frequency, default severity, and the timing of defaults. The marginal impact of these factors on a subordinate CMBS's yield varies according to each security's price and exposure

---

[1] Mark Snyderman, "Update on Commercial Mortgage Defaults," *The Real Estate Finance Journal* (Summer 1994).

to loan losses. In general, securities sold at a very deep discount tend to recover the present value of their purchase price more quickly than securities sold closer to par. In effect, the high coupon in conjunction with the discount price paid for the bond generates an exceptionally high positive carry. As a result, the earlier years in the life of these securities are the most critical in terms of the investor's yield.

Exhibit 7: Scenario Analysis Summarizing the Effect of Different Loss Rates on CMBS Yields

Original Principal Balance ($ MM)	69.74
Number of Loans	40
Loans Defaulting (No.)	9
Loans Defaulting ($ MM)	11.99
— Portion of Original Loan Pool (%)	17.20
Periods of default (Mos.)	18 to 60
Loss Severity (%)	30 to 50

Class	A1	A2 (IO)	B1	B2 (IO)	C	D	E	F	G
Rating	AAA	AAA	AA	AA	A	BBB	BB	B	Unrated
Size ($ MM)	48.82	NA	4.18	NA	3.49	2.79	4.18	3.49	2.79
Coupon (%)	8.34	1.24	8.60	0.98	8.81	9.44	9.57	9.57	9.57
Base Case Scenario — No Defaults									
Yield (%)	8.20	11.80	8.53	12.04	8.88	9.53	11.78	13.13	40.80
Avg. Life (Yrs.)	8.26	8.26	11.78	11.78	11.88	11.90	12.51	12.92	14.97
Mod. Duration (%)	5.64	3.49	7.17	4.35	7.10	6.87	6.55	6.10	2.37
Total Payments ($ MM)	82.48	4.99	8.43	0.48	7.14	5.93	9.20	7.80	6.79
Scenario #1: 17.2% Cumulative Default Rate — 30% Loss Severity									
Yield (%)	8.18	9.50	8.53	12.02	8.88	9.53	11.69	11.66	20.00
Avg. Life (Yrs.)	7.44	7.44	11.76	11.76	11.90	11.96	13.81	13.69	NA
Mod. Duration (%)	5.19	3.46	7.16	4.35	7.10	6.89	6.85	6.27	1.57
Total Payments ($ MM)	79.14	4.49	8.42	0.48	7.14	5.94	9.72	7.09	1.03
Scenario #2: 17.2% Cumulative Default Rate — 40% Loss Severity									
Yield (%)	8.18	9.99	8.53	12.09	8.88	9.53	11.65	7.27	16.61
Avg. Life (Yrs.)	7.62	7.62	11.84	11.84	11.90	12.32	14.45	12.80	NA
Mod. Duration (%)	5.28	3.48	7.19	4.36	7.11	7.00	6.98	6.16	1.52
Total Payments ($ MM)	79.88	4.60	8.45	0.48	7.15	6.04	9.97	4.75	0.95
Scenario #3: 17.2% Cumulative Default Rate — 50% Loss Severity									
Yield (%)	8.19	10.47	8.53	12.11	8.88	9.54	11.62	-3.72	15.07
Avg. Life (Yrs.)	7.81	7.81	11.86	11.86	11.92	13.04	14.83	8.08	NA
Mod. Duration (%)	5.38	3.50	7.20	4.36	7.11	7.21	7.06	5.01	1.50
Total Payments ($ MM)	80.63	4.71	8.46	0.48	7.15	6.23	10.13	2.36	0.92

For example, class G yields are reduced by one-half under the 30% loss severity assumed in scenario 1. However, despite the complete loss of the bond's $2.79 million face value in the fifth year of the security's life, a 20% yield is generated because the aggregate coupon payments to the security ($1.03 million) are well in excess of the purchase price of the bonds ($697,379). As the loss severity increases from 30% to 50%, the marginal effect on the bond's yield is minor because the earlier coupon payments are not affected and most of the additional loss is absorbed by the class F securities. Even under a 50% loss rate, the high positive carry provides the investor $919,395 of coupon payments for a yield of 16.61%.

In the case of the class F securities, however, the bond offers a much smaller positive carry and is therefore more sensitive to the level of loss severity. In scenario 1, under a 30% severity of loss, the class F security receives aggregate payments of $7.09 million, a comparatively moderate reduction from its $7.80 million of scheduled payments. In scenario 3, under a 50% severity of loss, the securities' payments are reduced by $5.44 million to $2.36 million. This drastic reduction triggers a -3.7% yield over the life of the bonds.

Timing of Defaults and Loan Amortization

Scenario analysis also may be used to explore the timing of loan defaults. Exhibit 8 presents one of the default scenarios discussed previously in Exhibit 7 and compares this scenario to one in which the defaults occur four years later in the life of the securities, i.e., between months 66 and 108, rather than between months 18 and 60. As a result of the four-year delay, bond classes F and G are able to add 3.66 percentage points and 20.53 percentage points, respectively, to their yields to maturity. The forces underlying these changes are exactly the same as those forces affecting the scenarios shown in Exhibit 7. For example, the principal balance of the class G tranche is eliminated in both scenarios but, in scenario 1, the last dollar of principal is lost in the fifth year of the bond's life while, in scenario 2, the last dollar of principal is lost in the ninth year. The four-year delay allows an additional $1.1 million of interest payments to pass through to the investor.

These considerations help explain the recent activity in subordinate CMBSs by real estate funds. With the commercial mortgage market apparently having reached a low point in 1993 and having registered slight gains in 1994, the real estate cycle appears to be in a favorable stage for investing in high-yield CMBSs. If widespread, systematic losses are held in check over the next several years, the return from subordinate debt is likely to be well above what could be obtained through a traditional commercial mortgage portfolio or even certain forms of real estate equity.

CMBSs that avoid defaults during their early life also benefit from the amortization of mortgage principal. As payments begin to reduce the outstanding principal on the pool of loans, the LTV ratio is reduced as well, increasing the chance of recovering the balance of the loan if the borrower defaults.

Exhibit 8: Scenario Analysis Summarizing the Effect of the Timing of Loan Defaults on CMBS Yields

Class	A1	A2 (IO)	B1	B2 (IO)	C	D	E	F	G
Rating	AAA	AAA	AA	AA	A	BBB	BB	B	Unrated
Size ($ MM)	48.82	NA	4.18	NA	3.49	2.79	4.18	3.49	2.79
Coupon (%)	8.34	1.24	8.60	0.98	8.81	9.44	9.57	9.57	9.57
Base-Case Scenario — No Defaults									
Yield (%)	8.20	11.80	8.53	12.04	8.88	9.53	11.78	13.13	40.80
Avg. Life (Yrs.)	8.26	8.26	11.78	11.78	11.88	11.90	12.51	12.92	14.97
Mod. Duration (%)	5.64	3.49	7.17	4.35	7.10	6.87	6.55	6.10	2.37
Total Payments ($ MM)	82.48	4.99	8.43	0.48	7.14	5.93	9.20	7.80	6.79
Scenario #1: 17.2% Cumulative Default Rate Between Month 18 and Month 60 — 40% Loss Severity									
Yield (%)	8.18	9.99	8.53	12.09	8.88	9.53	11.65	7.27	16.61
Avg. Life (Yrs.)	7.62	7.62	11.84	11.84	11.90	12.32	14.45	12.80	NA
Mod. Duration (%)	5.28	3.48	7.19	4.36	7.11	7.00	6.98	6.16	1.52
Total Payments ($ MM)	79.88	4.60	8.45	0.48	7.15	6.04	9.97	4.75	0.95
Scenario #2: 17.2% Cumulative Default Rate Between Month 66 and Month 108 — 40% Loss Severity									
Yield (%)	8.20	11.36	8.53	12.01	8.88	9.53	11.66	10.93	37.14
Avg. Life (Yrs.)	8.05	8.05	11.75	11.75	11.90	12.06	14.15	13.16	NA
Mod. Duration (%)	5.55	3.45	7.16	4.35	7.11	6.92	6.92	5.92	1.99
Total Payments ($ MM)	81.62	4.86	8.42	0.48	7.15	5.97	8.66	6.28	2.06

Prepayment Risk

In addition to default risk, investors must also consider the prepayment risk of CMBSs. In general, the variability of CMBS prepayments is considerably less than for residential MBSs or other forms of ABSs. The limited exposure to prepayments may be attributed to prepayment provisions in the underlying mortgage collateral and the relatively high cost of refinancing a commercial mortgage. Prepayment provisions may be categorized within three basic types: (1) percentage of outstanding balance, (2) lockout clause, and (3) yield maintenance.

The *percentage of outstanding balance* type of penalty requires the borrower to pay a stated percentage of the remaining principal balance of the loan, usually according to a declining schedule over a limited period of time. Under a typical schedule, such as "5-4-3-2-1," the borrower would pay a penalty equal to 5% of the prepaid principal balance in the first year, 4% in the second year, and so on.

Under a *lockout clause*, any attempt to prepay during the lockout period is considered a technical default under the terms of the mortgage note. Lockout provisions typically extend for three or four years, after which another form of prepayment protection often applies for several more years prior to the loan's maturity.

Under a *yield maintenance clause*, the borrower is allowed to prepay at any time, but must compensate the lender for any give-up in yield during the yield maintenance period, assuming the pre-paid principal is reinvested in risk-free Treasury debt.

The most prevalent prepayment clause combines two or more of the previous three forms of call protection. For example, a 10-year loan might contain a lock-out feature for the first four years, followed by a 5-4-3-2-1 penalty, with no penalty for a prepayment during the final year prior to maturity. As another example, a 10-year loan might require a penalty payment equal to the greater of 1% of the remaining principal balance or a yield maintenance payment during the first nine years of the loan's term.

Prepayment penalties are often designed to diminish over time and are usually eliminated entirely between six months and a year prior to a loan's maturity. Since most commercial loans require a substantial balloon payment at the end of the loan's term, this structure provides a refinancing window during which the borrower may obtain a new loan to meet the balloon payment.

An additional variable affecting a borrower's incentive to refinance is the cost of securing a new loan. In the commercial mortgage market, the underwriting process is extensive and closing costs must cover environmental and engineering reports in addition to an independent appraisal, title search, etc. These costs are subject to economies of scale and are therefore more onerous for smaller loans ranging between $1 million and $5 million. For these loans, the total cost of refinancing is likely to reach as much as 3% or 4% of the loan amount, acting as an effective deterrent in addition to the prepayment penalty. For loans subject to yield maintenance, there should never be a financial incentive to refinance because the cost of refinancing and the yield maintenance payment will always exceed the savings from a lower coupon payment.

Exhibit 9 provides an example of two loans and the refinancing incentives under a range of interest-rate scenarios throughout the loans' 10-year terms. In the exhibit, a 5-4-3-2-1 structure is assumed after a 4-year lock-out period. The incentive to refinance is defined as the present value of the difference between the old and the new monthly payments for the remaining term of the original loan, reduced by the prepayment penalty and the present value of incurring origination costs prior to the original loan's maturity.

For example, in the case of a $5 million loan with a 10% coupon refinanced at 9.5% in the 49th month of an original 10-year term, the present value of the difference in loan payments is equal to $105,866. This sum must then be reduced by the prepayment penalty (equal to 5% of the remaining principal) and the present value of the loan-origination costs six years earlier than anticipated. Collectively, these two costs equal $272,999, far in excess of the present value of the reduced payments.

As shown in Exhibit 9, refinancing typically becomes an attractive option after the lock-out period if interest rates fall between 100 and 150 basis points. However, during the last two years of the loan's term, a progressively smaller interest rate movement puts the refinancing option in the money.

Stiff prepayment penalties are an important source of stability for the cash flow of CMBSs. However, should a prepayment occur, a further benefit for CMBS investors is the higher cash flow generated by the prepayment penalty or yield maintenance payment. Prepayment penalties are typically distributed to those investors most affected by the prepayment.

Exhibit 9: Present Value of Refinancing a Commercial Mortgage Under Various Interest Rate Scenarios

$1 million loan

Change in Rates (Bps)	Present Value of Refinancing for Each Month in Which Prepayment Occurs ($)					
	49	61	73	85	97	109
- 50 bps.	-36,998	-28,481	-20,296	-12,490	-5,116	1,766
-100 bps.	-16,130	-10,682	-5,738	-1,357	2,399	5,458
-150 bps.	4,417	6,844	8,595	9,605	9,798	9,094
-200 bps.	24,627	24,082	22,693	20,386	17,076	12,670
Penalty:	5%	4%	3%	2%	1%	None

$5 million loan

Change in Rates (Bps)	Present Value of Refinancing for Each Month in Which Prepayment Occurs ($)					
	49	61	73	85	97	109
- 50 bps.	-167,133	-127,140	-88,949	-52,804	-18,978	12,217
-100 bps.	-62,790	-38,142	-16,161	2,860	18,596	30,680
-150 bps.	39,946	49,487	55,507	57,668	55,591	48,859
-200 bps.	140,994	135,675	125,997	111,574	91,979	66,740
Penalty:	5%	4%	3%	2%	1%	None

Assumptions

Initial coupon rate(%)	10.0
Amortization (Yrs.)	30.0
Term (Yrs.)	10.0
Prepayment Provisions:	4-year lock-out, followed by 5-4-3-2-1 and one year no penalty
Refinancing Costs:	2 point origination fee plus $18,000 (for the $1MM loan) and $25,000 (for the $5MM loan) for engineering, appraisal, attorney, title search, etc.
Amount Refinanced:	$1MM and $5 MM, respectively.
Discount Rate (%)	5.5

For example, prepayment penalties and yield maintenance payments may be allocated in one of the following ways: (1) pro-rata to one or more classes (such as an IO and corresponding class receiving the prepaid principal), based on the reduction of the principal balance as a result of the prepayment; (2) sequentially to each class with an outstanding principal balance; or (3) according to a predetermined percentage assigned to an IO or other security.

It should also be noted that the allocation of prepayment penalties may differ from the allocation of yield maintenance payments, although both provisions are present in the same pool of loans. Further, as implied by the sample allocation formulas shown above, the penalty allocated to an IO or higher yielding security may not be sufficient to maintain the anticipated yield of such security.

In short, prepayment protection provides two essential functions for CMBS investors. First, borrowers are given a strong economic incentive not to prepay their loans, thus minimizing prepayment rates over the term of the securities. Second, should prepayments occur, CMBS structures typically use the additional cash flow to offset all or a portion of the lost yield for those securities most affected by the early return of principal.

THE RELATIVE VALUE OF CMBSs AND COMMERCIAL MORTGAGES

Investments in commercial mortgages have traditionally served an important role in an institutional portfolio. Commercial mortgages are attractive to institutional investors because they generally offer above-average yields and long-term average lives that can be matched against long-term liabilities.

In addition, commercial mortgage returns are partly tied to the performance of the commercial property market, which is not closely correlated with the general returns of the fixed-income market. Consequently, commercial mortgages offer an important form of diversification for most portfolios. Nevertheless, commercial mortgage investments also have several drawbacks, including a relative lack of liquidity and a limited opportunity to manage portfolio risk.

In the past, illiquidity was a relatively minor concern because many institutions originated mortgages under a buy-and-hold investment strategy. However, from 1990 to 1992, the downturn in the commercial property market coincided with the application of regulatory pressure for many financial institutions to reduce their exposure to real estate related risk. In the period that followed, several of these institutions turned to securitization as the most effective way to create commercial mortgage liquidity and maximize the value of their assets. Although institutions are now under less pressure to reduce their exposure to real estate, the need for liquidity remains.

In the CMBS market, securities can be placed or removed from the balance sheet much more quickly than in the case of direct lending, thereby reducing the time required to implement or alter an investment strategy. In practice, CMBSs are not listed on public exchanges, but several firms act as dealers of such securities and a competitive purchase or sale may often be accomplished within several days.

In addition, the presence of credit tranching in CMBSs allows investors to target more effectively a specific level of risk and return based upon each security's exposure to default from a specific pool. Investors seeking the highest levels of credit quality would be attracted to triple-A and double-A rated securities. Such highly rated classes are the most liquid form of CMBSs and are generally priced at a 50 to 60 basis point discount to comparably rated corporate debt.

Although all classes of CMBSs offer higher yields than their corporate counterparts, investing in the highest-rated CMBSs provides the least risky way to take advantage of this disparity. In the context of a diversified portfolio, investments in triple-A rated CMBSs also may be viewed as the most conservative type of exposure to real estate.

At the other end of the credit spectrum, subordinate securities are structured to provide high returns, but with little or no credit enhancement outside of the underwriting standards of the loan pool. More importantly, the most junior tranches are exposed to the performance of every loan in the pool, an amount far in excess of their principal balance. This means that a comparatively small loss with regard to the pool could greatly reduce or eliminate the principal balance of the subordinate securities.

The Benefits of a Diversified Pool

The greater exposure and sensitivity to loan defaults represent the primary risks of subordinate securities. At the same time, the higher risk profile of these CMBSs must be interpreted carefully. The default risk for each underlying loan is independent of other loans in the pool and therefore does not increase or decrease with the size of the loan pool. Thus, subordinate securities are exposed to losses from a large number of loans, but the probability that any given loan will incur a loss is not combined with the probability of loss from other loans in the pool.

In contrast to individual loan performance, aggregate defaults are driven, in part, by the default correlation among the loans in the pool. However, the returns among different property types and regions are not perfectly correlated, so the volatility of defaults for diversified pools will be less than for non-diversified pools. Consequently, loan diversity by location and property type is an important variable in CMBS pricing.

The degree to which a pool's default volatility is reduced will indicate the marginal value of diversity for any given CMBS. In general, this marginal value increases as the level of subordination decreases because diversification will play a larger role in limiting the losses of riskier tranches. However, diversification is only useful if the principal value of a particular class of securities is not eliminated by one or two defaults. In other words, diversity only retains value when a given class of securities is large enough to benefit from the lack of correlation among the underlying loans.

CMBS Spreads

Exhibit 10 presents spreads in the CMBS market at the beginning of 1995 and 1996. At the beginning of 1996, spreads for investment grade CMBSs (rated triple-A through triple-B) ranged from 85 to 195 basis points over Treasury debt of comparable maturity. These spreads may be compared to average spreads ranging between 165 and 225 basis points over Treasury debt for most institutional quality commercial mortgages.

Exhibit 10 also shows that spreads have tightened between 5 to 10 basis points for higher rated CMBSs and approximately 45 basis points for lower-rated, investment grade CMBSs. The across-the-board spread tightening in 1995 is partly due to improvements in the commercial mortgage market and partly due to a higher level of comfort with the performance and liquidity of CMBSs.

Maximizing Returns from Commercial Mortgage Portfolios

The ability to refine a portfolio's risk/return profile through the process of credit tranching suggests that a portfolio of CMBSs can be tailored to outperform a portfolio of whole loans within any specified range of default rates. As long as defaults stay within the projected range, the yield on the securities can be tailored to exceed those of a portfolio backed by similar collateral in which there is no credit tranching.

Exhibit 10: CMBS Spreads (in Basis Points): 5-Year to 10-Year Terms

Rating	Spreads as of January, 1996	Spreads as of January, 1995
AAA	85 - 105	95 - 110
AA	113 - 120	118 - 125
A	137 - 143	160 - 175
BBB	175 - 195	220 - 240
BB	450 - 600	475 - 650
B	600 - 750	600 - 800

Source: Prudential Securities Impact Database

Exhibit 11: Hypothetical Portfolio Returns of Commercial Mortgages and CMBSs

Whole-Loan Portfolio		Base-Case YTM (%)	YTM with 17.2% Cumulative Default and 50% Loss Severity	Difference (BPs)
		9.65	8.56	-109

CMBS Portfolio		% of Portfolio	Base-Case YTM (%)	YTM with 17.2% Cumulative Default and 50% Loss Severity	Difference (BPs)
Class	Rating				
A1	AAA	33.33	8.20	8.19	-1
D	BBB	33.33	9.53	9.54	+1
E	BB	33.33	11.78	11.62	-16
	Total	100.00	9.91	9.92	+1

An example of this strategy is shown in Exhibit 11, for which a portfolio of CMBSs was constructed equal to the $69.7 million of the face value of the whole-loan pool presented previously. The CMBS portfolio assumes an equal weighting of the face value of triple-A, triple-B, and double-B rated CMBSs. In the exhibit, a 17.2% cumulative default rate is applied to the whole-loan portfolio used to generate the hypothetical CMBSs. Under a 50% severity of loss, the aggregate yield of the whole-loan portfolio falls 109 basis points, over a 15-year holding period.

If the loans underlying the CMBS portfolio perform as the loans in the whole-loan pool, the CMBS portfolio will consistently outperform the whole-loan portfolio under the default patterns discussed previously. Exhibit 11 illustrates the yield for each portfolio under the base case (no defaults) and a 17.2% cumulative default rate with a 50% loss severity. As shown in the exhibit, the CMBS portfolio outperforms the pool of whole loans by 26 basis points in the case of no defaults and 136 basis points under the default scenario.

Interestingly, the CMBS portfolio with a 17.2% cumulative default rate and 50% loss severity also outperforms its no-default scenario by one basis point. This can be explained by the changes in the modified duration of the three classes of debt used to construct the portfolio. In the case of the triple-A rated security, which is priced at a premium, defaults lead to principal prepayments, thereby reducing its duration and yield.

In contrast, the durations of the higher yielding double-B and triple-B rated CMBSs increase in the default scenario because their principal payments are delayed slightly due to the losses from the loan pool. As the triple-B rated security is priced at a slight premium, its yield rises slightly, while the yield for the double-B rated security, priced at a discount, declines by 16 basis points. When combined, the weighted duration of the portfolio increases from 6.41 to 6.63, triggered by the changes to the higher-yielding double-B and triple-B rated CMBSs. The effect of this shift is to extend the average life of the portfolio from 10.89 years to 11.89 years and to add one basis point in yield.

CMBS REGULATORY TREATMENT

To date, most government entities have recognized the need for distinct regulatory treatment of commercial mortgage investments and CMBSs. Consistent with this view, the federal government recently extended the Secondary Mortgage Market EnhancementAct (SMMEA) to all multi-family and commercial "mortgage related securities." This change was included in the Riegle Community Development and Regulatory Improvement Act of 1994. Under the Act, SMMEA provisions will become effective after the implementation of appropriate regulatory guidelines through the Office of the Comptroller of the Currency. Such guidelines have been proposed and are likely to be adopted by mid-1996.

When SMMEA provisions take effect, eligible CMBSs rated in one of the top two rating categories of a nationally recognized rating agency will be granted special regulatory treatment in the areas of security registration, state investment restrictions, and margin requirements. In essence, "mortgage related securities" are exempt from state registration requirements and are treated as U.S. government obligations in regard to state investment restrictions.

Along with SMMEA eligibility, CMBSs have typically been afforded favorable treatment under the capital reserve requirements developed by the National Association of Insurance Commissioners (NAIC). Under the NAIC's guidelines, reserve requirements for commercial mortgages are 3.0%, regardless of the perceived credit quality of the individual loan. Fixed-income securities are assigned to a separate risk category, however, for which reserve requirements range from 0.03% to 1.0% for investment-grade debt. When accompanied by the necessary structural features to warrant an investment-grade rating, CMBSs therefore provide a regulatory advantage when compared to commercial whole loans.

SUMMARY

As the recovery in the commercial property market proceeds, CMBS will be used increasingly as a source of liquidity and a means to enhance the returns from commercial-mortgage and fixed-income portfolios. In particular, CMBSs provide the opportunity to target a specific level of risk within a diversified pool of loans. In addition, the credit enhancement and stability of highly rated CMBSs generally receive more favorable regulatory treatment than commercial mortgages or noninvestment-grade corporate bonds.

Chapter 14

Investing in Interest-Only Commercial Mortgage-Backed Securities

Jonathan Adams
Vice President
Fixed Income Research
Prudential Securities Inc.

Inna Koren
First Vice President
Fixed Income Research
Prudential Securities Inc.

Lina Hsu
First Vice President
Fixed Income Research
Prudential Securities Inc.

In Chapters 12 and 13, commercial mortgage-backed securities (CMBSs) were discussed. In this chapter, we discuss the risk and rewards associated with investing in triple-A rated interest-only (IO) securities backed by commercial mortgages. As we will explain, several unique features of commercial mortgages are reflected in the structure of CMBS IOs, thus distinguishing them from other, more volatile IO securities.

CMBS IOS AND COMMERCIAL-MORTGAGE OPTIONS

In structured CMBSs, it is common for the average coupon of the underlying collateral to exceed the coupon of the security. This extra cash flow, referred to as excess interest, is often "stripped" from the pass-through rate and used to either pay down the principal on the rated bonds in the CMBS structure, thereby retiring these bonds at a faster pace, or create an IO security.

The allocation of excess interest to the principal balance of a single class of securities will shorten its average life and eventually create overcollateralization as a cushion against losses from the underlying loans. This structure was common in a number of RTC transactions.

When excess interest is used to create CMBS IOs, the derived security's yield is determined by the cash flow generated by the underlying loans. If the principal balance of a loan is paid prior to its maturity, the IO's yield will decrease, while an extension of the loan will increase the IO's yield. The actual term of each underlying mortgage is a function of the option to prepay the loan and the probability of a loan default.

The prepayment option might be exercised when the present value of the new coupon payments and the total costs of securing a new loan fall below the present value of the existing coupon payments (excluding amortization). A loan default is likely to occur when the value of the property falls below the outstanding value of the mortgage.

Loan defaults typically are analyzed as a put option held by the borrower to put the property back to the lender. As a result, a CMBS IO investor is in the position of selling both a call option with regard to prepayments and a put option with regard to the property's value. However, the value of these options is reduced considerably by various forms of call protection and credit enhancement in the underlying mortgage debt.

THE VOLUNTARY PREPAYMENT OPTION

A commercial-mortgage prepayment option is, in certain respects, similar to the prepayment option in a residential mortgage. However, the value of this option is reduced greatly by various forms of call protection, including stiff prepayment penalties and the relatively high cost of refinancing. Prepayment provisions may be broken down into three basic types.

Percentage of Outstanding Balance (5-4-3-2-1 Structure)

This type of penalty requires the borrower to pay a stated percentage of the remaining principal balance of the loan, usually according to a declining schedule over a limited period of time. Under a typical schedule, such as "5-4-3-2-1," the borrower would pay a penalty equal to 5% of the prepaid principal balance in the first year, 4% in the second year and so on.

Lockout Clause

Under a lockout clause, any attempt to prepay during the lockout period is considered a breach of contract under the terms of the mortgage note. In practice, should a borrower need to prepay the loan, an acceptable premium may be negotiated to allow the prepayment, at the discretion of the lender. Lockout provisions typically extend for three or four years, after which another form of prepayment protection often applies for several more years prior to the loan's maturity.

Yield Maintenance

Under a yield-maintenance clause, the borrower is allowed to prepay at any time, but must compensate the lender for any give up in yield, assuming the prepaid principal is reinvested in risk-free Treasury debt. When loans are subject to yield maintenance, the incentive to refinance is eliminated because the cost of refinancing and the yield-maintenance payment should always exceed the savings from a lower coupon payment.

The most prevalent prepayment clause combines two or more of the previous three forms of call protection. For example, a ten-year loan might contain a lockout feature for the first four years followed by a 5-4-3-2-1 penalty, with no penalty for a prepayment during the final year prior to maturity. As another example, a ten-year loan might require a penalty payment equal to the greater of 1% of the remaining principal balance or a yield-maintenance payment during the first nine years of the loan's term.

Prepayment penalties often are designed to diminish over time and usually are eliminated entirely between six months and one year prior to a loan's maturity. Since most commercial loans require a substantial balloon payment at the end of the loan's term, this structure provides a refinancing window during which the borrower may obtain a new loan to meet the balloon payment.

Commercial-Mortgage Origination Costs

An additional variable affecting a borrower's incentive to refinance is the cost of securing a new loan. In the commercial-mortgage market, the underwriting process is extensive and closing costs must cover environmental and engineering reports in addition to an independent appraisal, title search, etc. These costs are subject to economies of scale and therefore are more onerous for smaller loans ranging between $1 million and $5 million. For these loans, the total cost of refinancing is likely to reach as much as 3% or 4% of the loan amount, acting as an effective deterrent when added to the prepayment penalty.

THE DEFAULT OPTION

The credit quality of the underlying properties is a primary consideration for a CMBS IO holder. In most cases, any loan losses are absorbed readily by the transaction's subordinated tranches, but the liquidation of a defaulted property will lead to a partial prepayment of notional principal and reduction in IO cash flow. As a result, the yield on the IO is reduced as the life of the security is shortened.

CMBSs benefit from rigorous stress testing by the rating agencies and very conservative underwriting criteria for newly originated debt. In addition, commercial-mortgage pools are benefiting from the improving conditions in the commercial-property market. Although the recovery of the commercial market has been a long time in the making, the current low levels of supply and increasing demand for commercial property should generate an impressive period of stable property performance. These factors should translate into higher values, lower default rates and therefore greater yield stability for CMBS IOs.

The likelihood and impact of mortgage defaults may be evaluated by analyzing the quality of the underlying collateral and the security's structure. As a general rule, the CMBS market has favored diversified pools backed by newly originated loans. Diversified pools contain a large number of loans from many borrowers, often representing several property types in different geographic markets, thereby reducing the volatility of the loan pool's performance. Newly originated loans are based on current pricing and usually employ more conservative underwriting criteria than the criteria used for older, seasoned loans. With regard to underwriting requirements, the following characteristics of each loan should be reviewed to evaluate a pool's inherent credit risk: (1) loan-to-value (LTV) ratio, (2) debt-service coverage (DSC), (3) rate structure, (4) term, and (5) economic, borrower, and property characteristics.[1]

---

[1] For more information see Jonathan Adams and Lina Hsu, *Analytical Techniques for Investing in Securitized Pools of Commercial Mortgages*, Fixed-Income Research, Prudential Securities, Inc., October 1995.

Exhibit 1: Summary Data for a Hypothetical Securitization of a Commercial-Mortgage Loan Pool

Collateral Value ($MM)	100
Weighted-Average Coupon (%)	8.40
Weighted-Average Maturity (Years)	12.3
Weighted-Average Life (Years)	10.9
Amortization Terms (Years)	
— 66.6% of the loan pool	25
— 33.3% of the loan pool	20

CMBS Loan-Pool Servicing

Aside from cautious underwriting and significant subordination levels in CMBS structures, the cash flow available to commercial IOs is supported by servicer advancing and the possibility of loan extensions. Should a borrower default, most servicers are obligated to advance bond payments to the investor to the extent that these payments can be recovered through the property's liquidation.

If a borrower is unable to refinance a loan at its balloon date, many servicers are enabled to modify the terms of the loan to avoid the cost of a lengthy foreclosure proceeding. This option is beneficial to the IO holder because the cash flow will then extend beyond the maturity date and increase the yield on the IO.

Restructuring loan terms also is a viable option for loans that become delinquent because such an adjustment may meet the servicer's goal to maximize the cash flow to the trust. In the case of a loan default, the effect on the IO depends on the interaction of the change in coupon, amortization and term. Establishing a lower coupon would reduce the cash flow available to the IO, while an extended term or diminished amortization would increase the yield of the IO.

VALUING THE OPTIONS IN A CMBS IO

To illustrate the impact on IO yields due to voluntary prepayments and defaulting principal, we generated a hypothetical CMBS transaction with a structure similar to a conduit generated mixed-loan pool. The hypothetical transaction employs a simple multi-class structure with a single IO receiving excess interest payments from the investment-grade securities. Exhibit 1 summarizes the collateral assumptions used in this hypothetical transaction. Consistent with CMBSs backed by a newly originated, diversified loan pool, the investment-grade securities were structured to equal 85% of the $100 million pool.

Exhibit 2: Prepayment Vector Applied to the Hypothetical Loan Pool

Month	Percent
1 to 48	0.0
49 to 72	1.5
73 to 84	2.0
85 to 96	4.0
97 to 108	7.0
109	100

Estimating Prepayments and Defaults

The vector of voluntary prepayments realized by a loan pool will depend on the direction of interest rates and the precise prepayment provisions of the mortgage collateral. Our analysis employed a four-year lockout period followed by a 5-4-3-2-1 penalty structure, leaving at least one year to prepay the loan without penalty. Although most commercial-loan pools contain a mix of prepayment provisions, our uniform assumption reflects the aggregate call protection in a typical loan pool. Under these prepayment provisions, interest rates would have to rally by more than 100 basis points in order to trigger substantive prepayments during the first seven years of the pool's life.[2]

   Exhibit 2 illustrates the voluntary prepayment vector applied to the hypothetical loan pool. Because the call protection declines notably after the first seven years of the pool's life, we have assumed a corresponding increase in prepayment speeds beginning in month 85.

   Of course, prepayments also may be triggered by debt consolidation or the sale of the property, regardless of the financial barrier to prepayment. As a result, our prepayment vector incorporates modest prepayments even when they ordinarily would be unlikely (during the first seven years of the loan pool's life). Further, we conservatively assume that any remaining loans prepay at the beginning of the ninth year of the pool's life — the first month in which the prepayment penalties fall to zero.

   To incorporate the effect of loan defaults, we applied an aggregate default vector equal to 18.75% of the pool's principal balance, as shown in Exhibit 3. This vector approximates the default pattern identified in an in-depth empirical study of 10,955 commercial mortgages analyzed between 1972 and 1986.[3] To generate a reasonable worst-case scenario, we also concentrated loan defaults in the first few years of the pool's life, since loan

[2] For more detailed information on the efficacy of prepayment provisions, see "Spread Talk, The Mortgage- and Asset-Backed Securities Strategist," *Fixed-Income Research*, Prudential Securities Inc., October 27, 1995.

[3] See Mark Snyderman, "Update on Commercial Mortgage Defaults," *The Real Estate Finance Journal*, Summer 1994.

performance in the early years of the loan pool has the greatest effect on the IO's yield. Eighteen months after each loan's default, 65% of the principal balance was assumed to be recovered and passed through to certificate holders sequentially.

The Aggregate Cost of Prepayments and Defaults

The prepayment and default assumptions described above were applied in a cumulative fashion to four scenarios, designed to convey the unique contribution of each assumption to an IO's yield. To begin this type of analysis, we priced the IO at a 500-basis-point spread to the curve, assuming no prepayments, no prepayment penalties and no defaults (Base-Case Scenario, as shown in Exhibit 4).

Exhibit 3: Default Vector Applied to the Hypothetical Loan Pool

Time of Default (Months)	Level of Default (%)
18	3.20
30	3.20
42	2.50
54	1.80
66	1.80
78	1.50
90	1.50
102	1.25
114	1.00
126	1.00
Total	18.75

Exhibit 4: Scenario Analysis Summarizing the Yield Impact of Defaults and Prepayments on the Hypothetical CMBS IO

Scenario	Base Case	1	2	3
	No Prepayments No Penalties No Defaults	Prepayments No Penalties No Defaults	Prepayments Penalties Passed Through No Defaults	Prepayments Penalties Passed Through Defaults
Yield (%)	10.88	8.90	9.59	8.38
Spread (BPs)	+500	+308	+376	+258
Average Life (Years)	9.1	8.2	8.2	7.7

Exhibit 5: Example of the Yield Fluctuation on Residential Mortgage IOs

Deal ID:	FNMA Trust 257 IO
Collateral (%):	7.00
Price (32nds):	27-16
Yield (BPs):	13.83
Spread (BPs):	+845
Notional Average Life (Years):	7.7

	Interest-Rate Scenarios*						
	-300	-200	-100	NC	+100	+200	+300
Yield (%)	-13.70	-10.29	-2.07	13.83	15.46	16.12	16.32
Average Life (Years)	1.9	2.3	3.6	7.7	8.6	8.9	9.6

*Based on PSA prepayment vectors.

Source: PSI's IMPACT database as of 2/14/96

Scenario 1 shows the sensitivity of IO yields to voluntary prepayments. However, for this interim step, we assumed no prepayment penalties were passed through to the holder of the IO. Based on our vector of voluntary prepayments, the yield on the IO drops 198 basis points, from 10.88% to 8.90%, and the average life (of the notional principal) shortens one year. In Scenario 2, we assume the same prepayment vector as in the first scenario, but all prepayment premiums are passed through to the IO holder. The receipt of prepayment premiums raises the yield on the IO by 69 basis points to 9.59%, illustrating the importance of this additional cash flow.

Scenario 3 takes the analysis one step further and incorporates the default curve described previously. The combined effect of the voluntary prepayment vector and the default vector is to drop the original yield of 10.88% by 250 basis points. However, on a spread basis, the bonds still yield 258 basis points over the curve. Note, once again, that Scenario 3 uses very conservative assumptions, yet the absolute yield and spread are still attractive compared to alternative products.

To distinguish the yield behavior of commercial IOs, we conclude with a comparison to residential IOs. Exhibit 5 illustrates the risks of a typical residential IO, in this case FNMA Trust 257 backed by 7% collateral. The yields and prices on residential IOs are a function of the absolute level of interest rates, the shape of the yield curve and seasonality/burnout factors.

Comparing the base case for each product, the initial yield and spread currently are higher on residential IOs (13.83% for our selected trust IO versus 10.88% for the CMBS IO). However, residential IOs exhibit a greater degree of yield and spread volatility when interest rates change. In Exhibit 5, a 100-basis-point downturn in interest rates is sufficient to generate a yield of -2.07%. In contrast, the cost of the prepayment option and default option present in a commercial-mortgage IO is reduced considerably by prepayment provisions and structural features protecting against loan defaults.

Part III: Structuring Considerations

Chapter 15

Structuring Efficient Asset-Backed Transactions

Len Blum
Managing Director
Head, Asset-Backed Banking Group
Prudential Securities Inc.

Chris DiAngelo
Partner
Dewey Ballantine

INTRODUCTION

Securitization allows an issuer to dissect the risks and rewards of investing in a pool of receivables. The risks can be allocated to those market participants that are in the best position to understand and absorb them and thus would do so at the lowest cost. The rewards can be allocated to those market participants who will pay the highest price (or will receive the lowest yield) for those rewards. Allocation of risk and reward, however, must be done in a way so that the transaction is acceptable given tax, legal, regulatory and accounting constraints. Furthermore, the structure must make sense within the originator's/issuer's financing plan. Optimally, the securitization should give the originator a form of sustainable, competitive advantage.

The investment banker's first goal is to understand the issuer's objectives. The securitization structure should address the issuer's needs; however, as discussed in this chapter, each of these needs must be analyzed with respect to the current market environment. Some issuer objectives may be absolute, whereas others may represent trade-offs and optimizations. Generally, consideration will be given to the amount of financing desired, the tenor of financing, cost considerations, cash flow requirements, accounting and tax objectives, as well as the originator's ability to retain risk and/or service the assets.

Once the investment banker has assessed the originator's goals and constraints, a deal team is assembled. Securitization teams tend to be fairly large and comprised of members that specialize in various facets of asset-backed finance. Examples of such sub-specialties are law, accounting, investment banking, securities modeling, origination practices, credit underwriting procedures, credit rating, and servicing practices.

The team's initial goal is to dissect the issuer's origination practices, pool of receivables, and servicing procedures. These factors are considered within the framework of the originator's operating position and environment.

Generally, once the deal team has analyzed a pool of receivables (and its servicing) and identified the risks and rewards that reasonably can be allocated out, the team often will bid the risk out to providers of credit enhancement. They also may decide to allocate certain risk to investors (for example, buyers of subordinated securities). The team will structure the securities with an eye towards specific investors who have expressed appetite for securities with characteristics that reasonably can be created from the pool. In many cases, the determination of structures will be based on estimates of what the parties will demand, because the actual marketing of the securities cannot take place until the structure is already set.

Information Flow and Pool Identification

The securitization process often provides feedback to the originator. As risks and rewards are analyzed, the specific costs of asset characteristics are made explicit. For example, if certain receivables are included in a pool, the cost may increase (either through more costly credit enhancement or higher security yields). In certain cases, a finance company, having gone through the securitization process, will make certain changes to its origination and/or servicing practices. In other cases, an originator may retain its origination practices and instead cull securitization pools, while selling or retaining those assets that cannot be securitized efficiently. The deal team often stands in the middle of this process and attempts to identify new risk and reward profiles of the asset pools and market participants as they arise. Not surprisingly, finance company treasurers/secondary marketing executives often have one foot on the loan origination side and the other in the asset-backed market.

Definition of Securitization

A securitization is a transaction in which a company effectively issues securities for which it is generally not corporately liable. The securities are backed by assets. Yet, securitizations can take on a broad variety of attributes that raise unique structuring issues.

COMPARISON TO OTHER FINANCING VEHICLES

Prior to discussing specific structural issues, it may be helpful to compare securitization with other corporate financing vehicles. This will provide a backdrop for many of the issues discussed in this chapter. Also, this will highlight the hybrid nature of securitization; securitization is neither a secured corporate financing nor a sale of assets. Rather, it incorporates certain aspects of both, while utilizing many of the well-accepted and fundamental legal, regulatory, tax, and accounting concepts commonly found in other financial transactions.

Whole-Loan Sales versus Securitizations

One market-driven feature that often distinguishes an asset-backed transaction from a whole-loan sale is that, while asset-backed transactions generally are done on a servicing-retained basis, whole loans usually are sold servicing-released because the purchaser (often itself an originator and servicer of such assets) will want to service the assets. This will, among other things, allow the purchaser to build portfolio scale economies, earn servicing revenue, cross-sell other products, and influence underlying borrower credit dynamics.

A second feature that distinguishes an asset-backed transaction from a whole-loan sale is the retention of credit and prepayment risk. In a whole loan sale, the seller often sells 100% of the credit risk and prepayment risk in the pool, yet it may make representations and warranties in connection with the sale and thus retain certain risks. Like a financing, the originator typically may retain credit risk. Yet, for the reasons described below, it is rare that the securitizing originator would transfer all of this risk; in most instances the issuing company economically retains at least the expected risk of loss on the asset pool, with the risk of certain disaster scenarios resulting in an unanticipated high level of credit losses being allocated either to a third-party credit enhancer, if any, and/or to investors.

A whole-loan sale may result in a premium execution, whereas an asset-backed sale usually does not involve an execution materially in excess of par (although premium execution may be achieved either directly or through the use of interest-only securities, as discussed later in this chapter). One reason that new issue securitizations, in most markets, generally trade at or near par is that premium securities create unique prepayment risk for the investor and typically are not found in the new issue market. Also, the issuer in an asset-backed transaction sometimes will retain a subordinate interest in the principal of the receivables pool or the issuer may make "excess servicing" (the difference between (1) the net pool coupon and (2) the bond coupon and other expenses) available for credit support (thereby precluding at least part of its use for backing the bond premium), or a combination thereof.[1] In other words, it frequently is not possible, for credit reasons, to exceed a par execution. Furthermore, even if it were possible for credit reasons to exceed par, the investor market is frequently not interested in premium execution or may demand a yield premium for such securities.

Securitizations are also distinguished from whole-loan sales by their cash-flow timing. In a securitization, flows from the assets often are reinvested in short-term investments, resulting in a payment lag feature in which investors receive their payments later than the dates on which these payments were received by the servicer. Payments from the loans also may be reinvested in additional loans of a similar type (this often occurs in credit card and trade receivables transactions), thereby causing the securities to have a longer average life than that of the underlying pool. When certain asset pools, such as credit card portfolios, are sold (rather than securitized), both the accounts and the receivables that arise pursuant to such accounts are transferred (whereas a securitization would be backed only by the receivables arising pursuant to the accounts). Furthermore, securitization

---

[1] Sometimes the availability of principal and interest (from a credit perspective) may be enhanced through the use of cash reserves or other features; however, there are economic implications (as discussed later) of such methods.

uses various forms of credit enhancement that protect the investor from losses on the loan pool (although certain forms of credit enhancement also can be found in whole-loan sales) and generally provides the investor with a more liquid holding.

Secured Financing versus Securitizations

Securitizations often are compared to secured financings. From a legal perspective, there is one primary feature that most distinguishes an asset-backed transaction from a receivables-secured financing. In an asset-backed transaction, although typically resulting in the issuance of notes or certificates (collectively referred to herein as "securities"), an issuing company is not *corporately* liable on its asset-backed securities. Investors primarily look only to the asset pool, together with any credit enhancement thereon.

The concept of asset-backed transactions resulting in the issuance of securities for which the issuing company is not itself generally liable is not immediately obvious. A helpful point of entry into the discussion of this peculiar issue is a familiar principle in corporate finance, that of defeased securities — outstanding corporate debt, that, after its issuance, is secured by the establishment of a Treasury escrow that results in the release of the original issuer from general corporate liability.

Defeased Debt versus Securitization

Corporate bond indentures often contain "defeasance" provisions. Such provisions allow a company that previously issued corporate debt to deliver to the bond trustee an escrow account; this account is pledged to repay the debt. The account typically must consist of Treasury bonds. It is structured such that the principal and interest payments on the Treasuries match, as closely as possible, the required principal and interest payments on the debt. A defeasance escrow typically is structured to minimize excess funds that may remain after payment of debt service. If any funds remain, they typically will flow back to the company. Defeasance is used when a company would like to redeem its debt, perhaps to relieve itself from restrictive covenants, but optional redemption is not currently available. A defeasance provision provides that, once the company has pledged the Treasury escrow, it will be released from paying the debt as a matter of corporate liability. Bondholders must thereafter look only to the escrow account to service the debt. Defeased debt, then, is somewhat unusual in that, post-defeasance, it looks like debt of the company, but it is debt for which the issuing company is not liable. Instead, the company's corporate liability has been replaced by the Treasury escrow.

Securitization achieves a similar goal for an issuer; namely, it provides for the issuance of securities by a company for which the company itself is not corporately liable. Instead of funding a Treasury escrow to support a pre-existing liability, a securitization establishes a receivables pool on day one. The company often will never be corporately liable on such debt. However, many of the economic risks may remain; the issuer, or an affiliate thereof, may continue to service the assets and the issuer (or an affiliate thereof) may have made representations and warranties about the loan pool and the transaction.

BANKRUPTCY FIREWALLS AND THE ISSUANCE VEHICLE

For most companies, the mitigation of corporate liability requires the establishment of a separate legal entity. Securitizations generally are structured such that this entity is the legal owner of the assets. As a result, the receivables pool would not legally be part of the company's property in the event of the company's bankruptcy. One exception to this rule is, to some extent, securitization for U.S. banks because federal banking laws are more favorable to creditors of insolvent banks than comparable provisions of the Bankruptcy Code are to creditors of Bankruptcy Code debtors. (Note that finance companies generally are subject to the Bankruptcy Code.) The only other common exceptions to the rule would be insurance companies that are subject neither to the Federal Bankruptcy Code nor to the federal banking laws but rather to state insolvency laws relating to insurance companies, and municipalities, that are subject to special provisions of the Federal Bankruptcy Code.

The type of legal entity that must be constructed to achieve the desired bankruptcy goals varies depending upon the structure of the transaction. The most commonly used legal entity in securitization is the common-law trust. This type of trust is generally referred to as a "business trust." It is quite different from testamentary or estate-planning trusts that individuals frequently establish. In most states, a business trust is an entity that conducts a business activity. Yet, like a corporation, it is a separate entity from its security holders. In this regard, a trust is similar to a corporation or a partnership.

There are several reasons why trusts are favored over corporations and partnerships as issuing vehicles. As a legal matter, a trust will tend to have fewer rules in terms of its establishment than will a corporation or a partnership. A corporation invariably requires articles, bylaws, officers, and directors. It also is required to issue at least one class of common equity. Similarly, a partnership requires partners, including at least one general partner, and a partnership agreement. Both corporations and partnerships generally are required to file certificates with the state in which they are formed. Although certain states, such as Delaware, have statutory provisions that allow the establishment of a statutory business trust that is more corporation-like than a common-law trust, in most cases this is not done unless some particular goal is sought. The common-law trust that generally is used does not require any particular formalities, except a declaration that a trust is being created.

The types of securities that a common-law trust can issue include various classes of debt and equity and generally are limited only by the imagination. The trust, being a separate legal entity, can also enter into other agreements, such as servicing agreements and indentures. Equity securities issued by a trust generally are structured as participation interests.

In a nutshell, the common-law trust is the most flexible issuing entity. There are fewer rules governing its establishment and operation. There is a lack of restrictions on the types of securities that a trust can issue. Furthermore, trusts can be used to achieve accounting sale treatment of the receivables pool (assuming other tests are met) by providing an easy vehicle for the issuance of participation interests. Yet, there may be, and frequently are, substantial federal income tax concerns, that, as a practical matter, limit the types of securities that a trust can issue.

Except for the federal income tax considerations discussed later, a trust generally is treated as a "pass-through entity." On the one hand, it is a separate legal entity for state and corporate law purposes; it can enter into contracts, issue securities and conduct ancillary activities. However, it is not an entity for federal and most state income tax purposes. Rather, it generally is a consolidated entity for tax purposes that will be consolidated into whatever entity owns the majority of the equity in the trust.

The establishment of a trust, however, is often not enough. Typically, in a securitization transaction, a *special purpose financing vehicle* (SPV) also is formed. An SPV is generally a corporation established (for bankruptcy purposes) as a separate legal entity from the seller/servicer. This is necessary because the seller/servicer usually ends up retaining at least the expected risk on the portfolio. This risk may be embedded in subordinate securities, subordinated excess servicing, or cash reserves. If the issuer itself were to hold this retained subordination, a bankruptcy risk may exist that, in the event of a bankruptcy of the originator/seller/servicer (that is holding the retained subordination), a bankruptcy court could recharacterize the entire transaction as an issuance of secured debt of the originator/seller/servicer. This could leave the senior security holders with only a security interest rather than an ownership interest in the receivables pool. At the very least, this would create timing problems by subjecting the security holders to the risk of an automatic stay (commonly referred to as "stay risk").

Apart from stay risk, the bankruptcy law provides that secured creditors are entitled only to "adequate protection" rather than the exact protection that they may have thought they received at closing. Although specific outcomes are not fully known, the presumed risk is that the bankruptcy court could redirect cash flows or collateral to the detriment of the senior security holders, or force a sale of the collateral to repay the senior security holders and generate immediate cash for the bankruptcy estate. Having the subordinate interests that are issued by the trust held by an SPV mitigates these risks.[2]

A legal opinion generally is given in connection with the securitization transaction to the effect that, in the event of a bankruptcy of the seller/servicer, counsel issuing the opinion believes that the SPV and the seller/servicer's estates would not be consolidated as a single entity for bankruptcy purposes. The SPV, although often set up as an affiliate of the seller/servicer, is established pursuant to a formula that ensures its separateness in a bankruptcy. In other words, it should be treated as a third-party entity vis-à-vis the seller/servicer, even though it may be a wholly-owned subsidiary.

In a typical SPV structure, the seller/servicer legally will sell the assets to the SPV. The SPV, in turn, will sell the assets to the trust. The trust then issues participation interests in the asset pool to investors, with the subordinate interest being retained by the SPV. For both generally accepted accounting principles (GAAP) and federal tax considerations, the sale from the originator to the SPV is meaningless because the SPV will be consolidated as part of the parent company's accounting and tax financial statements.

The sale by the SPV to the trust, in and of itself, does not trigger an event for GAAP or tax reporting. However, the sale of the participation interests to investors (i.e., a sale outside of the affiliated group of originator-SPV-trust) may effect a GAAP and tax event (that may or may not receive parallel treatment depending on the transaction's structure). This is contrasted with the bankruptcy analysis, in that the sale from the company to the SPV is treated as a sale for Federal Bankruptcy Law purposes. One result of using the SPV structure is the isolation of the asset pool from the reach of the originator's general creditors or other secured creditors by transferring the pool, as a legal matter, to the SPV. The sale from the SPV to the trust, although potentially also resulting in a sale for bankruptcy purposes, may be less important to the bankruptcy analysis, where the key goal is to remove the asset pool from the legal property of the company.

Not all asset-backed transactions use trusts. The most frequent alternative to the establishment of a trust is simply the issuance of debt from an SPV. This technique typically is used when the issuer does not want or need to achieve GAAP sale treatment. GAAP financing treatment also could be achieved using a trust; however, if such treatment is unnecessary or undesirable and debt is the goal, the trust structure is likely unnecessary.

---

[2] Yet even very conservative parties generally will allow at least some level of subordination to be held directly by the issuing seller servicer.

Securitizations should not only be "bankruptcy remote," but also be "bankruptcy proof." As discussed, bankruptcy remoteness is achieved in two principal ways. First, the assets are legally sold to the SPV. Second, the SPV is established and operated in a manner that ensures it could not be consolidated with the company in the event of the company's bankruptcy. However, additional protection is usually required as well. The SPV should be constructed so that it cannot engage in activities that would expose it to undue risk on its own (as distinguished from risks arising through consolidation). Among other things, an SPV generally is restricted from incurring recourse debt and engaging in an operating business (such as originating or servicing loans).

In summary, the principal elements on the bankruptcy checklist are as follows:

- Has a sale of the assets occurred to legally remove them as property of the company and make them property of the SPV?
- Could the SPV be consolidated with the company in the event of the company's bankruptcy?
- Is the SPV constructed so as to mitigate the risk that it could go into its own bankruptcy?

One final bankruptcy issue relates to the bankruptcy opinion (often called a "true sale" opinion) that is given by legal counsel in an asset-backed transaction. Bankruptcy courts refer to themselves as "courts of equity" rather than "courts of law." This means that the courts have significant discretion to use their judgement within the guidelines of the Federal Bankruptcy Laws. As a result, structuring bankruptcy-proof transactions is more of an art than a science. The opinions that are given by even the most competent counsel tend to be "reasoned" opinions. They reflect both sides of the argument and often only give their conclusions in a tenuous manner.

Some people incorrectly believe that the true sale opinion is the last word on the issue and that the opinion itself makes the transaction isolated from a bankruptcy point of view. This is not true. Legal opinions from a private law firm, unlike court opinions rendered by a judge, do not conclusively establish a result. Opinions, however, do let the rest of the deal team know that a presumably competent lawyer has studied the bankruptcy implications of the transaction and has concluded that, on balance, the transaction should achieve the desired bankruptcy result. The opinion also transfers some liability to the law firm (and its insurance carrier) to the extent that the opinion is wrong. As a practical matter, however, given the reasoned nature of most of these opinions, the chances of liability are slim.

UNDERLYING CONSIDERATIONS OF FINANCING VERSUS SALE FOR GAAP AND TAX

An asset-backed transaction can be structured, within certain limits, for GAAP and tax reporting, either as a financing or as a sale. What many issuers want to accomplish when they first hear about asset-backed finance is to try to achieve the best of both worlds, namely, an accounting sale and a tax financing.

An accounting sale transforms the receivables into cash without creating a related liability (basically, cash is debited and receivables are credited). Depending on the use of proceeds, such a transaction can enhance leverage ratios and improve capital velocity. Conversely, if the transaction is structured as a GAAP financing, the assets remain on the balance sheet, the cash account is debited, and a corresponding liability is credited. (The characteristics of accounting sales and financings are covered in greater detail in Chapter 25.) For "above-water" assets (generally those assets with coupons approximately at current market rates) that have relatively long average lives (e.g., mortgages), GAAP sale treatment can trigger a material gain (as a percentage of the pool), that can enhance earnings in the period of sale.

Tax sales and financings often result in the same expected aggregate tax liability over the life of the transaction. However, a sale can trigger a taxable gain at the time of the transaction, thereby accelerating taxes that otherwise would be due during the asset's life. Due to cash flow and time value of money considerations, most originators would rather defer this tax liability over the life of the pool.

Although sometimes a worthwhile goal, as a practical matter, financing-for-tax treatment is often inefficient for several asset classes (for example, home-equity and manufactured-housing loans). The inefficiencies required to accomplish this treatment frequently outweigh the benefits from having the result. (As discussed below, however, such treatment is readily available for certain asset classes, such as credit card accounts and trade receivables). In many instances, the most economically efficient structure would result in a sale transaction for tax purposes. To demonstrate this, it is useful to provide an overview of one of the most basic, as well as one of the most difficult concepts, in the general area of tax law: the difference between debt and equity.

Tax Debt and Equity

For tax purposes, securities are naturally equity in form. If a company issues only a single class of securities, those securities would be treated as an ownership interest (equity); the security holders would be entitled to receive all the revenues generated by the entity after the payment of expenses. To distinguish debt from equity, the purported debt needs to be given some characteristics and/or form to distinguish it from the equity. This is normally not a problem with an operating company. An operating company's debt, in addition to its contractual payment requirements, typically has a precise form, for example, a set interest rate, a payment frequency, a maturity date, and other characteristics that are taken for granted when an operating company issues debt. Its contractual payment is not directly correlated to the cash flows from the company's operations.

The issue becomes more complex, however, in a securitization because the issuing entity is not an operating company; instead, it only holds financial assets in the form of a receivables pool. The receivables in a pool are typically themselves debt instruments. They typically pay monthly pursuant to their debt-service schedules. Asset-backed securities also are often monthly pay. Because of this high correlation between debt service and revenues, it is often difficult to conclude that any securities issued in such an arrangement, whether styled as debt or as equity, are anything other than equity, especially when they account for a vast majority of a trust's revenues. This is different from the operating company, where revenues are not based on a schedule. Corporate debt, furthermore, is not typically monthly pay, but may rather be semi-annual pay, yet the company may receive revenues on a daily basis. Therefore, it is unlikely that corporate debt would be seen as constituting an ownership interest in the revenues of an operating company, at least in part, because the debt service requirements on the corporate debt are so clearly distinct from the revenues of the company.

In the United States, as distinguished from certain European countries, the economic substance of a transaction, rather than its form, governs (or at least greatly influences) the tax characterization. In other words, the form of a security does not dictate its classification. For example, if a company were to (1) transfer $100 million dollars in receivables that bear interest at 8% to a trust, (2) issue notes with a face amount of $100 million dollars that bear interest at 7.9%, and (3) construct the debt service schedule on the notes such that principal was payable on the notes only when the trust itself received principal payments on the underlying receivables, it would be difficult to conclude that the company had done anything other than sell a receivables pool. The "debt" that purports to be "secured" by the pool looks just like the pool itself. Characterizing this transaction as an issuance of debt typically would not fly as a matter of tax law.[3]

Of course, form may help in the determination of whether a security is debt or equity. To make a security "look like debt," it is helpful to

---

[3] In contrast, the form of a transaction can dictate (or influence) its treatment under GAAP. Under SFAS 77 and under SFAS 125, effective after December 31, 1996, for a transfer of receivables to be treated as a sale, it must purport to be one. This would preclude sale treatment for asset-backed transactions that issue securities in the form of "notes" or "bonds."

call it debt (for example, to refer to the security as "notes" or "bonds" rather than "certificates").

For tax purposes, besides simply calling securities debt, it is usually necessary to distinguish the debt from some equity component of the issuing entity. When a trust issues debt it will typically issue some other type of security as a residual interest that may be represented by certificates. Also, as a general matter, the less debt that a company is trying to raise against a given pool of collateral, the easier it is to conclude that the securities will be treated as debt. In general, if the originator retains a larger interest, it is easier to conclude that the assets have not been sold for tax purposes because the risk of ownership of the assets remains with the issuer.

Securities look more like debt when an issuer "breaks the chain" between its revenues and its debt service. In the true corporate context, this is usually the case when an issuer's revenues are not tied to any fixed schedule, but its debt is. In asset-backed transactions, the revenues are tied to a fixed schedule. Unless the debt is consciously disengaged from this schedule, it may resemble equity.

Often, to create tax debt, payment features are altered. For example, the interest rate on the debt (for example, fixed rate) can be set independent of the interest rate on the receivables pool (for example, floating rate), the payment frequency of the debt (for example, semiannual pay or quarterly pay) can differ from that of the receivables pool (for example, monthly pay), or the debt can have a maturity date that does not correspond with that of the receivables. Yet such measures often are economically inefficient. For example, disengaging the interest rates of the receivables and the debt not only introduces risk to the residual holder, but also may introduce negative marketing characteristics. For example, if fixed-rate receivables were to back an available-funds floater, investors may be concerned with the cap if the weighted-average coupon of the pool was too low (obviously, this also may create credit enhancement implications). Creating quarterly or semiannual-pay securities from monthly-pay assets creates reinvestment risk during the period between receipt on the assets and payment on the securities. Also, these funds generally must be invested in low-yield, short-term instruments. Mismatching maturity dates may create the need for costly maturity guarantees or reinvestment accounts.

Credit Card Securitizations

As mentioned, certain types of collateral lend themselves more easily to the creation of debt. Revolving accounts (for example, credit card accounts and commercial trade receivables accounts) are prime examples. Since the medium-term asset-backed debt is closed-end (i.e., not revolving), but is backed by short-term receivables arising pursuant to accounts, there is a significant mismatch between the underlying receivables (at any point in time) and the outstanding debt. Given the fact that in a credit card securitization the receivables pool itself fluctuates up and down, and revolves, credit card deals typically are treated as the issuance of debt by the credit card issuer for tax purposes. For GAAP accounting purposes, however, these transfers of assets are treated as sales if they meet the requirements of SFAS77 or SFAS 125 after December 31, 1996. Because they are issued in certificate form, they purport to be sales. Other than for estimable credit losses, there is no recourse to the issuer (for example, the issuer does not guarantee the market value of the pool). Call options generally are de minimus (5% to 10%) and investors cannot "put" the receivables back to the issuer (this "no-put" requirement will be eliminated under SFAS 125).

Mortgage Securitization

It is difficult to achieve tax debt treatment for closed-end mortgages for a number of reasons. First, unlike credit card accounts, mortgages do not revolve and are long-term. Second, because of their high credit quality, most mortgages may be monetized at or near par. As noted above, the higher the advance rate, the more difficult it is to conclude that the issuer has issued debt backed by the pool. Also, "chain-breaking" features tend to introduce economic inefficiencies. For example, a company could issue semi-annual- or quarterly-pay securities backed by a pool of monthly-pay mortgage loans; however, this would potentially expose the issuing company to negative arbitrage. The reinvestment rate on the monthly receipts may not cover the interest rate on the asset-backed debt since the monthly receipts would generally be reinvested in "cash-equivalent" investments. A company may issue floating-rate securities backed by fixed-rate mortgages (or vice versa); however, this introduces interest-rate risk and available funds concerns. Of course, a company may issue securities for materially less than the par amount of the mortgages; however, for most issuers, this would not be desirable.

In addition, for mortgages there are a series of interlocking federal tax requirements, primarily the real estate mortgage investment conduit (REMIC) rules and the taxable mortgage pool (TMP) rules. The REMIC rules were created by the Tax Reform Act of 1986. These rules provide that a REMIC can issue multiple classes of "regular interests" (similar to debt), but only one "residual interest" (similar to equity). They essentially create a safe harbor for mortgage-backed securities by alleviating the risk of double taxation, since REMICs are not taxed at the entity level. The residual holder generally is taxed in a similar manner to a partner in a partnership.

Largely due to REMIC, the asset-backed community has devised multi-class, mortgage-backed structures that are almost 100% efficient. A study of non-conforming mortgage deals (i.e., deals not involving Fannie Mae, Freddie Mac, or Ginnie Mae) from 1990 to 1995 shows an evolution beginning with retained subordination transactions, in which the issuing company received less than a 100% advance rate, and often had payment mismatches. Transactions then evolved to "spread account deals" that involved setting up a reserve account and funding it from excess servicing. From there, the current and widely accepted Prudential Accelerated Credit Enhancement (PACE) structure evolved, in which excess servicing is used to accelerate the amortization of the asset-backed securities relative to the amortization of the underlying mortgage loans.[4] As a result, this creates a subordinate security (that may be a residual) over time. Spread account and PACE structures often give the issuer an advance rate of par or near par at the time of issuance.

The REMIC rules are flexible and appreciated by the asset-backed community. Yet, the REMIC rules also require that the issuing company treat the transaction as a tax sale. For GAAP purposes, depending on the specifics of a transaction, a REMIC can be treated as either a sale or a financing.[5] The taxable mortgage pool rules further complicate the issue by providing that any multi-class transaction that can be done as a REMIC, namely, just about any multi-class transaction involving mortgage loans, must be done as a REMIC (except pro-rata pay classes that may differ in payment priority). This means that it is difficult to do an asset-backed transaction with a pool of mortgage loans other than as a transaction that achieves a tax sale. One of the sinister beauties of the interlocking federal tax statutes regarding the issuance of mortgage-backed securities is that even a REMIC transaction that is styled as debt is unlikely to achieve debt treatment for federal income tax purposes for the issuer.

Although most REMICs are accounted for as GAAP sales, it is not difficult to achieve non-parallel, GAAP-financing treatment. This can be done, for example, by introducing put or call options under SFAS 77. A structure that is sometimes used in higher interest-rate environments is the "underwater" REMIC. In such a transaction, assets worth less than their amortized tax basis are securitized, thereby triggering a tax loss. Yet the introduction of a material put or call agreement under SFAS 77 ensures that an accounting loss will not be accelerated because for GAAP purposes, the assets have not been sold.

---

[4] Two of the advantages of the overcollateralization structure are: (1) the elimination of the negative arbitrage that results from the cash reserve account; and (2) the shortening of the weighted-average life of the asset-backed securities, thereby bringing them "down the yield curve" and creating a lower cost of funding in an ascending yield curve environment.

[5] This fact should not be confused with the further fact that REMIC also provides that "regular interests" issued by the REMIC will be treated as debt in the hands of the security holders as a matter of the REMIC law. This aspect of the REMIC treatment is also non-parallel treatment, but deals with looking at a REMIC transaction from both the issuing company's point of view (sale) and from the security holder's point of view (debt).

Currently proposed legislation generally would extend REMIC benefits to other asset classes such as auto loans and credit card receivables. This legislation would create a new tax vehicle, the financial asset securitization investment trust (FASIT), which, although under a separate statutory authorization from REMIC, would generally work similarly to REMIC. Although Congress appears receptive to the adoption of the FASIT legislation, it has yet to be passed.

Since non-conforming mortgage deals are thus currently structured as REMICs to achieve almost 100% efficiency, any non-REMIC, debt-for-tax, sale-for-GAAP structure would have to be overpoweringly useful in its tax-deferral achievements to beat this almost perfect economic efficiency. Any "chain-breaking" necessary to achieve debt-for-tax treatment potentially would introduce substantial economic inefficiencies and make the transaction impractical, absent other compelling objectives, such as a need to maximize after-tax proceeds in the short term, even though the long-term cost implications would be suboptimal.

Other Asset Securitization

Between trade receivables and credit cards, on one side of the spectrum, and mortgage loans, on the other, fall many other asset classes, such as auto loans and equipment leases. Although these asset types generally do not revolve as credit card accounts do, they typically do not lend themselves to the extreme efficiency that residential mortgages do. For example, for credit and other reasons, it is usually not possible to achieve a a par or near par advance rate. Since the advance rate is lower for these asset classes, fewer efficiencies need to be created to construct a debt-for-tax, sale-for-GAAP structure.

Although auto loans themselves do not revolve, one can make the pool artificially revolve by adding receivables over time to the initial pool. The practice has thus developed to achieve non-parallel treatment in the form of debt-for-tax, sale-for-GAAP with auto loans and similar types of assets to have a revolving structure such that, for a certain period, principal amortization on the asset pool, instead of being paid through as a payment in principal to the security holders, is used to purchase more assets, thus making the securities "interest-only" during the revolving period (an obvious break in the chain from the underlying receivables that themselves amortize every month). This revolving feature, together with a less-than-100% advance rate and a few other miscellaneous bells and whistles, has been known to achieve debt-for-tax, sale-for-GAAP treatment.

In summary, it is possible to achieve sale-for-GAAP/financing-for-tax treatment for any type of asset pool. The issue rather is the trade off between the benefits of the tax deferral on the one hand versus the cost of adding debt-like features on the other. Transactions have become more economically efficient (aside from tax considerations) and credit-related efficiencies have made transactions more difficult to do as tax financings. Furthermore, not all of the costs of adopting a debt-for-tax structure may be known at the time of the transaction. For example, the cost of a semi-annual pay structure on the securities to "break the chain" from a monthly-pay receivables pool will be largely driven by reinvestment rates during the transaction. Consequently, debt-for-tax, sale-for-GAAP remains, at least outside of credit card, trade receivables, and certain other transactions, an increasingly elusive goal.

EFFICIENT ALLOCATION OF RISK — CREDIT RISK

The market for asset-backed securities is in large part a "triple A" market. In other words, asset-backed securities generally are rated in the highest rating category by at least one (and often two, but sometimes more) of the nationally recognized statistical rating agencies (Moody's, Standard & Poor's, Fitch Investors Service, and Duff & Phelps). Note, however, that asset-backed securities also are issued at the AA, A, or BBB levels and, once in a while, even in noninvestment grade or unrated designations. To enable a pool of receivables to back high-grade, fixed-income securities generally requires credit enhancement.

External Enhancement

There are two major types of credit enhancement: external and internal. External enhancement can take the form of an insurance policy issued by a financial guarantee insurance company, a letter of credit issued by a bank, a corporate guarantee, or a reserve account funded by a third party. These credit enhancements rely on a party other than the asset pool itself to provide protection to security holders.

The simplest form of external credit enhancement is an insurance policy that covers 100% of the principal and interest on the asset-backed securities (other forms of credit enhancement often cover less than 100%). This type of insurance is issued by monoline insurance companies, which themselves have a AAA-rated claims-paying ability.

Internal Enhancement

Internal credit enhancement takes a variety of forms, although the most prevalent are senior/subordinated ("overcollateralization") structures, internally funded reserve accounts, and PACE structures. In a relatively simple senior/subordinated structure, the advance rate of issuance of the receivables pool, for example, is 90%. The 10% subordinated interest could be retained by an SPV affiliate of the company. Losses, in effect, would be charged against the subordinate security before the senior security holders would begin to suffer losses.[6] Note that more than one level of subordination can be utilized in a single transaction. For example, a transaction can be structured where the most subordinated interest (which may be a reserve fund or a subordinated interest) is retained by an SPV and mezzanine tranches are sold to investors. In a reserve account structure, the excess servicing funds an account pursuant to a formula. Available monies from the reserve account are used to cover losses as they occur during the life of the transaction.

Time tranching, which is discussed in more detail below, can be an important tool in structuring subordinated securities. Subordinated securities can be either structured as *pro-rata* or *sequential pay*. (Such tranching has important tax implications.) In a typical pro-rata pay structure consisting of one senior and one subordinate security, both securities will receive principal during the life of the transaction. Assuming no losses are allocated to the subordinate security, the level of subordination (the percentage interest that the subordinated security bears to the pool as a whole) will remain constant. In a sequential-pay structure, the subordinate security may only receive principal once the senior security has been paid in full.[7] In such a transaction, the level of subordination increases over time, which may allow for a lower level of initial subordination and/or may make the senior securities more marketable (of course, with a potential corresponding decrease in the marketability of the subordinated interest). Additionally, senior security holders may find such a structure more desirable if losses on the pool are expected to be relatively back-loaded. Consideration should be given to static loss curves when engineering such structures.

Combining External and Internal Enhancement

Even transactions that have external credit support such as an insurance policy will also have internal enhancement. This is most obvious again in the case of monoline insurance, where the monoline insurers typically will not insure the senior security unless the senior security is rated at an investment-grade level independent of the insurance policy. Although monolines have the power to insure transactions that have an internal rating of less than BBB, their economics of doing so diminish rapidly because, at least in part, the insurers themselves are subject to regulation in the form of the analysis of their capital adequacy by the rating agencies.

---

[6] Yet, if losses (and/or anticipated losses) are higher than originally anticipated (even when the senior interest is not being allocated such losses), the market value and/or the credit rating of such securities may deteriorate due to the reduced level of actual and/or expected protection afforded by the subordinate interest.

[7] Other variations are possible. For example, the subordinate security could receive principal once certain targets or formulas are met.

Sometimes mezzanine and senior classes within the same transaction are both afforded the enhancement of an insurance policy. This is often referred to as a "super-senior" structure. In such a transaction, the pool typically would be enhanced to at least a BBB level. This could be achieved through the use of a reserve account, a retained subordinated interest, PACE structuring, or some other method. The resulting investment-grade interest is then further credit tranched, with a mezzanine interest that enhances the senior interest to, say, a AA or AAA level. Both the mezzanine interest and the senior interest are then guaranteed by a monoline. The resulting mezzanine and senior bonds would both achieve AAA ratings. The mezzanine bond would achieve this level because of the guarantee, but the senior bond would enjoy this level of support from both the enhancement afforded by the subordinated and mezzanine classes, as well as the guarantee. This structure has sometimes been used when investors in the senior securities require "belt and suspenders" enhancement or are concerned about saturation in their portfolio (or the market in general) for a particular monoline's credit.

Providers of external credit enhancement generally do not expect to themselves suffer any losses as a result of the performance of the receivables pool. This distinguishes, for example, a monoline insurer from a company that sells life insurance. The life insurer expects to have claims under its policies while the monoline would be surprised if a loss was charged against one of its transactions.

Conceptually, the monolines provide catastrophic risk coverage. In addition, they perform their own due diligence prior to closing and conduct an important surveillance function during the life of the transaction. They also may be more likely than a trustee (or other transaction participants) to step in and take action if there are material servicing problems. They also potentially make investor credit risk easier to analyze, which can add value particularly to a transaction involving a new issuer and/or new asset class.

Credit Enhancement Decisions

Credit enhancement decisions generally are made based on relative costs. The investment banker will typically consider various forms of credit enhancement and present them to the issuer. Generally, there are two major considerations: allocations to third parties and retained risk by the originator.

If the banker has an understanding of the costs of assuming risk by various parties, the decision of how to allocate third-party risk is fairly straightforward. In a very simple example, once a pool is internally enhanced to the BBB level, either BBB securities could be sold or a monoline could guarantee the securities to a AAA level. The decision between these two alternatives will be based, along with other qualitative and economic factors, on the spread differential between wrapped, AAA, senior securities and unwrapped, senior BBB securities on the one hand, and the premiums charged by monolines on the other.

These alternatives also could be compared to a mezzanine structure, where the risk could be further tranched into multiple securities, for example, AA, A, and BBB bonds. In such a structure, however, one must also consider deal size (a small pool would only allow creation of small tranches, which may trade poorly due to liquidity or "hassle factor" considerations) and loss severity (a credit loss to a smaller security will have a relatively larger impact). When analyzing such a structure, however, the banker must consider the effect of the structure on all of the sold bonds. For example, if mezzanine subordination is used versus a surety wrap, investors may view the risks of the AAA senior bonds differently. On the one hand, they neither would carry surety event risk (the risk of a negative credit deterioration of the surety) nor expose the investor to saturation of any given insurer. Yet they would have a lower percentage of enhancement and may have less ongoing surveillance, as well as be more difficult to analyze.

Qualitative issues also should be considered. For example, non-investment grade or unrated servicers potentially could not be used in a senior/subordinated structure when highly rated securities are to be issued (unless, of course, a creditworthy master servicer was retained or other transactional features, such as triggers — which are often found in credit card deals — are used). Also, some third-party insurers may have sufficient familiarity with the issuer or asset class to facilitate the credit analysis process. Due to competition or service quality considerations, some parties also may offer quicker turn-around and greater flexibility.

The amount of risk retained by the originator is often, at least in part, dictated by its cost and availability of capital. As a general rule, as the issuer's capital cost increases (or availability decreases), the more desirable it is for the issuer to sell a larger percentage of the pool. For example, an originator could either retain a large subordinate security and sell AAA bonds or retain a small subordinate security and sell BBB bonds. In the first instance, the issuer's savings on the sold securities (based on the fact that the issuer is retaining more risk and passing along less risk to investors) potentially could be outweighed by the cost of carrying the larger subordinate interest.

Furthermore, retaining the larger subordinate interest may negatively impact the issuer's ability to grow (by decreasing the velocity of its capital), accounting ratios (by decreasing liquidity and reducing funds that potentially could be used to reduce leverage) and earnings in the period of sale (by selling less of the asset and thereby recognizing less of a gain in such period). Conversely, the issuer may be in the best position to understand the risks of the assets and control or at least influence them through proper servicing. In this case, even for a capital-constrained entity, it may be preferable for the issuer to retain larger amounts of risk. In some cases, such as the securitization of risky, servicing-intensive assets, investors take additional comfort when the issuer has retained significant credit risk and "servicing upside."

Determining Credit Enhancement Levels

Credit enhancement levels for asset-backed securities are typically based on two primary factors. The first factor is the asset pool itself — the creditworthiness of the borrowers on the underlying receivables, the diversity of the pool, and to what extent the receivables themselves are secured. The second factor is servicing.

As may be expected, when the credit quality of the underlying asset pool is low, servicing practices are more important. A portfolio of weaker receivables would presumably require more work to extract a given level of payments than would a higher quality pool. In one extreme example, a Treasury bond portfolio requires no servicing other than maintaining a filing cabinet in which to keep payment records. Contrast this to many of the so called "sub-prime" markets in which lenders make loans to borrowers who would be unable to obtain credit from more traditional sources. Such loans often are serviced in a more rigorous fashion.

Enhancement requirements often are set at high multiples of historic performance. To ensure high credit quality of structured securities, which is reflected by high credit ratings, transactions are structured to withstand extreme stress-case scenarios. Also, enhancement levels reflect servicing risk and the risk that servicing could deteriorate during the life of the transaction. Also note that as a particular asset type becomes more familiar to market participants, credit enhancement requirements tend to decline. Still, there often are things that a transaction team can do to reduce required enhancement. A detailed discussion of these is beyond the scope of this chapter; however, some of the more common concepts are as follows:

- The deal team should ensure that the risks of the pool are adequately understood by enhancers, investors and the rating agencies. This should include static and dynamic pool analysis gathered over a significant period, and an analysis of underwriting, servicing, and collection practices. All risks should be adequately disclosed. Not only is this an essential general practice, but also it may enhance marketability. As a general rule, astute investors prefer to assume the risks they comprehend rather than to assume potentially lower risks that they do not clearly understand.
- The originator should analyze how its origination and servicing practices affect its securitization program. In certain circumstances, it may pay for the servicer to upgrade its operations and/or

tighten its underwriting criteria. Sometimes, transaction participants, such as a credit enhancer, will require that a master servicer
be retained. Also, profitable high risk loans potentially can be
culled from the pool and retained or sold in the whole-loan market.

- Structural triggers should be analyzed. These triggers are commonly found in revolving structures. Triggers can require the build
up of additional enhancement or the early amortization of securities in the event of a credit deterioration. Generally, the tighter the
triggers, the lower the required credit enhancement. Yet tight triggers present greater cash flow, interest-rate, and availability risk to
the issuer.

- Allocating specific risks to third parties should be considered. For
example, residual value insurance can increase advance rates in
operating lease transactions.

- Cross collateralization among transactions or among specific pools
within a transaction should be considered. Sometimes, third parties will reduce required credit enhancement if subordinate instruments from a series of transactions are allowed to be cross
collateralized. Yet this can decrease the issuer's flexibility in later
financing or selling such subordinated interests.

TARGETING SPECIFIC INVESTORS

Besides the risk of credit loss, pools of receivables may contain prepayment
risk or have average lives, principal windows and maturities that are relatively less attractive to investors. Time and prepayment tranching can be
used to address these concerns and optimize execution.

Investment bankers constantly monitor the secondary market. From
day to day, they are aware of specific investor preferences. When relatively
strong investor demand exists in a particular sector (or weak demand exists
in another), they can use that information to structure a transaction targeted
to the preferences of the market.

Time Tranching

Tranching often involves the issuance of several series of securities against a
single pool of receivables in a sequential-pay structure. Generally, all of the
series receive interest during their lives (although this does not have to be
the case); however, the first series receives all of the principal from the
underlying pool until it is paid in full, after which the second series begins
to receive principal. This process is repeated with subsequent classes until
all of the securities are retired. In this way, a pool of receivables can be
carved into a number of securities that may feed the appetites of particular
investors or classes of investors.

As a mechanical matter, the expected characteristics of a particular time-tranched security generally will depend on the underlying pool and the principal balance of the security itself, as well as the principal balances of the other securities issued. To illustrate, imagine a pool of receivables backing two time-tranched (fast-pay/slow-pay structure) securities. As the principal balance of the fast-pay security is increased, its expected maturity, expected average life and expected principal window also will increase. At the same time, the maturity of the slow-pay security will remain unchanged (its final payment will not be affected), yet its expected average life will increase (because its earlier cash flows have been allocated to the fast-pay security), and its expected principal window will shorten (because it will receive principal over a shorter period of time). This concept can be applied to a larger number of tranches with more complex, yet similar, results.

In some market environments, the more time-tranched securities that can be created (up to a limit, of course), the lower the issuer's all-in cost will be. This may allow the issuer to target specific investor demands, take advantage of the shape and slope of the yield curve and shorten principal windows. Please note that certain asset types lend themselves more to tranching than do others. Also, the creation of a large number of tranches often requires a large asset pool because a small asset pool may result in very small tranched securities, which generally would be illiquid and demand a yield premium. Appropriate time tranching also allows for the reduction of specific tranche sizes, thereby alleviating concerns of sector saturation.

Time tranching also allows pricing of specific securities at premiums and discounts. For example, in a given transaction and market environment, buyers of longer tranches may demand pricing at a discount from par (hence a lower coupon), whereas buyers of shorter tranches may accept premium pricing (hence a higher coupon).

Coupon and Volatility Tranching

More elaborate tranching mechanics besides the relatively simple "sequential pay" structure also have been devised; however, they have been slower to catch on in the asset-backed markets than in the mortgage-backed markets. Perhaps this is partially because asset-backed collateral presents less prepayment risk; therefore, there is less need to allocate this risk to various classes of investors. One fairly common tranche in auto and home-equity transactions, however, is the interest-only security. Interest-only structuring often is especially appropriate with payment-stable assets, such as autos, where the perceived risk of purchasing such a potentially volatile security is lower.

Interest-only securities can increase net proceeds to the issuer and can be created when the coupon rate on the receivables pool is high relative to the sum of the market-driven coupon on the securities, ongoing transaction expenses, and the amount of excess servicing required for credit enhancement. Of course, another way to increase net proceeds is to issue premium securities with high coupons. Premium securities can possess additional prepayment risk relative to par securities and may be less desirable to investors, which may cause the spread on those securities to widen. Instead, this cash flow can be allocated to an interest-only security. Although the spread to Treasuries on the interest-only security may be relatively wide, this spread only will apply to a very small security; conversely, a wider spread on the entire transaction would apply to a larger amount of cash flow, potentially creating a higher all-in financing cost.

Interest-only securities can be issued as strips (that may carry a high degree of the prepayment risk of the underlying collateral) or as planned-amortization-class (PAC) securities (that contain less prepayment risk). PAC securities generally are structured to pay according to a pre-specified schedule as long as underlying prepayments remain constant and within a pre-specified band.

In its PAC form, the interest-only security generally is sized such that, as long as prepayments remain below the upper level of the band, investors will not be exposed to yield reduction (interest is not paid on prepaid assets in the pool). Depending on the transaction's structure, investors, however, may have an upside if prepayments go below the lower band. The planned-amortization security is senior in prepayment priority to a companion security (which may be the residual interest in the pool and is backed, at least partially, by excess spread from the underlying assets). In general, the higher (lower) the upper band, the lower (higher) the proceeds, but the lower (higher) the yield and spread to comparable Treasuries. By establishing the upper band at a higher level, investors are protected against fast pool prepayments. As a general matter and depending on transaction specifics, as the lower band goes down, investors may require a higher yield. This is because their chance of "upside" from additional cash flow resulting from slow prepayments may be diminished.

EMBEDDED OPTIONS AND FLOATING-RATE MISMATCH

Underlying assets can be based on different indices than the securities that they support. Fixed-rate assets can back floating-rate securities (or visa versa). Adjustable-rate assets (assets that float according to an index, but may be limited by periodic or lifetime caps and floors, as well as teased initial rates) can back floating-rate securities (which, of course, may also be subject to specific caps and/or floors). Assets that float based on one index (for example, the prime rate) can back securities that float based on another (for example, LIBOR). Such structures often are created to address specific investor demands or allocate risk to particular parties. Several issues, however, must be considered when structuring such securities:

- Tax implications are important. Competent tax counsel should carefully examine the structure. Mismatches generally will work in debt-for-tax or REMIC structures. The anticipated adoption of FASIT legislation also should facilitate such issuance.
- Credit enhancement considerations are paramount. If excess servicing is compromised due to market movements, less cash flow may be available to credit enhance the securities.
- The risk in such "mismatch" transactions often is largely allocated to the issuer's retained interest. The issuer should carefully analyze this risk.
- Options and/or swaps can be used to hedge or mitigate mismatch risk. The cash flow of these derivative instruments can be allocated to investors or, conversely, an issuer may wish to retain them "outside of the transaction" to manage its own risk.

Often, an "available-funds cap" is placed on the securities. In such a case, the rate paid to security holders never can exceed a certain rate, generally based on the rate that the underlying assets pay minus ongoing expenses and any "cushion" that may be required by credit enhancers. When an available-funds cap is used, the investor is generally short an interest-rate option(s). In certain markets, due to inefficiencies in pricing risk, the present value of the implied yield premium demanded by investors for this short position exceeds the price at which such an option can be purchased from a third party. In these scenarios an arbitrage opportunity exists, and options can be purchased and imbedded in the security, a process that raises several structuring challenges.

Embedding options and swaps not only raises tax and other legal issues (for example, ERISA considerations or SEC registration requirements), but also potentially introduces prepayment and credit risk. For example, it may be difficult to structure such instruments to amortize with the notional value of a pool, which itself is subject to prepayment risk.[8] Also, the holder of such instruments is exposed to the credit risk of the counterparty (and the counterparty may need to publicly disclose information that it does not wish to disclose). Furthermore, should payments be required by the holder (for example, in a swap contract), the availability of such cash flows and their effect on the payments due security holders should be analyzed.

---

[8] If it is not possible to make the notional value of the option amortize with the pool's actual performance, the option's notional amortization schedule can be set as a zero-prepayment schedule (which may be costly) or at a very slow prepayment schedule (which introduces risk to investors to the extent that the pool actually pays at a rate slower than that used in projecting the schedule).

Public versus Private Execution

Securities can be issued in the public or private markets. Public securities are registered pursuant to The Securities Act of 1933 (the "Act"). Privately placed asset-backed transactions generally are issued in transactions exempt from the Act.[9] Within the private placement market, three general types of transactions exist: (1) transactions pursuant to Rule 144A, which may enjoy more liquidity than traditional privately placed securities; (2) traditional private placements; and (3) confidential private placements, which usually involve confidentiality agreements executed with potential investors and other parties.

In general, issuers consider the following issues when deciding the market in which to issue:

- Public securities are often more liquid and generally trade at lower yields. This is especially true of larger transactions, higher rated securities, and assets that are well understood by the market.
- Public securities may include greater up-front expenses, such as Securities and Exchange Commission fees (currently $\frac{1}{29}$ of 1% of the principal balance of the offering) and financial printing (this is really an optional expense; some public issuers are now photo-copying prospectuses).[10]
- Public securities historically have been more prone to unsolicited credit ratings.
- For non-generic transactions, the private market can sometimes offer the most efficient execution because of the ability of investors to have greater involvement in documentation and transaction structuring and the lack of liquidity advantage such transactions may otherwise have in the public markets.
- Private transactions can be executed confidentially. Typically, offering documents contain information relating to a company's underwriting guidelines or other statistics (for example, customer concentrations in trade receivables financings), that an issuer may not want to put in the public domain.

---

[9] Transactions issued by "exempt issuers" (for example, a bank) generally are not exempt from the Act in the asset-backed markets. This is because the trust, not the issuer, is considered the registrant of the securities for Act purposes. Note, however, that credit enhancement, such as a surety bond or option contract, is considered a security. If such enhancement is from a non-exempt issuer, it may be subjected to registration requirements.

[10] Many people are under the impression that a public transaction is more difficult to document than a private placement (thereby running up more legal time). This is arguable and may not even be the case at all. The documentation requirements for most asset-backed transactions are pretty much the same whether the securities are offered on a public or private basis, and generally consist of a set of principal contracts to establish the asset pool, issue the securities, and provide for servicing, as well as an offering document.

- Private transactions can be more easily amended or restructured subsequent to issuance.
- Private transactions often subject the issuer to risks of delayed closing due to investor negotiations. Sometimes (but, of course, not generally) private transactions subject the issuer to the risk of renegotiated pricing or structuring between the dates of pricing and closing.

In late 1992, the Securities and Exchange Commission made the public offering of asset-backed securities considerably easier when it broadly allowed for asset-backed shelf registration statements. The rules permitting asset-backed shelf registrations have generally mitigated "SEC review risk" (i.e., the risk that the SEC will fully review a potential public offering, thus potentially subjecting the issuer to delay). Another result of the asset-backed shelf rules has been the establishment of underwriter shelves, also called "rent-a-shelves." In a "rent-a-shelf" transaction, the originating seller/servicer sells its assets to the entity that has previously established an asset-backed shelf (often an affiliate of the underwriter). The "rent-a-shelf" concept allows an infrequent issuer that would like to do a public offering that cannot itself justify the time and expense necessary to establish a shelf registration statement to access efficiently the public markets. In addition, shelves reduce cost by eliminating the requirement of delivering red herrings and creating de novo documentation for subsequent offerings. They further potentially familiarize potential investors with upcoming offerings; they help investors to be knowledgeable about the issuer's shelf in general.

Tax Efficiency

The major tax law consideration in structuring pools is often to avoid creating an entity for federal income tax purposes that is treated like a corporation. The technical term for such an entity is an "association taxable as a corporation." A corporation in the United States (other than a closely held "S corporation") is taxable as a legal entity separate from its owners. This can be distinguished from, for example, a partnership, in which the income is attributable to the partners and not to the entity that is the partnership.

REMIC legislation allows a corporate type of entity — not necessarily a corporation but an entity for corporate law purposes, such as a corporation, a partnership, or a trust — to elect to be treated as a REMIC for federal income tax purposes. Most REMICs are trusts. However, if one had a particular result in mind and created a mortgage-backed security issuer as a corporation in form and had that corporation elect to be treated as a REMIC (or a FASIT, should the pending legislation be adopted), the REMIC election would supersede the general rule that a corporation's income is subject to a corporate tax.

A REMIC is not an entity. Instead, it is a tax election that an entity may make. Although it is perhaps not so confusing to see this with REMICs, the confusion becomes much greater when other types of federal tax law constructs, for example, partnerships, are considered. A partnership is both a federal income tax law status as well as a corporate entity concept. For example, a partnership for state partnership law purposes could elect to be treated as a REMIC for tax purposes; further, a trust for state corporate purposes may elect to be treated as a partnership for tax purposes.

On May 9, 1996, the IRS issued proposed regulations that simplify the process for determining if an entity will be treated as a corporation or a partnership for tax purposes. Under the proposed regulations, certain types of state law and foreign entities will be treated as per se corporations. All other entities can elect to be treated as either partnerships or as corporations with the additional provision that entities that do not make an election will "default" into partnership status. A trust created as a securitization vehicle would therefore default to partnership status if the IRS were to determine that it did not qualify as a trust for tax purposes.

These proposed "check-the-box" regulations will apply for periods beginning after the date the regulations are issued in final form. IRS officials have stated that they expect to issue final regulations by the end of this year. The current "four factor test" for classifying entities will continue to apply until the proposed regulations become final. The proposed regulations state, however, that the IRS will not challenge the characterization of existing entities for periods which the current rules apply if the entity had a reasonable basis for its claimed classification.

The four factor test refers to the requirement under current IRS regulations that to be regarded as a partnership an entity must lack at least two of four characteristics not common to both corporations and partnerships. These characteristics are continuity of life, centralization of management, limited liability, and free transferability of interests. After the "check-the-box" regulations become final, trusts drafted to have a partnership fallback will not have to meet the four factor test requirements. Further, existing entities will then be able to drop partnership fallback provisions and still claim partnership status if their characterization as a trust is successfully challenged by the IRS.

The rules regarding publicly traded partnerships, however, have not been changed. Partnerships treated as publicly traded partnerships are taxed as corporations. Therefore, to avoid taxation as a corporation, an effective partnership fallback will continue to require provisions restricting the total number of holders of equity or deemed equity interests in order to avoid publicly traded partnership status upon a recharacterization of the trust.

As a general matter, when legislators created technical rules relating to whether or not a particular entity is treated as an "association taxable as a corporation" for federal income tax purposes, it appeared that they were attempting to prohibit multiple classes of ownership interests in one of these entities. As a general rule, the tax laws pretty much allow for only one class of equity interest to be issued in any of these entities. A REMIC, for example, is required to issue one and only one class of equity interests in itself, which is called the residual interest. A grantor trust, which is a tax election frequently used for asset-backed transactions involving types of non-revolving assets other than mortgages (such as auto loans), permits multiple classes of ownership but does not permit for the shifting of certain risks among the various classes of ownership. For example, one cannot as a general rule create a "sequential-pay" structure in a grantor trust, although through some rather intricate drafting one can come pretty close, but probably will not match the flexibility that can be achieved for mortgage securitizations that use a REMIC election. So as one moves away from mortgage loans as an asset class and into other types of assets (and does not use an efficient debt-for-tax structure), there may be many more restrictions that may effectively prohibit the dicing and slicing of the asset pool into the types of securities that one would ideally like to offer to feed particular investor appetites.

Almost all of these federal income tax restrictions that apply to asset pools other than mortgages are rules against multiple classes of ownership interests in the asset pool, or rules that narrowly prescribe the type of ownership interests that can be issued. In other words, the restrictions are restrictions on multiple classes of equity, as opposed to restrictions on multiple classes of debt. Therefore, many multi-class, non-mortgage transactions have been structured as the issuance of debt rather than the issuance of ownership interests in the form of certificates.

As discussed above, debt treatment is often difficult to achieve. This is the case even when the transaction is structured to be debt in form. One of the principal difficulties in structuring debt, of course, is the necessity of having a class of equity from which we can distinguish the debt. Using equity to distinguish debt often is used in what is commonly called an "owner trust." An owner trust basically works as follows: a trust is created and capitalized with the receivables pool. The trust then issues certificates of equity ownership in itself. The trust then also effectively enters into an indenture and issues debt. The debt of the trust typically is sold to third-party investors as rated, fixed-income securities. The equity ownership in the trust may be retained by the company, or a portion may also be sold to investors. As long as such a transaction is structured to comply with SFAS 77, it may be accounted for as a GAAP sale.

There are few or no restrictions on the type of debt that an owner trust may issue. Therefore, the debt (if it is properly characterized as debt) may, for example, be structured as a "sequential pay" series of notes. One of the trade-offs that should be evaluated by an issuer of non-mortgage, non-revolving assets would then generally be the following: is it more advantageous to use an owner trust/debt structure that allows for the carving up of the asset pool into multiple classes of debt, thus allowing its investment bank to target specific investors with narrowly constructed securities, but suffer the downside that an economic equity interest must now be created and presumably held? Or, should it structure the transaction as the sale of pass-through equity interests in the issuing trust, recognizing that the types of securities that can be created may not be specifically targeted to individual investors due to the more restrictive provisions of federal income tax law relating to the creation of multiple classes of ownership?

Deal Size

A larger transaction, other things being equal, provides scale economies and more structuring opportunities to allow for the targeting of specific investors and enhanced liquidity. Transaction sizes can be increased through two distinct avenues: pre-funding accounts and the issuance of joint securities through securitization conduits.

Pre-Funding Accounts

A pre-funded transaction generally allows the issuer to close the securitization when only part of the collateral can be delivered to the trustee. The trustee then holds some of the cash proceeds in an account (the pre-funding account) and releases that cash to the issuer when and if subsequent collateral is delivered within a specified time period. Although the issuer is not contractually obligated to deliver the pre-funding collateral, issuers generally feel not only a moral obligation to do so, but also understand the importance of doing so if they wish to issue subsequent pre-funded transactions and have them accepted by the market.

Subsequent deliveries must materially conform to a pool description that is disclosed to investors in the offering document. If this collateral is not delivered to the trustee by the issuer, the cash in the pre-funding account is paid to investors. The transaction's operative documents will specify how this cash would be allocated among investor classes. For an established issuer that can be expected to materially fill the pre-funding account, a pre-funded deal (with a reasonably sized pre-funding account) should trade (and generally does) comparably to a transaction that has all of the collateral on the closing date.

Other considerations of pre-funded transactions are as follows:

- The issuer and its banker should carefully consider how the final pool will be parametized. Defining the pool too narrowly inhibits flexibility; yet, defining it too broadly deteriorates marketability.

- The pre-funding account effectively allows an issuer to hedge its production because the funding cost of the subsequent deliveries has been set at the time of pricing.
- The pre-funding period must be carefully tailored. If it is too short, it may make it difficult for the issuer to deliver the additional collateral. If it is too long, it may increase cost, and supplemental interest would have to be funded into a capitalized interest account to cover potential shortfalls between the yield on the cash investments in the pre-funding account and the bond coupon. Maximum terms also are effectively set by the REMIC rules for mortgage collateral. A subtle point is that, as the allowable pre-funding period increases, investors may make longer average-life assumptions, as newly originated collateral could be delivered at a later date.
- The pre-funding account gives the originator more flexibility in timing the market, as securities can be sold prior to the full formation of a pool.
- The pre-funding account gives the originator enhanced flexibility for determining how much collateral to sell in a given period. Subsequent deliveries can take place within the same accounting period as the initial sale, thereby allowing GAAP sales treatment for a greater amount of collateral within a given period.
- Careful legal analysis should be conducted. For example, as of this writing, certain ERISA considerations apply to prefunded transactions.

Conduits

The word "conduit" has yet to develop any single meaning. Yet it generally refers to the idea that smaller originators who lack name recognition in the capital markets and scale economies may still access the securitization market by entering into conduit relationships with larger, more seasoned issuers. One distinguishing characteristic of conduit relationships is the extent to which a participant retains an ongoing interest in its loans. Some conduits buy whole loans, usually at a premium, such that they purchase the receivables pool entirely from the smaller originator. Other conduits purchase the receivables pool at its par and give the participant an ongoing interest in its loans over time, thus paying out the premium on an as-earned basis.[11] The latter conduit relationship is similar to the idea of a conduit participant issuing its own asset-backed securities by "piggy backing" its asset pool onto the asset pool of a larger originator. These structures are in fact referred to as "piggy-back securitizations." A second distinguishing characteristic of con-

---

[11] Combinations of these methods can be used. For example, a modest premium could be paid at closing and a reduced amount of ongoing cash flow could be passed through during the time that the securitization is outstanding.

duit relationships is whether or not they allow for the retention of servicing by the originator, to the extent that the originator or an affiliate thereof is itself a servicer.

STRUCTURING DEALS — A GENERAL APPROACH

The investment banker must understand both issuer objectives and current investor preferences. To structure an efficient transaction, he must optimize the trade-offs between both and be knowledgeable about the constantly evolving intricate rules briefly highlighted herein.

Not every problem ultimately will be solvable. Yet, most structuring problems can be overcome or at least alternatives can be proposed. Then the issuer can decide whether or not to pursue one strategy over the other.

Creativity is critical, and structuring asset-backed securities offers a myriad of opportunities to be creative. But before a banker or lawyer can suggest creative options, they first must master the technical details, which requires years of specialization and seasoning. A less desirable approach is to study one, two, or at most a small number of prior transactions to use as a model for the transaction that they have been asked to structure. This generally produces inefficiencies; if you study only several models you tend to think of those models as embodying rules rather than as being examples of what can be accomplished given a particular set of evolving constraints and opportunities.

Chapter 16

A Rating Agency Perspective on Asset-Backed Securitization

Suzanne Michaud
Director
Fitch Investors Service, L.P.

INTRODUCTION

Securitization is the method by which non-tradable financial assets are converted into tradable securities. In this process, a company ("the issuer") sells assets off its balance sheet to a bankruptcy-remote special purpose corporation, which then issues securities collateralized by these assets. "Asset-backed securities" (ABS) refer to transactions backed by assets other than commercial or residential first mortgages (although securitizations backed by home-equity loans or manufactured housing are generally considered to be asset-backed rather than mortgage-backed).

Since 1985, securitization has increased in volume and importance. Initial growth in the public ABS market came from three sectors: automobile loans, credit card receivables, and home-equity loans. During the early to mid 1990s, growth was fueled by the securitization of products such as manufactured housing and student loans, and other new asset types. During 1995, the market witnessed tremendous growth (44% increase to $108 billion), much of which stemmed from credit cards. Expansion (via private placements and 144A transactions) also reached into more exotic markets: sub-prime assets (automobiles, home equity), future receivables, cross-border transactions, tax liens, timeshare loans, as well as automobile and equipment leases.

The market is highly fragmented — the top 30 public issuers for 1995 accounted for just 22.5% of total public ABS issuance. The investor base has also continued to broaden as traditional corporate and mortgage-backed buyers searched for higher spreads, less credit volatility, and more predictable cash flows. The market has witnessed increased demand from non U.S. investors.

ISSUER CONSIDERATIONS

Securitization offers a company many benefits. It allows the company to achieve higher credit ratings on securities backed by the assets than it could otherwise obtain based on its own financial strength, thereby lowering its cost of funds. For banks and thrifts, the sale reduces the need for capital under regulatory accounting practices (RAP). For industrial and finance companies, the removal of assets under generally accepted accounting principles (GAAP) provides increased borrowing flexibility and reduces capital requirements imposed by rating agencies and lending institutions. Securitization provides access to an important and efficient funding source — the capital markets — for even small and relatively new companies. The mechanism also ensures predictable tax treatment of assets.

INVESTOR CONSIDERATIONS

For investors, ABS securitizations have broadened the selection of fixed income alternatives, most with higher credit ratings and lower credit volatility compared to corporate bonds and more stable cash flows than mortgage-backed securities.

Even so, investors should remember that not all ABS transactions are created equal. In the most general terms, ABS securities should contain strong asset pools that, with specified amounts of credit enhancement, can withstand recessionary and, at certain rating levels, even depression-like scenarios. In addition, each transaction's structure should ensure that collections on the underlying receivables will proceed, so that investors will continue to receive their contractual interest and principal, even when the company selling the assets becomes insolvent and subject to a bankruptcy or receivership.

RATING AGENCY CONSIDERATIONS

There are four critical elements to analyzing an ABS transaction — credit quality of receivables, seller/servicer evaluation, cash flow stress and financial structure, and legal structure.

CREDIT QUALITY OF RECEIVABLES

Evaluating the characteristics and credit quality of the underlying collateral is essential to understanding any transaction. Depending on the asset type, the analysis should differ. For transactions involving consumer loan obligations such as mortgages and auto loans, two basic theories apply — the borrower's ability to make monthly payments and the amount of equity the borrower has provided. Borrower's may lose their ability to pay when they suffer a personal or financial crisis, such as divorce or loss of employment. The equity theory states that the borrower's perceived equity (downpayment) in a loan dominates the decision to default in times of financial distress. Equity is also a good indication of the borrower's credit profile.

For a seller's historical portfolio of receivables to serve as a benchmark for the credit quality of the securitized pool, the characteristics of the pool should be representative of the seller's own portfolio. Loan attributes to consider include borrower profile, geographic concentration (performance is affected by changes in local economic conditions), loan size, original loan term, loan-to-value, loan coupon, seasoning, and new versus used status (borrowers who purchased used cars, for example, are general perceived to have weaker financial wherewithal). Trends in delinquencies and losses should also be evaluated. Once these factors are evaluated and determined to be comparable to the seller's portfolio, the appropriate level of credit enhancement can be sized according to the desired rating category.

Credit Enhancement

Credit enhancement is a source of capital built into every transaction as a cushion against losses. Losses occur due to uncollectibility (for consumer loans, the borrower's failure to pay back a loan). Sources of credit enhancement vary substantially, but often include one or more of overcollateralization, excess spread, reserve accounts, collateral interest, spread accounts, letters of credit, subordinated interests, agreements to purchase defaulted receivables, financial guaranties, and surety bonds. Credit enhancement is sometimes categorized according to whether it is first loss or second loss protection. From a rating agency's perspective, credit enhancement should be sufficient to cover a multiple of historical losses. The multiple of coverage required will vary depending on the desired rating, the collateral being securitized, and the predictability of the static pool data being provided.

Related Risks

For trade receivables (intercompany receivables), *dilution risk* is important to consider. Dilution is the occurrence of events unrelated to the creditworthiness of an obligor which "dilute" or cause a reduction in the outstanding balance of a receivables pool. Dilution results from an obligor's unwillingness to pay because of returns on goods sold, disputes, offsets, credits, rebates or warranty claims. Even a AAA (denoting the highest quality) obligor may refuse to pay a receivable because of a dilution-related cause.

Liquidity risk is prevalent in asset-backed commercial paper and medium-term note programs — when collections on receivables are not fast enough to meet the repayment of asset-backed notes. This is a result of a mismatch between the asset (the underlying receivable) and liability (the security), and occurs frequently when there is a revolving pool of underlying assets and the securities are offered on a continual basis. A source of liquidity must be established to bridge this gap. The most common form is a liquidity facility provided by a syndicate of banks having a rating commensurate with the rating of the ABS. Unlike providers of credit enhancement, providers of liquidity support are not expected to bear the risk of uncollectibility.

SELLER/SERVICER EVALUATION

Other than residential mortgages, which are frequently originated to meet specific standards for sale to Fannie Mae (Federal National Mortgage Association) or Freddie Mac (Federal Home Loan Mortgage Corporation), consumer loans are not standardized. Because each lender's underwriting guidelines are unique to the financial institution, analysts must review the lender's historical loss and delinquency performance, which is generally in the form of a static pool analysis. The loan pool is plotted over time to determine its life cycle and payment behavior (its average life, slope, and peak loss period). With the data, future losses and delinquencies can be forecast.

The seller/servicer of the receivables should have been in business for several years, preferably three to five. Predictability of receivable performance is more reliable for sellers with a track record of many years spanning several economic cycles. Because servicing is an important component of maintaining the credit quality of the collateral pools, rating agencies typically visit the servicer prior to issuing a rating.

Red Flags for Non-Investment Grade Companies

Investors should take extra caution when evaluating issues from a non-investment-grade company, particularly if it is securitizing for the first time, has a limited track record, or is securitizing unusual assets. Careful scrutiny should be placed on the management team in place — what is their tenure and relevant previous experience? Analysts should be wary of past bankruptcy filings or lawsuits, and incidents of fraud.

Information on the company's strategy, operating history, and experience in underwriting and collecting should also be obtained. A fundamental component of the analysis is to evaluate static pool data over several economic cycles to determine likely and worst-case scenarios. A start-up company would not be able to provide such basic data.

Analysts should also consider the rate at which the company is growing. Controlled growth is optimal. If a small company grows too quickly, it may not have the depth of management to maintain its underwriting and collection guidelines or it may not have adequate capitalization. Financial integrity and access to sources of capital are also critical elements. Three years of audited financials should be obtained on the company, with indicators such as leverage, profitability, and capitalization determined.

Back-Up Servicing

If a servicer's ability to perform its duties is questionable, a backup servicer should be in place to run parallel to the primary servicer — receiving copies of the servicer's monthly accounting and reporting tapes. The backup servicer would run the tape off its own system and compare the information to the servicer's reports. If the servicer was unable to perform the servicing, the backup would be able to assume the servicing without any timing delay or impairment of the receivables.

CASH FLOW STRESS AND FINANCIAL STRUCTURE

Credit enhancement adequacy is also determined by a review of the financial structure and cash flow analysis. Common structures are found within different asset categories, such as master trust structures for credit card receivables or grantor trust structures for auto loans. The issuer chooses the structure based on the type of collateral and its payment rate behavior, and whether the assets are amortizing or revolving. The structures themselves differ in terms of payment priorities, bond amortization schedules (controlled amortization, bullet, etc.) and how excess cash is applied. Issuers and their investment bankers are now adding investor maturity preferences into the equation.

Financial Structure

The financial structure must match cash flow payments of the receivables. The scheduled debt maturity should be sufficiently beyond the maturity date of the longest term receivable. The interest rate of the receivables must be adequate to cover the investor coupon, servicing fee, and any other expenses for which the issuer is liable. Loss and delinquency assumptions, payment rates, and interest rate scenarios are built into the structure to determine if credit enhancement levels are sufficient. Depending on the structure, stress scenarios should be run to test for timeliness of payment, as well as adequacy of excess spread to provide credit enhancement and ensure that all classes are paid in full at maturity.

Trust Structures

A stand-alone trust involves a one-time sale of a discreet asset pool. There may be various classes of securities offered. When the issuer wants to issue more securities, it must set up a separate trust to which it would designate new receivables. In contrast, a master trust structure allows an issuer to sell multiple securities backed by a common pool of receivables from the same trust. Here, the issuer has flexibility to add more receivables to the trust, and offer more securities if needed. A grantor trust allows only pro-rata pass-through payments, meaning all interest and principal is paid to investors based on their percentage ownership. Senior and subordinate classes repay at the same rate, unless the subordinate class is written down due to losses.

Pass-Through Structures

For a pass-through structure where principal and interest payments are distributed as received, the only consideration is sufficient liquidity to meet scheduled interest payments. If credit enhancement is in the form of over-collateralization (where bonds are supported by receivables having a principal amount greater than the value of the bonds), the financial structure must include a cash reserve account to be drawn on if receivable delinquencies increase to a level where interest collections are insufficient to pay the investor coupon.

Multi-Class Structures

If the transaction is structured with multiple classes of various maturities, several cash flow stresses should be evaluated. Multiclass structures involve complex payment priorities and contain classes having either short-term ratings assigned to them or maturity dates that occur earlier than the receivables' final payment date. Because F-1+ (one year or less) and AAA ratings address timeliness of payment as well as ultimate payment, the timing of receipts must be sufficient for each class to be paid off by its final payment date.

Excess Spread

Excess spread may be used as partial credit enhancement. This is the excess interest generated on a receivable net of investor coupon, servicer fee charge-offs, and other fees for which the issuer is liable. Excess spread is often placed in a reserve account which builds over time to a required level. In certain deals, it is only available on a "use it, or lose it" basis, where it is not captured in a reserve account. This means that if it is not needed to cover delinquencies or losses in a given period, it is released to the seller as income. Analysts should be conservative when evaluating the level of excess spread available for protection. Factors such as changes in interest rates, prepayments, and losses will cause excess spread to shrink. Assumptions regarding these variables should be built into the cash flow analysis.

LEGAL STRUCTURE

The issuer of the asset-backed securities must be independent from the seller/servicer of the receivables in order for the asset-backed debt to achieve a rating higher than the seller's. The issuer must be a special-purpose, bankruptcy-remote entity as verified by an opinion of legal counsel. To accomplish the legal separateness, the seller would sell the receivables to a subsidiary that was established specifically to own the receivables, issue debt to finance those receivables, and not enter into any transactions other than similar securitizations which are of same credit quality. To give further proof that the subsidiary will remain separate from (i.e. not substantively consolidated with) the parent/seller in the event of a bankruptcy, books and records, bank accounts, and other such elements should be maintained separately. An opinion of counsel should be obtained stating that the sale of receivables to the trust is a true sale. An additional opinion should state that no substantive consolidation of the assets would occur in the event of a bankruptcy of the parent/seller.

Another critical element to separate the credit risk of a pool from that of the seller is to ensure that collections on the receivables are not mixed or commingled with the parent/seller's funds at any time during which the parent might become subject to a bankruptcy proceeding. Therefore, a parent/seller may choose to commingle as long as its ratings remain in a stated investment-grade category. If the ratings fall below an acceptable level, then collections should be transferred to a separate account in the name of the trustee for the benefit of investors.

CONCLUSION

There is more to analyzing an ABS transaction than meets the eye. If these investments are structured properly, investors have the benefit of a bankruptcy-remote legal structure, a diversified pool of receivables, credit enhancement sized to cover a multiple of historical losses, and a highly rated investment.

Chapter 17

Credit Enhancement in ABS Structures

Lina Hsu
First Vice President
Fixed Income Research
Prudential Securities Inc.

Cyrus Mohebbi
Senior Vice President
Fixed Income Research
Prudential Securities Inc.

INTRODUCTION

A key element in ABS transactions is the credit enhancement associated with the structure. Credit enhancement levels are determined by the characteristics of the underlying collateral, historical delinquency and default statistics, underwriting guidelines, and the industry outlook regarding the robustness of future cash flows. Credit enhancement could either involve a third party enhancement or utilize a self-insurance feature generated internally from the cash flows. Most transactions have structures utilizing a combination of internal and external credit enhancement techniques. The exact selection of the type of enhancement tools is based upon minimizing the all-in issuance cost. A description of the various credit enhancement tools is discussed in this chapter.

EXTERNAL CREDIT ENHANCEMENT

Third party credit enhancement tools in ABS securitizations range from wraps provided by monoline insurers, corporate guarantees, letters of credit, and cash collateral accounts.

Monoline Insurance

Within the genre of external credit enhancement, the most common technique is a guarantee provided by monoline insurance companies, such as Municipal Bond Investors Assurance (MBIA), Financial Guaranty Insurance Co. (FGIC), Financial Security Assurance (FSA), or Capital Markets Assurance Corporation (CAPMAC). These entities typically insure investment grade rated (BBB-/Baa3 and above) cash flows to higher ratings desired by the issuer or the underwriter for an upfront fee and/or an on-going fee. The higher the desired insured rating, the higher the fees. Monoline insurers are able to insure cash flows at higher ratings as they are required by rating agencies to reserve a certain amount of capital for each insured transaction to protect bondholders against any losses on the underlying assets due to credit defaults, standard and special hazards, fraud, and bankruptcy up to the amount sustainable by the desired rating. For an insured AAA/Aaa rating, the monoline insurer guarantees investors timely payment of interest and eventual payment of principal.

Issues guaranteed by monoline insurers are subject to the credit standing of the insurers as the insured rating is dependent upon the claims paying abilities of the insurer. Monoline insurance may provide coverage for the entire issue or specific classes within the issue. It is most commonly used in transactions where the underlying collateral is home equity loans, unguaranteed portions of small business loans, leases, auto loans, and other exotic receivables. The following table details the rated claims paying ability of various monolines by the rating agencies.

Insurer	Rating Agencies	Rating
CAPMAC	S&P, Moody's, Duff & Phelps	AAA/Aaa/AAA
FGIC	S&P, Moody's, Fitch	AAA/Aaa/AAA
FSA	S&P, Moody's	AAA/Aaa
MBIA	S&P, Moody's, Fitch	AAA/Aaa/AAA

Recently Fannie Mae (FNMA) and Freddie Mac (FHLMC) have also ventured into the insurance business in limited asset types, such as home equity loans, as the monoline insurance methodology has been a very popular form of credit enhancement. However, both agencies have very stringent sets of guidelines and are very selective in the quality of the collateral which is insured. Like other monoline insurers, both agencies would insure cash flows which have a minimum stand alone rating of BBB-/Baa3.

Corporate Guarantees

Similar to the monoline insurance policy, a corporate guarantee protects bondholders from losses due to default, bankruptcy, fraud, and standard and special hazards of the underlying assets, with full recourse to the guarantor. The rating of the security is directly affected by any upgrade or downgrade of the guarantor as the highest rating an insured security can obtain is the rating of the guarantor. Corporate guarantees could be issued for the entire transaction or just specific classes. In a number of transactions, the issuers themselves provide the guarantee on certain lower rated classes. Unlike the monoline insurance policy, a corporate guarantee can be applied to below investment grade cash flows while a minimum of BBB-/Baa3 rating is required by any monoline insurer.

Letter of Credit

A letter of credit (LOC) is an insurance policy issued by a financial institution. Under the aegis of most LOCs, the institution is obligated to reimburse losses up to a specified amount. Similar to monoline insurance and corporate guarantees, a LOC provider cannot provide any enhancement with a rating above its own rating and therefore any downgrades of the LOC providers will directly impact the rating of the insured securities. With the scarcity of higher rated banks, which have been traditional providers of LOCs, this method of credit enhancement is infrequently used.

Cash Collateral Account

A cash collateral account (CCA) is a very common sources of credit enhancement for credit-card receivables. A CCA is a loan to the issuing trust with the proceeds reinvested in some short-term eligible investments. The loan amount can be paid down via excess spread from the transaction. The trust is usually charged a spread over short-term deposit rates such as LIBOR. Any classes covered by a CCA will be reimbursed on any shortfalls via proceeds from the account. CCAs were initially introduced in the early 1990s and have been the choice for many issuers who were unable to retain subordinated classes of issued structures. Unlike all other third party enhancement discussed above, the rating of a class covered by a CCA is the originally assigned rating and does not change upon the rating of the provider as the insurance is secured by cash.

INTERNAL CREDIT ENHANCEMENT

One major drawback of most third party enhancement tools is that the insured classes are often susceptible to the risks of downgrade of the credit enhancement provider. At the same time, with the growth of particular types of credit enhancement techniques concerns regarding counterparty credit risk with respect to the providers also have a tendency to increase. Internal credit enhancement removes these third party risks because a part of the actual cash flows from the underlying assets are used to credit enhance the structure. Internal credit enhancement tools include the creation of subordinated classes, turbo structures with overcollateralization, and spread account(s).

Senior-Subordinated Structures

In general, senior-subordinated credit structures could be created with a single or multiple subordinated credit class depending on the subordination levels. The credit structure could be designed to have credit classes pay pro-rata and/or sequentially with losses allocated first to the outstanding junior classes. Typically, credit enhancement levels determined by a rating agencies are also affected by the paydown of principal rules in the deal structure in addition to the characteristics of the collateral.

Generally, a structure with pro-rata paying credit tranches receives a higher subordination level than one with credit tranches that pay sequentially. This is because the subordination level of the senior classes of a sequentially paying credit structure increases over time whereas the subordination level remains the same for a pro-rata paying credit structure in the absence of defaults. Hence, if the same credit enhancement level were to be assigned to a pro-rata paying credit structure versus a sequentially paying structure, the credit support for the former would erode much faster in the event of defaults.

Structures with sequentially paying credit tranches are common among manufactured housing deals where any tranches with a rating below

AAA/Aaa or AA/Aa have a certain lockout period and pay sequentially with certain senior pieces subsequent to the lockout period. Similar sequential structures have also been used in the securitization of credit cards, where typical deals contain A, B, and C classes with the C class being the collateral invested account (CIA). While the CIA has been referred to alternatively as collateral interest and enhancement invested amount, it is essentially a privately placed interest in a trust which serves the same purpose as a CCA.

Another alternative senior/subordinated structure encompasses a shifting interest feature. This shifting interest structure is commonly used in most non-conforming type mortgage-backed transactions. The structure is designed such that all prepayment amounts that would otherwise be allocated to the subordinated class are paid to the senior classes instead. This increases the subordination level of the senior classes as the deal amortizes. The amount of prepayment shifted from the subordinated classes to the senior classes gets reduced as the deal ages subject to meeting certain delinquency and loss tests. A recent innovation in shifting interest structure is the addition of a senior support class, often referred to as the AAA mezzanine class. This structure, widely known as the super senior/senior support structure, creates additional support for the super senior classes. The AAA mezzanine class resembles the payment characteristics of a subordinated class during the prepayment lockout period, after which the amount of prepayment which is allocated to this class steps up over time as the deal amortizes and certain trigger events are not violated.

Overcollateralization

Another type of commonly used internal credit enhancement is overcollateralization. Asset types such as home equity loans or B and C mortgages typically bear higher interest rates than other assets, such as single family mortgages, mainly to compensate the lender either for the subordinated lien status of such loans or the poor credit quality of the borrower. Overcollateralization credit enhancement structures utilize the excess spread, which is the amount of interest coupon after payment of all fees and bond coupon expenses to pay down the principal of the structured bonds. This payment structure, also known as a turbo structure, accelerates the principal paydown of the bonds thereby creating an overcollateralization cushion for losses.

Overcollateralization provides a higher collateral to bond balance ratio in a structure. In case of losses, the bonds are protected from any write down by the amount of overcollateralization. Excess spread provides extra cash flows for payment of bond interest and principal, and thereby creates additional credit support.

If more than one asset group is included in a transaction, such as fixed-rate and adjustable-rate loans or home equity loans and home improvement loans, excess spread from one group is first used to enhance the bonds created from cash flows from the same group. Any excess spread is then used to enhance the bonds created from other collateral groups. This type of enhancement is known as cross collateralization.

Depending on the amount of excess spread available at the inception of the deal, an initial deposit may not be required for the transaction. However, in cases where an initial deposit is required, overcollateralization is required at the inception of the deal resulting in a reduction in the overall proceeds received by issuers.

Many issuers use overcollateralization for internal credit enhancement along with monoline insurance. Generally, the usage of overcollateralization brings the cash flows to a BBB-/Baa3 rating causing the resultant securities to be eligible for insurance by a monoline insurer in order to obtain a AAA/Aaa rating. A major advantage of the usage of overcollateralization is that issuers are allowed to reinvest excess spread at the gross collateral coupon rate, rather than at some short-term rate. Another interesting feature of an overcollateralized structure is that principal windows of bonds in such transaction are usually tighter than the collateral as interest cash flows are used to pay down bond principal. As a result, more short average life and tight window bonds can be created which causes a significant improvement in the execution of the transaction, particularly in an upward sloping yield curve environment.

Spread Accounts

An alternative to overcollateralization as credit enhancement is through the application of spread account(s). Similar to the overcollateralized structure, a spread account is built up to some predetermined levels specified by the rating agencies through excess spread in the transaction. Unlike the overcollateralized structure, the excess spread is accumulated in an account as cash and reinvested as some short-term eligible investments. Depending on the structure, a spread account could be created for all bond classes or be specifically used to credit enhance certain classes. Similar to the overcollateralized structure, the build up of the spread account can be designed for the cash flows to obtain a BBB/Baa3 rating. Based upon this internal credit enhancement, the cash flows are then eligible to be insured by a monoline insurer. Issuers typically choose an overcollateralized structure over a spread account structure because of the advantages discussed above.

As mentioned above, most issuers use a combination of different types of credit enhancement tools either internally or externally to obtain the most proceeds for the least cost of funds. In general, internal credit enhancement enables the transaction to be independent of any risks external to the collateral. However, a structure with sole internal credit enhancement such as a senior/subordinated structure could be extremely expensive for first time issuers or to deals with exotic assets as rating agencies tend to adopt a conservative stance in such cases. Additionally, ABS credit tranches have less investor appeals on first time issuances due to the paucity of data and lack of name recognition.

Chapter 18

Early Amortization Triggers

Anand K. Bhattacharya
Senior Vice Pressident
Director of Fixed Income Research
Prudential Securities Inc.

REASON FOR EARLY AMORTIZATION TRIGGERS

Early amortization triggers are included in ABS structures in which the underlying collateral pool requires the ongoing addition of receivables. In contrast to structures in which the collateral pool is static in nature (such as mortgages), the changing nature of the collateral exposes the transaction to risks that are attributable to the financial health of the issuer and the ongoing quality of the collateral originated by the issuer. In structures that are collateralized by static pools, the probability of the occurrence of defaults and the severity of these losses over the life of the transaction can be assessed. However, in the case of open-ended transactions, where the present performance of the collateral may not necessarily be an indicator of future performance, the investors are exposed to the risks of reduction in collateral quality and the possibility that the issuer and associated parties, such as the servicer and the credit enhancement provider, may not be able to discharge their contractual obligations.

In view of these considerations, such transactions typically involve the incorporation of early amortization triggers, which can shorten the life of the transaction contingent upon the occurrence of certain events. Typically, the securitization of trade receivables involves the establishment of a bankruptcy remote special purpose subsidiary to purchase the receivables from the seller and simultaneously resell these receivables to a trust that issues the certificates to finance the purchase of the receivables. The certificates are then sold as securities in the capital markets and the proceeds are transferred to the seller. Since the turnover rate of most receivables is high, the life of the structure is extended by purchasing additional revolving receivables from the funds collected from the existing receivables after paying expenses and debt services charges. In the event of certain specified conditions regarding deterioration in collateral quality, the structure begins to early amortize, based upon the amortization method incorporated in the structure. Typically, receivable securitizations are structured as hard bullets or soft bullets; as controlled amortization structures or as pass-throughs. Alternatively, changes in financial health of the issuer, servicer and credit enhancement provider, such as bankruptcy may lead to early amortization concerns on the part of investors.

For instance, in the case of credit-card receivables, where the securitization vehicle involves the ongoing addition of revolving receivables, the securitized structures have provisions to begin immediate amortization in the event the trust fails to generate sufficient income to cover expenses of investor coupon and servicing fees over a pre-determined period of time. When income from the receivables (net of losses) fails to support expenses, an immediate payout shields investors from further deterioration in the quality of the portfolio. In addition to such expense coverage conditions, credit-card securities may have additional triggers based upon portfolio loss levels, where the early amortization event could be triggered by aggregate losses in excess of a threshold level. Portfolio yields could decline due to increases in chargeoffs or as a result of reduced interest rate charges and annual fees in the face of increased competitive conditions. Typically, portfolio loss triggers are more conservative early amortization possibility tests than expense ratio triggers as loss triggers may be invoked even if there is sufficient income to support the expenses of the trust. Therefore, the portfolio loss trigger conditions for early amortization usually requires the approval of some stated percentage of the bondholders.

In general, as noted by Moody's, early amortization triggers are designed as a protection against the following events.[1]

- Significant changes in the nature and scope of the issuers business, such as bankruptcy.
- Attainment of collateral performance triggers, such as certain threshold delinquency levels, charge-off rates, minimum pool balances, reduction in payment rates and dilution rates.
- Significant regulatory and tax changes that cause changes in collateral cash flows, such as proposed legislation to cap interest rates charges on the receivables.
- Reduction of credit support, either through structural reasons or by the downgrade or bankruptcy of the credit support provider.
- Changes in the contractual nature of cash flows not related to collateral factors, such as the downgrade or bankruptcy of the swap or cap counterparty.
- Default of the servicer.

EFFECT OF EARLY AMORTIZATION

While early amortization triggers have existed since the inception of receivable securitizations, especially in credit-card transactions, manifestations of these triggers have been minimal. The first early amortization of a public transaction occurred in 1991 when the Southeast Bank Credit-Card Trust was unwound upon the collateral pool attaining a yield threshold. While there have been no other actual occurrences of early amortization in the public markets, it is an issue that immediately comes to the fore front of valuation anytime there are increases in delinquency and charge-off rates, increased competitive conditions forcing downward adjustments in underwriting standards or negatively affecting excess spreads, changes

[1] See *Moody's Approach to Rating Trade Receivables Term Securitizations*, Moody's Investors Services, June 1994.

in the economic climate or proposed regulatory and legislative changes. For instance, recessionary conditions in the economy may raise concerns about deterioration in the quality of the collateral pool. Alternatively, legislative initiatives to change usury laws which would affect the excess spread in credit-card transactions by limiting the interest rate charged on balances could cause concerns about deterioration in performance triggers, possibly leading to early amortization.

From the viewpoint of the issuer, it is beneficial to prevent early amortization by seeking to revise the performance triggers which would cause the structure to early amortize in order to maintain their capability to tap the capital markets for asset-backed financing. However, from the view point of the investor, an early amortization event can lead to prepayment risk and reinvestment risk, especially when the securities are priced at a premium as principal repayment would be at par, leading to investor concerns about premium erosion.

Due to such concerns on the part of investors, there have been certain structural innovations which have mitigated the likelihood of early amortization. For instance, the incorporation of an optional discount mechanism, where the issuer has the option to convey receivables to the trust at a discount alleviates excess spread erosion concerns. The discount portion of the receivables is conveyed to the trust as finance charge receivables and increases the amount of excess spread to absorb credit losses. The flexibility offered by this discount mechanism allows for an increase in portfolio yield even when the actual returns from the portfolio are low.

THE CHARMING SHOPPES EXAMPLE

As an example of the dynamics of an early amortization event and the implications of such events for investors, consider the recent example of Charming Shoppes Master Trust 1994-1, a private label credit-card structure. In October 1995, the threat of the bankruptcy of Charming Shoppes raised concerns as to the early amortization of the structure. In contrast to the widely held belief that an early amortization event signals a rating downgrade, history and experience indicate that rating changes are likely to occur only when the event triggering the early amortization signals a fundamental and material deterioration in the nature of the cash flows.

In the Charming Shoppes case, sales and profitability had declined sharply in 1995 leading some market participants to suggest that company might be forced to seek bankruptcy protection unless additional financing could be obtained. As with most credit cards, since bankruptcy of the issuer is one of several events that can trigger early amortization, spreads on the securities widened from approximately 45 basis points to around 60 over the 3-year Treasury note yield.[2] In the event of an early amortization event triggered by a bankruptcy filing, bondholders typically have the right to decide whether or not to permit the early amortization. This election should not present a problem in the case of discount priced securities. However, when the issue is priced at a premium, bondholders must weigh the risk of loss of principal if they choose not to have an early amortization versus the certainty of a loss of yield associated with an early payout. While the early amortization effects of the bankruptcy of the issuer should be defined in the pooling and servicing agreement, since there is a paucity of precedent associated with actual early amortization events, history suggests that it is not clear whether the bankruptcy of the issuer automatically triggers an early amortization or whether a bondholder vote is required on concerns that bankruptcy may lead to a deterioration in credit quality of the receivables. For instance, both Macy's and Federated Department stores filed for bankruptcy protection, reorganized and returned to profitability. During the course of the bankruptcies, neither experienced a significant deterioration in quality of securitized charge accounts.

In general, despite the fact that the actual occurrence of early amortization events has been minimal, the issue always takes center stage anytime there are changes either in the competitive arena that threaten excess spread or in the economic environment that leads to heightened concerns about deterioration in the credit quality of the underlying receivables. While the risk of principal loss is virtually non-existent in the case of early amortization, the event could be associated with yield losses for premium securities and reinvestment risk.[3] In this respect, the evaluation of early amortization conditions should be an integral part of the relative valuation process. At the same time, structural innovations such as the optional discount mechanism are likely to alleviate concerns about potential early amortization.

---

[2] As of this writing, Charming Shoppes had been able to gather additional financing to ward off the threat of immediate bankruptcy. While this alleviated immediate concerns regarding early amortization, it appears that the issue is still of relevance based upon concerns regarding the ultimate financial viability of the issuer. In the event of bankruptcy, there is a greater likelihood that retail customers would become delinquent and default than would a group of VISA or Mastercard accounts.

[3] This statement must include the caveat that principal losses could occur if there was sufficient immediate deterioration in the cash collateral account due to a high degree of defaults so as to prevent the satisfying of principal obligations.

Chapter 19

Home-Equity Loan Floaters

Lirenn Tsai
Vice President
Fixed Income Research
Prudential Securities Inc.

Cyrus Mohebbi
Senior Vice President
Fixed Income Research
Prudential Securities Inc.

INTRODUCTION

With the increase in the securitization of adjustable-rate home-equity closed-end loans (HELs), one unique structure that has resulted is the creation of LIBOR-based floating-rate tranches. These securities are collateralized by adjustable-rate HELs, typically indexed off 6-month LIBOR, with a small percentage indexed off Constant Maturity Treasury, Eleventh District Cost of Funds (COFI), and other indices. However, the coupon of the structured securities is typically indexed off more liquid and widely accepted indices, such as 1-month LIBOR, in order to enhance the investor appeal of these securities. The HEL floater is a unique structure that allows investors the opportunity to invest in securities with coupons determined by more acceptable and liquid indices despite the fact that collateral cash flows are a function of another index. This development effectively breaks down limitations associated with the type of securities that can be issued using floating-rate collateral. While most of the usage of this technology has been in the closed-end non-prime HEL market, the structuring methodology could be employed in virtually any floating-rate sector as long as the characteristics of the collateral and structural considerations permit the effective management of the basis risk between the collateral and the security indices.

As with most securities collateralized by mortgages, there are embedded options in the HEL floater structure. Specifically, the security may be decomposed as being short a call option from the loan holder, short a series of periodic caps and a lifetime cap, and long a series of floors and a lifetime floor. The short call option is essentially the same type of prepayment option that is standard in most MBSs and is a function of the loan holder's propensity to refinance. In general, prepayments on closed-end HELs, especially on lower credit loans, are less sensitive to interest rate changes which makes the call option less valuable, thereby increasing the value of these securities relative to MBS. The other options in the HEL floater structure are the coupon caps which are the unique feature of these securities. Like most adjustable rate-mortgages, the underlying collateral in HEL floater deals is associated with periodic and lifetime caps.[1]

DETERMINANTS OF CAPS

One of the major differences between the cap option in the HEL floater and other securities is that the HEL floater cap is dependent on the cash flows of

---

[1] The periodic caps are typically 1% semiannual caps. These caps generally are the most significant since there is a reasonable likelihood that they will be hit at some point due to normal interest rate fluctuations. The lifetime caps are generally about 6% above the loan origination rate. Most loans are originated with teaser rates around 1-2% below fully indexed levels

the underlying collateral which results in a variable strike rate. The variable nature of these caps is the result of the following four factors.

(1) the initial teaser period,
(2) the index mismatch between the security and collateral indices,
(3) the reset frequency mismatch of the collateral and the security coupon, and
(4) structural enhancements such as acceleration and overcollateralization.

The initial teaser period, which typically lasts for about a year, is a crucial period for HEL floaters because the level of interest generated by the collateral is less than it would be if the collateral was fully indexed. However, the security coupon does not have a teaser period, which results in a somewhat lower margin during the teaser period. A number of enhancements, which are discussed below, have been introduced recently to mitigate the risk of hitting the available funds cap during this period.

With respect to the index mismatch, changes in the relative levels of the coupon index, say 1-month LIBOR and collateral index, say 6-month LIBOR, will affect the amount of funds available to make coupon payments. For example, once the collateral is fully indexed, if 1-month LIBOR increases while 6-month LIBOR remains unchanged, then the security coupon will reset up and move closer to the cap rate. Conversely, if 6-month LIBOR increases while 1-month LIBOR remains unchanged, then the collateral will reset up and the cap will be farther out of the money.

In terms of the reset mismatch, the timing of the changes in the level of the collateral index and the security index affects available funds cap levels. In most HEL floater deals to date, the security coupon resets monthly while the collateral resets semi-annually. This mismatch can reduce the available funds margin temporarily even if the collateral and security indexes move together. For example, if the structure is collateralized by newly originated collateral with 6-months to the first roll date and both indexes increase by 1%, the security will reset in one month on the next coupon payment date. However, the collateral will not reset until six months on the next payment reset date. Therefore, the available funds margin decreases by 1% for five months before the collateral can reset up.

The fourth factor, structural enhancements such as overcollateralization and acceleration, also affect the amount of funds available to make coupon payments. In the case of overcollateralization, the par amount of collateral backing a deal exceeds the par amount of securities issued. The obvious result of the overcollateralization feature is the generation of a larger amount of funds with which to make coupon payments. The acceleration feature is designed to increase the speed at which the securities are retired. This is accomplished by utilizing excess collateral interest to pay down security principal. As the amount of outstanding security principal declines relative to the collateral principal, the amount of interest available to pay the security coupon also increases. All other things being equal, the result is an increase in the available funds cap rate. In most deals, there is a build-up stage where any excess interest is used to pay down the security principal until it reaches a target percentage of collateral at which point any excess interest is returned to the issuer.

COMPUTATION OF AVAILABLE FUNDS CAP

The coupon of the HEL floater is determined by a formula that is a function of an index value plus a margin in a manner similar to other floating-rate structured securities. The unique feature of this security is the cap, which limits the extent of the coupon reset. In a typical floater, the strike of the cap is a fixed level which is defined as a percent of par. In contrast, the strike of the HEL floater cap is a variable level which is dependent on the amount of funds which are generated by the net coupon on the principal, less any fees and surety spread requirement. If the coupon of the security is greater than the effective cap rate, then the cap is in the money.

As an illustration of the computation of the available funds cap, consider the deal described in Exhibit 1 that was issued by Aames Mortgage Trust. In our analysis, we have assumed that the entire collateral pool rolls at the same time and by the same amount. In practice, the actual roll schedule and coupon resets are used to calculate the exact collateral weighted average coupon (WAC) and available funds caps. A diversified collateral pool will have a distribution of reset dates which will smooth out collateral coupon changes and thus has the effect of reducing the cap cost. However, as a practical matter, issuers tend to securitize newly originated product which results in reset concentrations of around two quarters of the year.

Periodic Caps

The initial available funds cap for this security can be calculated as follows:

Gross Coupon − Servicing Fee − Other Fees − Surety Spread

$$11.045 - 0.50 - 0.155 - 0.50 = 9.89\%$$

Surety Spread is defined as the minimum interest strip that the surety provider requires as credit enhancement and is therefore included as interest in the determination of available funds. Assuming, the collateral index (6-month LIBOR) remains unchanged, the coupon index (1-month LIBOR) can increase by 3.3775% [9.89%−(6.0625%+0.45%)] in the first six months before the available funds cap is hit. Mathematically, this is stated as:

Initial available cap funds cap − (Coupon Index + Margin)

Exhibit 1: Summary of an Aames Mortgage Trust
Security Description

Issue:	AAMES 1995-B
Class:	A2
Coupon:	1-month LIBOR +45 basis points
Average Life:	4.017 years at 18 CPR/21 HEP

Collateral Description

Weighted Average Gross Coupon:	11.045%
Weighted Average Gross Margin:	6.372%
Weighted Average Life Cap:	17.039%
Servicing Fee:	50 basis points
Surety Spread:	50 basis points for first 6 months and 125 basis points thereafter
Fees:	15.5 basis points
LIBOR-1M:	6.0625%
LIBOR-6M:	6.1875%

The amount that the security index can reset without hitting the cap is referred to as the available funds margin. A table summarizing the dynamics of available funds cap and available funds margin at changing values of the collateral index is presented in Exhibit 2. In this example, the available funds cap would only be hit if the LIBOR yield curve became significantly inverted (index mismatch risk) or the curve shifted up by more than 3.375% before the collateral could reset upwards (reset mismatch risk).

After the initial 6-month period, the surety spread requirement increases from 50 basis points to 125 basis points which effectively reduces the cap level by 75 basis points. However, the collateral gross WAC will reset up by 1% from its initial teaser rate of 11.045% to 12.045 after six months. The fully indexed rate of 12.5595%(6.1875% + 6.372%) is 1.5145% greater than the initial teaser rate but the periodic cap prevents the collateral from achieving this level on the first reset date. Therefore, even though the surety spread increases by 75 basis points, the gross WAC increases by 100 basis points for a net increase in the cap level of 25 basis points after the first six months.[2]

---

[2] Assuming no change in rates, the collateral will continue to reset up the remaining 51 basis points to the fully indexed rate after one year. At this point, the available funds cap and available funds margin will be 76 basis points higher than at the inception of the deal. This is a simplified example to illustrate the mechanics of the collateral and cap resets. The actual reset schedule is smoother since all of the collateral does not roll at the same time.

Exhibit 2: Available Funds Cap and Margin

Date	Gross WAC (%)	Available Funds Cap (%)	Security Coupon (%)	Available Funds Margin (BPs)
07/15/95	11.0450	9.8876	6.5125	338
10/15/95	11.0450	9.8876	6.5125	338
01/15/95	12.0450	10.1376	6.5125	363
04/15/96	12.0450	10.1376	6.5125	363
07/15/96	12.5595	10.6521	6.5125	414
10/15/96	12.5595	10.6521	6.5125	414
01/15/97	12.5595	10.6521	6.5125	414
04/15/97	12.5595	10.6521	6.5125	414
07/15/97	12.5595	10.6521	6.5125	414

Lifetime Cap

Another factor which affects the security coupon level is the life cap level. Returning to our example, with a weighted average gross life cap level of 17.039%, the life cap can be calculated by substituting the collateral life cap for the gross coupon in the previous formula for the available funds cap.

Weighted Average Life Cap: 17.039%
Less Servicing (50bp):   16.539%
Less Fees (15.5bp):   16.385%
Less Surety Spread (125bp): 15.134%

The same calculation can be applied to determine the lifetime floor level by substituting the collateral weighted average life floor for the weighted average life cap.

STRUCTURAL ENHANCEMENTS

In recent years, several structural enhancements have been made in HEL floater structures to alleviate investor concerns emanating due to the deterioration of available funds margins. This has occurred as a result of the proliferation of the origination of teasered loans, potential coupon shortfalls and average life extension concerns arising due to the volatility of interest rates. At the same time, attempts have also been made to provide structural relief to issuers to offset the cost of some of these enhancements for investors.

With the increase in teasered issuance, and the resultant tight margins, structural innovations were incorporated in deal structures to provide investors with more available funds. The first approach involves buying a strip of amortizing (at a predetermined amortization rate) interest rate caps to offset the tight margins during the teaser period. This is a fairly straight forward approach but can be expensive depending on the levels in the cap market. In this arrangement, the cap provider will pay the difference between the prevailing indexed rate and the cap rate for a specified period of time and does not take any prepayment risk. In such arrangements, any excess cash flows from the interest rate caps due to faster amortization of the securities are paid to the issuer to offset the cost of buying the strip of caps to uncap the available funds. In addition, the issue may also sell higher strike caps to recoup the premium by using an interest rate corridor strategy. An alternative approach involves the prepayment of some of the ongoing fees for the teaser period. However, the level of fee expenses has a direct impact on the margin. As such, if fees are prepaid, then the margin during the period that was prepaid will be higher and the cost of prepaying those costs can be priced into the deal.

Other features have sought to structurally alleviate potential extension of the securities in bearish interest rate scenarios. One way of addressing extension concerns has been to enhance the cleanup call provision so that it would be exercised on the first available date or the investor would receive a higher coupon rate. This step-up feature is usually a significant increase over the normal coupon rate and all but assures that the bonds will be called. In the example deal mentioned above, the cleanup call step-up feature adds 100 basis points to the coupon rate after the 10% cleanup call date subject to available funds. Other innovations have served to enhance available fund caps by using some of the cash flows from the fixed-rate portion to enhance the floating-rate portion in mixed collateral deals. One such feature provides for a strip from the fixed-rate tranche to be made available for available funds of the floating-rate tranche. This had the effect of raising the available funds cap by the cash provided by the fixed-rate strip amount and causing the cap to move out of the money. The result has been decreased cap costs which have allowed the deals to be priced at tighter spreads. In addition to the issuer benefiting from tighter execution in the asset securitizations, in such cases if the lifetime cap of the collateral is out of the money, then the fixed-rate strip accrues to the issuer.

The last significant enhancement to the HEL floater structure was the inclusion of an interest shortfall accrual provision whereby any interest not paid out due to the available funds cap will accrue at the floater coupon rate and be paid out of residual cash flows when it is available. In effect, the available funds cap does not limit how the floater coupon can go but rather delays payment for any interest above the available funds cap rate subject to the life cap. As with any security, the delay of payment does have an impact on the value of the security and timing of cash flow. However, since interest shortfall occurs at the current floating rate, the yield impact of the shortfall will be significantly mitigated. It is important to note that if a deal has an interest rate shortfall feature, all interest shortfall accrual may be forfeited once the deal has been called at the 10% optional cleanup call, which is beneficial from the point of view of the issuer.

CONCLUSION

HEL floaters are becoming an increasingly important sector of the ABS sector. There are several key issues involved in the evaluation of these securities. The underwriting standards of the issuer are significant in that each issuer has its own servicing and issuing guidelines. These guidelines ultimately affect the quality of the collateral backing the securities. If the issuing or servicing guidelines are weak, then there is a greater likelihood of loan delinquency or foreclosure. Similarly, the structural credit enhancement is a key determinant in the likelihood of any delinquencies or foreclosures being passed through to the bond holders. If the credit support is inadequate for the level of delinquencies, then there will be insufficient funds available to meet interest payments on the securities. From the investor's perspective, the riskiest period in terms of the available funds cap is typically the teaser period. If the collateral loans were predominantly issued with teaser interest rates, the level of discount and length of time until they reach fully-indexed levels can add a significant amount of risk of interest shortfall, particularly if the market rallies during the teaser period. Other considerations such as the inclusion of interest shortfall reimbursement, overcollateralization, and acceleration may mitigate the risk of the securities.

Chapter 20

Dynamics of Cleanup Calls in ABS

Thomas Zimmerman
First Vice President
Fixed Income Research
Prudential Securities Inc.

INTRODUCTION

Cleanup calls are common features in many ABS transactions. While investors are aware of the existence of cleanup-call provisions in ABS structures, the exact variety and significance of these features may not be widely known. These calls are typically optional, but the likelihood of them being exercised can be high since there are significant economic benefits associated with exercising the call. In this chapter we discuss the dynamics of these cleanup-call provisions.

CALL FEATURES

The call feature can take one or more of the following forms.

Percent of Collateral

Percent of collateral is by far the most common form of call feature in regular amortizing issues. When the current balance of the issue's collateral reaches a predetermined percentage of the collateral's original balance, the remaining collateral can be called and any outstanding bonds are redeemed at par. The most common call percentage is 10% of the original collateral.

Percent of Bonds

Percent of bonds call structure is similar to the percent of collateral call. However, this type of call typically is used in accelerated deals in which excess collateral interest is used to pay bond principal. This makes it difficult to use a predetermined percent of principal as the trigger event. When the number of bonds outstanding reaches a predetermined percentage of the original number of bonds issued, the remaining bonds can be called.

Percent of Tranche

Percent of tranche feature is common in deals in which there is more than one collateral type. For example, in a home equity loan (HEL) deal with an available-funds floater backed by adjustable-rate mortgages (ARM) collateral, the floater might be called when the outstanding ARM collateral reaches a predetermined percentage of the original ARM collateral. This type of call also could be structured to make the issue callable after one bond has reached a predetermined factor. For example, a deal can be called after a derivative tranche has finished paying.

Auction Call

An auction call feature is triggered by a date and will then be exercised dependent on market conditions. For example, after a predetermined date, the remaining collateral will be made available for bids on a servicing released basis. If the bids result in a price greater than par, then the bonds would typically be called with the premium going to the trustee and ultimately to the issuer through the residual. This feature is common in HEL deals, especially those with available-funds floaters.

Call on or After Specified Date

A call on or after date feature is similar to the call feature for corporate or agency securities. Rather than a percentage of collateral as the trigger event, the issue can be called after a predetermined date.

Latter of Percent or Date

With latter of percent or date type of call, if the percent of collateral outstanding reaches a predetermined percentage of the original balance before the call date, then the deal can be called. If the percent of outstanding collateral is above the predetermined level but the call date has passed, the deal can be called.

Insurer Call

Insurer call feature is different than the other call features described above in the sense that the trigger event is based on cumulative defaults rather than how the collateral pays down or a date. For example, if the cumulative loss history of the collateral reaches a predetermined level, then the deal can be called by the insurer.

ISSUER PERSPECTIVE

Most of the call features described above are intended as a method to protect the issuer from enduring unnecessary and excessive costs associated with maintaining a deal with small outstanding loan balances. Since there are fixed costs associated with maintaining a deal and the servicing income declines as the collateral pays down, the incremental cost for each loan becomes prohibitive at some point. For the purpose of structuring deals, this point can be measured in terms of the percentage of outstanding collateral. For example, if a package of loans is securitized, the issuer pays fees to the trustee and the rating agencies. Furthermore, there are costs associated with maintaining the credit enhancements such as overcollateralization and spread accounts. These costs are usually either fixed or have a floor. Therefore, as a deal pays down, the net servicing spread will decline to a point at which it is more cost effective to call the remaining collateral in the deal.

Beyond the cost savings mentioned above, issuers also may benefit from tighter pricing levels because of the tighter principal window that results from the cleanup call. Furthermore, if an auction call is exercised, the residual holder, who is typically the issuer, may make a windfall profit on the difference between the bid levels received and par.

After a cleanup call is exercised, the issuer has a few options in terms of what to do with the outstanding loans that are no longer securitized. The first option is to sell the collateral as whole loans. This is particularly true when there is an auction call that is in the money. However, the issuer can retain the loans and continue to service them or possibly roll them into a new issue. Putting them into a new issue yet to be priced is fine, but using them to fund a prefunded issue may be a problem, since the collateral guidelines for these issues may limit the range of allowable seasoning of pools that are included in the collateral. Alternatively, a new deal composed entirely of seasoned collateral conceivably could be structured, but the number of loans would have to be very high because of the small loan balances. Moreover, the weighted average maturity of the collateral would be very short. Since few deals have reached the call decision point, it remains to be seen if this is a viable option. However, in theory, it is possible to create a deal consisting of all seasoned collateral.

INVESTOR PERSPECTIVE

From the investor's perspective, the benefits of the cleanup call are both quantitative and qualitative. When the call is exercised, the investor receives the remaining principal amount at par. Obviously, if the bonds are trading at a discount, this results in a pickup of yield and total return. If the bonds are trading at a premium, the exercise of the call would decrease the yield and total return of the security. However, premium callable bonds should trade at wider spread levels compared to par or discount callable securities. Furthermore, if the bonds are priced to call, they effectively roll down the curve, which results in a spread pickup. Depending on the investor's perspectives, the tighter principal window and shorter average life resulting from the call could be considered benefits. On a qualitative basis, most investors avoid securities with long tails because they are a nuisance to account for. The call eliminates this tail and results in a much cleaner cash flow.

It is also worth noting that the cleanup call in a tranched deal only affects the last few securities in the structure. Naturally, in a sequential pay structure, the shorter average-life bonds will be paid off before the cleanup call is triggered. In addition, when a deal includes a floating-rate tranche, this tranche is typically a pass-through structure from a separate group of collateral. As such, the call on the floating-rate security is independent from the call on the fixed securities and will be triggered when the factor on the floater reaches the predetermined level.

Exhibit 1: Effects of the Cleanup Call on a Tranched HEL Security

Issue:	Money Store1994C-A6
Collateral:	Fixed / Adjustable Rate
Yield(%):	7.78
Net/Gross WAC (%):	10.07 / 10.57
WAM (Mos.):	22.351
Price (32nds):	102-09
Spread (bps):	+152

	Immediate Parallel Interest-Rate Shift (bps)						
	DI 300	DI 200	DI 100	NC	UI 100	UI 200	UI 300
VCPR(%)	30	27	24	21	18	14	10
To Maturity							
Yield	7.87	7.88	7.89	7.91	7.92	7.93	7.94
Spread / WAL	155	154	153	152	151	148	145
Avg. Life	13.58	14.86	16.21	17.49	19.35	21.62	24.06
Total Return	32.87	25.01	16.62	7.99	−0.72	−9.37	−17.59
To Call							
Yield	7.67	7.71	7.75	7.78	7.81	7.84	7.88
Spread / WAL	151	153	154	154	154	155	155
Avg. Life	6.62	7.37	8.29	9.12	10.29	12.04	14.29
Total Return	20.87	17.36	13.08	7.88	1.97	−4.90	−12.60
Yield (%) Comparison: To Maturity Versus To Call							
	−0.20	−0.17	−0.16	−0.13	−0.11	−0.09	−0.06
Average Life (Yrs.) Comparison: To Maturity Versus To Call							
	−6.96	−7.49	−7.92	−8.37	−9.07	−9.58	−9.77
Total Return (%) Comparison: To Maturity Versus To Call							
	−12.00	−7.65	−3.54	−0.10	+2.70	+4.47	+4.99

Source: PSI IMPACT Database.

Exhibit 1 contains an analysis of the yield and total return effects of the cleanup call on the last fixed-rate tranche of a HEL structure. In this case, since the security is priced at a premium, exercising the call results in a decrease in total return and yield. In such callable securities, as the likelihood of the call being exercised increases, the current spread is likely to reflect the expectation that the security will be called at the first possible opportunity. In the event the security was priced at a discount, the call would enhance the yield in all interest rate scenarios and the total return in the bearish interest rate scenarios. However, the pricing spread would less likely reflect the beneficial effects of the call being exercised.

Chapter 21

ABS B-Pieces

Thomas Zimmerman
First Vice President
Fixed Income Research
Prudential Securities Inc.

INTRODUCTION

The senior/subordinate structure is one of the principal credit-enhancement techniques used in the asset-backed securities (ABS) market. Some issuers retain the *subordinate* piece, or *B-piece*, but, in many instances it is sold, either publicly or as a private offering. The B-piece, itself, usually is supported by one or more credit enhancements in order for it to receive an investment-grade rating, often at the single-A level. Because subordinate classes are more exposed to loss than senior triple-A classes, B-piece investors naturally are more concerned about the probability of loss than are senior-tranche investors. Also, ABS issues are backed by a wide range of collateral and each asset type has its own unique pattern of losses. These characteristics can, on occasion, make it difficult for investors to identify relative value in the ABS B-piece market.

In an effort to aid the investor in evaluating ABS B-pieces, this chapter briefly reviews the ABS B-piece market, explains the various ways loss data is presented, reviews the loss data for several major types of ABSs, and describes how various credit-support mechanisms are used to provide protection for B-pieces.

THE ABS B-PIECE MARKET

B-pieces are a common part of many ABS issues. As Exhibit 1 shows, from 1990 to 1995, a large number of B-pieces were issued in each of the major sectors of the ABS market. Credit cards and autos are the sectors with the largest B-piece volume. Most transactions in these sectors contain a B-piece and these two sections have the largest volume of issuance in the ABS market.

In both cards and autos, B-pieces accounted for around 6.5% of issuance in 1991 and 1992. In the card sector, B-piece issuance slipped to 4.0% in 1993/1994 and then rebounded to 6.9% in 1995. The swing reflected a changing composition of credit support. For example, in 1993/1994, several new issuers chose to rely entirely on collateral invested amounts (CIAs) rather than on subordination. In the auto sector, the decline in the B-piece ratio reflects a change to alternate forms of credit support, as well as reduced issuance by the Big Three U.S. auto companies. GMAC tended to rely on subordination more than other auto issuers, and they currently account for a much smaller percentage of ABS auto issuance.

In the home-equity loan (HEL) sector, the use of B-pieces has declined over the past few years and they are no longer used frequently (credit support in HELs usually relies on overcollateralization or a reserve fund and a surety wrap). In the manufactured-housing (MH) sector, several levels of subordination are used frequently, and the combined volume of support bonds as a percent of total issuance is much higher in this sector than in other ABS sectors. This reflects the higher rate of loss typically found in MHs. However, the level of losses and, consequently, the required level of support has dropped sharply from the 1991 to 1992 recession years. Today, subordinate bonds account for around 9.2% of MH issuance, about one-half the level of 1991 to 1992. In addition to the sectors listed in Exhibit 1, B-pieces also have been used with some of the smaller and less frequently issued types of ABSs, such as student loans, trade receivables, and equipment loans and leases.

Depending on the complexity and novelty of the underlying collateral, issuers and underwriters have used a wide range of policies with respect to placing B-pieces. On simple, straightforward transactions, such as credit cards and autos, the B-piece usually is rated and sold publicly. As the collateral becomes more novel or losses become more difficult to project, other options are chosen, including rating the B-piece but placing it privately, as in some HEL deals. In some cases, the B-piece is not rated and is sold privately to an investor who is both familiar with the underlying industry and the particular issuer. The due diligence required in this case is much less than if the security were rated or the general investing community were expected to become comfortable with the credit of the security. This last approach has been used with the B-pieces from some equipment-lease backed transactions. Finally, in a fair number of transactions, the B-piece is retained by the issuer.

Exhibit 1: Volume of Public ABS B-Pieces by Sector

	Credit Cards					Autos		
	Number	Issuance				Number	Issuance		
	B-Piece Bonds	B-Piece ($BB)	Total ($BB)	B-Pieces as % of Total		B-Piece Bonds	B-Piece ($BB)	Total ($BB)	B-Pieces as % of Total
1990	12	1.0	25.2	4.0	1990	6	0.6	12.9	4.7
1991	18	1.4	22.1	6.3	1991	16	1.2	18.4	6.5
1992	18	1.1	16.5	6.7	1992	20	1.4	21.7	6.5
1993	18	0.8	19.8	4.0	1993	16	1.2	26.5	4.5
1994	36	1.3	32.1	4.0	1994	23	0.8	16.4	4.9
1995	78	3.4	49.1	6.9	1995	28	1.2	25.9	4.6

	HELs					MHs		
	Number	Issuance				Number	Issuance		
	B-Piece Bonds	B-Piece ($BB)	Total ($BB)	B-Pieces as % of Total		B-Piece Bonds	B-Piece ($BB)	Total ($BB)	B-Pieces as % of Total
1990	14	0.3	6.4	4.7	1990	8	0.17	1.42	12.0
1991	18	1.0	11.2	8.9	1991	9	0.25	1.34	18.7
1992	15	0.3	6.5	4.6	1992	13	0.59	3.07	19.2
1993	18	0.3	7.4	4.0	1993	6	0.26	2.74	9.5
1994	17	0.3	10.5	2.9	1994	23	0.45	4.66	9.7
1995	6	0.2	15.2	1.0	1995	35	0.53	5.76	9.2

Source: Prudential Securities' IMPACT data base

Exhibit 2: Credit Card B-Pieces
Credit Rating and Spread for the First Quarter 1995

	Class	Rating	Average Life (Yrs.)	Spread (BPs.)	A/AAA Spread (BPs.)
Advanta 1995-A	Sr.	AAA	5.2	1-Mo. LIBOR+18	20
	Sub.	A	5.5	1-Mo. LIBOR+38	
Sears 1995-2	Sr.	AAA	5.0	48	20
	Sub.	A	6.0	68	
Standard 1995-1	Sr.	AAA	10.0	60	20
	Sub.	A	10.0	80	
Neiman Marcus 1995-1	Sr.	AAA	5.0	48	15
	Sub.	A	5.3	63	
Chase 1995-1	Sr.	AAA	3.0	1-Mo. LIBOR+13	15.5
	Sub.	A	3.6	1-Mo. LIBOR+28.5	
Spiegel 1995-A	Sr.	AAA	5.0	52	23
	Sub.	A	5.5	75	
MBNA 1995-A	Sr.	AAA	9.4	1-Mo. LIBOR+27	18
	Sub.	A	9.5	1-Mo. LIBOR+45	
Chevy Chase 1995-A	Sr.	AAA	5.0	1-Mo. LIBOR+20	15
	Sub.	A	5.0	1-Mo. LIBOR+35	
Peoples 1995-1	Sr.	AAA	5.0	1-Mo. LIBOR+20	15
	Sub.	A	5.0	1-Mo. LIBOR+35	

Source: Prudential Securities' IMPACT data base

Most B-pieces from card and auto issues, which comprise the largest percentage of all ABS B-pieces, are single-A rated. Issuers of MHs, like issuers of whole-loan mortgage-backed securities (MBSs), have utilized support tranches with a range of ratings, including single-A, double-A, and triple-B. ABS issues backed by sub-prime auto loans and other collateral with higher than usual losses may have some support tranches that are below investment grade.

ABS B-Piece Spreads

The spread on an ABS B-piece reflects two major factors, the spread on the senior class in the deal and the senior/subordinate (single-A/triple-A credit) spread. For example, consider the B-piece credit-card spreads shown in Exhibit 2. The B-pieces in the exhibit were issued in the first-quarter 1995. Virtually all of them were rated single-A. Note that they were all priced at about the same spread (15 to 20 basis points) to their corresponding senior class regardless of the spread at which the senior class itself traded to Treasuries. The senior class/Treasury spread, of course, will vary with the average life, remaining maturity, asset quality and size of the issue, as well as the perceived credit quality of the issuer. In contrast, the spread between the B-piece and the senior class is driven largely by the general perception of the value of the credit pickup to triple-A from single-A, and is similar for most of the issues.

Exhibit 3: Credit Card B-Pieces
Credit Rating and Spread for the Fourth-Quarter 1995

	Class	Rating	Average Life (Yrs.)	Spread (BPs.)	A/AAA Spread (BPs.)
Standard 1995-1	Sr.	AAA	10.0	51	13
	Sub.	A	10.0	64	
Chemical 1995-2	Sr.	AAA	5.0	40	15
	Sub.	A	5.1	55	
MBNA 1995-1	Sr.	AAA	5.0	1-Mo. LIBOR+17	10
	Sub.	A	5.1	1-Mo. LIBOR+27	
AT&T 1995-2	Sr.	AAA	4.9	40	15
	Sub.	A	4.9	55	
Standard 1995-10	Sr.	AAA	3.2	32	14
	Sub.	A	3.2	46	
Mellon 1995-A	Sr.	AAA	5.0	1-Mo. LIBOR+19	11
	Sub.	A	5.0	1-Mo. LIBOR+30	
Sears 1995-5	Sr.	AAA	7.1	48	12
	Sub.	A	8.3	60	
First USA 1995-6	Sr.	AAA	4.9	1-Mo. LIBOR+17	16
	Sub.	A	4.9	1-Mo. LIBOR+33	

Source: Prudential Securities' IMPACT data base

Exhibit 3 shows credit-card spreads in the fourth-quarter 1995. Senior/subordinate spreads tightened 5 basis points from the first quarter which was in line with the tightening that occurred in 5- and 7-year financial corporate single-A/triple-A spreads over that period.

As in the card sector, most auto issues contain a B-piece for credit support but, on occasion, in the auto sector the subordinate piece is retained by the issuer. Also, frequently in auto transactions the credit support is in the form of a *super-senior structure*. This type of support includes a subordinate bond to enhance the senior bonds, the entire deal is wrapped by a monoline insurer, and both the senior and subordinate pieces receive a triple-A rating.

The NationsBank 1995-A auto deal shown in Exhibit 4 is a typical grantor trust structure with a B-piece credit support. With this structure the B-piece is usually priced 14 to 15 basis points behind the senior piece. The same spread is common on tranched issues. When an auto deal is wrapped, as in the UAC 1995-D and Western Financial 1995-5 issues, the typical senior/subordinate spread is reduced to seven to nine basis points. Note that in the Premier 1995-4 and Olympic 1995-E deals, the subordinate bonds are slightly longer than the senior bonds and hence, carry several more basis points of spread than the spread ranges just mentioned would indicate. The senior/sub auto spread differentials in the fourth-quarter 1995 shown in Exhibit 4 are similar to those of the first-quarter 1995. In large part, this reflects the fact that the spread between 2-year single-A and triple-A corporates was about the same in the fourth quarter as it was in the first quarter.

Exhibit 4: Auto-Loan B-Pieces
Credit Rating and Spread for the Fourth-Quarter 1995

	Class	Rating	Average Life (Yrs.)	Spread (BPs.)	A/AAA Spread (BPs.)
Premier 1995-4	A4	AAA	3.0	35	18
	B	A	3.3	53	
UAC 1995-D	A	AAA	1.9	52	8
	B	AAA*	1.9	60	
Olympic 1995-E	A3	AAA	2.0	45	13
	B	AAA*	2.3	58	
NationsBank 1995-A	A	AAA	1.5	46	14
	B	A	1.5	60	
Western Financial 1995-5	A	AAA	1.8	52	7
	B	AAA*	1.8	59	

* Surety wrapped to triple-A.

Source: Asset Sales Report

Exhibit 5: Manufactured Housing B-Pieces

	Class	Rating	Average Life (Yrs.)	Spread (BPs.)	Sr./Sub.* Spread (BPs.)
Vanderbilt 1995-B	A4	AAA	7.2	73	—
	A5	AAA	9.8	92	—
	A6	Aa3	12.9	125	25
	B1	Baa2	6.7	135	62
	B2	Baa2	12.6	167	67
Green Tree 1995-10	A4	AAA	7.1	71	—
	A5	AAA	10.3	94	—
	A6	AAA	17.2	145	—
	M1	Aa3	12.6	140	40
	B1	Baa1	8.3	145	63
	B2	Baa1	17.2	177	32

*Subordinate-class spread less interpolated spread from triple-A tranches.

Source: Prudential Securities' IMPACT data base

The MH B-piece sector is smaller than the auto and card B-piece sectors, but it offers a wider range of credits. Typically MH transactions, like many whole-loan mortgage deals, are structured with a series of support classes, ranging from triple-B to double-A. Some examples of MH B-pieces are illustrated in Exhibit 5, which shows two typical MH issues.

ABSs backed by collateral such as equipment leases, student loans, and C and D auto loans often rely on subordination for credit support and hence are also a supply of B-piece securities. However, in these sectors, senior/subordinate spread differentials are not as consistent as in the card or auto sectors. Sometimes, they are considerably wider because the collateral is less familiar or the expected loss rates are more difficult to ascertain.

Exhibit 6: Single-A/Triple-A Spread Differentials for 5-Year Financial Corporates

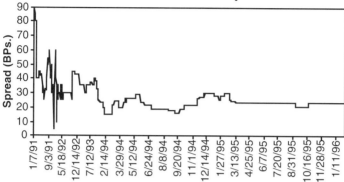

Source: Prudential Securities' IMPACT data base

Exhibit 7: Financial Single-A/Triple-A Spread Differentials Versus Senior/Subordinate Credit Card Differentials*

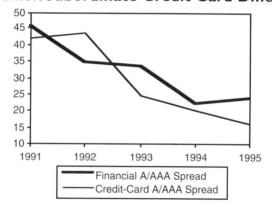

* Annual averages.

Source: Prudential Securities' IMPACT data base and Moody's Investors Services

ABS Spreads versus Corporate Spreads

Single-A/triple-A credit spreads in the corporate market can be used as a benchmark for single-A/triple-A spreads in the ABS market. For example, Exhibit 6 shows single-A/triple-A spreads since 1991 for 5-year financial corporates. As Exhibit 6 shows, corporate single-A/triple-A spread differentials can vary widely over the business cycle. In the 5-year sector, they widened to +80 basis points during the recession of 1991, whereas today they are around 12 to 15 basis points.

Exhibit 7 compares the average spread differential on 5-year single-A/triple-A financial corporates and senior/subordinate spreads on credit cards over the period from 1991 to 1995. Although the two series are not perfectly correlated, they are quite similar. This is not surprising since, among the ABS sectors, credit cards are the best understood, have readily available loss histories, are well known by many investors, and are the closest to the corporate-bullet structure. For these reasons, investors treat the senior/subordinate credit risk on a credit card virtually the same as the credit risk between a single-A and a triple-A corporate issue.

THE EVALUATION PROCESS FOR CREDIT RATING

The question that a B-piece investor must ask is whether the credit pickup from the ABS B-piece is more or less than the single-A/triple-A credit pickup available in other ABS or corporate sectors given the credit risk of the bonds under consideration. To address this question, the investor must go through a process similar to the one rating agencies go through when rating a B-piece security.

A rating-agency evaluation of a B-piece includes the following.

1. an understanding of the historical loss data for the particular type of collateral underlying the deal.
2. a determination of the historical loss rates for the particular *issuer* and whether that performance is changing.
3. from this information, estimation of *expected losses* for the pool of loans under normal and stressed economic conditions.
4. given the expected loss estimate under various scenarios, determination of the level of *credit support* needed to achieve the desired rating on the senior and subordinate securities.

Once the rating agency has determined the required level of credit support, the issuer and the underwriter will determine the least-cost method of structuring the transaction, choosing from among a variety of credit-support mechanisms.

Investors should perform a similar evaluation by using historical loss data to develop an estimate of future losses and by reviewing the deal structure to determine the level of protection provided the B-piece.

HISTORICAL LOSS EXPERIENCE BY SECTOR

The following section describes loss data for various types of ABSs, including autos, credit cards, HELs, and MHs. Before examining the data, however, those not familiar with the numerous methods used to present loss data may wish to review the appendix to this chapter, which contains a detailed description of loss terminology. Understanding loss data is no small task because it is reported in a variety of ways. It is reported for portfolios and for pools, as dollars and as percentages, as net losses and gross losses, as a percent of current receivables and a percent of original balance, and for a single period and on a cumulative basis. The appendix reviews these various methods of presenting loss data.

Auto Loans

In general, cumulative losses over the life of most auto issues average about 1% to 2% of the initial balance, but there is a good deal of variation from company to company depending on underwriting and servicing standards. Exhibit 8 shows annual portfolio-loss data for several of the major ABS auto-loan issuers. The data were taken from company prospectuses and shows a fairly wide variation. The Big Three U.S. auto companies have fairly comparable loss rates, running roughly between 0.5% and 1.5%. In contrast, some of the foreign car companies, such as Volvo and Daimler Benz, have much lower loss experiences. This appears to reflect the higher credit characteristics of the typical buyer of those upscale cars. However, even though Honda, Toyota, and Nissan all have similar customer profiles, they have very different average loss rates, which suggests that their underwriting and collection standards vary considerably.

Auto-loan losses also are sensitive to economic cycles. As shown in Exhibit 8, losses mounted during the last recession only to decline in recent years as the economy recovered. When reviewing loss data, it is important to have historical data covering at least one complete business cycle to see how the collateral performs during a recession or serious slowing of the economy.

Exhibit 8: Net Portfolio Losses for Major Auto-Loan ABS Issuers
(as a Percent of Outstanding Receivables at Year End)

	1988	1989	1990	1991	1992	1993	1994
Chrysler		0.83	0.98	1.21	0.97	0.75	0.73p
GMAC	0.93	1.13	1.11	1.08	0.89	0.64	0.57p
Ford	1.40	1.57	1.31	1.29	0.90	0.69	0.59p
Daimler Benz		0.30	0.54	0.55	0.90	0.46	
Volvo	0.12	0.06	0.19	0.51	0.26p		
Honda		0.24	0.43	0.51	0.40	0.41	
Nissan	1.18	2.42	3.19	1.99	2.40	2.78	0.99p
Toyota	1.30	1.33	1.01	0.85	0.69	0.49p	
World Omni	1.60	1.82	1.68	1.87	1.22	0.93	
Olympic					0.22	0.52	0.66
UAC	0.63	1.29	0.80	0.71	0.64	0.69	1.08
RCSB	1.19	1.29	1.02	0.95	1.33p		
Western Fin.			1.21	1.40	1.73	1.53	1.09

p = preliminary

Source: Moody's Asset Credit Evaluations

Exhibit 9: Cumulative Losses for Selected Auto-Loan Deals as a Percent of Original Balances

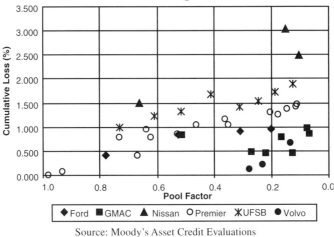

Source: Moody's Asset Credit Evaluations

While portfolio data can give a general picture of overall losses, it is also important to look at losses on individual pools of auto loans. Exhibits 9 and 10 show cumulative losses for a number of individual auto-loan pools through the third-quarter 1995. Exhibit 9 shows losses as a percent of the original balance, while Exhibit 10 shows losses as a percent of the balance paid down. The pools range in age from a few months (pool factors greater than 0.800) to nearly three years (pool factors less than 0.200). Exhibit 9 shows a clear pattern for the different companies. As the pools age and losses increase, the cumulative losses rise in a fairly uniform manner. By extrapolating to the end of the period, one can estimate total losses for a pool.

As discussed in the appendix, the cumulative data in Exhibit 10 (i.e., loss as a percentage of the balance paid down), is easier to interpret because it takes into account the changing level of the outstanding balances and thus gives an ongoing estimate of the level total cumulative losses are likely to reach over the life of the pool.

The pool data in Exhibits 9 and 10 show a slightly different picture than the portfolio data in Exhibit 8. The portfolio data show that, in recent years, the Big Three have had roughly the same level of losses, but the pool data show that Chrysler (Premier) pools have had the largest losses, followed by the Ford pools, and then the GMAC pools. It should be noted, however, that the relatively low loss experience on the GMAC pools is due, in part, to GMAC using more seasoned loans in some of their securitizations. Since the largest loss rates on auto loans occur in the second year, a pool comprised largely of loans seasoned for two years or more will show a lower loss rate than a pool of recently originated loans.

Exhibit 10: Cumulative Losses for Selected Auto-Loan Deals as a Percent of Balances Paid Down

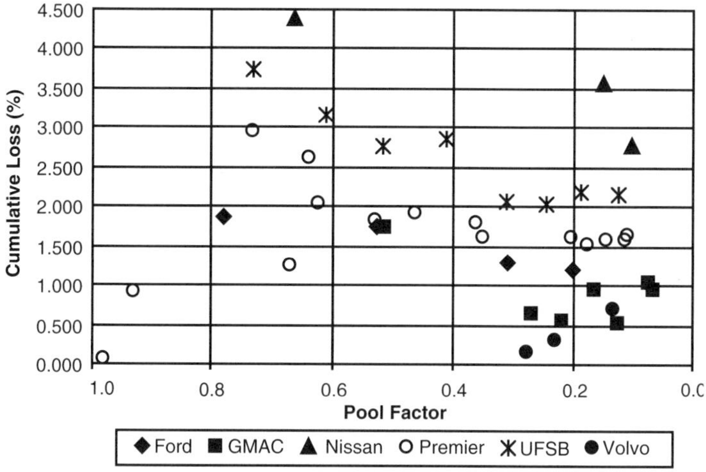

Source: Moody's Asset Credit Evaluations

The data in Exhibit 10 also show that because the auto-loss curve peaks at around 20 to 24 months, pools with factors in the 0.800 to 0.500 range often have higher cumulative loss rates than do older pools with lower factors. This also means that the cumulative rates observed on pools in the 0.800- to 0.500-factor range may overstate the final loss rate on the pools. This can be seen in Exhibit 10 for both UFSB and Chrysler, where the loss rates decline as the pool factors decline below 0.500.

It is important to understand that loss rates are driven by company-specific underwriting and servicing standards, as well as by the overall economy, and that those factors change over time. Historic data, such as that shown in Exhibits 8, 9 and 10, can only give a rough estimate of likely losses. Developing a sound projection of losses for a particular deal requires a careful examination of the latest information available with respect to the issuer, the industry and the general economy.

Credit Cards

Credit cards have one of the highest loss rates in the ABS market. There are two reasons for this. First, average balances are much lower on card accounts than on auto or home-equity loans, so card issuers will lend to individuals with lower credit. Second, there are fewer recoveries in the card business since a credit-card line is an unsecured line of credit. On the other hand, credit cards typically have the highest interest rates of any source of consumer credit. These high finance rates are required to offset the high loss rates. On a month-to-month basis, a much larger amount of excess spread is used to offset losses in cards than in most other ABS sectors.

Exhibit 11: Credit-Card Master Trust Charge-Off Rates

	1987	1988	1989	1990	1991	1992	1993	1994	1995
Advanta MT	6.46	6.05	4.50	4.23	4.78	4.83	3.85	3.02 (3)	
American Express MT			0.98	1.18	1.31	1.18	0.99	0.82 (6)	
Chase Manhattan MT		4.06	3.64	3.86	5.08	5.79	5.23	4.68	4.24 (3)
Discover MT		3.51	3.28	3.90	4.33	4.37	4.11	3.69	3.79 (6)
First Chicago MT	4.19	4.43	4.48	5.00	5.96	5.67	5.20	5.34	5.78 (3)
First USA MT				3.77	3.89	4.41	3.59	2.48	2.21 (3)
MBMA MT		1.98	2.17	2.56	3.47	3.80	3.41	3.28 (6)	
MBNA MT II						3.88	3.48	3.12	3.23 (6)
Sears MT I			2.45	2.89	3.59	4.10 (3)			
Capital One MT (a)						6.06	2.84	1.91	2.28 (3)
Standard MT 1									
Old Series		5.50	5.46	5.86	7.37	7.62	6.87 (9)		
New Series						6.10	5.01	3.79	3.99 (3)

Parentheses indicate the latest month that data were reported.
a = formerly Signet MT.

Source: Moody's Asset Credit Evaluations

Exhibit 11 shows historic charge-off rates for a number of the larger master-card trusts. Several items are noteworthy in the data.

- The average level of portfolio losses, between 3% and 5%, are high compared to losses on other ABS loan portfolios that typically fall in the 1% to 2% range.
- There can be a fairly wide range of losses between issuers, reflecting underwriting standards, and market segmentation.
- Losses reflect economic cycles. The recession of 1990/1991 saw credit-card losses rise, while the recent period of economic growth has seen loss rates fall.

Note that all credit-card securities issued from a common master trust will show the same delinquency and charge-off rates. This is not the case in other sectors of the ABS market where loss rates on individual pools may differ significantly from the loss rate on the overall portfolio.

However, each series from a common trust will have its own credit support level. Therefore, when charge-offs increase, the level of protection varies for the different series. Cumulative loss data, as illustrated in Exhibits 9 and 10 for auto loans, are not used to describe loss data on a pool of receivables, since the pool of receivables is being replenished constantly as principal is paid down and losses charged off.

A convenient way to track average losses on credit-card trusts is to follow the *Aggregate Credit Card Charge Off Index* published by Moody's. Exhibit 12 shows this index through September 1995. The index was in the low 3% range in late 1989, peaked at over 6% in the summer of 1992, and declined below 4% in late 1994. The index turned up in mid 1995 and may rise further given the general deterioration in consumer credit and a slower pace of economic activity. Moody's also publishes a delinquency index that is a good leading indicator of future losses. While an index is no substitute for data specific to an individual issuer, Moody's indices are useful for following broad credit trends in the credit-card industry.

HELs

The home-equity loan market typically does not use a senior/subordinate structure for credit support. Rather, it relies almost exclusively on 100% surety wraps. Consequently, there are few B-pieces backed by home-equity-loan collateral. However, some investors are approaching their maximum exposure limits on certain monoline insurers, suggesting that some issuers may turn to the senior/subordinate structure in the future. As a result, we have included an analysis of the HEL market in our review of historic ABS loss data.

Exhibit 13 presents portfolio losses for several major issuers of HEL securities. As the data show, losses on HELs vary a great deal over time and from issuer to issuer. Portfolio losses have ranged roughly between 0.5% and 1.5%, with some companies reporting losses as low as 0.05%.

Exhibit 12: Moody's Aggregate Credit Card Charge-Off Index

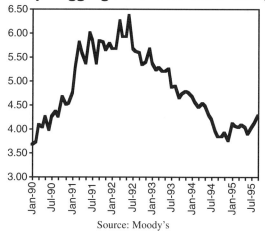

Source: Moody's

Exhibit 13: Net Portfolio Losses for Major HEL ABS Issuers
(As a Percent of Outstanding Receivables at Year End)

	1991	1992	1993	1994	1995
EQCC	0.30	0.47	0.65	0.55	0.57 (9)
Conti Mortgage	0.21	0.20	0.24	0.06	
Advanta	0.46	0.75	1.33	1.69	0.90
First Alliance	0.00	0.05	0.14	0.12	0.10 (9)
UCFC	0.41	0.59	0.88	0.84	0.57 (9)
Money Store	0.47	1.13	1.06	0.54	0.32 (9)

Parentheses indicate the latest month that data was reported.

Source: Company prosectuses

Exhibit 14: Cumulative Losses for Selected HEL Deals as a Percent of Original Balances

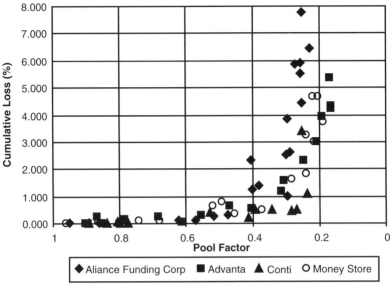

Source: Moody's Asset Credit Evaluations

Exhibit 14 shows cumulative losses as a percentage of original balances for a group of HELs from several issuers. The data not only differ between companies, but show some large differences within companies. The most noticeable difference is the very high cumulative loss rates on virtually all deals that have pool factors of less than 0.350. One might think this is an indication that HELs suffer very large losses late in a deal's life. In reality, those pools were issued in the 1990 to 1991 period and, for several reasons, HELs of that vintage suffered unusually large losses. First, they were hit with the 1990 to 1991 recession, which increased loss rates on many consumer-loan categories, especially those related to housing. Second, some issuers expanded their programs and experimented with new underwriting guidelines, which also led to higher than usual losses. The combined result was high loss rates. Several deals from that period are likely to reach cumulative losses of 6.0% to 8.0% or more of the original balance.

The HEL issues with factors greater than 0.400 are more representative of the issues from the last several years. These deals appear to be on a trend to have total cumulative losses of around 1.00% to 2.00%. However, to get a good sense of how any new HEL will perform, it is necessary to carefully examine the issuer's current underwriting and marketing strategy, since some have changed their target audience over the years.

Exhibit 15: Net Portfolio Losses for Major MH ABS Issuers
(As a Percent of Outstanding Receivables at Year End)

	1989	1990	1991	1992	1993	1994	1995
Green Tree		1.37	1.41	1.60	0.92	0.60	0.41 (9)
Security Pacific	0.98	0.97	1.17				
Oakwood	1.02	0.81	0.80	0.97	0.63	0.60	0.75 (9)
Vanderbilt							
Co. Orig.	0.35	0.42	0.32	0.41	0.17	0.07	0.04 (6)
Total	0.53	0.59	0.89	1.10	0.64	0.30	0.20 (6)

Parentheses indicate the latest month that data were reported.

Source: Company prospectuses

Manufactured Housing

Manufactured housing deals typically are structured with one or more subordinate tranches for credit support. While MHs resemble MBSs and HELs in the sense that they are loans for housing, they resemble auto loans in that the collateral is a depreciating asset. Because of this, prepayments on MHs are much less interest-rate sensitive than prepayments on HELs or MBSs. Historically, MHs have suffered from a rather poor image because home owners with lower credit ratings often turn to MHs as an alternative to site built homes. Consequently, defaults and losses on MHs have been high compared to other ABS classes. However, in recent years, some of the major MH manufacturers/issuers have tightened their underwriting standards. That action, combined with quality improvements in the product and a trend to a higher-income clientele point to lower loss rates on MH deals in the future.

Historical MH portfolio data are presented in Exhibit 15. Green Tree, by far the largest issuer of MH securities, shows a significant improvement in 1994 and early 1995 compared to the previous three years. The same is true for Oakwood and Vanderbilt. In particular, the losses on the Vanderbilt originated portfolio for 1995, at 0.04%, were minuscule.

Cumulative-loss data for a large number of MH deals is presented in Exhibit 16. The data are rather closely bunched and shows that some of the older pools, say those with pool factors less than 0.600, already have cumulative losses in the 5% to 7% range and probably will end up with total losses of 7% to 8%. In contrast, the newer pools have started off with relatively low losses, reflecting the improved underwriting by Green Tree and others. Here again, historical data can give a broad picture of what loss levels to expect, but understanding recent changes in the industry and issuer underwriting standards is critical in projecting loss rates going forward.

Loss Curves

When looking at historical losses, it is important to identify the seasoning pattern of losses as well as the magnitude. Each type of ABS collateral has its own unique default curve. For autos, for example, there is a distinct pattern with losses increasing during the first two years or so, holding at an elevated level for a brief period, and then declining during the later years of the pool. Rating agencies start with these standard default curves when setting credit-support levels. Their approach is to make certain that the credit-support level is adequate at all points along the maturity spectrum. Because losses are low in the early months of an ABS pool's life, a low support level is acceptable for the first few months. The most common manifestation of this approach is the requirement that the reserve account be built up during the first year or so in the recognition that the highest default rates will occur only after the loans are partially seasoned.

CREDIT ENHANCEMENT AND THE ROLE OF THE B-PIECE

The previous section dealt with the issue of obtaining historical-loss data on which to base a sound forecast of future losses for various types of ABS collateral. Once an expected loss curve has been determined, it is then necessary to consider the structure of the deal in order to understand what level of stress the deal can withstand before the B-piece is affected.

The B-piece, itself, is an integral part of the credit structure since it supports the senior bonds in a deal. Some B-pieces are first-loss pieces, but usually they are supported by one or more credit enhancements, themselves. The choice of credit support is determined by relative costs and also, to some extent, by tradition (e.g., virtually all HEL deals have surety wraps), as well as by an issuer's own particular preference.

Exhibit 16: Cumulative Losses for Selected MH Deals as a Percent of Original Balances

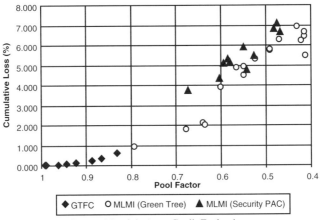

Source: Moody's Asset Credit Evaluations

Excess Spread and Spread Account

The first level of support in an ABS transaction is excess spread. Each month, excess spread, i.e., interest received in excess of that required to pay the coupon on the bonds, servicing fees, and other transaction costs, is available to cover losses. To the extent that interest income exceeds those uses, the excess is deposited into a spread account, up to a specified amount, and is available to cover losses in subsequent months. Any funds remaining in the spread account at the end of the deal typically revert to the issuer.

As discussed earlier, monthly losses can be quite high on credit cards, but so is the excess spread each month. On the other hand, HELs have lower monthly losses but they have lower levels of monthly excess spread. In both of these instances, and for most other types of ABS collateral, excess spread will cover monthly losses under normal economic conditions. However, the rating agencies, insurers and investors are concerned about the additional levels of support that are needed to protect the structure if losses increase to the point where they no longer can be covered by excess spread.

Other Types of Credit Enhancements

Since various combinations of support can achieve the desired credit rating, issuer and underwriter work together to find the combination that will meet the rating agencies' requirements at the least cost. In addition to a spread account, one or more of the following types of credit enhancement typically are used.

- *Cash-Reserve Account (CRA)*. The issuer places cash into an excess spread account at the beginning of the deal to protect against losses in the first few months of the deal. The account is built up over time from excess spread payments. The money in the fund not used to cover losses reverts to the issuer at the end of the deal.

- *Cash-Collateral Account (CCA)*. Cash is borrowed from a bank and placed in a CCA. Over time, excess spread is used to pay down the amount borrowed. Losses are first paid out of the part of the CCA that has been contributed from excess spread. If losses exceed the excess-spread contributed amount, the loss comes from the borrowed amount. As with a CRA, cash remaining at the end of the deal reverts to the issuer.

- *Collateral Invested Amount (CIA)*. A CIA is essentially a C-piece that supports the A and B classes in an ABS structure. CIAs, of late, are used frequently in credit cards rather than CCAs. Commercial banks are the primary investors in CIAs. Instead of lending money, as in a CCA, a bank will buy an ownership interest in an issue. The owner of the CIA receives coupon income and, at the end of the deal, a return of principal to the extent losses have not reduced the CIA.

- *Overcollateralization (O/C).* An extra amount of collateral is used to support the deal. Monthly cash flows are larger than needed to cover bond payments under normal circumstances. The extra cash is used to cover losses and to accelerate the paydown of the bonds.

- *Letter of Credit (LOC).* A commercial bank provides a guarantee that covers losses, usually an amount equal to the support level indicated by the rating agency. This form of support is used infrequently today because the credit level obtained from an LOC can be no greater than the credit of the LOC issuer, itself, and few banks today have the desired triple-A rating. When used today, such agreements require that, in the event of downgrading, the bank put up sufficient cash to insure the bonds.

- *Subordination.* Junior class(es) of bonds, i.e., B-pieces, absorb losses and protect the senior classes. This is a popular and efficient structure, often used in conjunction with one of the other credit-enhancement techniques discussed above.

- *Shifting Interest.* During the first few years, all prepayments on a shifting-interest deal flow to the senior class, which causes the senior class to pay down faster than the subordinate classes. Over time, the level of support increases to meet the rising level of losses. The shifting-interest structure is a very cost-effective means of providing an increasing percentage of support bonds as a deal ages.

- *Surety Wraps.* Monoline insurers, such as FGIC, FSA, and MBIA, insure payment of principal and interest on the bonds. A surety wrap is sometimes used when there is greater than usual uncertainty about likely loss levels and obtaining a triple-A rating would be too expensive using other credit-enhancement techniques. In most recent HEL issues, the surety wrap guarantees 100% of the bonds. In a few ABS issues, a surety guarantee is used like an LOC and covers only a portion of the issuance amount.

Exhibit 17 shows the order in which various types of credit support will absorb losses with the ones on the bottom, i.e., monthly excess spread, and the excess spread account absorbing losses first. After these come a cash revenue account, overcollateralization, a cash-collateral account, or a letter of credit. Next in line are a CIA or non-investment grade subordinate class. The last level is a surety wrap or investment grade subordinate bond. In a super/senior structure, both subordination and a surety wrap are used to support the senior tranches which are often triple-A without the wrap. Of course, in any specific deal, the order may differ and usually only two or three of these alternatives are employed, but the exhibit gives a general picture of how the various types of credit enhancement are usually layered. Note that when a surety company is involved, the level of credit support needed to obtain a particular rating often is negotiated between the insurer and the rating agency.

Exhibit 18 shows some examples of the types of credit support recently used in the ABS market. Note that in each asset class a "standard" credit structure has evolved. Credit cards typically have a B-piece supported by a cash-collateral account or collateral invested amount; autos also have a B-piece and a cash-reserve account or overcollateralization; MHs make use of a tiered B-piece structure; HELs have, to date, relied largely on 100% surety wraps.

B-PIECE PROTECTION

As discussed above, the B-piece usually will be protected by excess spread and a spread account, and often by one or more layers of additional credit enhancement. An investor should compare the total protection for the B-piece to the likely levels of loss in order to understand the risk exposure of the B-piece. A B-piece that is protected by a CIA, CCA or C-piece may not be more secure than one that takes a first-loss position if the expected losses are lower on the deal in which the B-piece takes the first loss.

Furthermore, in the absence of additional credit support, the relative size of the B-piece is also an important consideration. Just as in the case of a second mortgage position that is subordinated to a first mortgage, the larger the B-piece relative to the deal size, the less risk there is. To see this, consider the two bonds described in Exhibit 19. The only credit enhancement is a 10% B-piece for bond A and a 5% B-piece for bond B. If losses amount to 1% of the deal (beyond the excess spread and spread account), the bond A B-piece holder will experience a 10% loss, while the bond B B-piece holder will experience a 20% loss. The larger the B-piece, the less risk taken.

Exhibit 17: Typical Sequence of Credit Enhancement on an ABS Issue

Triple-A Senior Securities		
100% Surety Wrap	or Investment Grade Subordinate Bonds or	Super Senior (Subordination + Surety Wrap)
CIA or Non-Investment Grade Subordinate Bonds		
CRA or LOC or O/C or CCA		
Excess Spread Account		
Monthly Excess Spread		

Exhibit 18: Representative Credit-Support Structures

Credit Cards		
Standard 1995-11 (11.0%) B-Piece (6.0%) CCA (5.0%)	MBNA 1995-J (13.0%) B-Piece (4.5%) CIA (8.5%)	Capitol One 1995-4 (20.0%) B-Piece (13.0%) CIA (7.0%)
Autos		
Ford 1995-B (6.5%) B-Piece (6.5%)	PAT 1995-4 (11.5%) B-Piece (3.75%) Overcol. (4.25%) CRA (3.5%)	UAC 1995-C (11.0%) B-Piece (6.75%) CRA (4.75%)
MHs		
Green Tree 1995-10 (17.0%) Mezzanine (9.0%) B-1 Class (4.0%) B-2 Class (4.0%)	Vanderbilt 1995-B (19.0%) Mezzanine (8.0%) B-1 Class (6.0%) B-2 Class (5.0%) Limited Corp. Guaranty on B-2 Class	
HELs		
Money Store 1996-C (17.0%) 100% MBIA Surety Wrap		

Source: Asset Sales Report, various issues

Exhibit 19: Impact of B-Piece Percentage on Loss

	Bond A (%)	Bond B (%)
Triple-A	90	95
B-piece	10	5
Loss on B-piece		
1% Loss	1%/10%=10%	1%/5%=20%

On the other hand, if two deals contain additional credit support beyond the B-piece, and the total support is the same in two deals, it usually is preferable to own the smaller B-piece. This is so because the smaller B-piece will have a larger level of additional support. Exhibit 20 illustrates this. Bond A has a 5% B-piece with 5% support ahead of the B-piece. Bond B has a 7% B-piece with 3% support ahead of the B-piece. For a loss of up to 3%, neither B-piece suffers. At a loss of 4% to 5%, only the B-piece on the B bond suffers. For losses greater than 5% both B-pieces are impacted, but the relative impact is always greater on the B-piece from the B bond. These examples show that of the two factors, B-piece percentage and level of additional protection, the level of additional protection is the most crucial.

Exhibit 20: Impact of B-Piece Percentage with Additional Credit Support

	Bond A (%)	Bond B (%)
Triple-A	90	90
B-piece	5	7
Other Support	5	3

Loss Level (%)	Loss on B-piece (%)	
0 to 3	0	0
3 to 5	0	0 to 2
6	1/5=20	3/7=42.9
7	2/5=40	4/7=57.1
8	3/5=60	5/7=71.4
9	4/5=80	6/7=85.7
10	5/5=100	7/7=100

Also, it is important for investors to monitor the amount of support remaining in a deal as the deal ages. What may be sufficient protection at the beginning of a deal can erode with time. The B-piece investor will want to track the pools performance by obtaining pool performance data from Bloomberg or another financial data service.

SUMMARY

In a period of tight spreads, such as mid-1996, more investors are being compelled to go down the credit curve in search of yield. One way to do this is through single-A ABS B-pieces, which provide an additional 10 to 20 basis points in spread compared to triple-A senior classes. The spreads available are a function of the expected losses on the collateral and the general credit spread between single-A and triple-A credits. Often, an investor can pick up more spread by going down the credit curve in the ABS market rather than in corporates. Hence, we feel that it behooves investors to become familiar with the B-piece sector of the ABS market. The analysis is not always straightforward and some effort is required, but the incremental advantage from this sector should make the effort worthwhile.

APPENDIX
LOSS-DATA ANALYSIS AND TERMINOLOGY

This appendix reviews the numerous methods used to present loss data. Since issuers, rating agencies, and other sources of loss data may use any one of these methods, it is important to understand the different methods and how they relate to one another.

Portfolio Versus Pool

Historical loss patterns may be presented using either portfolio or pool data. Portfolio data have a well known drawback in that, for a growing portfolio, loss data have a downward bias because losses normally peak after one or more years (depending on the type of loans). Therefore, a large percentage of new loans will lower the average loss rate on a portfolio. This problem does not exist with static pool data. On the other hand, portfolio data are based on a much larger sample than pool data and, to the extent that pool data are not representative of an entire portfolio, it may present its own biases. For these reasons, it is best to look at both types of data.

Dollars Versus Percent

While dollar losses are what investors ultimately are concerned with, percentages are most useful for analytical and comparative purposes. Consequently, all of our discussion is in percentage terms, although dollar amounts are the raw material from which percentages are derived.

Gross Versus Net

Net losses are more meaningful than gross losses, since the former are what drive credit ratings and are what matter to the B-piece investor. For example, some home-equity lenders that target B and C borrowers may have high gross loss rates, but, because they require low LTVs, their net losses are very small. Unless otherwise noted, we always refer to net losses.

Remaining Balance, Original Balance, or Amount Paid Down

It is most common to report losses as a percent of remaining balances or outstanding receivables. This is true for MBSs, as well as for ABSs. However, rating agencies also report pool-loss data as a percent of original balance since credit-enhancement levels are based, in part, on that number. At times, the agencies also report losses as a percent of the amount paid down. All three approaches are useful in analyzing and projecting losses.

Period Loss Versus Cumulative Loss

Pool data reported by the rating agencies usually include both period (monthly) and cumulative statistics, since both are needed for credit analysis. A large loss in a single month can trigger a payment from a support structure, while cumulative losses above a certain level may signify an early amortization or credit problem. Expected cumulative losses as a percent of the original balance in a pool is a key statistic in determining the amount of credit support required for a particular transaction. On the other hand, cumulative loss data for a portfolio are not meaningful, since new loans are constantly being added and old ones retired. Therefore, portfolio-loss data are reported for a specific period, say for a month or a year, and not on a cumulative basis.

Period loss data, whether for a portfolio or for a pool, are virtually always presented as an annual rate. For example, if losses in a month are 0.1% of outstandings, they will be reported as a 1.2% loss rate.

Summary of Alternative Methods for Reporting Loss Data

Exhibit 21 gives an overview of the various ways to represent loss data discussed above. A different basis is used for calculating the loss rates in each column as follows: Column A = remaining balance, Column B = original balance, and Column C = amount paid down. The graph in Row 1 in each column illustrates how the basis changes over time under those three alternatives. For example, the graph in Column A, Row 1 shows a pool's remaining balance as it declines over time.

The second row of graphs in each column shows the amount of loss each month in dollars for a hypothetical static pool. These graphs are the same in each column.

The graphs in Row 3 show the dollar losses as a percent of the basis in Row 1. Column A, Row 3 shows monthly losses as a percentage of remaining balance (on an annualized basis.) This is the form in which ABS losses are most often reported. Most types of ABS collateral have loss curves that follow a common pattern. They rise sharply during the first year or so, peak in the second year, and then decline as the pool seasons. Loss curves will vary from issuer to issuer and by the credit level of the borrower, but the general pattern is quite similar within each asset category.

Column B, Row 3 shows the monthly losses as a percentage of the original balance. This graph drops off sharply in the later years since it reflects both the lower rate of loss as the pool seasons and the fact that the pool has paid down.

Row 4 shows cumulative losses. This is simply the sum of the monthly data shown in Row 2 and, like Row 2, is the same for each basis.

Row 5 shows the cumulative losses as a percent of the basis in Row 1. In Column A, Row 5 the graph climbs almost vertically near the end of the pool's life. As the pool's balance goes to zero, the loss rate goes to infinity. Clearly, this is not a useful presentation of loss data.

Column B, Row 5 shows cumulative losses as a percent of original balance. This curve, when based on expected losses, is a key factor in determining the required support level for an ABS transaction. Also, this curve, when based on actual loss data and plotted against the amount of credit support in the deal, can be used to monitor the amount of protection still in the deal.

The final graph, Column C, Row 5, also can be useful in monitoring loss data on an ongoing basis. After the pool is partially seasoned, this graph will give an approximation of the final total loss as a percent of the original balance. In fact, the graphs in Column B, Row 5 and Column C, Row 5 will converge to the same level as the pool approaches maturity.

Exhibit 21: Comparison of Loss Data Based on Remaining Balance, Original Balance, and Amount Paid Down

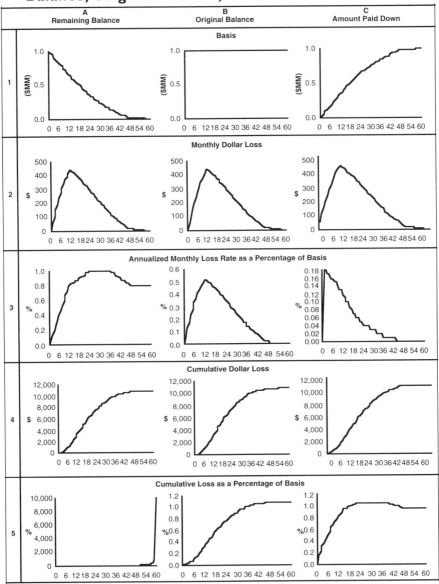

Source: Prudential Securities Inc.

Exhibit 22: Comparison of Period, Cumulative, and Total Losse for Autos*

	Year	1	2	3	4	5
A. Loss Rate as % of Remaining Balance		0.80	1.00	1.00	0.80	0.80
B. Pool Factor		0.65	0.36	0.15	0.02	0.00
C. Loss Rate as % of Original Balance		0.33	0.44	0.25	0.07	0.01
D. Cumulative Loss as % of Original Balance		0.33	0.77	1.02	1.09	1.10

* End of period values.

Exhibit 23: Comparison of Period, Cumulative, and Total Losses for MHs*

	Year	1	2	3	4	5	10	15
A. Loss Rate as % of Remaining Balance		0.50	1.80	2.30	2.30	2.00	0.50	0.50
B. Pool Factor		0.91	0.81	0.71	0.62	0.53	0.20	0.00
C. Loss Rate as % of Original Balance		0.25	1.02	1.56	1.52	1.22	0.11	0.01
D. Cumulative Loss as % of Original Balance		0.25	1.27	2.83	4.36	7.45	7.45	7.67

* End of period values.

Impact of Average Life

The preceding discussion can be used to point out key relationships that exist between two types of loss data: (1) monthly losses as a percent of remaining balances, and (2) cumulative losses as a percent of original balance.

For short average-life loans, such as auto loans, the total cumulative loss (as a percent of the original balance) is often similar to the monthly loss figures (reported as a percent of the remaining balance). Hence, monthly loss data can give a rough idea of what the total losses on the pool will be. For longer average-life ABSs, such as MHs and HELs, the monthly loss rates are only a fraction of the final cumulative loss. This difference is illustrated in Exhibits 22 and 23.

Exhibit 22 shows period loss rates, pool factors, and cumulative losses for a typical auto deal with a 5-year final and a 1.6-year average life. Reported losses (row A) range from 0.80% to 1.00%. Because the pool pays down rapidly, loss as a percent of the original balance (row C) drops off sharply after year two and is negligible in the last two years. The sum of these losses over the 5-year period amounts to 1.10% of the original balance, roughly the same as the monthly reported loss rates.

Contrast this to the MH loss data in Exhibit 23. The paydown rate on loans in this hypothetical MH pool is much slower and the average life, at 6.1 years, is much longer than the auto example. During the middle years, losses (row A) run in the 1.8% to 2.30% range. Losses as a percent of the original balance (row C) remain in the 1.02% to 1.56% range for several years. Cumulative losses amount to 7.67% as a percent of the original balance, four to five times the reported monthly rate. In this case the reported monthly rate is not a good gauge for projecting total losses.

The relationship just described for pool data also is useful when looking at portfolio data. Portfolio losses for auto issuers are similar to the monthly reported pool losses, which, in turn, are similar to the total cumulative losses on the pools. However, for MHs and other longer average-life ABSs, historical portfolio losses are similar to reported monthly losses but are smaller than the expected total cumulative losses on a pool from that portfolio.

Part IV: Relative Value Considerations

Chapter 22

Prepayment Nomenclature in the ABS Market

Anand K. Bhattacharya
Senior Vice President
Director of Fixed Income Research
Prudential Securities Inc.

INTRODUCTION

The asset-backed securities (ABS) market has experienced tremendous growth in recent years. With increases in different types of assets in the market, it is important to understand general prepayment nomenclature in the ABS market, such as ABS, HEP, PPC, MHP and MPR. In this chapter, we outline the basics of asset-backed prepayments and offer a succinct definition of each prepayment measure, some of which are specific to each segment of the market.

BASICS OF ASSET PREPAYMENTS

Amortizing versus Non-Amortizing Assets

Most assets can be categorized as amortizing or non-amortizing. For fixed-rate amortizing assets, such as fixed-rate mortgages, home-equity loans (HELs) and automobile loans, the monthly scheduled payment, consisting of scheduled principal and interest payments, is constant throughout the amortization term. If the borrower pays more than the monthly scheduled payment, the extra payment will be used to pay down the outstanding balance faster than the original amortization schedule. If the outstanding balance is paid off in full, the prepayment is a "complete prepayment;" if only a portion of the outstanding balance is prepaid, the prepayment is called a "partial prepayment," or curtailment. Prepayments can be a result of natural turnover, refinancings, defaults and partial paydowns.

Non-amortizing assets, e.g. credit cards and home-equity lines of credit, do not have a fixed payment schedule. There is usually a minimum payment and the unpaid interest portion is added to the outstanding principal. Thus there is usually no "prepayment" for non-amortizing assets because there is no predetermined amortizing schedule; the borrower has a flexible repayment schedule.

Loan- versus Pool-Level Prepayment Analysis

Prepayments can be analyzed on both the loan and pool level. Loan-level prepayment analysis, which requires detailed loan level information, is more accurate and computationally intensive than pool-level prepayment analysis. Loan-level analysis involves amortizing each loan individually, tracking the prepayment on an individual loan basis and aggregating the prepayment amount to calculate prepayment speeds.

For pool-level analysis, the pool (which is composed of many loans) is treated as a virtual loan.[1] The gross weighted average coupon (GWAC) and weighted average maturity (WAM) are used to amortize the pool as if it were one single loan.

---

[1] A theoretically correct way to treat the pool is as an infinite number of loans of infinitesimal size, such that each loan can be prepaid without altering the amortization schedule.

If a pool is composed of a large number of homogeneous loans, e.g., agency mortgages, pool-level analysis is usually sufficient. However, for many ABSs, the underlying loans have very different characteristics and, in those cases, loan-level analysis is generally more accurate and reliable.

Due to the diversity of asset classes falling under the genre of ABSs, a variety of measures, such as SMM, CPR, PSA, ABS, HEP, MHP and PPC are used to define prepayment behavior in this market.

GENERAL PREPAYMENT NOMENCLATURE

Single Month Mortality (SMM)

SMM is the most fundamental measure of prepayment speeds; it is the unit upon which all other prepayment measures are based. SMM measures the monthly prepayment amount as a percentage of the previous month's outstanding balance minus the scheduled principal payment. For example, if the pool balance at month zero is $10,000,000, the scheduled principal and interest payments are $2,920.45 and $100,000 in month one, respectively. If the actual payment in month one is $202,891.25, the SMM rate is 1%, calculated as:

$$SMM = \frac{202,891.25 - 100,000 - 2,920.45}{10,000,000 - 2,920.45} = 1\%$$

If an asset prepaid at 1% SMM in a particular month, this means that 1% of that month's scheduled balance (last month's outstanding balance minus the scheduled principal payment) has been prepaid.

Conditional/Constant Prepayment Rate (CPR)

CPR is the most popular unit used to measure ABS prepayment rates. CPR is the annualized or compounded SMM. The formula to convert from SMM to CPR is similar to standard compounding formulae:

$$1 - CPR = (1 - SMM)^{12}$$

Its annualized nature makes CPR fairly intuitive — if an asset continues to prepay at a monthly SMM rate for one year, it is equivalent to the annualized CPR rate. For example, if an asset prepays at 1% SMM every month for one year, it is equivalent to 11.4% CPR, which means 11.4% of the asset will be prepaid in a year. Furthermore, CPR methodology does not have a built-in seasoning ramp, which makes it easy to understand and use.

Exhibit 1 provides a table of SMM to CPR conversions.

Exhibit 1: SMM to CPR Conversion Table
Conversion Formula CPR (%) = $1 - (1 - SMM)^{12}$

SMM (%)	CPR (%)	SMM (%)	CPR (%)
0.5	5.8	13.5	82.5
1.0	11.4	14.0	83.6
1.5	16.6	14.5	84.7
2.0	21.5	15.0	85.8
2.5	26.2	15.5	86.7
3.0	30.6	16.0	87.7
3.5	34.8	16.5	88.5
4.0	38.7	17.0	89.3
4.5	42.5	17.5	90.1
5.0	46.0	18.0	90.8
5.5	49.3	18.5	91.4
6.0	52.4	19.0	92.0
6.5	55.4	19.5	92.6
7.0	58.1	20.0	93.1
7.5	60.8	20.5	93.6
8.0	63.2	21.0	94.1
8.5	65.6	21.5	94.5
9.0	67.8	22.0	94.9
9.5	69.8	22.5	95.3
10.0	71.8	23.0	95.7
10.5	73.6	23.5	96.0
11.0	75.3	24.0	96.3
11.5	76.9	24.5	96.6
12.0	78.4	25.0	96.8
12.5	79.9	25.5	97.1
13.0	81.2		

PSA

While there is a fair degree of standardization in the prepayment nomenclature for MBSs, there is no such commonality in the ABS markets. In the mortgage markets, the PSA curve is the normal benchmark for expressing prepayments. A prepayment rate of 100% PSA assumes a prepayment rate of 0.2% CPR in the first month of mortgage origination and an additional 0.2% CPR in each subsequent month until month 30. Hence, speeds on traditional agency mortgages usually increase in the first 30 months and then reach a plateau of 6% CPR at month 30. Exhibit 2 displays the 100% and 200% PSA curves.

Note that the PSA curve is a relatively good measure of agency prepayment speeds in the absence of refinancings. The refinancing component, which does not exhibit an aging pattern, could significantly distort the PSA curve, which is a major reason that PSA is used mainly to measure discount and current-coupon prepayments, while CPR is used to measure premium-coupon prepayments.

Exhibit 2: PSA Curves

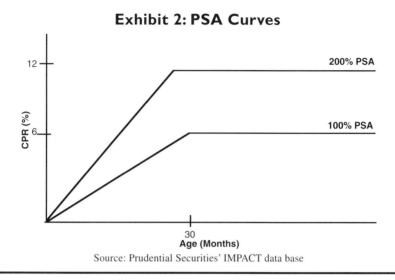

Source: Prudential Securities' IMPACT data base

ABS PREPAYMENT UNITS OF MEASURE

While the expression of prepayments in PSA terms is fairly standard in the MBS markets, a variety of descriptions are used to express the paydown behavior of different asset types in the ABS market. The most commonly used measures are ABS, HEP, MHP, MPR and, more recently, PPC.

ABS

The ABS model defines an increasing sequence of prepayment rates (SMMs). The formula to convert between SMM (%) and ABS (%) is:

$$\text{SMM} = \frac{100 \times \text{ABS}}{100 - \text{ABS} \times (M - 1)}$$

$$\text{ABS} = \frac{100 \times \text{SMM}}{100 + \text{SMM} \times (M - 1)}$$

where M is the number of months after loan origination.

ABS is used to measure prepayments on auto loans, primarily because auto prepayment speeds tend to exhibit increasing prepayment rates as the loans season when measured on an SMM basis. However, measured on an ABS basis, auto prepayment speeds exhibit greater stability.

Exhibit 3 shows a conversion table from ABS to SMM. For example, If an auto pool prepaid at 2% ABS at month 11 after loan origination, its corresponding SMM rate can be calculated as:

$$\text{SMM} = \frac{100 \times 2}{(100 - 2(11 - 1))} = \frac{200}{(100 - 20)} = 2.5\%$$

Exhibit 3: Conversion Table from ABS (%) to SMM (%)

Loan Age (Months)	ABS (%)									
	0.50	0.75	1.00	1.25	1.50	1.75	2.00	2.25	2.50	2.75
	SMM (%)									
1	0.50	0.75	1.00	1.25	1.50	1.75	2.00	2.25	2.50	2.75
2	0.50	0.76	1.01	1.27	1.52	1.78	2.04	2.30	2.56	2.83
3	0.51	0.76	1.02	1.28	1.55	1.81	2.08	2.36	2.63	2.91
4	0.51	0.77	1.03	1.30	1.57	1.85	2.13	2.41	2.70	3.00
5	0.51	0.77	1.04	1.32	1.60	1.88	2.17	2.47	2.78	3.09
6	0.51	0.78	1.05	1.33	1.62	1.92	2.22	2.54	2.86	3.19
7	0.52	0.79	1.06	1.35	1.65	1.96	2.27	2.60	2.94	3.29
8	0.52	0.79	1.08	1.37	1.68	1.99	2.33	2.67	3.03	3.41
9	0.52	0.80	1.09	1.39	1.70	2.03	2.38	2.74	3.13	3.53
10	0.52	0.80	1.10	1.41	1.73	2.08	2.44	2.82	3.23	3.65
11	0.53	0.81	1.11	1.43	1.76	2.12	2.50	2.90	3.33	3.79
12	0.53	0.82	1.12	1.45	1.80	2.17	2.56	2.99	3.45	3.94
13	0.53	0.82	1.14	1.47	1.83	2.22	2.63	3.08	3.57	4.10
14	0.53	0.83	1.15	1.49	1.86	2.27	2.70	3.18	3.70	4.28
15	0.54	0.84	1.16	1.52	1.90	2.32	2.78	3.28	3.85	4.47
16	0.54	0.85	1.18	1.54	1.94	2.37	2.86	3.40	4.00	4.68
17	0.54	0.85	1.19	1.56	1.97	2.43	2.94	3.52	4.17	4.91
18	0.55	0.86	1.20	1.59	2.01	2.49	3.03	3.64	4.35	5.16
19	0.55	0.87	1.22	1.61	2.05	2.55	3.13	3.78	4.55	5.45
20	0.55	0.87	1.23	1.64	2.10	2.62	3.23	3.93	4.76	5.76
21	0.56	0.88	1.25	1.67	2.14	2.69	3.33	4.09	5.00	6.11
22	0.56	0.89	1.27	1.69	2.19	2.77	3.45	4.27	5.26	6.51
23	0.56	0.90	1.28	1.72	2.24	2.85	3.57	4.46	5.56	6.96
24	0.56	0.91	1.30	1.75	2.29	2.93	3.70	4.66	5.88	7.48
25	0.57	0.91	1.32	1.79	2.34	3.02	3.85	4.89	6.25	8.09
26	0.57	0.92	1.33	1.82	2.40	3.11	4.00	5.14	6.67	8.80
27	0.57	0.93	1.35	1.85	2.46	3.21	4.17	5.42	7.14	9.65
28	0.58	0.94	1.37	1.89	2.52	3.32	4.35	5.73	7.69	10.68
29	0.58	0.95	1.39	1.92	2.59	3.43	4.55	6.08	8.33	11.96
30	0.58	0.96	1.41	1.96	2.65	3.55	4.76	6.47	9.09	13.58
31	0.59	0.97	1.43	2.00	2.73	3.68	5.00	6.92	10.00	15.71
32	0.59	0.98	1.45	2.04	2.80	3.83	5.26	7.44	11.11	18.64
33	0.60	0.99	1.47	2.08	2.88	3.98	5.56	8.04	12.50	22.92
34	0.60	1.00	1.49	2.13	2.97	4.14	5.88	8.74	14.29	29.73
35	0.60	1.01	1.52	2.17	3.06	4.32	6.25	9.57	16.67	42.31
36	0.61	1.02	1.54	2.22	3.16	4.52	6.67	10.59	20.00	73.33

Exhibit 4: Principal Paydown Comparison: 2% SMM Versus 2% ABS

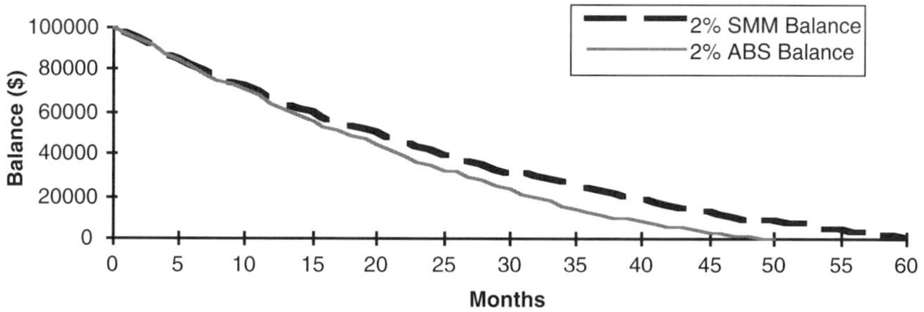

Source: Prudential Securities' IMPACT data base

Exhibit 4 compares the principal paydown of a 60-month auto pool at 2% SMM versus 2% ABS. Note that the 2% ABS paydown is similar to the 2% SMM paydown during the early part of the life of the pool. However, prepayments accelerate toward the later part of the life of the pool. In fact, usage of the 2% ABS convention shortens the final maturity of the pool by ten months.

Home-Equity Prepayment (HEP) Curve

In the closed-end, fixed-rate HEL market, prepayments are expressed using the HEP curve, which was developed by Prudential Securities based on the prepayment experience of $10 billion home-equity loan deals. The HEP curve captures the faster seasoning ramp for HEL prepayments. While there may be disagreement regarding the actual length of the seasoning ramp, it is a fairly well accepted fact that HELs exhibit a faster ramp than single-family agency mortgages.

HELs season much faster than traditional single-family loans, making the PSA ramp an inappropriate descriptive for HEL prepayments. At the same time, the very pronounced HEL seasoning ramp makes a single long-term prepayment projection somewhat inappropriate. The ineffectiveness of a single prepayment projection is especially apparent for a tranched pool of home-equity loans. Prudential Securities developed the HEP curve to address these issues in HEL valuation.

Usage of the HEP curve leads to more accurate estimates of HEL average lives. The HEP curve reflects the observed behavior in historic HEL data — it has a ramp of ten months and a variable long-term CPR to reflect individual issuer speeds.

A faster long-term speed means faster CPRs on the ramp because the ramp is fixed at ten months regardless of the long-term speed. For example, a 20% HEP projection would mean a ten-month ramp going to 20% in the tenth month from 2% in the first month and a constant 20% thereafter.

Exhibit 5: HEP Curves

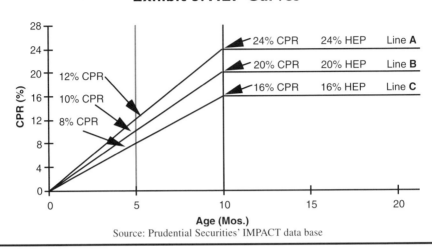

Source: Prudential Securities' IMPACT data base

In other words, speeds will increase 2% per month until they level off at 20% in month ten, as shown by line B in Exhibit 5. Line A in the exhibit shows monthly speeds for an HEL with a projected speed of 24% HEP. The speeds on the ramp start at 2.4% in month one and grow at 2.4% CPR per month. Line C shows the monthly speeds for a 16% HEP projection.

Prospectus Prepayment Curve

A recent addition to the HEL prepayment terminology is the Prospectus Prepayment Curve (PPC). PPCs are issue specific and differ from HEP mostly in the seasoning ramp. 100% PPC is defined as the base-case assumption. However, there is no industry standardization for the usage of this terminology, as it is issue dependent and specified in the issue prospectus. For example, for one particular issue, 100% PPC may be defined as prepayment speeds starting at 5% CPR at month zero, increasing 1.5% CPR a month until month 11 and then plateauing at 21.5% CPR. For another issue, however, 100% PPC may be defined with different starting points and with a different seasoning ramp. Investors should carefully investigate how 100% PPC is defined for each particular issue.

Manufactured Housing Prepayment (MHP)

MHP is a measure of prepayment behavior for manufactured housing, based on the Green Tree manufactured housing prepayment experience. MHP is similar to the PSA curve, except that the seasoning ramp is slightly different. 100% MHP is equivalent to 3.6% CPR at month zero and increases 0.1% CPR every month until month 24, when it plateaus at 6% CPR. Exhibit 6 shows the prepayment speeds at 50% MHP, 100% MHP and 200% MHP.

Monthly Payment Rate (MPR)

MPR is used mostly for measuring credit-card payments. Because there is no amortization schedule on credit-card payments, the concept of prepayments essentially does not apply to this asset class. MPR measures the monthly payment, including principal/interest payments and finance charges, of a credit-card portfolio as a percentage of debt outstanding in the previous month.

For example, out of a $100 million credit-card portfolio, a 15% MPR rate means that the payment for that month is $15 million, including all relevant finance charges. Because most credit-card issues are under a master trust structure, the payment rate usually does not alter investment cash flow unless the MPR slows to extremely low levels, which might cause extension on principal payments.

MPR is also important because rating agencies require that card issues include a minimum MPR as an early amortization trigger event. The credit rating agencies reason that, if the MPR were to drop to a very low level, there might not be enough cash flow to pay off all of the principal if an early amortization occurred for any reason.

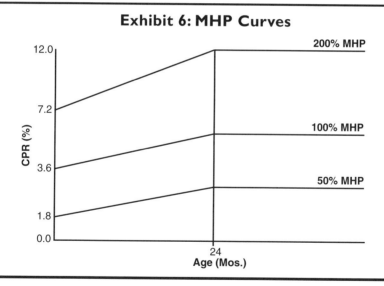

Exhibit 6: MHP Curves

Chapter 23

Evaluation of ABS Prepayments

Anand K. Bhattacharya
Senior Vice President
Director of Fixed Income Research
Prudential Securities Inc.

INTRODUCTION

In general, asset-backed securities (ABSs) are considered to be prepayment "safe havens" because of their cash-flow stability. There is a wide range of ABSs, from mortgage like home-equity loans (HELs) and commercial mortgages to more traditional ABSs, such as credit cards and auto loans. To a certain extent, all collateral backing ABSs is subject to prepayments, either voluntarily or involuntarily. Certain asset types, such as credit cards and automobile loans, are less prepayment sensitive, primarily due to contractual characteristics and the relative insensitivity of the loans to interest rates. However, other asset classes, such as HELs and manufactured housing (MH) contracts have prepayments characteristic that are relevant in the valuation process. In this chapter, we discuss prepayment characteristics for assets such as fixed-and adjustable-rate HELs, Title I home-improvement loans, Small Business Administration (SBA) loans, and MH loans and leases.

For mortgage like ABSs such as HELs, prepayments are much more important in the valuation process. Even though HELs cannot readily prepay, either because of lower credit or some sort of prepayment penalty, prepayments tend to fluctuate over time as a result of either voluntary prepayments or involuntary defaults. The correlation between HEL prepayments and interest rates is a function of the credit quality of the HEL borrower. The higher the borrower's credit quality, the more the HEL behaves like an agency mortgage, and the more responsive the HEL's prepayments to changes in interest rates. Thus, prepayment rates on HEL issuers, especially in the B and C market, are more stable than some HELs originated by banks that target A- credit borrowers. For some new types of ABSs, such as equipment leases and SBAs, the voluntary prepayment is minimal, while default related prepayments play a very important role. For equipment leases, there is usually a hell-or-high-water clause that essentially bars a lessee from prepaying a lease. However, if a lessee upgrades equipment or defaults on a lease, a prepayment could result. The reason for defaults, to a large extent, depends on the general condition of the economy and the particular credit of the borrower. For SBA loans, prepayment levels are strongly correlated with the original term of the loan and whether or not the floating-rate loan has a life cap. Furthermore, approximately half of SBA prepayments are the result of defaults, which is not surprising given the high failure rate of small businesses.

ABS PREPAYMENT COMPONENTS

Similar to mortgages, all ABS prepayments consist of four components, even though the relative importance of the four components may be different. These components are: turnover, refinancing, defaults and partial prepayments (or curtailments).

Turnover

The turnover component happens over the "natural" course of the life of the asset. The loan is "paid off" as soon as legal control of the asset is "turned over." For mortgages and HELs, the turnover component corresponds to prepayments from relocating or selling the property. The home mortgage turnover component depends on general economic conditions, the real estate market and borrower demographics. For equipment leases, an upgrade in equipment contributes to the turnover component of prepayments. For SBAs, turnover in the control of a business (e.g., as a result of a merger or acquisition) could cause a prepayment. For autos, an upgrade or sale could result in a turnover prepayment.

Refinancing

The refinancing component is largely driven by interest rates. When a borrower replaces the old loan with a new one, which usually carries a lower interest rate, the old loan is refinanced. Refinancing is bad for the investor, as borrowers tend to refinance when interest rates are low, causing prepayments and forcing investors to reinvest at lower rates. For most ABSs, the refinancing component is relatively low compared with agency mortgages. Lower-quality HEL borrowers cannot readily refinance due to their impaired credit. Equipment leases cannot refinance because of the hell-or-high-water clause in most lease contracts. SBA and auto loans are hard to refinance owing to limited availability of alternative financing sources.

Defaults

The default prepayment component is probably the least understood. When a loan defaults, it usually goes through 30-, 60- and 90-day delinquency stages before the foreclosure process starts. Once the asset is foreclosed and liquidated, there will be a prepayment to the bond holder if there is credit support to absorb the defaults. For SBAs, defaults can run as high as half of the total prepayments.

Partial Prepayments

The partial prepayment component (or curtailment) occurs when borrower pays more than the monthly scheduled principal and interest amount in order to build equity. Partial prepayments are usually only a minor percent of total prepayments. For HELs, partial prepayments usually represent less than 1.5% CPR.

FIXED-RATE HELS

The securitized HEL market has grown steadily over the past few years, with annual issuance reaching $15.2 billion in 1995. With this growth has come increased diversity; the market now includes fixed-rate and adjustable-rate

HELs, Title I home-improvement loans, home-equity lines of credit (HELOCs) and multi-family (commercial) HELs. Despite the impressive growth in this market, investors do not have a solid understanding of the differences between HELs and agency mortgages. The most important distinction is the credit profile of the borrower. While agency mortgage borrowers generally have the highest credit standing, HEL borrowers typically have impaired credit histories and are assigned credit ratings ranging from A- to D.

HEL Characteristics

Contrary to popular belief, most HELs are actually first lien, not second lien mortgages, largely as a result of debt consolidation of mortgage, credit-card debt, and other personal debt. The original terms on HELs generally vary between 15 and 30 years. As previously mentioned, HELs differ from agency mortgages primarily in the credit rating of the borrower. Agency mortgage borrowers usually possess A credit ratings, but HEL borrowers can have widely disparate credit standings, from A- to D.[1] The lower credit profiles of HELs directly impact the credit enhancement of HEL issues as well as the pattern of prepayment speeds.

HEL Prepayment Stability

As the HEL market develops and more information becomes available, more market participants understand the relative stability of HEL prepayments and the driving force behind it, which is the credit standing of the borrowers. There is an inverse relationship between credit rating and prepayment sensitivity of the loan. The better the HEL borrower credit profile, the more interest-rate sensitive the prepayment speeds. The rationale is that higher credit borrowers are more likely to refinance when interest rates drop due to the availability of attractive refinancing opportunities and their higher degree of financial sophistication. On one end of the credit spectrum are agency mortgages, which have exhibited a higher degree of prepayment gyration in the past few years. On the other end of the credit spectrum are C/D HELs, which have exhibited a consistent, stable prepayment pattern.

For example, from 1994 through 1995, interest rates exhibited major swings. Such large-scale changes in interest-rate levels provide a good indication of possible prepayment speed extremes. When interest rates rose by more than 200 basis points in 1994, agency mortgage speeds slowed to as low as a few CPR. The subsequent 200-basis-point drop in 1995 caused speeds to reach as high as 40% CPR. Changes in HEL speeds during the

---

[1] The A-/B/C/D credits are defined according to the number of delinquencies a borrower has had on mortgage payments and the guidelines may vary from one issuer to another. For example, a typical set of guidelines would be based on the previous year credit history and might look as follows: A-: twice 30-day delinquent; B: three times 30-day delinquent; C: at most four times 30-day delinquent and once 60-day delinquent; D: at most five times 30-day delinquent, twice 60-day delinquent, and once 90-day delinquent.

same period were far less dramatic. A- speeds dropped to the low teens in 1994 and increased to the low 20s CPR during the 1995 rally. During the same period, B/C credit speeds ranged from a low of around 20% CPR to a high of 30% CPR. Exhibit 1 compares aggregated HEL prepayment speeds versus agency mortgage speeds during this period. Clearly, HEL speeds were far more stable in this period, demonstrating far less optionality embedded in securities backed by HEL collateral.

HEL Prepayment Components

Similar to other mortgages, HEL prepayments consist of four components: housing (natural) turnover, refinancing, defaults, and partial prepayments. However, the relative importance of these four components is very different for HELs than for agency mortgages. For example, defaults are minimal for agency mortgages, but play a more important role in HEL prepayments. We comment below on the four components of HEL prepayments, particularly the default and refinancing portions.

Defaults The delinquency and foreclosure rates of HELs are typically much higher than those of traditional agency mortgages. Usually, the foreclosure process begins when a loan is more than 90 days delinquent. Depending on how aggressive the lien holder is and the jurisdiction of the loan, it may take from a few months to more than one year before the loan is liquidated. From the viewpoint of the investor, once a loan is liquidated, it normally translates into a prepayment. In some cases, the servicer may purchase and remove some delinquent loans from a pool before foreclosure, effectively prepaying those loans.

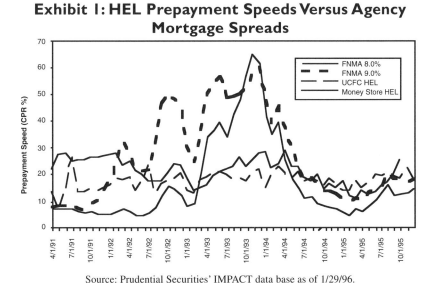

Exhibit 1: HEL Prepayment Speeds Versus Agency Mortgage Spreads

Source: Prudential Securities' IMPACT data base as of 1/29/96.

Despite relatively high foreclosure rates, principal losses to investors in senior (triple-A) HEL bonds have been nonexistent. To our knowledge, none of the HEL bond insurers, such as MBIA and FGIC, have had to pay for any principal loss from insured public HEL issues. The low loan-to-value (LTV) ratio on HELs, combined with solid structural protection, such as spread accounts, overcollateralization (OC), and insurer wraps, provide more than an adequate cushion for investors. The actual loss rates for HELs serviced by a few major issuers, such as The Money Store, Advanta, and United Companies Financial Corporation (UCFC), have been under 1% for recent years.

According to the National Delinquency Survey and Consumer Credit Delinquency Bulletin, as of June 1996, the average 90-plus-day delinquency and foreclosure rates on first mortgages were 0.23% and 0.13% per month, respectively. For HELs, the 90-plus-day delinquency and foreclosure rates were both issuer dependent and normally run between 0.5% and 5%. The significant difference lies in the foreclosure percentage as far as prepayments are concerned. Remember, from an investor's point of view, once a loan has been foreclosed, it is effectively prepaid.

Credit is the key indicator for predicting defaults. The higher the credit rating, the fewer the loan defaults. Aside from trending with the general condition of the economy, defaults tend to follow a seasoning pattern, with default rates starting relatively low and gradually increasing in a year or so. It takes at least three months before a delinquent loan enters the foreclosure stage and, in some cases, foreclosed loans can be "worked out," which can cause a refinancing as discussed in the next section. For relatively high credit (A-) HEL issues, defaults usually contribute 2% CPR to total prepayments. For lower-credit (C) HEL issues, defaults typically comprise 6% CPR of total prepayments.

Refinancing There are typically two types of refinancing for HELs, namely *rate-driven refinancing* and *debt consolidation/workout refinancing*, both of which are highly correlated with borrower credit profile.

Rate-driven refinancings result when the borrower's credit improves. In such instances, the borrower can qualify for a lower rate loan or take advantage of a drop in mortgage rates. The motivation to refinance high-interest debt with lower-interest debt is similar in both HELs and agency mortgages. The rate-driven refinancing component is the primary source of prepayment for MBSs, since these prepayments typically occur in a declining interest-rate environment. For HELs, however, the opportunity to reduce interest payments often results from an improvement in credit quality and is, therefore, not always tied to a drop in interest rates. This is particularly true for B/C credit loans and has a stabilizing effect on the prepayment pattern of these loans.

The second type of refinancing for HELs is essentially uncorrelated with interest-rate movements and is often unfamiliar to traditional agency MBS investors. This type of interest-rate insensitive refinancing is a combination of debt consolidation and "workout" refinancing. Debt consolidation has been mentioned previously as a motivation for a homeowner to take out a HEL. It is also one of the primary reasons homeowners refinance a HEL. Workout refinancing, a much smaller refinancing component, is when a HEL borrower experiences difficulty in paying the loan. In such cases, the originator, instead of trying to foreclose the loan, "rewrites" it to reduce the borrower's monthly payment by extending the maturity of the loan, effectively refinancing the original loan. Prepayments that are not correlated with interest-rate movements, on average, do not hurt investors, since principal is equally likely to be returned when bonds are priced at a discount as when they are priced at a premium.

Issues backed by higher-credit HELs tend to have more volatile refinancing prepayment components than those backed by lower-credit HELs. For the reasons mentioned previously, refinancing of higher-credit HELs increases significantly in a declining interest-rate environment and slows during rising interest-rate periods. The refinancing component of lower-credit HELs is more stable since refinancing alternatives are not so strongly tied to interest-rate movements.

Turnover Housing turnover also contributes to HEL prepayments. For agency mortgages, the housing turnover component results in 6% to 8% CPR (or 100% to 133% PSA) of the total prepayments. For HELs, the housing turnover speeds are typically slower than those of agency mortgages. The primary reason is credit. Because most HEL borrowers have impaired credit histories and are not as mobile as agency mortgagors, the HEL turnover related component of speeds is slower. There are no precise statistics on the turnover component for HELs; our estimate is that the turnover component contributes 4% to 6% CPR to total prepayments. This component can fluctuate slightly under different economic conditions. In any case, it is a relatively small component when compared to total prepayments, which are typically around 20% CPR.

Partial Prepayments Sometimes mortgagors pay more than the monthly scheduled principal and interest, without prepaying the whole loan. The extra payments are called *partial prepayments* or *curtailments* — because such payments shorten the maturity of the loan. Partial prepayments could be either a result of mortgagors rounding up their monthly payments to a round dollar amount or as a result of mortgagors' desire to build up equity faster. Also, partial prepayments can increase slightly in a steep yield-curve environment when mortgagors are more inclined to use money that might otherwise be invested in lower-yielding CDs to pay off higher-interest debt. Partial prepayments play an insignificant role in total prepayment speeds, ranging up to 1.5% CPR for longer maturity loans.

Exhibit 2 quantifies the prepayment components for two typical primary A- and C HEL issues in the no-change base case and up/down 150-basis-point interest-rate movement scenarios. Note that the C HEL issue prepays faster in the base case than the A- issue owing to higher defaults and refinancings. However, the variation of C issue speeds in the up/down 150-basis-point scenarios (9% CPR) is less than the speed variation of the A-issue (16% CPR). The wider fluctuation in the refinancing component contributes to the wider swing in the A- issue prepayment speeds.

ADJUSTABLE-RATE HELS

The prepayment patterns of adjustable-rate HELs (AHELs) are relatively new and unclear to many HEL investors. This is not only because of the lack of prepayment history of AHELs but also as a result of the relatively small pool size backing AHEL tranches. Exhibit 3 shows the prepayment speeds for recently issued AHELs underwritten by Prudential Securities. AHELs have experienced significantly faster speeds than fixed-rate loans, due to the following reasons.

> *Payment shock.* When an AHEL coupon resets upward after the teaser period, the AHEL borrower would likely experience a payment shock. The unpleasant experience of writing a larger monthly payment check makes the borrower more aware of market rates and more likely to respond to refinancing opportunities.
>
> *Self-selection.* AHEL prepayment speeds are intrinsically faster than those of fixed-rate HELs. Similarly, agency ARMs are faster than agency fixed-rate MBSs. The reason behind the faster speeds is that, by the process of self-selection, adjustable-rate borrowers have a shorter horizon and are more mobile.

Exhibit 2: Quantifying HEL Prepayments

Prepayment	—Down 150 BPs.—		— Base Case —		— Up 150 BPs. —	
	A- Credit	C Credit	A- Credit	C Credit	A- Credit	C Credit
Housing Turnover	7%	5%	6%	4%	5%	3%
Partial Prepayments	1%	1%	0.5%	0.5%	0%	0%
Refinancings	18%	15%	9%	12%	5%	9%
Defaults	3%	6%	3%	6%	3%	6%
Total	29%	27%	18.5%	22.5%	13%	18%

Source: Prudential Securities' IMPACT data base as of 6/12/96.

Exhibit 3: Historical Speeds for Adjustable-Rate HELs

Issue HEL Deals	WAC (%)	WAM (YY-MM)	Age (Yrs.)	Amt. ($MM)	Orig. Pricing Speeds (HEP%)	CPR (%) 1995 Apr.	May	June	July	Aug.	Sep.	Oct	Nov.	Dec.	1996 Jan.	Feb.	Mar.	Apr.
Aames 1995A	11.5	28-09	13	41.1	21.0	2.6	2.2	13.5	24.2	18.2	35.8	11.6	12.7	35.4	33.2	23.1	13.6	45.5
Aames 1994D	11.3	28-04	15	29.5	18.0	3.8	24.2	13.9	16.0	17.1	15.3	5.0	7.6	25.1	36.8	11.2	17.2	25.7
Aames 1994C	10.9	27-09	19	14.9	18.0	5.9	21.2	34.2	27.1	28.8	28.1	1.0	44.5	45.4	27.0	32.6	6.0	42.4
Aames 1994B	10.3	27-03	22	15.9	23.0	9.2	14.2	11.5	20.3	24.1	14.6	28.2	38.4	28.0	15.9	8.6	22.9	16.7
Aames 1994A	9.8	27-05	24	6.8	25.0	16.0	7.1	12.2	44.1	40.0	48.8	23.1	40.8	28.0	9.0	7.1	49.0	22.9
Advanta 1994-2	10.9	26-11	29	15.1	22.0	8.9	14.8	21.9	43.5	26.1	43.3	29.5	21.1	22.7	NA	29.4	13.6	NA
First Alliance 1995-1	10.9	28-01	12	26.9	20.0	NA	NA	NA	NA	11.0	17.0	32.3	28.8	31.5	43.7	35.0	31.5	NA
First Alliance 1994-4	10.6	27-09	15	23.1	21.0	4.0	13.3	14.9	12.9	20.6	28.6	21.1	5.3	29.6	42.6	56.2	38.3	NA
First Alliance 1994-3	10.5	28-01	19	24.9	24.0	16.7	16.7	26.9	31.5	22.8	44.2	28.3	37.4	40.1	31.4	12.8	35.0	NA
First Alliance 1994-2	9.2	27-05	23	33.3	18.0	14.4	12.1	8.7	22.5	15.7	21.0	38.4	13.7	39.9	24.9	26.3	14.2	NA
First Alliance 1994-1	10.8	27-08	26	61.3	25.0	19.8	19.3	20.5	15.0	25.6	31.8	19.7	19.5	26.7	40.5	33.1	36.9	NA
First Alliance 1993-2	11.0	27-07	29	35.5	25.0	16.8	19.0	15.7	21.2	32.0	48.4	27.7	32.6	34.6	39.0	25.4	40.0	NA
First Alliance 1993-1	10.6	26-06	33	13.7	25.0	11.7	14.6	28.3	43.0	13.4	19.8	28.3	48.6	20.6	19.3	34.8	33.1	NA
Money Store 1995C	10.0	29-01	9	134.0	23.0	NA	NA	NA	NA	NA	NA	NA	NA	NA	11.2	16.4	18.7	NA
Money Store 1995B	10.4	29-01	7	310.6	18.0	NA	NA	NA	NA	NA	NA	NA	7.0	10.3	25.8	16.0	27.0	NA
Money Store 1995A	10.3	28-09	13	270.6	18.0	NA	5.8	3.7	6.2	11.2	13.3	13.6	16.8	21.7	29.1	29.1	32.3	NA
Money Store 1994D	10.1	28-07	16	179.4	21.0	6.3	4.5	5.3	6.3	15.7	22.8	16.4	25.9	27.4	27.8	29.4	27.5	36.8
Money Store 1994C	10.6	28-03	20	26.7	22.0	8.5	6.8	4.6	5.9	25.9	35.2	94.1	34.0	28.2	41.0	22.8	56.7	56.8
PSSF 1994-4	10.9	21-00	21	18.3	19.0	14.2	22.1	29.0	46.6	43.3	67.3	38.3	38.4	22.0	40.7	27.0	44.1	24.8
UCFC 1994C	11.5	26-01	18	7.4	22.0	7.8	0.2	14.9	14.3	74.0	74.9	50.5	46.3	64.9	43.1	58.1	16.1	33.9
UCFC 1994B	11.3	27-00	36	9.3	22.0	13.7	13.7	39.4	56.5	43.9	51.0	34.8	37.8	19.9	40.7	38.7	39.9	52.0
UCFC 1994A	11.4	26-05	43	5.5	22.0	53.2	53.2	41.8	36.6	12.8	50.2	55.8	31.8	57.4	27.6	44.2	55.5	62.3
UCFC 1993D	10.8	26-07	41	4.9	22.0	40.9	10.3	14.2	41.4	43.9	41.5	56.0	38.9	51.8	70.0	48.2	57.9	59.5
UCFC 1993C	11.0	26-11	37	8.5	22.0	48.6	30.8	44.0	18.6	30.8	50.6	38.5	37.3	53.3	45.8	28.3	44.1	NA

Source: Prudential Securities' IMPACT data base as of 4/19/96. Base mortgages rate: 8.13%

     Smaller outstanding amount. For small AHEL pools, it takes very few loans prepaying in order to reach a high prepayment speed. For example, a single $100,000 loan prepaying in a $20 million AHEL pool would result in almost 6% CPR. As a result, there are significant inter-month prepayments swings in the smaller AHEL deals.

     Dispersion on gross WACs. As a direct result of high gross WAC dispersion, there is always likely to be some degree of faster prepayment — this is typical in most HELs. The impact is just magnified when the outstanding amount is small.

In a stable interest-rate environment, AHELs are expected to prepay at around 30% CPR in the first few years, which is faster than that of fixed-rate loans. However, after a few years, the burnout effect will likely slow prepayments to the 20% CPR range.

HOME-IMPROVEMENT LOANS

Title I Loans

FHA Title I loans consist of home-improvement loans originated under Title I of the National Housing Act of 1934. Several types of loans may be made under the Title I loan program, including property improvement loans and manufactured home/lot purchase loans. Property improvement loans may be made by approved lenders to finance alterations, repair or improvement of existing homes. The Title I Loan Program is a co-insurance program. The lender is at risk for 10% of the principal balance and the FHA insures the remaining 90%, subject to an aggregate loss limit for each individual lender. The FHA charges a fee of 50 basis points per annum of the original balance for each loan it insures.

Due to the purpose of Title I home improvement loans, loan sizes are much smaller at around $15,000 compared to normal HEL sizes of $50,000. Unlike traditional HELs originated by finance companies, which are mostly first-lien mortgages, Title I loans are mostly second-lien mortgages. The fact that the first-lien mortgage is not consolidated with the second-lien mortgage suggests that the underlying first lien has a much lower rate.

Title I loans have extremely high LTVs. As many borrowers have relatively high first-lien LTVs to start with and require cash for home improvements. Their last resort is through the FHA Title I program, because no other lender is willing to lend against a high LTV mortgage.

Gross WACs normally have a high correlation with LTVs, everything else being equal. Lenders typically charge higher rates for higher LTV loans rates on Title I loans can be more than 150 basis points higher than HEL rates.

Exhibit 4: Prepayment Speeds of Money Store Title Is versus Traditional Money Store HELs

	WAC (%)	WAM (YY-MM)	Size ($ MM)	CPR (%) 1-Month	3-Month	6-Month
Title Is	13.15	13-08	54.7	17.4	18.2	16.4
Money Store 94D	11.21	21-09	373.2	26.6	27.8	25.7
Title Is	13.09	14-06	38.6	17.6	14.8	12.2
Money Store 95A	11.74	21-02	264.7	28.1	28.2	23.0

Source: Prudential Securities' IMPACT data base as of 6/19/96.

Exhibit 5: Default Rate Comparison of Title Is versus HELs
Percentage of Loan Entering Foreclosure (Annualized)

	MON 94D		MON 95A	
	Title Is	HELs	Title Is	HELs
3/95	3.61	1.00	NA	NA
4/95	2.70	0.48	5.46	0.97
5/95	4.91	3.33	3.35	0.25
6/95	8.32	0.94	0.43	0.22
7/95	8.53	2.26	5.98	1.38

Source: Prudential Securities' IMPACT data base as of 4/19/96.

Prepayment Characteristics

Due to the extremely high LTVs of Title I loans, they are much harder to refinance than lower LTV HELs. Thus, prepayment speeds on Title Is are expected to be more stable than HELs with lower LTVs. Historical prepayment speeds bear this out, as shown in Exhibit 4. Title Is have been prepaying around 17% CPR, which is significantly slower than the traditional HELs.

In contrast, Title I home improvement loans have higher default rates than normal HELs due to their higher LTVs. Exhibit 5 compares the annualized percentage of loans entering the foreclosure stage. Default rates on Title I loans can be four times as high as those on normal HELs. However as noted above, defaults tend to stabilize total prepayments under various interest-rate environments.

There is one caveat regarding the stability of Title I loan prepayments — the unknown first-lien mortgage under a mostly second-lien Title I loan. Because of the higher combined LTV, Title I loans are more difficult to refinance. However, once the loan is sufficiently amortized such that the combined LTV falls to the 75% range, Title I loan prepayments are likely to be more sensitive to changes in interest rates. As the potential to consolidate the higher-rate Title I loan with the underlying first mortgage could be realized.

SBA Loans

The SBA helps small businesses obtain more attractive funding than would otherwise be available to them by giving lenders a guarantee on a large percentage of loans granted to eligible businesses. SBA-guaranteed loans are typically prime based floating-rate notes.

The floating-rate nature of these loans, combined with the leverage provided by the SBA guarantee, substantially reduces the role of refinancing as a prepayment component. Companies that rely on these loans do not have equally appealing financing alternatives. Instead, defaults play a major role, accounting for about half of all SBA prepayments. The remainder, which we will label "voluntary prepayments," is due to such factors as ownership transfer, mergers, and liquidations.

In late 1993, Prudential Securities conducted an exhaustive study of SBA loan prepayments involving nearly 50,000 individual SBA loans underlying 2,280 SBA pools Our analysis suggests the following important conclusions regarding the two primary components in SBA loan prepayments. First, defaults have a tendency to peak after about 24 months and then decline. Second, voluntary prepayment are a less significant component in the early years of the life of the pool, but tend to increase throughout the pool's life.

The combination of these two factors creates a prepayment ramp that increases linearly to a plateau that is achieved after about a 30-month seasoning period. This plateau level is then maintained for the remainder of the life of the pool. The magnitude of the prepayment plateau depends primarily on the original maturities of the underlying loans. Longer maturities exhibit substantially reduced prepayments. In addition, the plateau is halved if an interest-rate cap is present. This reduction is partly explained by the fact that lenders generally offer interest-rate caps to their most creditworthy customers.

Exhibit 6 compares capped and uncapped SBA prepayment speeds of 10- and 25-year maturities. Note that the plateau level for 25-year uncapped SBA loans at approximately 8% CPR is much lower than the 15% CPR level for 10-year uncapped SBA loans. Capped SBA loans have lower plateau levels than their uncapped counterparts, as 25-year capped SBA loan prepayments peak at around 6% CPR versus much higher levels for 10-year capped SBA loans.

Exhibit 7 describes the plateau levels associated with both capped and uncapped loans in five representative maturity bands.

MANUFACTURED HOUSING LOANS

Manufactured homes, sometimes called "mobile homes," are primarily an alternative to renting an apartment or purchasing a site-built home. The quality of manufactured houses has improved over the years, attracting a higher-income group than in the past. As a result, about one of every five homes built in the United States is a manufactured home. As a general rule, manufactured housing prepayments are much more stable than those of agency MBSs. Exhibit 8 shows the prepayment stability of manufactured-housing loans. The major reasons for the stable prepayment speeds for manufactured homes are:

Exhibit 6: One-Year Historical Prepayment Speeds on 10-Year and 25-Year Capped and Uncapped SBA Loans

Uncapped

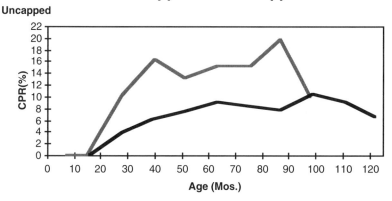

Capped

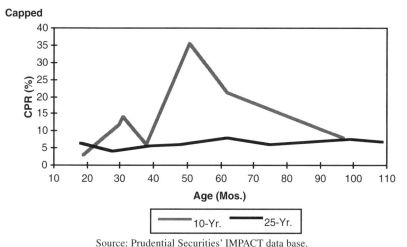

Source: Prudential Securities' IMPACT data base.

Exhibit 7: Plateau Levels Associated with Both Capped and Uncapped Loans in Five Representative Maturity Bands

Maturity Band	Plateau (% CPR)	
(Yrs.)	Uncapped	Capped
0-8	22	11-13
8-11	19	10-12
11-16	15	6-10
16-21	12	7-9
21+	8-10	5-7

Source: Prudential Securities' IMPACT data base as of 4/19/96.

Exhibit 8: Prepayment Speed Comparison: Manufactured-Housing versus 15-Year Pass-Through

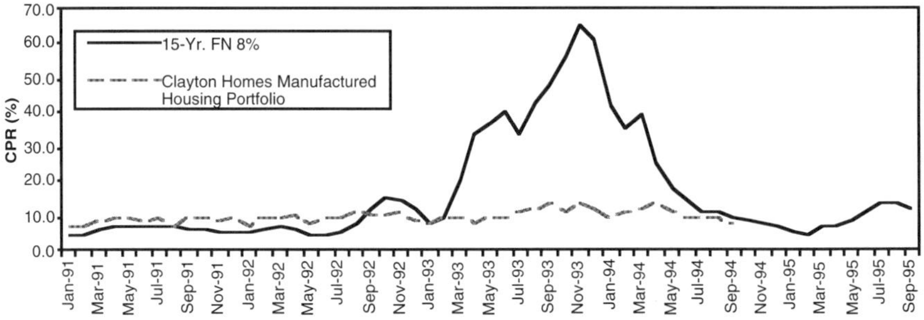

Source: Prudential Securities' IMPACT data base and Clayton Homes.

Loan size. The average loan size is about $30,000 with rates typically 2% to 4% higher than conventional mortgages. Thus, changes in mortgage rates have a much smaller impact on monthly payments.

Home depreciation. Manufactured homes generally depreciate over time. In the loan's early years, depreciation may exceed loan amortization, leaving the borrowers with lower equity and less ability to refinance.

Borrower income and fewer refinancing options. Manufactured home borrowers have a median household income of $21,000, resulting in fewer refinancing options.

Low credit quality. Many of the lower-credit borrowers of manufactured homes may not qualify for refinancing alternatives.

Prepayment Curve

Similar to single-family mortgages, manufactured housing loan pools exhibit a seasoning curve. *Manufactured housing prepayment* (MHP), which describes this prepayment curve, starts at few CPR in the first month and then increases in a linear fashion reaching a plateau in two years, after which it stays at that constant level. The base, or 100% MHP, begins at 3.7% CPR in month one and increases by 0.1% CPR each month until month 24, at which point it remains constant at 6% CPR. An MHP of 150% is simply the 100% MHP curve multiplied by 1.5. Manufactured housing pools are generally priced at speeds between 100% MHP and 175% MHP (i.e., with long-term speeds of 6% to 10% CPR).

LEASES

A lease is a contract between two parties, the lessor and the lessee. In an equipment lease transaction, the lessor obtains the equipment at the start of the lease term, usually by purchasing it from the manufacturer. The lessor then agrees to make it available to the lessee for a stated period of time in exchange for a specified schedule of payments. Often, the lease may contain provisions that give the lessee an option to purchase the equipment outright from the lessor on pre-specified terms when the lease expires.

The prepayment uncertainty of leases is relatively minimal because leases generally are structured without the prepayment option found in most loans. Exhibit 9 provides a prepayment speed comparison between FNMA 15-year MBS and Copelco 1994-A and Copelco 1995-A lease-backed deals. While a typical mortgage borrower may repay an outstanding loan balance at any time, a lessee must comply with the "hell or high water" provision that obligates it to make all contractual payments upon early termination. This economic disincentive to repay virtually eliminates refinancing related lease prepayments. However, there are three other categories of lease prepayments, namely equipment upgrades, outright prepayments and lease defaults.

> *Equipment upgrades.* Upgrades account for the majority of early termina-
> tions. With an upgrade, the lessee takes out a lease for new equipment
> and is permitted to repay the old lease, sometimes under liberal terms.
> Many lessors have policies that permit or even encourage lessees to
> upgrade to new equipment. Such upgrades are actually to the lessor's
> advantage, because they maintain the quality of the lease collateral.
>
> *Outright prepayments.* These are infrequent, but if a lessee decides to exit a
> business line or to purchase equipment earlier than the stated lease term,
> the lessee may prepay the lease and curtail the cash-flow stream, despite
> the cost of doing so.

Exhibit 9: Prepayment Speeds for FNMA 15-Year 8% MBS and Two Copelco Leasing Transactions

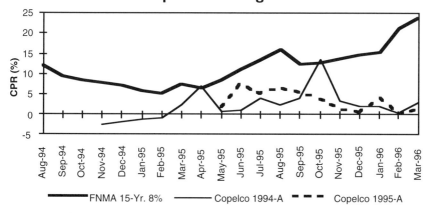

Source: Prudential Securities' IMPACT data base and Clayton Homes.

Exhibit 10: Prepayment Volatility of Different Assets on a Relative Basis

————————————— Prepayment Volatility ——————————————

Low	Medium	High
Credit Cards	Manufactured Housing	High-Credit HELs
Autos	Lower-Credit HELs	
SBAs		
Leases		

Source: Prudential Securities' IMPACT data base as of 1/29/96.

Lessee defaults. A lessee may default on lease payments. An originator's portfolio history is the best indication of how a particular pool will perform over time and, with respect to principal protection, the extent to which any default will be covered by a transaction's credit enhancement. Typically, however, a lease-backed transaction requires the amount of prepayments and defaults to be included in the principal paid to investors on the payment date after the month in which such prepayments or defaults occur.

CONCLUSIONS

The prepayment behavior of the collateral backing ABSs is much more stable than that backing traditional MBSs. Exhibit 10 summarizes the prepayment volatility of different types of assets on a relative basis. Credit cards are not subject to prepayments due to the revolving nature of most credit-card trusts. Assets with low prepayment volatility are autos, leases, and SBAs; manufactured housing and lower-credit HELs have medium prepayment volatility, while high-credit HELs exhibit relatively high prepayment volatility. The continued growth and evolution of the ABS market is expected to provide more information on gauging ABS prepayments.

Chapter 24

Z-Spreads

Anand K. Bhattacharya
Senior Vice President
Director of Fixed Income Research
Prudential Securities Inc.

Carol Sze
First Vice President
Prudential Securities Inc.

INTRODUCTION

One of the buzz words used in the relative valuation of asset-backed securities (ABSs) is Z-spreads. The nomenclature has its genesis in option-adjusted spread (OAS) analysis, which is one of the valuation metrics used for the evaluation of mortgage-backed securities (MBSs). With respect to the analysis of ABSs, since the prepayment behavior of the loans (with perhaps the exception of manufactured-housing and home-equity loans) is less of an issue than with the evaluation of MBSs, the metric is used in a slightly modified form. In the valuation of MBSs, OAS analysis measures the value of the embedded option using either a term structure of volatility or a constant-volatility assumption. The resultant measure provides the value of the short-call option embedded in the security. However, as it concerns ABSs, a variant of OAS methodology using a zero-volatility assumption, commonly known as Z-spreads, is used to assess the bullet equivalency of ABSs.

On a purely mathematical basis, Z-spreads (or for that matter, OASs) measure the spread over the Treasury yield curve. Since most amortizing structures, including ABSs, are priced at a point on the curve, any deviation between the spread over the curve (Z-spread) and the pricing spread at a point on the curve may be used to assess the relative value of the security. As explained in this chapter, since the calculations of Z-spreads do require a prepayment or paydown assumption, the appeal of this metric is greater for ABSs (as opposed to MBSs) due to the lesser prepayment sensitivity of ABSs.

FRAMEWORK FOR EVALUATION

In the evaluation of the bullet equivalency of ABSs, the main issue is whether the pricing spread is adequate compensation for the wider window associated with the structure. *In this sense, the inclusion of Z-spreads in the valuation equation is essentially tantamount to evaluating the window cost of amortizing structures.*

Our framework for evaluating the window cost is based on the fundamental tenets of finance. As a first step, consider the basic bond pricing equation that states that the price of a bond is the sum of the present values of the periodic cash flows discounted at the yield. Mathematically, this is stated as:

$$\text{Price} = \frac{CF_1}{\left(1 + \frac{y}{2}\right)^1} + \frac{CF_2}{\left(1 + \frac{y}{2}\right)^2} + \dots + \frac{CF_n}{\left(1 + \frac{y}{2}\right)^n}$$

where

CF_t = Cash flow in period t (t=1, ..., n)
n = Number of periods
y = Bond-equivalent yield

In the case of structured bonds, the CF (1 through n) in the bond pricing equation includes the interest, scheduled principal payments and any prepayments of principal incorporated in the cash flows.

Note that this pricing mechanism includes the following characteristics:

- For the same yield, the greater the cash flows in a given time period, the higher the present-value component of the set of cash flows. Stating the obvious, the present value of $2 is more than it is for $1 for any particular time period at any yield.
- For the same yield, the present value of a longer dated set of cash flows will be lower than it will be for a short dated set of cash flows.

These basic points form the foundation of our methodology for evaluating the window cost in structured bonds and thereby provide the motivation for the inclusion of Z-spreads in the relative-valuation equation. With this slight digression, we return to the issue at hand — the pricing of the window. In fact, we take it one step further and posit our analysis by incorporating into our evaluation the entire set of cash flows — the interest and both scheduled and unscheduled (prepayment) principal. As noted above, a common initial reaction in the evaluation process may be to perceive a wide principal window as a negative. While a wide window may be critical for the valuation of ABSs, such as autos, controlled-amortization credit cards and home-equity loans, wide principal windows are not necessarily undesirable features in structured bonds.

In the valuation of structured securities, the commonly accepted methodology is to benchmark the securities off of a reference point on the Treasury curve. Usually, the benchmark is determined as the closest match to the weighted-average life of the structured bond. However, if we make the assumption that a structured security is nothing more than a set of bundled cash flows from a series of one-period bonds, then the commonly accepted methodology of pricing these bundled cash flows at a particular point on the Treasury curve has certain current and future relative-value implications.

Under this framework, the price of the bundled cash flows is equal to the sum of the prices of the individual one-period bonds. The prices of the individual bonds are determined by discounting the periodic cash flows along the Treasury curve rather than at a single point on the curve. Therefore, any deviation between the spread determined by discounting the cash flows *along* the curve and the spread determined by discounting the cash at a *point* on the curve can be construed as a measure of the relative "cheapness or richness" of the security.

RELATIVE VALUE USING RICH/CHEAP ANALYSIS

Current Relative-Value Implications

As noted above, Z-spreads involve determining the spread of the security using discount rates along the curve. Since the actual pricing of the security is at a point on the Treasury curve, the evaluation translates to assessing the extent to which (assuming a positively sloped yield curve) the short dated cash flows (occurring prior to the maturity of the benchmark) are priced cheap and the extent to which the long dated cash flows (occurring beyond the maturity of the benchmark) are priced rich. In essence, the current relative-value assessment comes down to evaluating the relative richness or cheapness of the timing of the cash flows.

The influence of the relative magnitude of the cash flows also is significant. Consider that if a majority of a security's cash flows occur in a relatively short period of time, with the remainder of the cash flows comprising the "tail," the relative-cheapness factor of the cash flows will be substantially greater than the relative richness factor. Our discussion of present-value dynamics provides the key to this analysis.

The present value of a long dated set of cash flows is less than the present value of short dated cash flows, thus causing the relative impact of the longer dated cash flows on the valuation to be relatively minor. Furthermore, the relative-cheapness factor of the bond will increase in direct proportion to the amount of cash flows received in the earlier periods. This result also follows from the basic present-value principles discussed earlier. In a given time period, the greater the cash flows, the higher the present-value component of those cash flows.

In our analysis, we label this net amount of the "cheapness/richness" factor as the *cash-flow uncertainty cost*. Note that since "rich/cheap" analysis includes all cash flows received from a bond (interest and scheduled and unscheduled principal payments), the cash-flow uncertainty cost includes the cost of the long or short principal window. This evaluation is in addition to the determination of the relative value of the security using other measures such as OAS.

Future Relative-Value Implications: Effect of Yield-Curve Slope Changes on Cash-Flow Uncertainty Cost

An important issue in rich/cheap analysis is how cash-flow uncertainty cost changes as the shape of the yield curve flattens or steepens. Non-parallel shifts in the yield curve can change the dynamics of the cash flows and, by extension, the relative cheapness or richness of the short and/or long dated cash flows. Exhibit 1 graphically illustrates the dynamics of this issue.

Exhibit 1: Cash Flow of Structured Securities

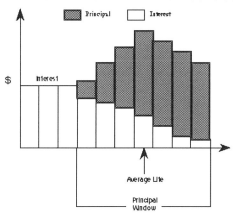

Exhibits 2 through 6 describe the cash-flow schematic of a fixed-rate structured bond backed by home-equity loans in various yield-curve environments as home-equity loans are affected by a higher degree of prepayment sensitivity than other ABS types, such as autos and credit cards.

Exhibit 2 shows that when the bond is priced at a spread over the Treasury yield corresponding to the average life of the bond, the entire set of cash flows is priced using a single yield. However, using our "rich/cheap" approach, assuming a positively shaped yield curve, cash flows occurring prior to the maturity of the benchmark are priced cheap. This is because the shorter dated cash flows are priced off of a longer dated benchmark. At the same time, the cash flows occurring after the maturity of the benchmark are priced rich because they are indexed off of a shorter dated benchmark. Depending upon the magnitude and timing of the cash flows, either the richness or cheapness factor will dominate.

The uncertainty cost of the structured bond will change as the shape of the yield curve changes. Exhibit 3 illustrates a yield curve flattening with the short end backing off and the long end remaining relatively stable. Since the long end does not move significantly, and assuming prepayments are unaffected, the cash flows associated with the bond also will remain essentially unchanged. However, the relative richness and cheapness of the cash flows changes. The relative-cheapness factor of the bond will decrease as the shorter dated cash flows are priced off of incrementally higher benchmarks. At the same time, due to a flattening of the long end, which causes the spread between the benchmark and the longer dated Treasury yields to tighten, the richness factor of the bond also will decrease. Depending upon whether the decrease in the relative-cheapness factor is matched by a corresponding decrease in the relative richness factor, the overall cost of cash-flow uncertainty either will decrease or increase. This concept is illustrated by comparing Exhibits 3 and 4.

Exhibit 2: Cheapness/Richness of Cash Flows

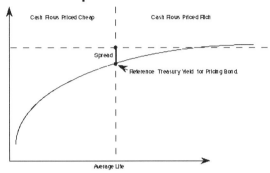

Exhibit 3: Yield Curve Flattens:
Short End Up/Long End Unchanged

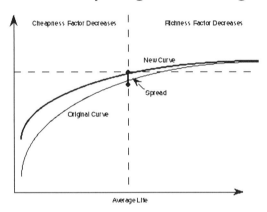

Exhibit 4: Yield Curve Flattens:
Short End Unchanged/Long End Down

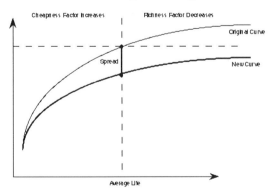

Exhibit 5: Yield Curve Steepens:
Long End Up/Short End Unchanged

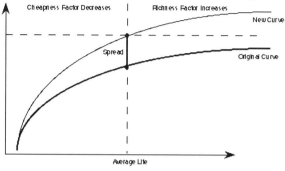

Exhibit 6: Yield Curve Inverts

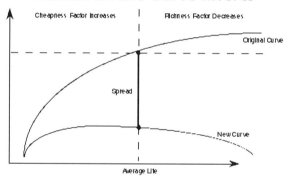

In the opposite scenario, in which the yield curve steepens without any significant change in the short end of the curve and a shift upward in the long end, prepayment speeds are likely to slow down. As illustrated in Exhibit 5, the result is that the relative cheapness of the shorter dated cash flows decreases, while the relative richness of the longer dated cash flows increases, assuming the cash flow has not changed significantly. In the event that the steepening occurs at the long end, the cheapness of the short dated cash flows essentially will be unchanged, while the richness factor of the long dated cash flows increases.

If the yield curve inverts, the decrease in long rates will likely cause prepayment speeds to increase and the average life of structured securities to decrease. In this scenario, shown in Exhibit 6, the decline in long rates causes the cash flows to be "front loaded" and thus the relative cheapness of the bond is enhanced. The cheapness factor is further boosted because, with the rally in the short end, the short dated cash flows are discounted using a lower set of benchmarks.

Exhibit 7: Z-Spread Comparison of Bullet Credit-Card, Structured Auto and a Tranched HEL Securities

Security	Bullet Credit Card	Tranched auto	Tranched HEL
Coupon (%)	6.06	6.10	6.20
Price (32nds)	101-07	100-24+	99-29
Yield (%)	5.69	5.82	6.22
Pricing Speed(%)	21.51 MPR	1.50 ABS	23CPR
Average Life (Years)	2.78	2.80	2.77
Payment Window	Bullet	2.3 to 3.3	0.1 to 9.8
Spread/3-Year Treasury (BPs)	+30	+43	+83
Zero-Volatility Spread (BPs)	+32	+45	+71
Price at Zero-Volatility (32nds)	101-05+	100-26	99-22+
Price Differential (32nds)	00-1+	00-1+	-00-6+

Treasury Yield Curve							
3-months	6-months	1-year	2-year	3-year	5-year	10-year	30-year
5.48	5.44	5.35	5.36	5.39	5.53	5.71	6.04

Analysis as of December 11, 1995.

Spread "Over the Curve" Factor in Rich/Cheap Valuation

As an example of the analysis of the uncertainty cost, consider the set of bonds in Exhibit 7. We examine a bullet credit card, a tranched auto and a short home-equity class with similar average lives and coupons.

In evaluating these bonds with respect to bullet equivalency, the main issue is whether the price differential of the various length of principal windows versus the bullet security is sufficient compensation for the non-bullet securities. In addition, there is a related issue regarding the performance of the bond(s) in different yield-curve scenarios.

As a starting point in our evaluation, we introduce the concept of a zero-volatility OAS. It is important for our analysis to recognize that this zero-volatility metric essentially is a measure of the spread over the curve. Once a positive volatility is introduced into the analysis and movements in interest rates are linked with the associated prepayments, the result is an OAS that measures the value of the embedded prepayment option. *In the present context, if the nominal spread reflects full compensation for the time value of money, then the spread over a single benchmark should be equal to the zero volatility OAS.*

Based on our argument above, the cheapness factor (cash flows occurring prior to the maturity of the benchmark) should balance out the richness factor. Therefore, if the spread over the curve (zero-volatility OAS) is greater (or less) than the spread over the single benchmark, then the aggregate set of cash flows is being priced cheap (or rich).

Exhibit 8: Relative-Value Impact of Changes in Yield Curve

Yield curve	Bullet Credit Card		Tranched Auto		Tranched HEL	
	Price (32nds)	Change (%)	Price (32nds)	Change (%)	Price (32nds)	Change (%)
Current	101-07	NA	100-24+	NA	99-29	NA
Steepen	103-10	2.07	102-26+	2.05	101-14	1.53
Invert	99-06	-2.01	98-24	-2.00	98-18	-1.35

Yield curve	3-months	6-months	1-year	2-year	3-year	5-year	10-year	30-year
Current	5.48	5.44	5.35	5.36	5.39	5.53	5.71	6.04
Steepen 200 BPs	3.48	3.78	4.02	4.36	4.73	5.20	5.71	6.04
Invert 200 BPs	7.48	7.10	6.68	6.36	6.05	5.86	5.71	6.04

Analysis as of December 11, 1995.

This analysis shows that the wider-window tranched HEL is cheap based on its higher yield and zero-volatility spread versus the bullet credit card and the tranched auto. While this is expected, it is interesting to note that our analysis shows that the tranched HEL is slightly rich relative to its benchmark by eight basis points (71 to 83 basis points) and the bullet credit card and tranched auto are slightly cheap by two basis points. To quantify this on a price basis, we use the spread to Treasury as the zero volatility and recompute prices, all other factors constant. The results show that the bullet and tranched auto currently are cheap by about 1.5/32nds, whereas the tranched HEL currently is rich by about 6.5/32nds.

USING Z-SPREADS TO DETERMINE FUTURE RELATIVE VALUE

Our framework is also useful for evaluating the effect of any changes in the shape of the yield curve on the future relative-value implications of tight- and wide-window bonds. We demonstrate this aspect of the valuation equation by determining the price performance of the bonds under various yield-curve environments by holding the zero-volatility OAS and cash flows constant. In our analysis, the yield curve shows a spread of 23 basis points between the 3-month Treasury bill and the 10-year Treasury note yields. For a steepening scenario, we shift the 3-month Treasury bill yield downward by 200 basis points while keeping the 10-year note yield constant. A similar twist is applied to the inversion where the 3-month bill is shifted upward by 200 basis points. The results of this analysis are presented in Exhibit 8.

Exhibit 9: Relative-Value Impact of Changes in Yield Curve

Yield Curve Environment	BondA Narrow Window		Bond B Wide Window	
	Price	Percent (Absolute) Price Change	Price	Percent (Absolute) Price Change
Unchanged (Yield curve as of 11/16/92)	98-09	NA	97-19+	NA
Flatter 7-year yield, -25 BPs 10-year yield, -50 BPs 30-year yield, -75 BPs	101-27	3.62 (3-18)	100-26	3.28 (3-06+)
Steeper 30-year yield, +118 BPs	98-03+	-0.17 (-0-05+)	97-09+	-0.32 (-0-10)
Inverted 5-year yield, -100 BPs 7-year yield, -200 BPs 10-year yield, -300 BPs 30-year yield, -400 BPs	106-26+	8.69 (8-17+)	107-09+	10.24 (10-0)

Exhibit 9 shows that, as the curve steepens, all three bonds appreciate in price since the relative cheapness of the cash flows occurring prior to the maturity of the benchmark decreases dramatically, while the cash flows after the maturity of the benchmark remain relatively unchanged. In the case of the inversion, the opposite happens in that all prices decreased since the cheapness of the cash flows dramatically increases. Note that in both shifts of the yield curve, the bullet credit card displayed the highest absolute price change and the wide windowed tranched HEL displayed the lowest.

CONCLUSION

One of the main issues in the structured asset market is the length of the window and the associated issue whether the nominal spread is adequate compensation for the amortizing structure versus bullet securities. As a general rule, all things being equal, assets with wider windows are priced at wider spreads to compensate for the diversion in the bullet-equivalency of the bond. However, if the securities are treated as a collection of one-period bonds with each cash flow priced at the appropriate discount rate, it can be argued that any deviation of the spread over the curve from the single spread over the benchmark can be viewed as an indicator of the net "cheapness/richness" measure of the pricing of the cash flows.

Specifically, based on a certain prepayment assumption, if the spread over the curve is greater (less) than the single pricing spread, the cash flows are priced net cheap (rich). While we cannot generalize from the example presented above, based on our analysis, it can be argued that wider-window bonds are cheaper than tighter-window bonds, definitely on an absolute basis and possibly on a relative-value basis.

At the same time, the current relative value of the bond is likely to change as the shape of the yield curve changes. Our analysis shows that as the yield curve inverts (steepens), the bonds become cheaper (richer) mainly due to the fact that the relative-cheapness factor of the shorter dated cash flows becomes more (less).

Part V: Accounting Considerations

Chapter 25

Introduction to ABS Accounting

Len Blum
Managing Director
Head, Asset-Backed Banking Group
Prudential Securities Inc.

Evan Mitnick
Vice President
Asset-Backed Banking Group
Prudential Securities Inc.

The authors would like to thank Marty Rosenblatt at Deloitte & Touche LLP for his comments and suggestions on the content of this chapter.

INTRODUCTION

Securitization is the process by which financial assets are transformed into securities and often involves the transfer of receivables from one entity to another. Depending upon the details of the transaction, this transfer may be accounted for as a sale or as a financing. Sale treatment is often desirable to recognize any gain on the transfer and to achieve off-balance sheet treatment. Reducing the level of debt on the balance sheet can help an issuer maintain a higher return on assets and better coverage ratios. Also, if the issuer uses the proceeds to extinguish on-balance sheet liabilities, the debt-to-equity ratio may be improved. The purpose of this chapter is to provide an introduction to the accounting treatment for asset-backed securities.

TREATMENT OF A RECEIVABLES TRANSFER

At the time of this writing, the primary authoritative literature used to determine the treatment of a receivables transfer is Statement of Financial Accounting Standards No. 77, "Reporting by Transferors for Transfers of Receivables with Recourse" (SFAS 77). Effective January 1, 1997, SFAS 125, "Accounting for Transfers and Servicing of Financial Assets and Extinguishments of Liabilities," will replace SFAS 77. SFAS 125 is discussed later in this chapter.

According to SFAS 77, for a transfer of receivables to be called a sale, it must meet four criteria:

1. the transfer must purport to be a sale;
2. the transferor must surrender its control of the future economic benefits relating to the receivables;
3. the transferor must be able to reasonably estimate its obligation under the recourse provisions; and
4. the transferee may not return the receivables to the transferor except pursuant to the recourse provisions.

What does "purport to be a sale" mean? There are several ways to analyze this: e.g. (1) the transaction is called a sale and is referred to as such in the legal documents; (2) the transaction is a sale for tax purposes; (3) the securities issued represent an interest in the receivables pool itself and not debt collateralized by the receivables pool; and (4) the transaction is a "true sale" as far as bankruptcy is concerned, that is, the transferred receivables would not be included in the bankrupt estate should the transferor file for bankruptcy. In many cases, these considerations are not always going to give the same result. For example, many asset-backed transactions are treated as debt for federal income tax purposes but are referred to in the transaction documents as sales (for example, credit-card securitizations). Under normal circumstances, if such a transaction meets the other three SFAS 77 requirements, it will receive accounting sale treatment.

The second requirement states that the transferor surrenders control of the future economic benefits from the receivables. This precludes the transferor from holding a material call option on the sold pool of receivables. The only exception to this prohibition is the "cleanup call" in which the servicer (normally the seller or an affiliate thereof) may repurchase the assets of the trust when the outstanding principal balance of these receivables is less than 5% or 10% of their principal balance when sold into the securitization. This cleanup call provision exists because, at a certain point, the expense of leaving the securitization outstanding (for example, the negative arbitrage associated with a reserve account when it is at its floor as a percentage of the transaction or the expense of administering a small transaction) outweigh its benefits. Furthermore, in many cases, investors prefer transactions with cleanup calls. Should the call be exercised, the securities' principal window can be significantly reduced (this is especially true for longer self-amortizing assets, such as home equity loans). Accountants have allowed that a cleanup call for a *de minimis* percentage of the trust assets (typically 10%, 5% for bank regulatory purposes) does not violate the "no call" provision of SFAS 77. The fourth requirement states that the transferee may not return receivables to the transferor (except for agreed-upon recourse). In other words, the transferee may not hold the equivalent of a put option on the transferred receivables.

Finally, the transferor must be able to estimate possible recourse. Most securitizations have some form of "recourse," often in the form of a subordinated ("first-loss") asset that may be retained by the seller. The size of this subordination generally is based upon rating agency criteria and typically results in a multiple of the previous loss history that the seller has had with similar receivables. An analysis of the dynamic and static pool history of the seller's receivables leads to a determination (by the rating agencies or a monoline insurance company) of the size of the expected loss that the receivables pool will suffer. The level of subordination required is a multiple of this expected loss.

If a transaction does not meet the SFAS 77 requirements for a sale, it will be considered a collateralized financing and the receivables and the associated debt will remain on-balance sheet. In such a case, the basic accounting entry that would be required to record the securitization would be as follows:

Cash	xxxx	
Long Term Debt Payable		xxxx

This entry simply recognizes the proceeds from the "loan" and the associated liability. The receivables remain on the balance sheet as this transaction is, essentially a collateralized loan.

When a transaction is accounted for as a sale, the accounting becomes somewhat more complex. In theory, the basic entry reflecting sale treatment, assuming a sale at par, no transaction costs, no retained interests, no taxes and no credit reserves, would be:

Cash	xxxx	
Receivables		xxxx

If the cash were more or less than the carrying amount of the receivables, a Gain or Loss on Sale would be recognized.

However, there are a number of components to a sale of receivables. Securitizations often are structured such that the interest from the receivables is used first to pay transaction expenses and the investor coupon and to meet any credit enhancement requirements with any excess going back to the seller. (In many cases when receivables are sold into a securitization, the seller continues to service the receivables.) The seller is entitled to a regular servicing fee to cover its administrative expenses for the receivables in the transaction pool. This servicing fee is recognized as earned over the life of the transaction. The remainder of the excess cash flow that is returned to the seller from the transaction is referred to as "excess servicing."

Treatment of Excess Servicing

Excess servicing is an asset recognized when receivables are sold and the seller retains the right to receive the difference between (a) the coupon on the loans and (b) the sum of the investor coupon, losses on the loans and other transaction expenses (including normal servicing). This would be the case in a securitization or in a whole loan sale where the receivables are sold with the servicing retained by the seller. Excess servicing typically is calculated by taking the excess of the anticipated cash flow to the seller over a "normal" servicing fee (which varies by type of asset) for each period in the future, assuming certain default and prepayment rates and discounting these cash flows by an appropriate discount rate.

The components involved in a securitization are: (1) the portion sold; (2) the portion, if any, retained; and (3) the excess servicing asset. Depending on the structure of a transaction, when receivables are sold into a securitization, the seller's basis in these three components must be allocated according to their relative fair market values to determine the gain or loss from the sale.

This "allocation of basis" concept was promulgated in 1989 through Emerging Issues Task Force Issue number 88-11 (EITF 88-11) because prior literature (including SFAS 65 which will be discussed below) was unclear as to the recognition of gain/loss on the "partial sales" of receivables. The following example will illustrate the proper accounting for a sale of receivables into a securitization (where the seller is the servicer, and the seller retains an ongoing interest in the transaction):

Assumptions:

1. Total receivables to be sold:	$100 million
2. Existing loss reserves:	2 million
3. Senior interest to be sold:	90 million
4. Subordinated interest to be retained:	10 million
5. Present value of excess servicing:	8 million

The relative fair values of the three components that make up the receivables are as follows:

	Amount (Fair Value)	Percentage of Total
Senior interest	$90 million	83.33
Subordinated interest	10 million	9.26
Excess servicing	8 million	7.41
Total	$108 million	100.00

Thus, the entry to record the transfer of receivables from the seller to the securitization vehicle is as follows:

Cash	$90.00 million	
Subordinated interest	9.26 million	
Excess servicing asset	7.41 million	
Loss Reserves	2.00 million	
Receivables		$100.00 million
Pre-tax Gain on Sale		8.67 million

Note that the Gain on Sale in this transaction results from the excess of the proceeds received for the sold senior interest over the basis allocated to this portion of the sold receivables. The assumptions used to capitalize the subordinated interest and the excess servicing asset take expected losses into consideration.

In another example, using a different set of assumptions, the seller may sell "underwater" assets to the issuing trust. However, if the originator's credit reserve has been adjusted accordingly (and the deterioration in value is due to credit), the sale should not yield a loss. For example, if loss assumptions and prepayment assumptions were different, the fair market value of the retained interest and the excess servicing may be lower as illustrated below:

Assumptions:

	Amount (Fair Value)	Percentage of Total
Senior interest	$90 million	91.84
Subordinated interest	5 million	5.10
Excess servicing	3 million	3.06
Total	$98 million	100.00

The entry to record the sale of receivables to the trust in this case would be as follows:

Cash	$90 million	
Retained interest	5 million	
Excess Servicing Asset	3 million	
Loss Reserves	2 million	
Receivables		$100 million

Note that the retained interest and the excess servicing asset in this example were recorded at the lower of their fair market value or their percentage of basis allocation. In the first example, the allocated basis was lower than the fair market value for both of these items so they were recorded based upon their respective allocation percentages of the transferred receivables.

Earlier, we discussed the calculation of the value of the excess servicing asset. Generally, this asset "amortizes" over the remaining life of the receivables. As the receivables pay down, the seller records the receipt of cash and the amortization of the excess servicing asset. Any differences are credited to interest income. If at any time during the receivables' life there are any changes in prepayment assumptions or loss assumptions that would have a negative impact on the value of the excess servicing, the asset should be written down at that time to reflect the real expected value. On the other hand, if changes in any of these assumptions were to increase the expected value of the excess servicing, the seller would not write up the value of the excess servicing but would instead recognize the higher than expected cash flow prospectively as interest income in the period of its receipt.

Clearly, the determination of the value of excess servicing is important in the determination of the gain or loss from sale that will be recognized from the sale of receivables. A significant gain may have a positive impact on a company's share price.

SFAS 125

Until now, SFAS 77 and EITF 88-11 have been the primary authoritative literature upon which companies have based their accounting for securitization. These pronouncements have helped companies and their auditors determine whether to recognize a transaction as a sale or a financing and how much, if any, of a gain or loss to recognize in the case of a sale. However, SFAS 77 was written well before securitization was in vogue. The transfer of receivables envisioned in SFAS 77 was generally the sale of receivables to a factor. Securitizations have characteristics which differ from a plain vanilla sale of receivables.

In response to this, the Financial Accounting Standards Board (FASB) adopted SFAS 125 that will supersede SFAS 77 as of January 1, 1997 (with no early adoption permitted). This Statement, entitled "Accounting for Transfers and Servicing of Financial Assets and Extinguishments of Liabilities," will cover not only securitizations but other transaction types as well, including loan participations, repurchase agreements, securities lending transactions and dollar rolls. Furthermore, the Statement will extend mortgage servicing guidance pursuant to SFAS 122 (see below) to servicing of receivables other than mortgage loans.

SFAS 125 gives the following conditions for a transfer of assets to be defined as a sale:

1. The transferred assets have been isolated from the transferor — put presumptively beyond the reach of the transferor and its creditors, even in bankruptcy or other receivership.
2. Either (a) each transferee obtains the right — free of conditions that effectively restrain it from taking advantage of that right — to pledge or exchange the transferred assets, or (b) the transferee is a qualifying special-purpose entity and the holders of beneficial interests in that entity have the right — free of conditions that effectively constrain them from taking advantage of that right — to pledge or exchange those interests.
3. The transferor does not effectively maintain control over the transferred assets by a concurrent agreement to repurchase them before their maturity.

The main theme behind these conditions is that the transferor has surrendered control of the assets. SFAS 125 will also incorporate EITF 88-11 in that retained interests will be recorded based upon their respective allocations of basis in the transferred assets (as discussed earlier), except that an issuer would also include "contractually specified servicing fees" as a separate retained interest. This was true for mortgage loans per SFAS 122 and now will apply to all asset types.

The key phrase in the first condition under the Statement is "beyond the reach of the transferor and its creditors." Accounting for a transaction as a sale would be appropriate only if there is evidence that the transferred assets would not be includable in a bankrupt estate should the seller go into bankruptcy or would not be accessible by a receiver for parties such as banks which are not subject to bankruptcy law. In most securitizations, counsel will issue a "true sale" opinion in which the attorneys express their view that the transferred assets may not be touched by creditors of the seller. Such an opinion would be one example (probably the most common example) of evidence that the "beyond the reach" standard is being met.

The second condition demonstrates the idea that the assets are no longer under the transferor's control. The transferee may do as it pleases with the transferred assets. Note that a separate reference is made to a "qualifying special-purpose entity." Typically, a special-purpose entity (SPE) is set up to buy the receivables, issue securities, collect payments on the receivables and make the required distributions to investors. This SPE exists separately from the seller, with its own books and records and a separate board of directors and it is generally not under the seller's control. Holders of beneficial interests in the SPE generally may freely transfer their interests as they see fit.

As discussed earlier, the inclusion of cleanup calls has not violated sale treatment conditions even under SFAS 77. However, the new Statement allows for call options to exist, even under sale treatment, as long as the underlying asset is commodity-like in nature such that an investor whose interest in a security is called by the seller would be able to take the proceeds and readily purchase such assets in the open market. Certain asset types that are commonly securitized may qualify as "readily obtainable." Also, put options will no longer disqualify sale treatment. Thus, certain transaction features, such as "maturity guarantees" may be offered by the issuer directly without the involvement of a third-party outside of the transaction.

ACCOUNTING FOR VARIOUS ASSET TYPES

Credit-Card Receivables

Typically, credit-card receivables are securitized through a revolving structure. In such a structure, credit-card receivables are sold into an SPE (what is actually sold are the receivable balances that arise pursuant to credit-card accounts from time to time, not the accounts themselves). As these receivables pay down, the cash generated from the payments is used to buy new receivable balances into the trust. This process continues for a certain period of time (the revolving period) after which the payments are used by the trust to repay investors (the amortization period). Issuers have found this structure to be useful; it allows them to fund for a longer term (for example, three to five years) using a short-term asset (for example, six to nine months).

However, the issue of how to account for this structure is not as clear. When investors purchase interests in the SPE, according to SFAS 77, they should have control over the cash payments received from the receivables. However, in a revolving structure, this cash is used instead to purchase more receivables from the issuer. The cash actually ends up in the hands of the issuer, not the investors.

The EITF met to discuss this issue and decided that as long as all conditions of SFAS 77 are met, and as long as investors do not receive more than their investor percentage of principal collections during the amortization period, a securitization using a revolving structure would qualify for sale treatment. The logic here is that investors do have control over the cash; they merely have agreed pursuant to a document executed at transaction inception to direct this cash to purchase new receivable balances from the issuer.

The consensus of EITF 88-22 was to allow sale treatment for securitizations using revolving structures. Late last year, the FASB discussed this issue and decided to continue to allow sale treatment for revolving structures despite opposition from some within the FASB. This treatment is included as part of the new FASB Statement discussed earlier without the prohibition of accelerated investor paydowns.

Leases

Leases of a number of asset types, including equipment, computers, autos and aircraft have been securitized in recent years. In deciding whether to treat a securitization of leases as a sale or a financing, it is important to determine the nature of the leases to be securitized.

From an accounting standpoint, there are two basic types of leases, operating leases and capital (finance) leases. According to SFAS 13, "Accounting for Leases," a lease is a capital lease if it meets any one of the following four criteria:

1. The lease transfers ownership of the property to the lessee by the end of the lease term.
2. The lease contains an option to purchase the leased property at a bargain price.
3. The lease term is equal to or greater than 75 percent of the estimated economic life of the leased property.
4. The present value of rental and other minimum lease payments equals or exceeds 90% of the fair value of the leased property (less any investment tax credit retained by the lessor).

In practice, classifying a lease can be quite complex and the subtleties are beyond the scope of this chapter. For example, some accountants believe that leases with significant economic residuals can be classified as capital leases if residual insurance is available and certain other tests are met. Non-parallel GAAP/tax treatment also may be available for certain transactions, which also is beyond the scope of this chapter.

From the lessor's standpoint, an operating lease represents the purchase of a capitalized asset that is depreciated over its life and has a monthly stream of rental income pursuant to the lease agreement. It is recorded as follows:

```
Cash                         xxx
     Rental Income                 xxx
Depreciation Expense    xxx
     Accumulated Depreciation      xxx
```

There is no receivable recorded for an operating lease; the revenue is recorded as it is "earned." Accordingly, the leased asset remains on the lessor's books.

For a capital lease, on the other hand, the leased asset is actually removed from the lessor's books and replaced with a receivable. The lessor also records unearned income representing interest income that will be recorded over the life of the lease and a residual value for the lease at the time of lease inception as follows:

Lease Payments Receivable	xxxx	
Residual Value of Leased Equipt.	xxxx	
Equipment		xxxx
Unearned Lease Income		xxxx

Note that for a sales-type lease where the lessor is recording a gain (or loss) on sale from the capital lease, Inventory would be credited instead of Equipment.

The lease payments receivable and the unearned lease income are recorded at the gross amount (not discounted to net present value). The unearned income is what discounts it to present value. Each month, as payments are received, the lessor records the decrease in the receivable and the recognition of the interest income as follows:

Cash	xxx	
Lease Payments Receivable		xxx
Unearned Lease Income	xxx	
Interest Income		xxx

Both operating and capital leases are securitized. There are different considerations which must be taken into account for each when determining which accounting treatment would apply for an issuer. Generally, accounting for the securitization of capital leases is governed by SFAS 77 and will be governed by SFAS 125.

A primary difference between an operating lease and a capital lease is that the lessor of an operating lease keeps the leased asset on its books while the lessee in a capital lease records the leased asset on its books. In an operating lease, the lessor records depreciation on the asset and may be able to take advantage of a depreciation deduction for tax purposes whereas the lessee will get this benefit under a capital lease.

This affects how an issuer will choose to structure a securitization. Quite often, an issuer whose leases are primarily operating leases will choose to structure a transaction as a financing in order to keep the leased assets on its books and continue to take advantage of the depreciation deduction for tax purposes. Securitizing such assets in a tax sale format (such as a grantor trust) is generally inefficient as investors typically would not value the attendant tax benefits accordingly. On the other hand, an issuer with mostly capital leases may prefer sale treatment in order to recognize the gain from the sale of the lease contracts to the SPE.

Mortgage Loans

SFAS 65, "Accounting for Certain Mortgage Banking Activities," has been the accounting standard that controls the accounting treatment for the origination, purchase and sale of mortgage loans and mortgage-backed securities. This Statement deals with a number of issues related to mortgage banking, including balance sheet classification and valuing the mortgage loans on the balance sheet. A key element of SFAS 65 is its discussion of mortgage servicing rights. According to SFAS 65, if mortgage loans are sold servicing-retained, meaning that the seller of the mortgage loans will continue to service the sold loans, and the servicing fee that will be received by the seller will differ materially from a "normal" servicing fee, the sales price should be adjusted for the difference between the actual sales price and the sales price that would have been obtained if a "normal" servicing fee were used. The entire gain or loss from this difference in the servicing rate to be received by the seller should be recognized at the time of sale. As you may recognize, this is the excess servicing of which we spoke in our discussion of EITF 88-11.

SFAS 65 also discussed the recording of the components of mortgage loans originated or purchased on the balance sheet. SFAS 65 differs in its accounting for loans purchased versus loans originated. The cost of purchased loans should be broken out between the cost of the loans and the cost of the servicing rights to those loans. The cost of the servicing rights would be the fair value of those rights and if that is not readily determined, then the allocated cost would be the present value of future net servicing income. For originated loans, on the other hand, all costs involved in the origination would be allocated to the loans. This led to a discrepancy in which loans sold servicing-retained that were originated by the seller would generate a lower gain (or a higher loss) on sale due to the fact that the entire cost of origination was allocated to the loans while loans that were purchased would generate a higher gain (or lower loss) on sale because some part of the cost of the loans was allocated to the servicing rights.

The FASB recognized this discrepancy and in May of 1995, passed SFAS 122 "Accounting for Mortgage Servicing Rights" as an amendment to SFAS 65. Under SFAS 122, which became effective for fiscal years beginning after December 15, 1995, mortgage loans receive the same accounting treatment whether they are originated or purchased by the seller. If the mortgage banking enterprise sells or securitizes these loans servicing-retained, the cost of the loans should be allocated between the servicing rights and the loans based upon their relative fair values if it is practicable to estimate those fair values. If it is not practicable to estimate those fair values, then the entire cost should be allocated to the loans. Elements of both SFAS 65 and SFAS 122 are included in SFAS 125.

Investor Accounting

Until now, we have discussed accounting for securitization from the side of the issuer. However there are also special considerations that must be taken into account by investors in asset-backed securities.

In May of 1993, the FASB issued SFAS 115, "Accounting for Certain Investments in Debt and Equity Securities." Prior to that point, accounting literature was not consistent in its treatment of accounting for debt securities. Generally, entities had to use lower-of-cost-or-market to evaluate their securities portfolio. However, this often led to an inaccurate evaluation of the portfolio because it would only take into account value depreciation, not value appreciation. This often led to companies manipulating the accounting for securities sold versus securities held to maturity (a company could sell a security with a low book value for its high market value and overstate the true gain on the portfolio). Furthermore, it became apparent that fair value information regarding debt securities would be far more relevant to users of financial information than the amortized cost of these securities. The FASB also felt that it was relevant to disclose the intent that a company would have regarding the different securities in its portfolio. After all, the fair market value of a debt instrument that will be held to maturity is perhaps less relevant than the fluctuations in the market value of a security that a company intends to sell.

SFAS 115 covers debt securities and equity securities that have readily determinable fair values. According to this Statement, investments in securities fall into three categories:

1) *Held to maturity securities:* securities that an entity has the positive intent and ability to hold until maturity.
2) *Trading securities:* securities that an entity buys with the intention of selling them in the short term (and making a profit).
3) *Available-for-sale securities:* securities that are not classified as held-to-maturity or trading securities.

The reporting differs for each category of securities. Held-to-maturity securities are reported at amortized cost. Trading securities are reported at cost when acquired and are then reported at fair market value with the unrealized gains or losses from fluctuations in market value included in current income/expense. Available-for-sale securities are also reported at fair value except that the unrealized gains and losses from market value fluctuations are reported in a separate component of stockholders' equity and are not included in earnings.

Securities classified as held-to-maturity should, indeed, be investments that the entity intends to hold until those investments mature. Securities should not be classified as held-to-maturity if they will only be held as such for an indefinite time and would be sold in response to certain circumstances such as changes in interest rates and prepayment expectations or a greater need for liquidity. Held-to-maturity securities may be recorded at amortized cost since fluctuations in market value will have no effect on their value to the company if held to maturity. Assuming no default on the part of the issuer, the investor will receive its predetermined stream of cash flows. Trading securities, on the other hand, have a much shorter time frame. They are purchased in order to be sold at a profit. Fluctuations in market value have a real impact on these securities and their carrying value must be constantly adjusted in order to properly disclose their actual fair market value. Available-for-sale securities will also be affected by market value fluctuations and should be reported at fair market value, as well.

There may be instances when a company's intent with regard to individual securities that it owns may change. The company would wish to reclassify a security from one category to another. According to SFAS 115, securities transferred between investment categories should be accounted for at fair value. On the date of the reclassification, any unrealized gain or loss on the security should be accounted for as follows:

1. For a security transferred from the trading category, the unrealized holding gain or loss at the date of the transfer will have already been recognized in earnings and shall not be reversed.
2. For a security transferred into the trading category, the unrealized holding gain or loss at the date of the transfer shall be recognized in earnings immediately.
3. For a debt security transferred into the available-for-sale category from the held-to-maturity category, the unrealized holding gain or loss at the date of the transfer shall be recognized in a separate component of stockholders' equity.
4. For a debt security transferred into the held-to-maturity category from the available-for-sale category, the unrealized holding gain or loss at the date of the transfer shall continue to be reported in a separate component of stockholders' equity but shall be amortized over the remaining life of the security as an adjustment of yield in a manner consistent with the amortization of any premium or discount. The amortization of an unrealized holding gain or loss reported in equity will offset or mitigate the effect of interest income of the amortization of the premium or discount for that held-to-maturity security.

Trading securities should be presented on the balance sheet as current assets. Available-for-sale and held-to-maturity securities should be presented either as current assets or noncurrent assets, depending upon the appropriate time horizon. Similarly, in the statement of cash flows, cash flows related to trading securities should be classified as cash flows from operating activities while cash flows related to held-to-maturity and available-for-sale securities should be classified as cash flow from investing activities.

SFAS 115 became effective for fiscal years beginning after December 15, 1993. However, there was enough confusion among Statement users regarding which securities were subject to SFAS 115 and how to classify various investment types that the FASB had to: (1) issue a special report in November 1995 entitled "A Guide to Implementation of Statement 115 on Accounting for Certain Investments in Debt and Equity Securities" to answer the most commonly asked questions regarding the adoption of SFAS 115; and (2) open a window from November 15, 1995 to December 31, 1995 during which companies could make a one-time-only reassessment of the classification of its securities. This window has been closed and all reporting of securities must be in accordance with SFAS 115.

Index

G

GAAP. *See* Generally accepted accounting principles
GEMS Mortgage Securities, 55
Generally accepted accounting principles (GAAP), 142, 244, 247, 270. *See also* Financing/sale for GAAP
accounting purposes, 249
financing, 246
purposes, 250
GAAP-accounting principles, 183
GAAP-sale, 76
GAAP/tax treatment. *See* Non-parallel GAAP/tax treatment
sale treatment, 246, 264, 266
structure. *See* Sale-for-GAAP structure
Geographic concentration, 161, 164, 271
Geographic location, 109
Germany, 54-57
activity, 54-55
economy, 54
legal/tax framework, 55-56
regulatory environment, 56
securitization background, 54-55
securitization growth potential, 56-57
Gestoras. *See* Sociedad Gestoras de Fundos de Titulizacion Hipotecaria
GLA. *See* Gross leasable area
GMAC, 88, 89, 306
pools, 93, 314
GNMA. *See* Government National Mortgage Association
Government National Mortgage Association (GNMA), 3, 12, 104, 110, 197, 198
Grading, 135-136
Green Tree Financial, 110, 111, 113, 120, 124, 125, 127, 319
Gross leasable area (GLA), 193-196
Gross losses, net losses comparison, 326
Gross weighted average coupon (GWAC), 332, 351
GWAC. *See* Gross weighted average coupon

H

Health maintenance organizations (HMOs), 182
Healthcare Operators Group 1, 33
Health-care providers, 182, 185
Health-care receivables, securitization, 179-186
introduction, 180-182
reform, impact, 185-186
Health-care transactions, structures, 182-185
Held-to-maturity, 381, 382
Hell-or-high-water clause, 342
HELOC. *See* Home-equity lines of credit
HELs. *See* Home-equity loans
HEP. *See* Home-equity prepayment curve
HFC, 35
HFC Bank, 27, 30
Historic data, 315
Historical loss experience, 312-320
Historical prepayment speeds, 96
HMOs. *See* Health maintenance organizations
Home depreciation, 354
Home-equity lines of credit (HELOC), 130, 131, 344
Home-equity loan floaters, 291-298
conclusion, 298
introduction, 292
Home-equity loan (HEL) origination, 134
Home-equity loan (HEL) securitization. *See* Multi-class HEL
market, 140
securitizations
Home-equity loans (HELs), 5, 10, 11, 13, 96, 98, 104, 113, 130, 131, 292, 300, 312, 317-323, 329, 332, 338, 342-344, 347, 350, 356, 359, 365, 366. *See also* Adjustable-rate HELs; Fixed-rate HELs; Loan-to-value
bonds, 346
characteristics, 344
deals, 301, 307, 337
floaters, 293, 296-298

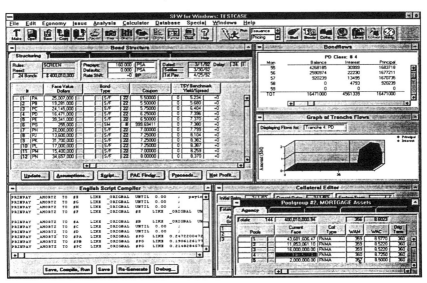

KPMG

The Global Leader

BIG IDEAS
GREAT SOLUTIONS

*AND THE WORLD-WIDE EXPERTISE
TO MAKE THEM WORK...FOR YOU*

STRUCTURED FINANCE GROUP

KPMG
ASSET-BACKED SERVICES

● ● ● ● ● ● ● ● ● ●

Financial Advisory
●
Structuring and Analysis
●
Asset-Backed
Transaction Services
●
Tax Reporting and
Bond Administration
●
International Securitization
●
KPMG *FAST*
Structured Finance Technology Tools
●
Systems Advisory and Development
●
Due Diligence
●
Training

For more information about our Structured Finance Services please call:

Washington

Michael Horn
*Partner and
National Director*
202-467-3236

Thomas Loughlin
Partner
202-467-3242

Patricia Cary
Partner
202-467-3245

Pedro Goitia
Partner
202-467-3533

New York

Karen Wiggins
Partner
212-872-5776

Los Angeles

Scott Carnahan
*Partner and Director of
Asset-Backed Securitization*
714-850-4329

Minneapolis

John Dee
*Partner and Director of
Tax Services*
612-305-5459

Why gamble with fixed income valuations?

Fixed income portfolio management is a tough game. Evaluating traded securities can be difficult. Accurately evaluating thinly traded securities is even worse. But Interactive Data puts the odds in your favor.

Get accurate fixed income valuations

At Interactive Data, we pride ourselves on unbiased valuations. We solicit market information from both buy- and sell-side sources. Then we integrate this information with our proprietary financial models to give you accurate, objective valuations.

For example, we generate CMO and asset-backed valuations using a sophisticated model that incorporates relative spreads and prices from multiple dealers. We also cover complex structures, such as inverse floaters and IOs. And our fixed income evaluators contact primary and secondary market makers throughout the trading day.

Boston   *Chicago*   *Hong Kong*

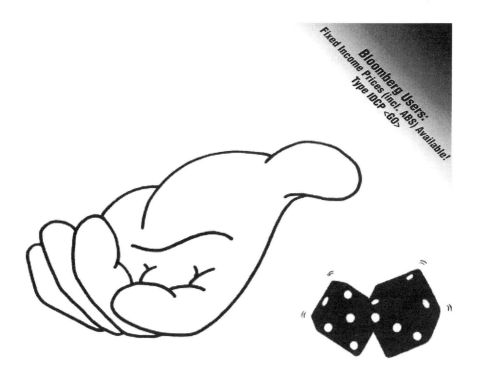

Get the full range of fixed income securities

Interactive Data gives you data on corporates, Eurobonds, municipals, MBS, money markets, ABS and CMOs. You get daily valuations every afternoon as early as 4:00 PM, continually-updated descriptive data 24 hours a day, and historical data as far back as 1968.

Get the best customer service in the business

Besides valuations delivered when and how you need them, you get direct access to our evaluators and analysts. And we offer local support with offices in six major financial centers.

Why gamble with your current fixed income vendor? Call Interactive Data today at 212-306-6999, or visit us on the Web at http://www.intdata.com.

Interactive Data
FINANCIAL TIMES Information

London   *Los Angeles*   *New York*

They're choosing up teams, again.

But this time...

The best players

Deloitte & Touche brings our size and experience to work for you.

As the largest securitization practice, we have worked on literally thousands of securitized transactions involving more than a trillion dollars in aggregate principal.

We currently serve most of the leading issuers and other participants in the securitization market, and are the only large player to offer a full range of consulting and technology services.

are on your side.

We're there from start to finish, and then some.

✔ Because of our **unmatched knowledge** of the market, we can help you identify potential problems faster and recommend better solutions.

✔ Our commitment to the asset securitization market doesn't stop with the transaction closing. We offer **consulting support** at every phase of the process, and our **market presence** allows us to respond quickly and effectively to your needs.

✔ We're with you for **the long run**. The systems we've developed for clients reflect our market knowledge and are designed to meet your needs in the future as well as the present.

With this team, you can win.

Deloitte & Touche LLP

Accounting, Tax and Consulting Services

If you are a serious player in securitization, you realize that it is more than a just a game. Let us give you strategies for your success.

Securitization Services

- Securitization Closing and Issuance Structuring
- REMIC, FASIT, and other relevant special purpose vehicle tax return preparation
- Master Trust
- Grantor Trust
- Bond Payment Calculations/Investor Reporting
- Due Diligence
- Tape Cracking-Data Verification

The Ernst & Young Vision

"Ernst & Young is changing, inspired by our vision of what we must be to be the unsurpassed leader in professional services. Our vision is about becoming more strategically driven. It is about reengineering the way we serve our clients, leverage technology and transfer knowledge. And it is about a good deal more."

Philip A. Laskawy, Chairman

Ernst & Young provides many financial advisory services including:

- Corporate finance services in conjunction with mergers, acquisitions and divestitures

- Valuation services associated with planned purchases or sales, insurance and business disputes

- Capital markets services to identify cross-border opportunities related to the taxation of new financial products

- Financial products services to determine if borrowings are structured in the most tax-efficient manner

- Corporate real estate advisory services, including strategic planning, consolidation studies, surplus property planning, valuations, outsourcing consulting and location analysis

≣ll ERNST & YOUNG LLP

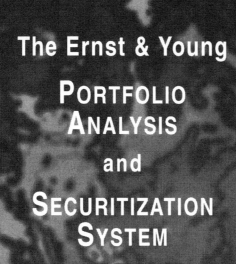

The Ernst & Young

PORTFOLIO ANALYSIS

and

SECURITIZATION SYSTEM

For further information call:

D.L. Auxier
(901) 577-6348

Gary Cole
(212) 773-1430

ERNST & YOUNG LLP

Data Migration and Scrubbing

- External Interface with Servicing System
- Data Scrubbing Routine
- Loan Matching against Loan Warehouse

Pool Selection and Analysis

- Pool Stratification and Summary Reports
- Loan Filtering
- Generation of Modeling Pools
- Optimization of Securitized Pool Using Internal Criteria

Collateral Cashflow Generator

- Utilize Market Standard Prepayment Models (PSA, CPR, HEP and ABS)
- Utilize SDA and CDR Loss Models with Recoveries and Servicer Advances
- Generate and Utilize Customized Prepayment Curves
- Generate and Utilize Customized Loss Curves
- Incorporate Custom Delinquency, Default and Recovery Methodologies

Bond Structuring

- Model Sequential and Pro-Rata Bond Tranches with the Ability to Easily Add, Subtract and Resize Tranches
- Model Pass-Through and Turboing Structures
- Model Floating Rate Tranches
- Generate Bond Equivalent Yields, Weighted Average Lives, Modified Durations and Decrement Tables for Bond Tranches
- Generate Price/Yield Matrices
- Export Information to Financial Printer

The Ernst & Young Vision

rub this

or, try conquest,

and get a better handle

on the future.

Frank J. Fabozzi / InformationManagementNetwork

present

Leading-Edge Summits On

Asset-Backed Securitization

Table of Annual Events

PROGRAM	LOCATION	DATE
ABS East	*Bermuda*	Early October
ABS West	*Scottsdale, AZ*	Early February
ABS Europe	*Call For Information (rotates annually)*	Mid June

Additional Comprehensive Events Include:

Music & Motion Picture Royalties,
Revenue & Receipts Securitization Summit

125 LTV Origination

125 LTV Investors' Summit

ABS - Asia

ABS - Latin America

Emerging Classes In Asset Securitization

Sub-Prime Securitization

Asset-Backed Commercial Paper

Home Equities Summit

For complete information:

Tel: (212) 768-2800 ext. 1 • Fax: (212) 768-2484
Email: imnreg@aol.com

The BARRA Cosmos System™

We are pleased to announce the most comprehensive suite of fixed income management tools in the financial industry—The BARRA Cosmos System.™ This completely Windows™-based suite addresses the most crucial tasks facing today's fixed income professional: managing domestic portfolios, controlling risk, managing global portfolios and analyzing structured products.

DECISION
MANAGE PORTFOLIOS

GLOBAL RISK MANAGER
MANAGE GLOBAL PORTFOLIOS

RISK MANAGER–U.S.
CONTROL RISK

PRECISION
ANALYZE STRUCTURED PRODUCTS

Challenge
"How can I assess the prepayment risk and cashflow distribution of my CMO and MBS portfolios?"

Action
Within the Cosmos framework, BARRA provides a Windows-based analytical module—PRECISION—that includes an extensive database of CMOs, REMIC, RE-REMIC, ABS and MBS deals. You can:

- Assess the relative value and total return profiles of various tranches by running vector analysis and contrasting existing tranches with combination trades and/or collateral.

- Conduct regulatory reporting on the portfolio including FFIEC, NAIC FLUX scores, NYS Regulation 126, FAS91, S&P and A.M. Best reporting.

- Project the future cashflow behavior of the portfolio under user-defined prepayment or interest rate scenarios.

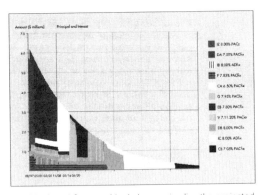

Precision's cashflow graphics help you visualize the projected behavior of any structured product.

2100 MILVIA STREET • BERKELEY CA 94704-1113 • 510.548.5442 • www.barra.com